Politics in India

SECOND EDITION

Rajni Kothari

Introduction
by
Prakash C. Sarangi

Orient BlackSwan

POLITICS IN INDIA (2nd Edition)

ORIENT BLACKSWAN PRIVATE LIMITED

Registered Office
3-6-752, Himayatnagar, Hyderabad 500 029, Telangana, India
e-mail: centraloffice@orientblackswan.com

Other Offices
Bengaluru, Chennai, Guwahati, Hyderabad, Kolkata,
Mumbai, New Delhi, Noida, Patna

First published in India by Orient Blackswan Pvt. Ltd., 1970
with the permission of Little, Brown and Company
Reprinted 1972, 1982, 1986, 1989, 1191, 1994, 1995, 2003, 2005, 2006, 2008
First Orient Blackswan impression 2009
Reprinted 2010
Second Edition 2012
Reprinted 2013, 2014, 2015, 2016, 2017, 2019, 2020, 2022, 2023, 2025

ISBN 978-81-250-4281-5

Typeset in Book Antiqua 10.5/13 by
Orient BlackSwan

Printed in India at
B.B. Press, Tronica City, Ghaziabad, UP 201 103

Published by
3-6-752, Himayatnagar
Hyderabad 500 029, Telangana, India
e-mail: info@orientblackswan.com

To
Raojibhai C. Patel
an early catalyst, a constant critic

Contents

Acknowledgements xi

***Politics in India*: An Introduction** xiii

Chapter 1
Theoretical Considerations 1
Context of political development. A comparative perspective. Significance of the Indian "model". Role of politics. The challenge of simultaneous change. Problem of performance.

Chapter 2
Historical Antecedents 21
The Hindu social order. The Muslim impact. The British impact. Political response. Charisma and reconstruction. The communal problem and national integration.

Chapter 3
Approach to Modernization 79
Significance of the antecedents. Approach to modernization. Issues of center and periphery. Factors of change.

Chapter 4
Institutional Strategy 102
Decision-making on the Constitution. Issues of consolidation and change. Center and periphery. Patterns of state politics.

Process of decentralization. Bureaucracy and political development. Institutionalization and legitimacy.

Chapter 5
Party System and Coalition-Making **155**
Competitive dominance. Salient characteristics. Evolution of the system. Identity and dissent. Social composition of parties. Interest articulation. Role of protest.

Chapter 6
Social Infrastructure **229**
Prevailing perceptions. Political dimensions of caste. Stages of articulation. New forms of aggregation. Other ethnic groups. Conclusion: process of reintegration.

Chapter 7
Political Culture and Socialization **255**
Perspective of History. Themes of political culture. Political socialization. Modernization of tradition. Conclusion: a comparative overview.

Chapter 8
Political Institutionalization and National Integration **299**
Approach to performance analysis. Dimensions of institutionalization. The demands of diversity. Conclusion: democracy and national integration.

Chapter 9
Political Economy of Development **344**
The broad strategy of transformation. The goal of self-sustained growth. Disequilibrium and development. Issues of distribution and equity. Conclusion: crises and development.

Chapter 10
Coping with the International Environment **390**
Growth of a policy. Challenges to national integrity. Changing context of international environment. Achieving economic independence. A period of transition.

Chapter 11
Future Perspectives **427**
The Indian "model". Emerging issue areas. Policy perspectives. The next phase.

Index **463**

Acknowledgements

First, I am deeply indebted to my colleagues at the Centre for the Study of Developing Societies for continuously providing me with an atmosphere of intellectual stimulation and primordial affiliation. (we have found that the two go very well together.) Much of what follows in this book is a product of collegiate intelligence at the Centre and not just my thinking.

Second, I am grateful to the Center for Advanced Study in the Behavioral Sciences, where a major part of this book was written, for providing me with ample time, good cuisine and bracing air, and the environment of a modern *ashram*. I am especially grateful for the high tolerance I received for my lack of involvement in the many temptations of sport and spirit.

Above all, I am grateful to Joan Warmbrunn of the Center for Advanced Study in the Behavioral Sciences, and M. Rajan of the Centre for the Study of Developing Societies, for their unstinting support of my various moods and meticulous handling of my illegible and often ill-constructed drafts.

Being an Oriental, not disposed to exhibiting his private affections in public, I prefer to keep the contributions of my wife and children to the writing of this book to myself.

Politics in India: An Introduction

Prakash C. Sarangi[1]

Rajni Kothari (b. 1928), widely regarded as an astute interpreter of Indian politics, "represents a serious blend of the theory and practice, or political reflection and political action" (Mohanty 1991: 151). He is a prolific writer and has attempted to theorise on several political issues. He is also one of India's premier voices of dissent against authoritarianism and anti-people development policies of the state. "Kothari's struggle against the forms of power in the contemporary political context of India must be regarded as the touchstone of his overall contribution to knowledge and of his interventions in the sphere of keeping democracy alive through mass actions" (Sathyamurthy 1991: 2100). Kothari is recognised as one of the early initiators of the 'alternatives movement' in ideas and assumptions about development and the role of the state. Starting in the form of critiques of development policies in India in the late 1960s, he joined in a number of such efforts worldwide. These efforts were aimed at producing both an alternative vision of man, society and state and a set of concrete ideas on how to move towards a more humane, equitable and democratic future, the 'victims of history', as he calls them. While Kothari's portrayal

1 Professor of Political Science, University of Hyderabad. Some parts of this piece are borrowed from his chapter on Rajni Kothari in his book, *Liberal Theories of State: Contemporary Perspectives* (New Delhi: Concept Publishers), 1996.

of the human condition is stark and often chilling, he seems to have an ardent faith in the capacity of human beings to intervene and change the course of history.

THE INTELLECTUAL JOURNEY

Pantham (1988) traces two phases in Kothari's writings with 1975–76 (Emergency in India) being the dividing line. These are two distinct "theoretical responses" to two different socio-historical phenomena. A product of the London School of Economics and Political Science, Kothari's writings from 1959 (when he published his first paper) up to the mid-1970s, were concerned with creating viable states and polities for the third world. Throughout the 1960s he mostly followed structural functional analysis culminating in his *Politics in India* (1970),[2] published in the developmental approach series initiated by Gabriel Almond and Bingham Powell. However, as Pantham notes, he went beyond structural functional "frameworking" and "theorized the autonomous role of the national political elite and the state in building up national and democratic political institutions and in pursuing social transformation and economic development" (Pantham 1988: 230).

Kothari founded the Centre for the Study of Developing Societies in 1963. This think-tank "recognised the need for historically sensitive theoretical and empirical research in social and political processes, in the cultural and philosophical anchorage of these processed and their implication for human choices" (1988c: 36). Its interdisciplinary focus with an attempt to bridge the gap between knowledge and action has its impact on Kothari's writings. One of his major concerns at the Centre has been to understand the theory and practice of democracy as it confronts the problems of social justice and human needs. Kothari was also involved in the World Order Models Project

[2] Unless otherwise mentioned, all the references in this chapter are to Rajni Kothari's works.

and was the Programme Director of the United Nations University's programme on Peace and Global Transformation. One result of this involvement is *Footsteps into the Future* (1974). It is an exercise in futurology, presenting a diagnosis of the present world, providing a design of an alternative and the strategies of action he finds necessary to realise the model. It presents his own worldview and its philosophical justification. As part of this exercise, Kothari became the editor of *Alternatives*, an international journal of ideas, institutions and policies. He edited the journal for ten years from its inception in 1975. He also edited *State and Nation Building: A Third World Alternative* (1976a). A related work, *Democratic Polity and Social Change* (1976b) is an application of his alternatives framework to the Indian context. It outlines the crisis in Indian polity and this work perhaps serves as a fine transition between the two phases of his works.

The second phase of Kothari's works is conditioned by the problems faced by the masses due to the techno-bureaucratic model of politics and governance and the crisis of the capitalist model of economic modernisation. "In this phase, the building blocks of Kothari's theoretical model of radical Indian social democracy are classes, masses and their struggles, non-party political formations, grassroots political movements, civil liberties movements, humaneness and justice at both the national and transnational levels and civilisational alternatives to Western modernity" (Pantham 1988: 230). Kothari became an intellectual-activist. He continued to write on theoretical issues on state, governance and human rights. The shift from global structures to the rights of the people also took him to the whole realm of civil society, the struggles for freedom and upholding of democratic values. He campaigned against the Emergency in India, got involved in the JP movement, and became a leader of the Civil Liberties movement. He questioned Indira Gandhi's and Rajiv Gandhi's use of state power against the democratic aspirations of the people. Kothari took the initiative to establish an action research centre named

"Lokayan" (meaning, 'Dialogue of the people'). It became a forum for interaction among activists, intellectuals and policy makers. During this phase, Kothari wrote extensively in newspapers, popular periodicals and scholarly journals. He delivered popular lectures. Gradually he changed the focus of his writings and speeches, now targeting common masses, rather than academics and scholars. Most of these papers were revised and published in five volumes: *State against Democracy: In Search of Human Governance* (1988a); *Transformation and Survival: In Search of Humane World Order* (1988b); *Rethinking Development: In Search of Human Alternatives* (1988c); and *Politics and the People: In Search of a Humane India* (1989), in two volumes.[3]

KOTHARI'S WORLDVIEW

Kothari's preferred world is a place in which each individual is free and enjoys autonomy for his self-realisation and creativity. The goal of social and political institutions is to protect individual freedom and to provide adequate opportunities for the fulfillment of individual potentialities and propensities. However, freedom and self-realisation of one individual does not provide justification for preventing other individuals from realising their freedom and potentiality. "Autonomy is not to be confused with individualism. While autonomy involves the principle of diversity, it also involves the need to modify the ill-effects of diversity in the form of domination of the many by the few by admitting the complementary principle of integration; for it is necessary that autonomy does not degenerate into the privilege of a few" (1974: 19). For Kothari diversity is an important component of the concept of freedom. Conflicts of interests are bound to emerge. "It is the function of institutions to manage these conflicts, reconcile them and resolve them so that not exploitation and oppression but solidarity and a sense

[3] Kothari's post-Emergency papers are in the second volume.

of community become the institutional expressions of the basic desire towards freedom and happiness" (1988c: 84).

Kothari's principal goal is to provide to the individual conditions for his self-realisation through a process of reason. A basic relationship between the process of reason and the process of freedom is expected to emerge. The process of policy, the utilisation of knowledge and intelligence, and statecraft as a whole are all embodiments of reason. Institutional structures of participation, justice and non-violence, on the other hand, are conditions of the individual's realisation of his freedom. However, Kothari does not envisage unrestrained autonomy to the ethic of self-control. He prefers a world where dehumanising social relationships of a consumption society are eliminated. Not only a minimum standard of living is ensured in such a world, but also a maximum ceiling is imposed and beyond which the extra resources are transferred from the haves to the have-nots. "The nation of a constantly rising material condition that men and nations are aspiring to achieve everywhere is not a utopia but in reality a dystopia" (1974: 11). Kothari suggests that a better standard of living should be measured in terms not only of material standards but also of cultural and ethical standards. This involves "limiting wants (restraining artificial simulation of needs) and making it possible for the individual to aspire to not simply freedom from inequity and exploitation but also to a higher freedom in which he seeks liberation from dependence on material acquisitions and attachments" (ibid). Kothari's ideas of self-control seem to echo Gandhian principles.

Thus the basic issue with which Kothari's framework is concerned is the ability of individuals to exercise choices, to actively intervene in the process of history. His conception of politics is based on such a possibility. Politics, according to Kothari, "ought to be neither *ad hoc* manipulation of events as they come nor adherence to a predetermined purpose as laid down in some closed system of thought (whether mystical or scientific). It should rather be an exercise of choice in the light of the concrete situation that faces man and the future that lies before him" (ibid: 40–41). It is evident that Kothari's conception of power emphasises the individual's capacity to intervene in the social process and to build ethical and institutional safeguards against unrestrained intervention. He assigns a central role to the human consciousness in defining the ends of politics and hence, of the power. This, according to Kothari, means two things: power should be purposive and not an end in itself; and it should be rationally distributed. He regards power as a necessary condition for autonomy. But for it to play that role it is imperative that its concentration be put to an end. Neither justice nor non-violence can be realised without an adequate distribution of power. Kothari argues that in his ideal world the specific values and institutional arrangements "would have meaning only in the larger context of providing conditions for the self-realisation of individuals in cooperation with other individuals, in the process imparting strength and dignity to human collectivities known as states" (ibid: 46).

Kothari argues in favour of a decentralised, humanist state, going beyond both classical liberalism and theoretical Marxism. Both the worldviews, according to him, are offshoots of the same philosophical pedigree of the enlightenment and the nineteenth-century mechanical humanism. There is a need to rethink regarding the role of the state in the large context of the present human condition. He regards the contemporary national state as a social institution (1988a: 15). The characteristics which make it different from the earlier regimes are: expansion of the base of political participation, extension of the reach of the state to cover economic tasks that are hitherto performed by diverse 'estates', and the emergence of the state as a mediator, indeed an arbiter, in conflicts arising out of divisions based on class and ethnic and nationality factors.

In a newly independent country the state has a special role. It has to secure, according to Kothari, nationhood for the large masses of the people both by providing security from external threats and through the achievements of a just social order. It is to be conceived through the transformation from a largely apolitical, non-national entity to a nation-state committed to the security and welfare of the whole population. Kothari suggests that there are generally four attributes of such a positive and purposive state, at least during the early phases in the life of a new state. He laments that these attributes gradually get eroded, as the euphoria surrounding the emergence of a new state vanishes (1988a: 90). First, the state is assigned a degree of autonomy in dealing with demands and pressures of various types. Second, the state with its functionaries, operating through appropriate institutions of government and party, enjoys a high degree of legitimacy. Third, the institutional edifice through which the state functions is generally elaborate, both in carrying out its formal law-giving administrative and judicial functions and in working out more substantive political tasks through competition and coalition-making, within and between parties and citizen groups, across the different regions and levels representing various socio-economic, cultural and ethnic components of the society. Fourth, such a state is generally a positive state which is assigned the task of mediating in and transforming the social order for the purpose of providing conditions of happiness and welfare for the purpose at large. The principal justification for concentrating in the state a wide array of powers is that these are necessary for it to serve the people. It is the state that is supposed to be a liberator from both the inequities of tradition and the inequities inherent in the capitalist order. It is supposed to uphold the interests of the people.

Kothari believes that there can be no freedom until the state itself becomes a condition of freedom instead of becoming an impediment to it. There is a need to humanise the enterprise called the state: "What is needed is to move from a government of humans to humane governance . . . [and] bringing back human concerns to the centre of regulating both the state and civil society" (1988a: 2). Such a state would be based on a grassroots model of mass politics in which the people would be more important than the state. Though the idea seems to be simple, it is a revolutionary idea in contemporary times when the dominant tendency is to place the state above the people and to regard the security of the nation-state as more important than people's security. Kothari believes that to restore to the people their sovereignty is not to undermine the role of the state but to transform it (ibid: 70). The transformation of the state is to be achieved through the transformation of the civil society, not the other way around in which the state is to be the author of social transformation. Kothari does not expect the centralised state apparatus to wither away; but it is to operate in concert with other centres as well as other institutional spaces in civil society. However, the state as an instrument of class and ethnic oppression should wither away and it should survive only as a mediator of conflicts and stresses in civil society.

In Kothari's model of decentralised polity, the state is expected to fulfil four essential conditions (1974: 16). First, there should be institutions for optimum participation of people at different levels, ensuring both representative structures of responsible government and more direct structures of deliberation and consensus at the level of the workplace, the local community and cultural institutions. Second, there should be institutionalisation of the principle of equity among individuals as a condition of justice, though not as a doctrinal principle. This is an area where politics and economics intersect. Third, there should be a balance between enlightened, centralised national institutions that can take a total perspective and are responsible to the people as a whole. This would mean a decentralised structure of decision-making, planning and implementation, so as to maximise individual freedom, social justice and cultural diversity and thus give rise to a vibrant federal polity. Fourth, there has to be a fundamental obligation that the nation-state and the units within it should preserve human rights, violation of which would lead to legitimate intervention by the national central authority.

The individual's participation forms the keystone of Kothari's political theory. It defines the limits of state activity and extends the scope of governance. He formally defines participation as "a process of arriving at a general consensus by a critical exchange of views in which the individual joins in active fellowship with others on the basis of his own choice and conviction and with the end of furthering a good life for him as well as for others: and for others because of him" (1988a: 206). There are three implications of this definition. First, participation is not an end in itself; it is only a means to an end. The end is to produce a certain quality of mind with which the individual shows the confidence and capacity to mould his own life in willing cooperation with his fellow beings, their good being as important to him as his own good. Second, participation is a process, not simply a form. Instead of viewing it as another form of communal behaviour, it has to be seen more as a method of reaching decisions, flexible in its working and producing a certain quality of human intercourse. Third, it is not participation *per se*, but a certain quality of participation that is desirable. Participation that is based on a metaphysical theory of society such as the corporate state, the class state or the historicist state endowed with a world mission can only lead to rigid conformity and the negation of individual freedom. Participation has to be based on individual self-consciousness with dignity and rights of the individual as its starting point. There is always the fear of converting the participation into a social myth (ibid: 205–6).

Rajni Kothari's conception of a decentralised pluralist state is not intended simply to limit its powers vis-à-vis the individuals, it is also supposed to be a purposive state with the task of transforming the society and creating a just social order. The positive aspect of state activity is built into his proposal for an alternative development strategy which aims at not simply economic growth but takes care of an equitable distribution in society. It is not supposed to be a more welfare state where the individuals thrive at the mercy of the state. He expects the humanist state to create conditions whereby every individual has a reasonable good standard of living and there is no concentration of wealth in a few hands. Kothari writes, "the modern state, projected as the main instrumentality of the domestic and anti-colonial struggle, was conceived as an instrument for social change. The role was to be carried out by a whole range of initiatives, from ameliorative measures vis-à-vis the poor to transformative strategies vis-à-vis the basic structure of society" (1991: 553).

While being critical of excessive centralisation and a hegemonical view of the state, Kothari does not ignore the creative role of the state "by intervening in the social process and providing mechanisms for liberation from age-old inequities and exploitative strangleholds" (1988a: 109). He thinks that the goal of the state is not just protection of life and liberty, but enhancement of the purpose of life through fashioning a humane, egalitarian and just social order. The state is supposed to be a necessary condition of human survival, "for without it both human conflicts and the ravages of nature could not be controlled and ordered" (ibid: 135). Kothari believes that the major source of injustice in today's world is to be found in structures of domination and inequality. The magnitude of the problem is accentuated by the fact that more and more human beings are impinging on a shrinking nature; there is encroachment of cities on rural areas and their sources of sustenance and there is a decline in the value of work and labour in a technological society. It is the task of the state to find constructive solutions to the system of domination in the prevailing institutional structures.

Kothari is sensitive to the implications of the post-colonial character of the Indian state which is needed to be nursed carefully. He is also conscious of the crucial role played by the elites in consolidating and integrating independent India and the traditional and primordial elements which are present in its political discourse. Moreover, Kothari is reacting to the turbulent periods of the 1960s and 1970s. This period witnessed not only mass struggles, movements and a national emergency, but also the need to find alternatives to the Congress party, rise in the consciousness among the masses to become effective demanders in the polity and a shift in India's economic strategy from planned development to gradual liberalisation. Kothari has seen it all: the use of a strong state in the 1950s to its misuse in the 1970s, the welfarist activities in the 1960s to the games of the market strategies in the 1980s. Therefore, he is apprehensive when the state becomes too powerful and repressive. He becomes equally suspicious when the state loses its autonomy and becomes a pawn in the hands of a few groups. He is elated when the masses have control over the classes. He is pained when the common man does not get his due from state activities which are influenced by the interests of the majority groups. His penchant for democratic values prompts him to regard the individual and the civil society to be the ultimate arbiter of state action. All these seemingly contradictory ideas have emerged because of the historical context in which Kothari has been writing.

Kothari's goal is to ensure liberty for the individual through a framework of the state but mediated through an effective group life. He does not envisage that freedom is to be gained not from the state, but in the state. He does not take the extreme pluralist position that the individual is incapable of resisting any action by a centralised state, or that the individual *per se* did not possess liberty except in the context of groups. Kothari accepts the autonomy of individuals. He gives importance to groups for the sake of decentralisation of authority. He does not specify the type of groups which should wield initiative and control over state activity, except to mention that grassroots movements would be effective means of democratic participation.

POLITICS IN INDIA

Rajni Kothari's *Politics in India* is considered as an outstanding introduction to the Indian political processes during the first two decades after Independence. This text is also an important landmark in the evolution of his intellectual contributions. In Kothari's own words, "of all my work *Politics in India* is the most important. . . . [It] remains the most systematic and comprehensive piece of work in which a lot of effort had gone and which covered a lot of ground. It is in the family of what can be preposterously known as 'classic' which stands apart from all the other work that I have done" (2002: 69). He further elaborates that it "is important in that it not only brought together my empirical work pursued over time in India but because it also laid out a set of ideas, a broad canvas of themes which then led me to new vistas of intellectual endeavour" (ibid). This text is not only an important cornerstone in Rajni Kothari's five-decade-long career as a political scientist; it is also an important landmark in the evolution of Political Science in independent India. Rudolph and Rudoph write, "to our knowledge it was the first work of an Indian political scientist to be given . . . international recognition"(Rudolph and Rudolph 2010: 568).

Rajni Kothari was influenced by two contextual factors—one historical and the other academic—while writing *Politics in India.* Firstly, he had a great faith in the relevance of the Nehruvian model of nation-building and of parliamentary democracy in post-colonial India. He writes, "I started as a confirmed democrat. Greatly moved by the Indian model of democratic nation-building, influenced by the Nehruvian mode of thinking, participating in the institutional layout of the Nehru period, and hoping to provide intellectual backing to what I later on came to call the 'Indian enterprise'. . . , I continued for a fairly long time to be an exponent of the Indian model of political and social development" (2002: 121).[4] He was fascinated by the distinctive characteristics of this model, which was different from the authoritarian structures prevailing in many newly independent Third World countries.

[4] It was much later that Kothari got disillusioned with this 'Indian model' of politics.

He emphasises on three aspects of the 'Indian model'. The Indian state[5] was expected to play a central role in bringing about social change, modernisation and empowerment. It was expected to be autonomous from entrenched interests, while relating itself to civil society to bring about a just social order. Another aspect of this model was the system of one-party-dominance, which Kothari described as the 'Congress System'. It was expected to be multi-factional in character, representing different interests, while remaining functionally democratic. Finally, India provided a unique model of centralising federation, while providing adequate space for multi-centred and multi-cultural structures.

The second influence was primarily academic and methodological: his acceptance of the so-called 'new political science', using empirical method leading to analytical understanding of political processes, going beyond the legal-institutional and normative approaches. Kothari writes, "The empirical grounding that I was able to provide to political science was based on a conviction that no theory of politics or political process is valid which is not based on clear understanding and interpretation of reality as it existed" (2002: 31).[6] He was clearly influenced by several American scholars, including Gabriel Almond, Karl Deutsch, Richard Park and Sam Eldersveld. Most parts of *Politics in India* were written in Stanford University, where Almond was a professor. Kothari was evidently influenced by the then dominant behavioural approaches. Structural Functional Analysis, which was popularised by Gabriel Almond as a tool of comparative politics, has been liberally used by him, with suitable modifications.[7] Kothari's use of this approach

[5] Unlike his later writings, Kothari does not use the word 'state' in this book. He sometimes uses the term 'system', following David Easton's term 'political system', which was popular at that time.

[6] He admits that he soon became 'restless about an exclusive empiricist approach'.

[7] Kothari's emphasis on a power structure that has autonomy from entrenched interests is distinctly different from the notion of political

is *Politics in India*'s both major strength and weakness. It provides a measure of coherence to arguments provided in the text. However, it does not allow easy generalisations for a diverse country like India, which was at a rudimentary phase of nation-building.[8]

As one may notice in the previous section on Kothari's worldview (which summarises his overall understanding of political process), his intellectual journey has had several twists and turns after the publication of *Politics in India.* He admits that his later writings have a different type of intellectual flavour. However, it is our humble opinion that Kothari's later writings continued to use the overall political objectives set in the *Politics in India*. Of course, the substantive differences in his writings during the two phases of his intellectual journey reflect the transformed historical context and the changed academic climate. The Nehruvian model of consensual decision-making gave way to partisanship and identity politics. Institutionalisation through 'Congress System' became no longer relevant in the face of political bargaining associated with coalition formations. Similarly, the claims of universality (*a la* natural science) by the behavioural approaches and

---

'system' in structural-functional analysis. He also coined the term 'intermediate aggregation' to suit Indian political reality. Despite his claims of having maintained a distance from structural functional approach, a discerning reader can find liberal use of this approach in *Politics in India.* An example of Kothari's later protest reads thus: "I had disagreed with the 'comparative methodology' advocated by a large number of Western social scientists, including the academic sponsors of the series under which my *Politics in India* was written and published. This was also something I was to take up in a controversy with the structural functional analysts of Europe who had come under the broad American intellectual impact" (2002: 32).

8 *Politics in India* was first published in the US in 1970 in Gabriel Almond's Little Brown series in Comparative Politics. Rudolph and Rudolph write, "[this book] advertised and legitimized the modernization theory and structural functional approach of the Almond-led Committee on Comparative Politics" (Rudolph and Rudolph 2010: 568).

structural-functional analysis were questioned. The relevance of these tools for non-western societies was debated.

One may notice, however, an element of continuity in the ideas surrounding major themes around which *Politics in India* is constructed. Kothari uses these ideas as a benchmark or standard to evaluate new developments in India in his later writings. Take, for instance, the idea of 'Congress System', existence of an identifiable political centre assimilating diverse interests and that political dissent operates within a dominant party as factions as well as outside as protest movements. While assessing the collapse of the party system in the context of 1996 elections, Kothari writes, "The 'collapse' that I have in mind here is not just of the Congress as the ruling party at the centre . . . but rather of the entire party system that I had more than 30 years ago characterized as the 'Congress system'. . . . A system that hinged so much on a functioning and many ways unique party system is suddenly being rendered impotent with the collapse of that party system and the considerable national consensus that it had so long represented" (1996: 1004). Or, writing on the problem of non-party grassroots political movements in India, Kothari writes, "Part of the Problem lies precisely in this wide array of problems, demands, oppressive structures. The diffusion and fragmentation are not borne out of conflicts of ideas and personalities; they are in a way built into the very process of transformation" (1984: 221). Kothari clearly laments the break-down of a party system which he thought would accommodate all dissenting forces and institutionalise them in the power structure.

Writing about his favourite theme, national integration, Kothari states in 1988, "It is this transition from a highly structured and institutionalised, inter-sectoral, inter-group and inter-elite framework of pluralist politics to the advent of a diffuse and unstructured and potentially malleable and homogenising mass politics . . . that opened the floodgates of populism on the one hand and a monolithic elite and reliance on charismatic power on the other. I intend to show that the two are closely related, that both are related to a process of deinstitutionalizing and ultimately depoliticizing the conduct of public affairs" (1988d: 2225).

Again, while writing on social movements in 1993, Kothari echoes his notion of political elites being at the forefront of interest aggregation: "the biggest failure of what are known as new social movements lies in their inability to become part of a united political movement. At bottom they are apolitical beings. In a way they are not really leaders of 'movements'. Intellectual movements are not really, in and by themselves, movements of history and because they are not movements of historical change they turn out to be at once anti-intellectual . . . and anti-political" (1993a: 1105).

Kothari uses his notion of developmental humanist state to assess the role of contemporary state in social transformation: "built into the positive thrust and progressive creed of the post-colonial state was an eventual encounter between the 'classes' and the 'masses' with the state providing a frame for mediation through which a confrontation of contending interests was translated into a series of transformative policies. . . . It is now clear that the expectation of such a role of the state, and the presumed alliance between the state and the masses in such an expectation, have been belied" (1986: 211–12).

Kothari continued to emphasise on the democratic reincarnation of caste system in India. Writing on the same subject in 1994, Kothari states: "the poorer and socially marginalized, including the ethnic and religious minorities, have started seeking out their own futures on the basis of their own identities and numbers. This has led to a mobilization based on caste, sub-caste (including within religious minorities), tribe, ethno-regional and such other identities. . . . The pluralism that has all along been there and has been accepted as inherent to the Indian social terrain is now being expressed in an upsurge of equity and social justice, not as a result of state policy but as a matter of right, hence sought to be acquired through access to state power. The traditional view of pluralism is now being countered by a more radical interpretation of it" (1994: 1590).

While assessing a contemporary theme like globalisation, Kothari banks on his old idea of the elites institutionalising the traditional structures in India. He writes, "To my mind [erosion of political institutions in India] has to do with the rapidly changing social base of the political process leading to a radically changed set of demands and conflict situation which the Indian state has been increasingly unable, and the Indian elite classes have been increasingly unwilling, to handle. . . . [S]uch dysfunctioning is a result of a growing lack of fit between governing institutions and social demands." Again, "Rediscovery of the vitality of traditions and drawing upon their innate wisdom and storehouses of knowledge and ideas can only take place if there is a shift from a freezing of the *status quo ante* to transforming diverse traditions through restructuring them, redefining goals and reorienting lost creativity. Only thus can the new waves of disbelief and growing lack of faith in the institutions of the modern state be handled through a new interface" (1995a: 627/630).

Kothari's assessment of the Indian state in an era of globalisation echoes his views on accommodating interests for generating national integration. "[T]he future of the nation-state in India depends on whether it becomes still more centralized and run from the 'centre', which then makes an alien presence and also makes it an easy target for global interests, or it becomes increasingly democratic internally and on the basis of that inner strength plays a democratic role externally. The nation-state is a highly complex world full of contradictions and tensions has to become catalyst for voices of diverse cultures and peoples and thus give rise to a dispersed and decentralized world order" (1995b: 1597).

One could go on adding examples from Kothari's later writings. It is evident that the perceived discontinuity in his ideas is often overstated. Kothari may have shifted the gear but not the model of his car. Use of some of the academic vocabularies may have changed; but the influence of *Politics in India* is clearly discernible in these works. If one were to assess the contribution of Rajni Kothari to political science, one cannot ignore this text. Also, if one were to assess the significant interpretations on India's political development during the first two decades after Independence, one has to give a prime status to *Politics in India*. This makes the text relevant even during contemporary times. One does not have to agree with the arguments presented in the text in order to appreciate them.

References

Kothari, Rajni. 1970a. *Politics in India*. New Delhi: Orient Longman.

______ (ed). 1970b. *Caste in Indian Politics*. New Delhi: Orient Longman.

______ (ed). 1974. *Footsteps into the Future: Diagnosis of the Present World and a Design for an Alternative*. New Delhi: Orient Longman.

______ (ed). 1976a. *State and Nation Building: A Third World Perspective*. New Delhi: Allied.

______. 1976b. *Democratic Polity and Social Change in India: Crisis and Opportunities*. New Delhi: Allied Publishers.

______. 1984. "The Non-Party Political Process". *Economic and Political Weekly*, February 4.

______. 1986. "Masses, Classes and the State". *Economic and Political Weekly*, February 1.

______. 1988a. *State against Democracy: In Search of Humane Governance*. Delhi: Ajanta.

______. 1988b. *Transformation and Survival: In Search of Humane World Order*. Delhi: Ajanta.

______. 1988c. *Rethinking Development: In Search of Humane Alternative*. Delhi: Ajanta.

______. 1988d. "Integration and Exclusion in Indian Politics". *Economic and Political Weekly*, October 22.

______. 1989. *Politics and the People: In Search of Humane India*. Vols. I & II. Delhi: Ajanta.

______. 1991. "State and Statelessness in Our Time". *Economic and Political Weekly*, 26.

______. 1993a. "The Yawning Vacuum". *Economic and Political Weekly*, May 29.

______. 1993b. *Growing Amnesia*. New Delhi: Viking.

______. 1994. "Rise of the Dalits and the Renewed Debate on Caste". *Economic and Political Weekly*, June 25.

______. 1995a. "Globalisation and Revival of Tradition". *Economic and Political Weekly*, March 25.

______. 1995b. "Under Globalisation: Will Nation State Hold?". *Economic and Political Weekly*, July 1.

______. 1996. "Elections without Party System". *Economic and Political Weekly*, April 20–27.

______. 2002. *Memoirs*. New Delhi: Rupa.

Mohanty, Manoranjan. 1991. "On Democratic Humanism: The Review of Rajni Kothari's Recent Works". *Contributions to Indian Sociology*, 25.

Pantham, Thomas. 1988. "Interpreting Indian Politics: Rajni Kothari and his Critics". *Contributions to Indian Sociology*, 22.

Rudolph, Susanne Hoeber, and Lloyd I. Rudolph. 2010. "An Intellectual History of the Study of Indian Politics". In *The Oxford Companion to Politics in India*, ed. Niraja Gopal Jayal and Pratap Bhanu Mehta. New Delhi: Oxford University Press.

Sarangi, Prakash. 1996. *Liberal Theories of State: Contemporary Perspectives*. New Delhi: Concept Publishers.

Sathyamurthy, T.V. 1991."Unique Academic Understanding of Politics". *Economic and Political Weekly*, 26.

1

Theoretical Considerations

IF "MODERNIZATION" is the central tendency of our times, it is "politicization" that provides its driving force. It is a force, moreover, that man has not yet learned to master, in part because he is still a prisoner of outdated perceptions. In the seventeenth and eighteenth centuries the main historical challenge was man's mastery of nature and religious bigotry, and in the nineteenth century his control of demographic and economic forces. In our times it is the increasing scope of government and politics in human life that has posed the biggest challenge to man's ingenuity: it is through his capacity to master the art and science of politics that he must find his salvation. All this calls for a new level of comprehension on the part of not only the academic social scientists but also the engineers of consensus operating at many levels, ranging from the very local to the international.

Many strata and organizations are involved in this process—political parties and electoral machines, media of public opinion, interest associations, both secular and sectarian, and the expanding ranks of the intelligentsia, the professions, and the bureaucracy. The spread and aggregation of the institutional framework of a modernizing polity involve all these strata into significant interactions, sensitize them to the great gaps that divide aspirations and opportunities, and by constantly increasing the demands on the political system, test the latter's efficacy and integrity in the context of shrinking world horizons and the growing diffusion of a world culture.

CONTEXT OF POLITICAL DEVELOPMENT

The "development" of old societies that have recently achieved nationhood status entails sharp discontinuities and a changed set of universals; the transformation entailed is far-reaching. The fact that social traditions militate against any radicalism during change should not mislead us into ascribing quiescence to an inherently volatile situation. For what is basic here is not the antecedent style of conducting the affairs of a society but rather the pervasiveness of the dominant ideology of change; it is the latter that holds the key for an understanding of the probabilities that the future holds in store. The antecedent style and structures of caste or tribal loyalties may be functional in the short run (as indeed they are in India); in the long run they must give way to bigger pressures, and the implication of both ideological and institutional factors that were deliberately enacted must be faced squarely. It is this long-run potentiality (this *telos*) that hangs heavily on the conscience of nation-builders. It poses the most tortuous problem in any program of purposive change: Will the long run be long enough? Will time oblige? The issue is not that in the long run we are all dead but rather that in the short run not much can be done. Political development, even more than economic development, is essentially a long-term process. And it is not necessarily unilinear and cumulative, nor can it be substantially affected by exogenous factors. The spread of new values and aspirations, on the other hand, once started is a fast and cumulative process, and is greatly influenced by exogenous factors. Hence the critical dilemmas of stability and legitimacy faced in all modernizing new nations. It is everywhere a race with time; the only difference is in the degree of volatility of the process.[1]

Conditions of political stability, however, differ according to the tasks that a particular polity is called upon to perform and the nature of relationships in which it stands with different sub-systems of society. One major distinction that can be made is between a highly centralized and elitist political system and a more pluralistic and participant political system, although undoubtedly there is nowhere a pure form of either.

The basic dilemma of relatively open political systems like India is that they are called upon to undertake functions that even "developed" political systems have been hesitant to undertake, while wholly lacking in economic, technological, and organizational resources of the latter. Historically speaking, the non-Western societies have taken over the ideological urges and social aspirations of Western societies without either the time the latter had to deal with primary issues of legitimacy or the economic and intellectual resources that were built up before they broadened their political base to include mass functions. The "shrinking of the world" has in this respect become a painful circumstance for developing regions as it has bequeathed to them social and political belief systems without the concomitant material and institutional props that are needed for stable and consistent change.

The dilemma can be seen all along. In India the legacy of a long tradition, the integrity of an historical culture, and the great solidarities that were built through religious and social movements that were characteristically Indian had for long acted as buffers against an inherently fissiparous situation. The social system provided a key to political stability. Now this very social system is undergoing profound change and has entered a process of continuous fluidity and fragmentation. The dilemmas facing the leadership arise from the fact that so long as the changes that erode the traditional bases of society are not channeled into a new pattern of institutional relationships, sustained by a new structure of opportunities, and legitimized through a new set of universals, problems of political development turn into problems of political survival, and it becomes difficult to attend to the concrete tasks of administration and the minutiae of institution-building. And yet, without attending to the latter, the former cannot be assured.

The context of political development in a new nation such as India, then, is that of an ancient land slowly seeking to incorporate into its womb the best elements of the culture of the modern world, without at the same time destroying its age-old traditions and diversities. Such an attempt has been endorsed in the form of a "democratic" pedigree that has been interacting with other and older pedigrees for more than a generation now within the framework of consciously adopted national and local institutions. The first generation of independent nationhood dominated by tall and inspiring men is now coming to an end and a new generation finds itself saddled with, on the one hand, a considerable consolidation of state power and a general consensus on the goals of the transitional polity, but on the other hand lacking the means, the instrumentalities, and the necessary authority to put the power they wield to effective use for the solution of pressing issues. Operating in the context of a still largely apolitical society, not yet fully convinced of the rationalist-positivist creed nor capitulated by a politicized interpretation of the common good, and lacking the ruthless dynamism of a Stalin or a Mao, the leadership is forced to rely upon the institutional forte and accumulated skills of a diffuse political structure for meeting domestic as well as world pressures of all kinds.

Politics in India thus is preeminently the politics of integration, where the problem of development is taken as a necessary and urgent objective, but one that is not sufficient for effective nationhood and must always be balanced against potential disintegrative consequences that rapid change involves for the political system in any long-entrenched and highly diversified society. The result is a less frantic developmentalism, which is ridden with ambiguity, feelings of inadequacy, and a great deal of wishful thinking, lacking in firmness and self-confidence, and hesitant and over-accommodating in national style. The deeper bases of an otherwise organized polity are therefore yet too embryonic. The directions are ideally set; and perhaps all that is needed is time. But time is the scarcest of all commodities. Much would depend upon the resilience of cultural and social traditions in providing cohesion in the face of adversity and a state of deprivation, and in restraining the cumulation of loads on the political system. The key parameter is: What is precisely the "mix" between antecedent and enacted institutions that is developing in India? How long would it take before the traditional roots of Indian society succumbed to the modernist onslaught? Will they endure till the spiral of economic "take-off" really takes off? And what would be the distinctive Indian "mix" between traditionality and modernity that will survive in the future? The tests of the performance of the political system derive from this interpenetration of social traditions, political power, and economic reality.

A COMPARATIVE PERSPECTIVE

It should be clear from the above that anyone trying to present a development profile of a polity with the kind of background, structural diversity, and encounter with the modern world which is found in India must, whether he likes it or not, approach his subject from a variety of vantage points. This is especially the case when the analyst is trying to explore the "relational whole" rather than any particular segment of political reality, and do this less in the manner of a provocative essay and more in the style of empirical generalizations at different thresholds of an analytical continuum. One of the phenomenological dilemmas of such an undertaking is that it must turn empirical relationships into analytical issues, and yet in order to escape the temptation of ascribing conceptual categories with propositional value, draw upon a variety of theoretical aids.

We have, in our study, drawn freely on the tools provided by the functional school of comparative analysis, have added themes of structural transformation, political culture, socialization, and reinterpretation of tradition as correctives to the comparative myth, have employed the conceptual framework of center and periphery in highlighting the issue of institutionalization and coalition-making, and have introduced at some length criteria of performance and problem-solving at various levels, and in different subsystems of the polity. In the process, no doubt, we have questioned the validity of some prevailing heuristic devices and models, and have given reasons of such questioning at various stages in our analysis. We have shown the incompatibility of viewing tradition and modernity as discrete opposites with the reality of development, cast doubt on various "social origins" and "prerequisites" models of political behavior, questioned the current notions of "identity crisis", disagreed with certain derivations of interest group theory such as the treatment of political parties and bargaining structures as discrete organizational variables, and shown the limitation of the "aggregation" model of the political process. In the course of such questioning we have, without always laboring the point, provided an approach to a more adequate understanding of the Indian experience in political development, and with some variations, possibly of other developing societies as well.

In viewing the process of development in a society where it is unfolding, as it were, before our very eyes, rather than through any benefit of hindsight, it is necessary to view it from the perspective of the members of such a society, and especially of those that are involved in bringing development about. Once we look at the political process from this perspective, we may still employ a broadly behavioral approach but we need also to restore two of its more neglected dimensions: institutional analysis and the role of elites. Thus in the case of India we see that it will not do to look at political institutions as some kind of a superstructure that presides over more basic relationships in society and economy, or to look at elites as simple recipients of inputs from society to which they respond in the form of various governmental outputs. Instead the whole process starts here through the establishment of a constitutional and political superstructure which then, through the *actions* of elites, penetrates into society at various levels and, by stages, leads to responses from below in the form of new coalitional structures. Elites and institutional forms can be seen here as creative actors in the process of integration and diversification, initiators of a far-reaching change in all spheres of life, and catalysts and mobilizers of a new vitality at various levels. Politics is the great creative force in such a situation, not just a representative mechanism which responds to outside pressures and aggregates outside interests.

Recognition of such an activist role of the political process has been spreading in recent literature of comparative politics, but the old images persist. The hold of an amorphous theory of secularism and the concomitant concern with a movement from "communal" to "associational" organizations colors the analysis of caste and tribal associations. The habit of treating political parties as essentially structures of competition that operate outside the governmental system leads to a neglect of the systemic functions of dominant parties which operate closely with governmental and planning structures and are concerned more with penetrating the periphery through co-optation and segmental mobilization than with simply contesting votes and seats. An almost paranoid concern with stability, often reinforced by the foreign policy perspectives of dominant nations, results in a preoccupation with "centrifugal tendencies" and the theory that political participation in a semi literate and socially fragmented society will lead to national disintegration. Part of this is simply a subtle carry-over of the colonial mind which considers political competition as a luxury that non-Western societies cannot afford, but part of it also stems from a sequential model derived from the Western experience according to which things like economic development and social mobilization must be established before the extension of franchise and political participation. Finally, the preoccupation with national identity as an overriding theme of political development leads to a neglect of intermediate mechanisms of containing political demand and the role of differential (including parochial) identities in political institutionalization. The lack of systematic attention to these intermediate identities has also resulted in another cliche of modern social science, namely the "revolution of rising expectations." The theory of such a revolution is based more on a projection of a demand-oriented polity found in the West, and the conceptual model derived from it, than on any sensitive empirical sense of what is happening in the new states.

Before articulating our own introductory thoughts on political development in India, it may be useful to consider the prevailing approach of the developed world toward the new nations in general and India in particular. Here one notices a strange reversal of criteria. Until recently it was generally held in the West—and it is still held in respect to Western societies—that mass participation in politics increases the legitimacy of a political system and strengthens its effectiveness. In referring to the relatively underdeveloped countries, however, it is apprehended that the same approach will not work as freedom of dissent and participation are likely to release centrifugal forces and undermine authority. Although the evidence in this regard is scanty—the number of new states in which participatory institutions genuinely exist is so small—this view is held rather widely. (It is only a variant of the judgement of colonial powers that the colonies are not fit for self-government.) In the light of such a general approach, India has so far been considered as a deviant case, one that must ultimately given way to the prophecies of doom.[2]

Hence, the frequent resort to unique explanations. At first it was the steel-framed bureaucracy left behind by the British; then it was Nehru's charisma; still later it was the dominance of the Congress Party. Now that all these explanations have lost their force, there is genuine puzzlement and an underlying feeling that something must go wrong somewhere, in the relationship between the center and the states, or in guarding the frontiers of the country against China and Pakistan, or—the perennial whipping boy—in economic development. Suffering from such a basic lack of empathy (except of course among the special caste of area specialists), the true dimensions of the Indian experiment—in terms both of real achievements and real failures—are lost on these onlookers. At the same time the earlier romanticism about democracy has given way to a crude cynicism characteristic of a cold war mentality.[3] (It is an irony that at a time when the unfolding of the Enlightenment is engulfing the whole world, the areas where it once flourished the most should show such signs of weariness and exhaustion.) Let us, however, give some thought to the Indian case in political development.

SIGNIFICANCE OF THE INDIAN 'MODEL'

The point about Indian development which gives it the character of an unprecedented undertaking is that while economic and social change is in important respects planned and directed from above, it is nonetheless carried on within the framework of an open and undirected policy. This means that manipulation of change in the image of a few dominant ideas gets conditioned by an accelerated pace of political competition, a changing structure of power and influence, and a widening base of political consultation and persuasion. The model is based less on coercing individuals and groups into new directions of action than on indulging them towards their own growth, albeit within a framework enacted from above. It is based less on the transcendence of individual self-interest by reference to "reasons of state" than on reconciling such self-interest with the common good as interpreted by a legitimized elite in an idiom of persuasion.

Moreover, the arena of power is not limited to a ruling oligarchy or an aristocracy of birth; it is increasingly being spread to society as a whole by drawing new sections into its ambit. This differentiates the Indian case both from the European case where, during the phase of rapid industrialization and social change, political participation was confined to the upper classes of society, and from the revolutionary experiments of both communist and non-communist varieties where, barring intraparty feuds and military coups, political competition was generally not allowed to interfere with the process of development. In India, politics is neither suppressed nor confined to a small aristocracy. On the contrary, politics provides the larger setting within which decision-making in regard to economic development and social change takes place.

For a time, this was not so clear. Although in theory there were adult franchise and a number of political parties, in practice the ruling group was small and united. With the passage of time and activization of the electoral process, however, fragmentation and diversification in the structure of political power have assumed decisive importance for the whole process of change. Alongside, other trends have developed—trends that seem inherent in the Indian approach to nation-building. The influx of the representative element in the administrative system, the pressures for the distribution of scarce resources, the close interactions between social factions and political factions, the secularization of traditional social cleavages, and the growth of new standards and criteria of status—these are some of the new factors that are conditioning both the political process and the development process taking place in the country.

On the other hand, it is important to remember that the development process in India started within the framework of a well-developed administrative structure. This has had an enduring legacy for subsequent development. All the more important programs—industrialization, community development, education, agricultural production, even local self government—have been approached in a framework that is essentially administrative and bureaucratic. Overlaying this framework is now found an increasing penetration of political structures and values.

Thus, two processes of nation-building are going on in India. One is the administrative-governmental process aiming at maximization, coordination, and uniformity in planned effort. The other is the political process leading on the one hand to the establishment of a dominant political center and on the other hand to processes of dispersal and diversification, and the activization of new centers of institutional and group activity. It is the interaction between these two approaches to nation-building, the blurring of the line between the two, and the subtle modifications of outlooks and attitudes in each that provides the larger framework within which development takes shape.

The transformation taking place in India is largely a political-bureaucratic transformation. India seems to us to be the clearest refutation of the reductionist viewpoint which takes politics and government as phenomena whose explanation must properly be sought in social and economic forces. In India, politics and government are something that cannot be explained away. To no small degree, the state has become the arbiter of society. This is not to deny the autonomy of social and economic factors in the development process; indeed it seems likely that with increasing diversification of centers of power, this autonomy will increase.[4] What is being stressed is the increasingly political orientation of social interests, in which the political process provides the inclusive setting within which these interests are found to interact.

Such changes are sometimes interpreted as an attempt on the part of one or more social groups to perpetuate or strengthen their respective positions in the traditional hierarchy, thus making the political system an instrument of the social structure, a favorite theme of the political anthropologist. As time goes by, however, the organizational nexus within which the process takes place and the political-bureaucratic values that it enforces assure that the general process of politicization reaches a point of no return. In fact, the conditioning of politics by local groups to buttress their respective positions is to be understood as part of the process of politicization itself. The striving for status gets politically oriented, in the process acquiring new criteria of status and power.[5]

ROLE OF POLITICS

In short, the Indian model of development is characterized by politicization of a fragmented social structure through a penetration of political forms, values, and ideologies. Operating against the background of an essentially *apolitical* condition of society, such a process involves the building of a political center, the diversification of this center through a network of benefits and obligations, and the mobilization of diverse sections of society in this network, thus closing the gap that has traditionally divided village society from the polity.

There is great novelty in all this. One of the principal failures, perhaps the greatest failure, of India throughout its long history was its inability to function politically, to construct a viable political authority. It failed to build a center. It is this that is meant when we characterize India as an apolitical society, not just some cultural predisposition. Against this background, the enormously innovative and creative role of India's contemporary political elite becomes clear. And this background shows why such an undertaking had to be at once the building of a center and its diversification throughout the subcenters of society. Central to both, however, is the role of the 'political' in social change.

It is important to grasp the implications of this. The theory of economic development that has succeeded in standardizing not only the terminology but the whole orientation toward the study of social change has given rise to a simple-minded, unicausal, unilinear and largely dichotomous view of the development process. This is particularly relevant for a country like India where, in spite of its distinctive approach to development, preoccupation with traditional models has impeded awareness and perception of reality, and has in consequence blurred vision and capacity for self- direction. For it is clear that neither the traditional sociological nor the traditional economic variables provide adequate categories by which political behavior can be explained, much less reduced. We are investigating a society where change is neither wholly induced by, nor is it a reflection of, a given balance of forces. Politics in a society like India is at once restricted in its effective social coverage and autonomous in whatever it covers. In a variety of ways, political decision-making determines priorities on allocation of resources, statuses, and goals. Even the "forms of politics" become relevant and critical. While the substance of politics has no doubt to be perceived beneath formal institutions of authority in terms of patterns of elite socialization and coalition-making, it is also the fact that the political-institutional forms assume a primacy and a dynamism of their own, define society's goals and means, and bring more and more of social reality under their area of control. The two aspects get mixed up: socialization of elites becomes inseparable from politicization of social groups, and the legitimacy of the political system depends essentially on the political restructuring of social forms and identities. The forms of politics themselves assume a dynamic quality. All of this calls for a different framework of analysis than is provided by traditional development theory.

Two points are involved here. The model on which India is set is one of modernization of an ancient and highly plural society in the context of an open polity. This implies modes of attending to social and economic arrangements that need to be clearly gauged if other considerations—or fixations—are not to distort the institutional scheme that the country has adopted by an act of volition. Second, under such a system even the traditional goals of development, such as the rate of economic growth, the degree of requisite social overheads, and the diffusion of new ideas and values, would to a considerable extent depend upon the performance of the political system and its ability to mobilize diverse elements into a framework of unity through growth. Such performance assumes a level of reality perception among the political and administrative elites, as well as leaders of opinion. To enable the political system to arrange and articulate social and economic relationships into a purposive model or development is not an easy task. It meets deep resistance not only from age-old traditions of conformity but also from the style and prejudices of the so-called modernist elite found in the professions, the bureaucracy, and the intelligentsia. Abstract constructs of development and ideological fixations inherited from an earlier age could prevent precisely the integration-through-confrontation model of development on which the country has set itself. The need is to ensure that the operational competence of such a sophisticated model of development is not frustrated by rigidities that originate in doctrinaire obsessions which get translated into an insensitive and capricious bureaucracy.

A more sophisticated conceptual framework is called for essentially because India has adopted a particular model of development: it is not just a concession to political ideology. It is slowly being realized that economic development is not just an economic process and that its success depends on progress on so many fronts. So far such a realization, however, is more in terms of "preconditions of economic growth" than a comprehension of the total process involved. The important point is that the nation and the society that economists assume as given to them to develop have yet to come into being. Development is as much a process of building a nation as to raise levels of living of some or all segments of the people. Mobilizing and involving masses of people in the productive process is not simply a function of the accumulation-and-saving construct but involves such imponderables as incentives, involvement, morale, motivation, participation, and articulation of demands. These call for a reconstruction of existing differentiations and relationships, the creation of mediating factors between macro and micro-dimensions of society, and consequent patterns of response through which the traditional society must pass in order to develop productive capacities and orientations. The role of the political system has to be discerned against such a framework of tasks. The conceptual scheme called for by the above comments is more than a simple interactional scheme of economics and politics, more than a mere assertion of linkages. It is a multi-systemic model in which a hitherto fragmented and plural society (structures and values) is exposed to a new set of universalist norms, confronted with a purposively adopted framework of institutions, directed to new purposes of national unification and planned production, and finds its rewards in the distribution of divisible benefits on the one hand and the dispersal of political opportunities on the other. In this process the traditional sectors are mobilized as much as the modern sectors. Such a formulation brings out the critical role of the polity in social transformation.

The transition to such a model is not easy. It took many decades before the attention of students of democracy in the West shifted from forms of government to the actual organization of interest and power in society as a way of studying a political system. An examination of a new polity in an economically underdeveloped and culturally complex society like India brings out even deeper aspects of the structure and organization of power and its purposive direction. The deliberate injection of incongruence in a society's arrangement of human affairs by the gradual introduction and adoption of alien forms of government introduces unprecedented stimuli and responses and brings forth new levels of awareness and new identification. These also produce, with the passage of time, criteria of governmental performance which often threaten the balance and stability of the established order. Since the actual course of development contains elements from both the traditional and the modern sectors, there seems to be no pre-ordained path along which constitutional government must, of necessity, move.

THE CHALLENGE OF SIMULTANEOUS CHANGE

It is an assumption of rationalist theory that the institutions enacted by a society and the developmental goals it sets before itself at a given time ought to be in consonance. This, however, does not necessarily follow. A noticeable feature of India's early development was a growing incongruence between adopted structures and their anticipated goals. Economic and political thinking in the country after the achievement of independence crystallized along: (I) adoption of the institutional framework of parliamentary government based on universal suffrage, depending for its success on a widening electoral base; and (2) setting up of the goals of speedy economic development and a take-off into self-sustained growth through centralized bureaucratic planning. Whether the detailed implications of these two dimensions of development could, in spite of their seeming discrepancy, be made to converge into cumulative nation- building, whether *such an institutional structure* could have enabled the State to *realize such goals*, would have depended upon certain crucial conditions.

One way was to have established and maintained over a long period of time an authoritative structure of political leadership providing undissipated administrative drive from the beginning, partly through a steel-frame bureaucracy indifferent to political pressure, partly through the operation of a parallel one-party machine, preferably through both. Such an approach presumably would have made centralization in nation-building the *sine qua non* of the Indian situation. Whereas politicization of the social structure might be pursued in order to arouse and guide the latter in new directions, political competition would have to be confined within very narrow bounds. Consultation with local groups and their mobilization for productive purposes would be pursued as a matter of tactics, but there would be little reason to turn these into an ideology of political participation. Finally, while social justice and equality might be viewed as legitimate ends to be realized as soon as resources permitted, both the philosophy of the welfare state and the politics of rising consumption would be rigorously controlled in the interests of long-range growth and material prosperity of the nation.

India has not chosen such a strategy of development. Other factors have outweighed the political compulsions of centrally planned economic development. Both in its effort to erect a unified national political coalition and in its attempt to work out the institutional mechanics of a mass democracy and its consequent preoccupation with the dynamics of power—an inescapable corollary—the leadership has been forced to compromise one after another the simple-minded canons of sacrifice and austerity it preached during the years following independence. It now seems clear that India has chosen to give precedence to the complex and difficult task of mobilizing intermediate and peripheral structures through a simultaneous pursuit of both aggregative and participatory goals, rather than simply to re-map its institutions for the primary purpose of extracting from the people a growing economic surplus for the state. The latter remains as one of the important goals, but the strategy of achieving it is less through authoritarian manipulation and the suppression of all other demands than as part of a total process of social and political mobilization.

Such an approach undoubtedly led to a great deal of groping and muddling through, for there was no clear model to follow: to attempt a simultaneous achievement of political and economic development while at the same time undertaking a reconstruction of a hardened social structure was a unique undertaking. On the other hand, it is not so clear any more that the authoritarian formula necessarily works, especially in cultures where the central symbols of secular authority have not penetrated into the regions and where subnational identities have yet to be woven together into a viable federation. Indeed it is more probable that the only way in which India could be ruled from New Delhi was by New Delhi's establishing a coalition with the centers of subnational identity which in turn had to accommodate other centers still lower down. A preference for political participation and adult franchise, under such conditions, was not simply an act of faith; it also provided a pragmatic design for national integration and social mobilization, including effective economic development. At any rate the Indian approach to nation-building involved such a preference for simultaneous goal pursuit rather than any sequential ordering through suppression of competitive goals. As it was in effect an alternative path to progress from the available historical models, there was bound to be a great deal of ambivalence and confusion initially. At the same time, as we shall see in the chapters on system performance, such a path proved crucial not only in the establishment and institutionalization of a political center and the integration of various diversities in it, but also in continually adapting economic and social policies when these were found to be faulty and unrealistic.[6]

Implied in what is said above is another point. The prevailing approach to the concept of nation-building stems largely from the Western experience of the establishment of centralized nation-states out of the break-up of empires, feudal social structures, and ecclesiastical authority. This conception of a strong central authority monopolizing political and coercive power has strongly influenced contemporary theoretical approaches. Hence, for instance, the great interest in national identity; hence also, an almost compelling concern with parochial tendencies in the new states. It is not by any means clear, however, that such an aggressive approach to the establishment of one central authority and the suppression of all parochial identities provides a feasible recipe for the new nations. Indeed, if we are empirically sensitive enough, it is possible to see that such an approach may well lead to disintegration rather than integration. The task facing the elites of these nations is to establish a center, penetrate the symbols of this center, involve other centers into its dominant framework through coalition-making and bargaining, and mobilize the population into this framework by socializing them into new commitments and loyalties, in the process often innovating in regard to political- federal forms. Such tasks and challenges place a prime value on political initiative and creativity and assign to politics and the political elite functions that in other ages and places were performed by specialized and autonomous groups. Looked at in this way, the significance of India's alternative path to development can be seen for what it is worth.

But there are other considerations too. In a country where politicization is given a free course and becomes the principal medium of modernization, it tends to break the autonomy of economic and social institutions and to subject the latter to intense pressurizing from both within and without. Its capacity to render its established supremacy over these institutions functional and efficient would, however, depend upon the degree to which the performance of a particular political system has itself shown competence in meeting the needs and aspirations of individuals and groups.

PROBLEM OF PERFORMANCE

This is absolutely vital. No scheme of institutions is in itself justified. Historical and ideological reasons are not enough for the legitimacy of a system. Ultimately, it must be judged on the basis of its competence to satisfy the aspirations of the people and the demands of the time. A multilateral and dynamic model of development must indeed devise modes of evaluation that relate to a particular point of time and space, to distinguish between problems of transition inherent in the development process and those that derive out of faulty strategies and leadership, and to evaluate the system against a set of dynamic criteria. But it does not rule out criteria, without which a society is likely to be trapped into a false pragmatism. The initial confusion and groping must before long give place to a realistic perception of relevant variables and their inter-relationships. Not all the variables could ever be known, and this is just as well; there would be no scope for political creativity if all factors were predetermined. But to leave everything to intuition and ad hoc thinking would be to deny the existence of any system, and hence of reason itself. It would also mean that critical decision—especially large decisions—are taken only under the impetus provided by crises and accumulated disequilibria, that only catastrophes lead to learning. We shall keep returning to these aspects of elite perception in the course of the book.

How far is the Indian polity able to organize and articulate into meaningful hierarchies the changing interest structure of society so that issues and opinions, articulated through perceived divisions and identities, are able to crystallize into policies and lead to significant results for the country's all-around development? Such articulation and crystallization depend on two things, one relating to the structure of institutions, the other to the values through which they have to operate. On the one hand, the processes and structures of politics should become functional to society. By means of a real confrontation with social and economic realities, they should pressurize the machinery of government towards significant decisions and their concrete and timely implementation. On the other hand, there is the general problem of ideation and reality perceptions that we have already mentioned. The operation of a modern democratic polity in a complex and tradition-bound society gives rise to highly complicated processes of change and adaptation, calls for a re-evaluation of problems that were so far dealt with in a simplistic and doctrinaire fashion, and strains the will and patience of the country's intellectual and administrative leadership. Problems of equality, pluralism, and mass participation take on new meanings that have to be absorbed as part of the intellectual culture of the nation. Failing this, the apprehension is that lags in performance will lead either to a cynical withdrawal from reality or a sharp reaction to the heritage of freedom that history has bequeathed to the Indian people.

Against these standards of consideration, the critical questions of the Indian polity begin to appear. Continuity in governmental forms gives rise in all societies to processes of penetration and evokes corresponding structural forms and modes of communications through the prevailing structures and levels of society. The crucial test relates to the capacity of drawing together the dispersed support structure of the polity into a framework of participation and goal orientation in accordance with the available legal and institutional means for doing so. This calls for a study of the relationship between (1) penetration of institutional and political forms, (2) response of society to such penetration, and (3) the performance of the political system in meeting the needs and resolving the problems generated at different levels of society. The main focus of such analysis must be the performance of the overall strategy of development. In order to evaluate with some perspective, however, we ought first to analyze the deeper dimensions of development, such as historical legacies, antecedent structures of society, and themes of political culture and socialization. We propose to undertake both these kinds of analysis in the body of this work, though it is obvious that we shall not be able to go as thoroughly into either of them as a more specialized treatment would have done. It should also be emphasized that we treat these variables essentially as they inform the political system and therefore necessarily avoid any exhaustive treatment of any of them. The specialist historian may not be satisfied with our analysis of "antecedents," the anthropologist with "social infrastructure," the psychologist with "political culture," and the economist with "political economy." For our perspective is somewhat different from theirs.

We divide the book into three parts—a historical overview (Chapters 1 to 3), an analysis of the contemporary political system (Chapters 4 to 7), and an evaluation of the system's performance (Chapters 8 to 11). Our principal focus is the relationship between institutional development and governmental output. In pursuing such a focus, we have emphasized a few themes and underemphasized others. Thus we have devoted considerable attention to the peculiarities of India's institutional strategy and its consummation in the party system. As both of these are closely informed by the interactions between traditional and modern forms and the underlying political culture, we have given a good deal of space to them too. But we do all this for approaching the ultimate pay-off of any developmental analysis, namely the system's capability to perform. To this we have given the last third of the book.

On the other hand, we have underplayed many of the traditional themes of comparative political analysis. Thus while we have discussed the peculiar Indian perspective on modern interest groups (in Chapter 5) we have not tried to document the development of modern voluntary associations and pressure groups in India. And we have given our reasons for under emphasizing this aspect of the political process. Also, while the analysis of social infrastructure and communications is provided, we have left out an analysis of mass media as found in the Western literature. Lastly, we have almost completely left out constitutional history, and developments in the legal and judicial spheres, on which we plead ignorance.

We have sought, through these emphases and omissions, to maintain the developmental focus of our analysis and to carry it through the body of the work.

NOTES

1. We speak here of volatility arising out of unfulfilled aspirations, not that which is often found as a reaction to change itself, although the two need not be mutually exclusive.
2. In the words of W.H. Morris-Jones, "It is India's fate to attract prophets of gloom. (Perhaps she encourages them by her own self-criticism, perhaps by her very success in maintaining stability in the face of gigantic difficulties—most infuriating for the 'news'-hungry lovers of alarm and crisis.) it is her achievement to disappoint them." Quoted from "Language and Region within the Indian Union" in Philip Mason, ed., *India and Ceylon: Unity and Diversity* (London, 1967).
3. Two years after the first general elections in India, the *Manchester Guardian* wrote: "Parliamentary institutions have not had a very good time in Asia .... Pericles said that Athens was the school of Hellas. Mr. Nehru without boasting may say that Delhi is the school of Asia." (June 5, 1954). Almost thirteen years later the correspondent of *The Times* in India .predicted in a series of articles, on grounds best known to himself, that the fourth general elections would be the last elections to be held in India. The prediction received a not too unsympathetic response throughout the West.
4. We have dealt at length with these trends in Chapter 9.
5. Such a process not only articulates and crystallizes the relevant aggregates of Interest; it also reinterprets and restructures the antecedent distribution of needs and loyalties. Once such a political system is stabilized and achieves a concrete institutional form, the interest aggregates will, no doubt, take on a more positive role in the articulation of demands and policies. Until then the "interest group" approach is of limited use.
6. The significance of this alternative model for economic development is only now beginning to be dimly perceived in the West. See, for instance, two papers by Charles E. Lindblom, "Political Democracy and Disciplined Development: The Case of India" and "Politics, Policy Making and Planning for Indian Economic Development" (manuscripts, 1968).

2

Historical Antecedents

WE WOULD BE in a better position to deal with the questions raised in the introductory chapter if we had some notion of the historical and institutional experience through which Indian society has passed, the ideological and technological influences to which it has been subjected, and its peculiar modes of responding to such stimuli. Political democracy, wherever it has succeeded, has been the product of a combination of contexts and processes. It is in distinctive traditions, the adaptive capabilities of a given social and normative system, external impacts, and the historical conditions under which a new pattern of responses is generated and institutionalized that the democratic propensities of individual nations have found shape.

Modern India, in its political aspects, is a product of a variety of influences spread over a long period of time. Three historical strands stand out distinctly as substantial influences. The first is Hinduism, the solid bedrock and unifying framework of Indian society. The second is the British impact of rational-legal authority wielded by a central power that managed to consolidate the whole subcontinent under it. Although operating mainly in the legal and administrative spheres, the British *Raj* also affected fundamental political beliefs and relationships. The third is the reconstructive nationalism of the pre-independence era, generated in response to the impact of a new world order as transmitted through the colonial power, and developed as a means to political independence and social reform in the context of a slowly expanding framework of democratic institutions. In what follows, we provide a brief survey of the background to modern India in terms of these three components of the Indian heritage and their mutual interaction.

THE HINDU SOCIAL ORDER

Indian History extends over thousands of years, and is composed of a variety of political forms, ranging from empires to petty kingdoms, and including monarchies, oligarchies, chieftainships, and republics. The Hindu period itself crystallized roughly between the fifteenth and the tenth centuries before the Christian era, when the Aryans, whose hordes had been trickling in for more than a thousand years from south Central Asia, populated in considerable numbers the north and the west of the subcontinent, in the process either subjugating or driving further southwards the original inhabitants. From then until about the tenth century A.D., the Aryans formed several kingdoms and ruled over the area, giving rise at times to empires such as the Mauryas, the Guptas, and the Harsha dynasty in the north, and the Cholas and Pallavas in the south. Hindu dynasties persisted in some areas long after the tenth century when the Muslim invasions began to undermine the political supremacy of the Hindus. Thus the Maratha rulers in west India held against the Moghul power as late as the sixteenth century and continued to offer resistance to the British when they succeeded the Moghuls as conquerors. Taking the subcontinent as a whole, however, a decline had set in after the tenth and eleventh centuries. There was no way then of stopping the foreign invaders, so that at last they gained full control of the territory.

The short period of great and flourishing "empires" has left behind a considerable historical and legendary record, as well as great works of literary and cultural value which, together with the Hindu Epics, have left a deep and powerful impression on the Indian mind. The memory of a great past and its reinterpretation strengthened the awakening of modern India, and in that lies the political significance of the long Hindu period. Its real achievements, however, are in directions other than strictly political—in the perfecting of a remarkable social order, and in the development of traditions and values that have had a lasting effect on all subsequent periods.

The precise steps by which Hindu society acquired its character are not known. Spread over a large and sprawling territory, lacking in antecedent political unities and traditions, and generally remote from centers of military and political power, the Indo-Aryans developed a social organization that answered to the several needs of such a people. It became structured along a hierarchy of four *varnas* which were superimposed on a loose and primitive system of "castes" that existed before the Aryans came. Such a hierarchy, while based upon primary ties of marriage and family, assumed importance in the division of secondary functions, including "political" functions such as the resolution and adjudication of disputes. Starting from a functional distribution of occupations and roles which were embedded in a legitimized status hierarchy, and providing for an informal machinery or arbitration in cases of ambiguity, the system developed its own pedagogy and mystique, created vested interests, and hardened with the passage of time.

THE CASTE SYSTEM

The four varnas in which the Aryans divided the caste system—Brahmin, Kshatriya, Vaisya, and Sudra—while meant to correspond to the four functions of knowledge, defense, wealth, and labor respectively, provide more the theory than the actuality of caste. There is no such four-fold division of people that a visitor to India would find. If it had been so, analysis would be more simple. There would be four strata or classes, although the principle on which the classes were divided would be different than in the West. In reality, the situation is much more complicated. Caste in fact is an endogamous kinship group known as *jati*, linked by marriage and lineage, and for the most part locally identifiable (although the spread varies between regions). Accordingly, there are not four but thousands of castes—or *jatis*—in which the social system is organized. These are governed at the local level through their individual caste *panchas* (a group of five or more leaders) and an organization of village elders also known as *pancha* or *panchayat* which more often than not draws its members from different castes. Furthermore, there is the lowly caste of Harijan or the "scheduled castes," which are lowest in the hierarchy and often are physically segregated from the caste Hindus by virtue of their "low" occupations and beliefs of pollution, but which in turn have developed an intricate *jati* system within themselves and are an organic part of the total Hindu system. Similarly, tribal groups that are now entering into the general stream of national life, special minority groups, and even the Muslims and Christians in India are found to adopt the caste (*jati*) form of social organization. On the whole caste has traditionally performed an integrating function by bringing not only different kinds of occupations but also peripheral groups such as the various tribal and semi-tribal people, different religious sects, and invading and immigrant groups into a common cultural and secular framework. We shall see in Chapter VI how this function of caste is now being taken over by political associations. But this background is important even for understanding such a process of change.

It is possible, nevertheless, to classify most *jatis* in accordance with the *varna* distinctions, although this is easier at the extreme ends of the social spectrum (Brahmins and Harijans) than in the middle ranges. Moreover, there have been many recent movements of organizing for political purposes several *jatis* under the single banner of a varna, and claims to higher status by identification with a particular *varna*, all of which underlines the modern relevance of the traditional rationale of the caste system.[1] The chief point for us to note is that the caste system provides a localized social structure, organized along primary group lines, and making for functional interdependence, individual identification (each individual is born to a particular position and is assigned a particular occupation), and social cohesion (by the resolution of inter-group disputes). Such a system could endure the vicissitudes of time, continuous warfare, and changes in political regimes, as well as the various invasions and cultural impacts that have taken place from time to time. Over the years, the internal balance of the system has undergone shifts, often motivated by political and military thrusts and the access of particular groups to military and governmental power, often by economic mobility, and sometimes by mere change in administrative arrangements, such as in the collection of revenue for the king or the emperor. Absorbing these changes, as well as absorbing the influx of new elements, new faiths, and ideas, the system has survived the test of centuries and provides perhaps the most persisting reality which any political system in India must confront and deal with.

APOLITICAL SOCIETY

The above discussion of the role of the caste system underlies important characteristic in the relationship between society and politics in traditional India. The Indian system was a loose accommodation between a remarkably stable social order and a transient and unstable political order. The former limited for the most part to the village or a network of villages, provided security and a sense of order. The latter, though set against a larger canvas and backed by superior force and the sanctity that custom had assigned to the ruler, made for disturbance and uncertainty. As we noticed in the last chapter, India's great failure in the past has been its inability to erect a political authority, a coherent and persistent center. Looked at in this sense, the traditional Indian community can be characterized as largely apolitical in its organization.

This does not mean that there were no politics in traditional India. There was no absence of politics in village India, but it was politics of a different order. It was, on the one hand, the politics of village dominance, of local cleavages and factions, in which family and linear ties were the raw material. It was, on the other hand, the politics of managing external authority and its unpredictable ups and downs by allowing it a role in the pattern of local dominance, such as arbitration in local disputes and periodic changes in the secular ranking of castes. While on the whole such a system settled the relationships between groups at various levels, its principal failure was in evolving a unified political framework.

LOCAL SOLIDARITY

Such a state of social and political organization engendered, and was sustained by, customary behavior and a system of values and attitudes that characterized traditional India. There developed a strong sense of local solidarity. This had two intimately related aspects: first, a primary group loyalty, loyalty to one's own family and kin group; second, loyalty to the larger group, a clan, or a village, or a caste. The structure of authority and the norms of the latter were binding on the individual and he felt them to be binding. Each individual not only was born in a particular station by virtue of his caste and kinship; his position in the larger social system also was determined by the occupation to which he was entitled, his relationship to customary authority, and his obligation as a family man or a dependent.

Duties were fairly well defined. In return for his due compliance with the responsibilities assigned by the system, the individual was well protected; individual differences and inadequacies were taken care of by the group; and the rise or decline in his own status was a result of the change in status of the group as a whole, thus providing a system of security and mutual aid. There was no uncertainty with regard to the individual's participation in channels outside the primary group, for the system was closely integrated. The secondary social groups and leaders (the panchayat, the revenue collecting authority, the administrative chief of the village known as mukhi or patel) and the various functional groups in the village (the village craftsmen, landlords and tenants, the merchants and the moneylenders, washermen and scavengers) performed their respective roles in the context of customary norms of behavior which, although not codified, were elaborate. Social cohesion was relatively powerful, the whole system being based on the strongest tie that has acted on man anywhere—the tie of blood. And this in turn made custom the binding force of social behavior. Lacking in larger political identities and given the remote and intermittent nature of political authority, Indian society assumed, over the centuries, a small-group orientation that has not been seriously eroded even to the present.

CODE OF ETHICS

The force of custom and deference to familial and social authority were supported by a code of ethics. The central concept is *dharma.* Sometimes narrowly translated as "religion." the term actually denotes a whole series of duties: personal, social, moral, and religious. It is the way in which one is expected to behave in different situations: toward one's kin and fellow men, the old and the young, husband and wife, the poor, the aged, the infirm, the priest, the warrior, the merchant, the landowner, the scavenger, the tanner, the servant, religion, God, and one's own soul. Every situation calls for a specific code of behavior, a specific dharma; indeed the conception of a common standard of behavior, of an "absolute" ethic, is alien to the Hindu way of life. Dharma is essentially a logic of behavior in a variety of settings; it forms the basis of customary virtue. To offend it in any of its specific aspects is immoral and renders one liable to various sanctions, ranging from mild reprimand and disapproval to social boycott, punishment by the pancha, justifiable revenge and recrimination, and finally the inevitable reckoning through a cycle of births and deaths. On the other hand, good and moral behavior is to be rewarded, both in this world through respect and status, and perhaps elevation into the council of elders, and, as the belief goes, in the other world through entry into the heavens, and freedom from bondage in this world.

The concept of dharma is more than a codification of duties and functions. It is also a philosophy of life. It involves a kind a Weltanschauung, a world-view—the world-view of *anasakti* or non-attachment. In considering various duties and functions, the devout Hindu is enjoined to think of them objectively, without any sense of attachment or interest. For the supreme dharma (and here it also can be translated as "religion") is the salvation of one's own soul. This being the highest virtue, it was to be valued above all social bonds and duties. In trying to reach that state, however, and so long as the ties of this world were not given up altogether, dharma consists in a faithful pursuit of the duties endowed to one's role and station in life. Because the principal emphasis is on "duties to " rather than "rights against," it was good to be satisfied with one's lot and not to crave that which did not belong to one. Hence the Hindu's emphasis on a limitation of wants and contentment with his lot, on tolerance rather than revenge, and on restraint rather than exuberance.

All in all, such a basis for social arrangement makes for group cohesion and the individual's sublimation, and a relatively low set of expectations from society and government. Being highly pluralistic in structure, Hindu society has been able to retain primary loyalties and thus make for a high degree of personal security and cohesion. Added to this are the metaphysical norms and orientations of tolerance, non-attachment, and contentment which help the society to absorb tensions and to blunt the edge of suffering. There is among the Hindus a marked tolerance of deprivation, a low sensitivity to humiliation, and cynicism with regard to the use and abuse of power. The combination of "small group orientation" mentioned above and the metaphysical emphasis on personal salvation makes for a peculiar kind of individualism, non aggressive and non-collectivist in orientation. At the same time, such a structuring of motivations and loyalties prevents the easy growth of larger identifications and commitments and restricts the mobilization potential of a large-scale economy. Is this balance of advantages and disadvantages inherited from the Hindu legacy functional or dysfunctional in the development of a modern democracy? We shall deal with this question in some detail when we discuss India's political culture.

It will be seen from the above that the more important developments in the long period of Aryan ascendancy and power lie in the consolidation of the Hindu social system rather than in the several political and dynastic changes that had taken place in various parts of the subcontinent. The former was more pervasive than the latter and provided a unifying framework of social existence. The great periods of political expansion and consolidation contributed to the strengthening of the system, of course, inasmuch as they provided stability at the higher levels, encouraged the growth of local industries and handicrafts, built roads and canals, and above all stimulated creative endeavors in the arts, literature, and religion. The cultural efflorescence of these periods greatly raised the level of the Hindu heritage by enriching the Sanskritic tradition and by repeatedly renewing the power and vitality of the Brahminic leadership which provided an important unifying symbol and direction to the Hindu social system as a whole.

ROLE OF ELITE

The pedagogic and civilizing role of the Brahmin in the Hindu tradition cannot be overemphasized. Standing at the top of the hierarchy and performing the functions of local and family priest, he also was instrumental in imparting learning, in interpreting the scriptures and customary law, and in spreading to the laity common doctrines and ideas from generation to generation, thus nourishing tradition and usage. It was through such a privileged elite drawn from a narrow social base and commanding institutionalized charisma and authoritative pedagogic and arbitrational roles that the pluralities of Hindu society were woven into a common social structure, symbols and traditions. What united the elite itself was neither a theology nor any other kind of uniform doctrine but rather a status in society whose function it was to provide authority and wisdom, a status it enjoyed by virtue of birth, privileged training, and deference that was due to those who were so born and trained. The skills that the Brahmins deployed were mainly sophistic and arbitrational, but even when he reinterpreted tradition or text, his work carried great authority. The availability as a critical ingredient of the system of such an educating elite greatly enhanced the unifying character and legitimacy of Hinduism throughout the centuries and accounts for its resilience and durability in spite of the strains and dislocations brought by nearly seven centuries of religious, economic, and political domination by foreigners.

MOVEMENTS OF DISSENT

While the Brahmins were the great preservers of the Hindu order, they also often tended to degenerate into a rigid orthodoxy, and failed to provide the requisite leadership for change and innovation. The latter function was performed by others, notably the Kshatriyas: both Buddha and Mahavira, the great dissenters of Hindu society, were princes. They have been followed by a whole line of dissenting and reformist movements throughout Indian history, right to the modern times. These movements of dissent, and the innumerable new ideological sects and cults that have cropped up from time to time, have played an important role in the enrichment of Indian civilization and, paradoxically, in its survival. They have not only imparted vitality to Hindu society, but by forcing an assimilation of massive dissent, lent strength and resilience to its basic structure.

Many of these movements were puritanical and sought to purify Hinduism from the corrupting influences of power and wealth and the incipient ritualism that had taken hold of the priestly and ruling classes. Of all these movements perhaps the most relevant for modern time is the Bhakti (devotional) movement that took place prior to the coming of the British. The movement was made up of "saints" coming from the highest to the lowliest of castes (including the Harijans), cuting across all regions of India and the distinctions of birth, status, and sex. (One of the most prominent among these saints was Meera, a Rajput princess, who had given up the comforts of palace life for a communion with like-minded devouts of both sexes and all classes.) An important off-shoot of the Bhakti movement was the rise of new sects with large popular followings, including the new and militant community of Sikhs who later played an important role in India's economic modernization. Many of the movement's leaders came from the south too and their teaching became part of the general Indian folklore. By being multiregional in character and employing the medium of popular dialects rather than the difficult idiom of Sanskrit, the Bhakti movement produced an atmosphere of cultural and political integration, a rare thing for a dissenting movement to achieve. At the same time, by emphasizing equality of all, it militated against the Hindu concept of hierarchy and prepared the minds of thinking men for the egalitarian impact of colonial and post-colonial times.

Thus, the social system, the doctrines enshrined in the Hindu Epics, the Brahminic elite, and the great dissenting movements together gave to Hinduism a unified character and a sense of continuity. India was not yet a nation, but it certainly was a society and a civilization, and there was widespread consciousness of being one. Without this deep based cohesion and identity it would not have been as smooth, as it later proved to be, for British administrators and nationalist leaders to endow India with political unity. On the other hand, despite this consolidation and in fact because of its peculiar style, the general gap between society and politics noted earlier continued throughout the Hindu period. This meant that changes in political fortunes did not greatly affect the business of social living. Dynasties rose and fell, empires spread and collapsed, but much of Indian society went on its own way. The task of creating a political community identifying with a single center was by and large left unaccomplished.

The long period of Muslim invasions and conquests that followed the Aryan period disturbed this pattern somewhat, but not fundamentally as we shall presently see.

THE MUSLIM IMPACT

The Muslims (Arabs, Afghans, Mongols) came as raiders and conquerors, starting sporadically as early as the eighth century in Sind and then more massively in the tenth and eleventh centuries, followed by the founding of the Delhi Sultanate in 1206 and the long rule of the Moghul dynasty from 1526 to 1707. The consolidation of the Moghul dynasty can be dated from 1555 with the accession of Akbar to the throne. The symbol of an "emperor" continued until after 1857 while the Empire formally ended in 1862.

There are four main characteristics of the period. First, the political organization of Muslim rule, though it made great strides in civil administration, retained a hard core of military character. The period taken to install Muslim rule in India was very long and even then the whole of India was not brought under one political authority. The long period of fighting that resulted led to much dislocation of life and economic misery. Though the reign was quite secure between 1555 and 1707, court intrigues were not uncommon, and there were continuous challenges from the Rajputs and the Marathas, as well as from regional warlords.

Second, the Muslims confronted the Hindus with a quite different religion and social system. Although by and large the government itself wanted the two systems to live side by side—Akbar was the great proponent of Hindu-Muslim amity—Muslim rule did make religious conversion attractive, and gave the Maulvis and the Sufis a free hand to go about converting local populations, especially in the north. Oftentimes this led to waves of repression, religious bigotry, and hatred on both sides. This did not allow free scope to the traditional Indian concept of tolerance, of "many roads to the same truth," and prevented social assimilation from taking place. Some adjustments and mutual influences no doubt took place, such as the adoption of certain forms of caste and occupational patterns by the Muslims, thus making them acceptable as neighbors, although more of this developed after the decline of Muslim power; the Hindus also adopted several social usages and conventions, artistic forms, patterns of administration, and forms of courtly behavior from the Moghuls. Rajput generals and outstanding Hindu ministers ranked high in the Moghul court. In architecture, arts, and letters, the Muslims made a substantial impact, and succeeded in creating urban centers of Muslim culture in which educated Hindus took part. But, with all this, the two religions and social systems remained separate and mutually exclusive, such being the origin of Muslim power in India, proselytizing on the one hand and imposing military superiority on the other. Insecurity and the need to keep numerous armed forces over the country added to this feeling of distance and estrangement between the two communities.

Third, the Muslims in India developed a dominant political style, an authoritative "center," and an extensive and efficient administration in the country for purposes of law enforcement and revenue collection. There came into being a hierarchy of officials ranked in military terms, and based on a division of the Empire into provinces and districts. These officials enjoyed considerable local autonomy and, in spite of the uniformity of Muslim rule, turned their distance from the center to their personal advantage. The British inherited such a system of administration and continued many of its forms, although in the process significant changes were made, the chief ones being the separation of the military from the civil function and a greater uniformity of civil administration, both following Britain's own political traditions

Fourth, however, such a development of political dominance and administrative hierarchy had no great impact on local institutions and village affairs, and still less on the habits, beliefs, and traditions of the masses of people that lives in the villages. For the most part, the old form of social and occupational organization continued; public issues continued to be settled through hereditary, customary channels. Modifications did take place in the ranking of particular castes and hereditary groups, depending upon their relationship to political authority and their place in the economic system as a result of modifications in the system of revenue collection or land rights. But, as noted before, such changes had taken place earlier, social mobility having always depended upon economic opportunity and the access of particular groups to military and political power. This did not change the nature of the social and political system, as the general gap between local and central power continued, and local institutions remained autonomous in most of their social and civilian functions. Indeed, even the Muslim population, wherever it inhabited the countryside, was found to fit into this system, taking to specialized occupations and developing a caste system among themselves. Moreover, in spite of developing a rationalized system of administration, public works, and revenue collection, the Muslims failed to penetrate the lower regions of Indian life, partly because of their alien nature which kept them by and large confined to the urban areas, partly because of the strength of local institutions that managed to keep central power at arm's length, and partly because the Muslims did not develop a hereditary aristocracy and preferred instead the system of farming out military and administrative functions in return for fixed sums of tributary payments.

IMPACT ON HINDUISM

However, in one respect Muslim rule in India considerably disturbed the pre-existing balance of the Hindu system. From the first raids of the Afghans, internal peace was upset by periodic fighting, ravaging, plundering, the destruction of holy-places, general disorder, and lawlessness. Military affairs were ferociously conducted—by both Muslims and their Hindu adversaries—and often involved much local suffering and hardships. The fact that substantial portions of the sub-continent still remained under Hindu rule, as in the south and the west, despite the attempt of the Moghuls to carve out a single empire, kept the tension high. In many ways the whole period was characterized by lack of peace and a disturbance of the morale of the people. It greatly upset the self-confidence of leaders of society and religion and threw Hindu society into a state of confusion and defeatism. Hindus responded by withdrawing into the web of exclusiveness provided by caste and kinship, and thus managed to survive. Caste now became a protective shell, a mechanism of isolation and withdrawal from an unkind environment. The value of other worldliness also became a prominent part of Hindu ethic now, under conditions of defeat and humiliation. In the process Hindu society lost its vitality and dynamism, hardened a great deal in its internal structure, and turned fatalistic and pessimistic in its approach to the larger world.

This was one aspect, and its effect was not permanent. Part of the damage (the failure of law and order and of decent government) was restored by the British, and the Indian people eventually came out of the debilitating influence of Muslim power. The impact of the Muslim period was shattering but not permanent except for the fact that it left behind a vast Muslim community throughout north India (from Gujarat to Bengal) as an integral part of Indian society. In part this reflected the comparatively stronger impact of the British rule that followed. Partially, it reflected the strength of Hindu tradition and its peculiar approach to such an external challenge: of withstanding and possibly absorbing it in the framework of an "agglomerative" society, and where this was not possible, of waiting for its self-exhaustion rather than meeting it in a headlong confrontation. This was also its approach to the British power later on.[2]

Of more lasting significance are two indirect contributions of the Muslim impact. One was a legacy which later turned into a problem. This is the so-called "communal" issue of Indian politics. The coexistence of Hindus and Muslims in India has gone through several stages. During the period of Muslim power and ascendancy, a feeling of estrangement and hostility prevailed between leaders of the two communities, in spite of a general mutual acceptance of each other at the level of ordinary people. During the period following, under British rule and the gradual settling down of local affairs, Hindus and Muslims learned to live side by side, grew tolerant of each other, carved out distinctive spheres of influence and occupation, and participated in many common activities. There came about a worsening of the situation, however, during the latter period of British rule, through a cumulation of cleavages at the national level. The result was the "communal" problem or what is sometimes known as "communalism" in India. We shall discuss the issue in detail later in this chapter.

The second indirect result of the Muslim impact was a reaction to it after its decline. The Indian renaissance that followed the establishment of law and order by the colonial regime was as much a product of the revival of Hindu culture and its traditions as it was a response to English education and "Westernization." Indeed the Western impact itself contained the revival of Sanskritic learning and a consciousness of past accomplishments to which European scholars themselves contributed not a little, in the process returning to the Hindu mind a self-confidence that had been shaken during the period of Muslim ascendancy. This peculiar combination of Western ideas and Hindu enlightenment is not as curious as it sounds especially if it is set against the violence and uncertainty of the preceding Muslim period. Both aspects— Hindu revivalism and "Westernization"—appeared like liberators from the long period of defeat and anomie that preceded the advent of the British.

A PERIOD OF CONFUSION

On the whole, then, the Muslim period left behind a mixed legacy, not profound, striking few deep roots in social traditions or in the minds of the majority of the people,[3] but making its mark on the social and administrative framework, on literary and artistic traditions, and on the manners and etiquettes of elite politics. The Moghul Empire in reality ended after the death of Aurangzeb in 1707 with the Europeans taking over one territory after another. Throughout the eighteenth and the early part of the nineteenth centuries the political picture was greatly confused, with a crumbling empire and wars of territorial acquisition waged by the foreigners. While the rule of the Moghuls had for a century and a half led to a remarkable centralization of political power, the continuous resistance to its power, especially by the Marathas, ultimately weakened its hold, created restlessness and infighting in the provinces, and oppression of the population by local *jagirdars* India, toward the end of the Moghul empire, was a land divided, lacking in "central authority, militarily and politically chaotic. The European era had already begun, and English power, which was the chief beneficiary of the European impact, gradually capitalized on the ruins of the great Moghul Empire.

THE BRITISH IMPACT

As is well known, the western impact came in stages: (1) the explorations of the Portuguese, the Dutch, the French, and the British in the fifteenth, sixteenth, and seventeenth centuries and the establishment of active trading posts; (2) the rule of the British East India Company that established its supremacy first by eliminating the French (aided by the Seven Years' War in Europe), then by subduing the already weak and tired Moghuls by procuring extensive trading privileges and territorial and financial rights, and finally by breaking the power of regional rulers such as the Peshwas and Marathas in western India, the independent Sultan of Mysore and the Nizam of Hyderabad in the south, and the Sikhs of Punjab in the north, either through direct fighting or through a system of "alliances" and financial quid pro quo; and (3) the replacement of the Company in 1858 by direct British rule administered by the Queen-in-parliament in Great Britain. For most purposes, the Company period till 1857 and the direct phase of British rule in India from 1858 to 1947 should be considered as a continuous story. The watershed between the two—the "war" of 1857 between the British and the feudal order of northern India—does, however, help to emphasize an important aspect of British rule in India.

THE 1857 REVOLT

Described in extreme terms as a simple "mutiny" of Indian soldiers in the British Indian Army on the one hand and a "war of independence" on the other, the 1857 struggle was in fact neither. It represented a revolt that was not a military revolt. The steps taken and measures introduced by the Company in India were of a momentous nature that shook the foundations of feudal India and the prevailing class structure of north Indian society. The measures taken in land settlement, in economic organization, and in the legal order created newly privileged classes and undermined the traditional structure of authority. The effects boomeranged and led to a sharp reaction. The revolt was mainly waged by the old landed classes, was restricted to the north of the subcontinent, and was dominated by the Muslim princely and landed families that had been shorn of their power by the all-encroaching foreigner, though no doubt a number of Hindu rulers also joined in. The revolt was suppressed but left behind much bitterness, especially among the Muslims, the British themselves adopting an anti-Muslim posture after 1857. But it created less impact on the minds of the Indians—it had aroused no interest outside of north India even while it lasted—than on the minds of the British themselves. The latter turned more cautious and conservative, recognised the impermanence of their rule, and lost their initial zeal for large-scale reforms. They henceforth lacked the capacity—and the will—to reorder Indian society, a task that really started only after 1947. At the same time, however, the memory of such an early challenge lived on and sought to remind Indians of the vulnerability of the British Raj. Although it had represented a defense of the old order, it continued to be invoked as a symbol of progressive and nationalist forces in India. Significantly, although the British had learned their lesson in 1857, adopting greater tolerance for local traditions and forms and ruling with more benevolence as announced in the 1858 proclamation of Queen Victoria, the more they tried to woo the Indians thereafter, the more dissatisfied the Indians appeared to be. British domination over India, although more efficient after 1857, was based on an unwilling subject, and never struck deep roots. Indeed 1857 was the first event of major significance that made clear the continuing dilemma of British rule in India: although revolutionary in its impact, it incurred reaction and revolt.

CONTRIBUTIONS OF BRITISH RULE

The impact of the British was indeed revolutionary. It was not deep because it was alien, but it was big and powerful and enduring. We shall consider the colonial impact as part of a more general analysis in the next chapter. Meanwhile let us look briefly at the chief legacies of the British period.

Establishment of Central Authority. The British for the first time brought the whole subcontinent under one imperial rule and kept it under that rule on a continuous basis without fear of either disruption from within or aggression from without. Although more than a third of the territory was left outside Britain's direct administrative control, in the hands of native princes, its paramountcy was recognized even there, and there was no question about its imperial authority. This was a major achievement and became the basis of much else that the British did in India. It also later provided that territorial basis on which India's unity as a nation was built.

Law and Order. From the point of view of the Indian population, the most beneficial effect of British dominance over the country was the provision of law and order. We have seen above how the Muslim conquests and the internecine struggles that followed had disturbed the peace of the subcontinent and had led to insecurity in the countryside. The British rule that followed such a long period of turmoil provided security, enforced a rule of law, and heralded a long period of peace and stability. Leaders of opinion in many regions expressed gratitude at this "blessing" of the British Raj.

New Notions of Administration and Justice. The British not only brought the whole subcontinent under a single authority, they also provided a unified administration. Building on the district pattern of the Moghuls, a hierarchical structure of administration was created from the center downward, with the provinces and the districts acting as subordinate agencies. The pattern was made relatively uniform. The outcome was an efficient structure of authority, based on new principles of law and administration. Although the functions prescribed by the Moghuls continued to be the basis of district administration in British India, the principles on which the relationship between the district and higher authority was based were wholly different. It was a wholly civil relationship. It gave discretion and authority to the officer-in-charge of the district, but he was a servant of the central authority and enjoyed no sinecure or rights to extort his subjects personally. Above all, the British created a modern bureaucracy in India, a unified service based on merit and open competition. These principles were tried out in India even before they were introduced in Great Britain. The result was the ICS (Indian Civil Service), at first manned wholly by British officers, to which later on Indians were added in increasing numbers, but always containing men of learning and ability, of "gentlemanly" background, and picked with great care. To these men was entrusted the task of nursing the districts in India, maintaining order, collecting revenue, and providing leadership and justice.

The men of the ICS were not only district officers; they also were district magistrates who administered justice. With the passage of time, a new system of courts was created, based on Anglo-Saxon principles and procedures of jurisprudence, and with their ancestry in the British common law and precedents. Still later, a structure of social and economic administration based on principles of collective welfare was brought into being and measures of reform striking at gross disparities and inequities were gradually introduced.[4] This further changed the nature of civil administration and introduced new ways of looking at man and society which, while it gave a jolt to traditional notions, fitted in well with the new ideas that were gaining currency.

Creation of a Middle Class. Following Macaulay's celebrated *Minute* of 1835, there came the most momentous decision of the British Raj: the decision to introduce English as a medium of instruction in Indian colleges and high schools. Already self-made men and those inevitably dazzled by the Westerners were reading the English classics, legal and scientific works, and constitutional treatises; the introduction of English made this possible on a much larger scale. It should be remembered that the decision came not as an imposition by the East India Company, which was in face more inclined to the use of vernacular languages, but rather as a result of agitation made by Indian leaders themselves, foremost among them being Raja Ram Mohan Roy. Generation after generation there came into being a wholly new class—English-educated, tutored in liberal ideas, full of admiration for the West, and prepared to serve as "clerks" under foreign superiors. Many of them took to law and practised it. Some became teachers. Still others took to commerce and industry. A few managed to go abroad—mostly to England—took advanced education, and more often than not aspired to become members of the ICS. Some took to social reform, journalism, and other professions like medicine and accounting. Still others took to politics.[5]

This was the new middle class of India. Through this class the British ruled the subcontinent. Through this class new ideas of individualism and constitutional government gained currency. This class manned the new professions. And from this class, political leadership emerged to challenge the might of the British Empire. The overall effect was profound. The new middle class, created by English education and drawn by the concepts of liberty, democracy, and socialism, was indeed the greatest legacy of the British Raj. This class eventually inherited power from the British and declared itself a modern nation and a "sovereign, democratic republic."

Social Reform. The fact that modernization was introduced to India by a small, English-educated, middle class also created one of the most acute problems of Indian nationhood—the gap between the elite and the mass. We shall later in this chapter see how this problem was eventually dealt with. Meanwhile, let us note that with the emergence of the new class there also arose new stirrings for change in the "condition of India." Starting with demands for social and political reform, these stirrings slowly led to a demand for complete independence from the foreign ruler and the establishment of India as a fully sovereign nation.

First appeared the great urge to reform Hindu society and its more objectionable practices. In this, the enlightened administrators sent out by the British found common ground with the leaders of the Indian renaissance. Indeed the revival of the Hindu spirit and the regeneration of ancient Indian glory were attempted by purifying Hinduism and denuding it of the distortions that had grown during its period of darkness. The first steps were taken as state measures during the eventful regime of Lord William Bentinck, Governor-General of India from 1828 to 1835, and under sustained pressure from Indian liberals like Ram

Mohan Roy. Chief among these were the abolition of *suttee* (a practice according to which on the death of the husband his widow immolates herself on the same funeral pyre), *thugee* (robbery and strangling of their victims by professional robbers), and female infanticide (a practice of strangling the infant according to a ritual followed by the devotees of the goddess Kali). Infanticide was declared a criminal offense and so were all sacrifices of human beings undertaken for ritual purposes. Steps were taken to prevent gross injustices against women. Jurisdiction for criminal offenses and for all offenses involving state laws was taken over from local councils and given to the newly established courts.

The crusading zeal of the early English reformers and their Indian counterparts suffered a brake after the revolt of 1857. The British government at home, which now assumed direct control of Indian affairs, followed the doctrine of *Pax Britanica*,a policy according to which local customs were not to be disturbed and India was to be governed from an ethically neutral position. Henceforward, social reform was achieved mainly by movements stimulated by Indian leaders and intellectuals, and far less by enlightened policies from above. To be sure, even during the first half of he nineteenth century when the government took steps to eliminate objectionable social practices, more often than not agitation for these steps came as much from educated and sensitive Indians as from Englishmen startled at these practices. The government itself played a limited role. And as time went by, it became even more limited.

APPROACH OF COLONIAL REGIME

It is important to bear this limitation of the scope of the colonial impact in mind, as also the fact that the scope got narrower with the passage of time. For all its revolutionary influence, the colonial regime in India lacked the capacity—and the will—to reorder Indian society. While it gave rise to a modern bureaucracy and an efficient framework of administration (including the rudiments of welfare administration), in regard to larger social and economic issues it continued to be a force for conservatism, and this at a time when large-scale imbalances in social conditions were being created. During the latter half of the nineteenth and the first half of the twentieth centuries India's population rose rapidly, but agricultural production failed to keep pace with it; per capita real incomes remained stagnant or declined slightly; the traditional strongholds of industry—cottage and household—were being impoverished by new forces, and, all this gave rise to growing conditions of scarcity and hardship. During the same period, however, urbanization was spreading; railways and other means of communication were rapidly expanding; news media developed; a sizeable middle class came into being; and associational groups proliferated. Thus many of the structural conditions for social regeneration were being laid.

In failing to purposefully mediate between such conditions of impoverishment on the one hand and the opportunities for their amelioration on the other, the British proved that they were not just politically conservative but socially conservative too. The revolutionary potential of such basic changes was, fortunately for the British, channeled in a movement for national independence. By not attending to the growing dimensions of the issue of social change, on the other hand, they passed on a host of accumulated problems to the Indians when they assumed power in 1947. Much of this should, of course, be expected; it is not the business of an alien power to indulge in fundamental changes although empires tend to differ widely in this respect. We mention it here only to highlight the enormously innovative role of the early pioneers of Indian modernization.

EARLY MODERNIZERS

Raja Ram Mohan Roy (1774-1833) was one of the earliest of these pioneers. A man of great learning, he strove for a synthesis between the values of Hinduism, Islam, Christianity, and liberalism. Well-versed in Arabic, Persian, and Sanskritic scholarship, and knowledgeable in Greek and Hebrew, Ram Mohan Roy wrestled with the problems of Indian religion and society even before he came to a study of English. Influenced by Sufism and then by Christianity, Ram Mohan was highly critical of the caste system and discrimination against women. A strong though not uncritical believer in the beneficial effects of British administration, he devoted his life to the education of his fellow men in the spiritual and political values of liberalism. But his distinctive contribution was in the sphere of religious innovation. He founded the Brahmo Samaj, a theistic society that advocated a peculiar mix of secular and religious beliefs. The Brahmo Samaj exercised a deep influence on contemporary intellectual and social life in India. It was a forerunner of many other voluntary societies, both religious and secular, that sprang up in all parts of India.

GROWTH OF ORGANIZATIONS

Ram Mohan Roy is the most prominent among a whole array of early social reformers, and the Brahmo Samaj only one among scores of social reform organizations. There is no space to mention all the other names here. The latter half of the nineteenth century was especially characterized by a phenomenal growth of voluntary associations. Not all these associations took the same line. There were, first, the clearly political organizations such as the British Indian Society set up in 1843, the various presidency associations organized in the Presidency towns of Calcutta, Madras, and Bombay (starting in 1851), and the Indian Association (Calcutta) established in 1876 by Surendranath Banerjea, a nationalist and persuasive orator. It is interesting to note that it was out of the National Conference convened by the Indian Association in 1883 that the idea of a "national organization" for all Indians fructified and led to the formation of the Indian National Congress in 1885.

The second group of associations was more strictly oriented to social reform, many of their leaders sincerely believing that social regeneration was a pre-condition of self-government, that the people should be prepared first before they were given the right to govern themselves. The leadership of this group ranged widely from the early innovators like Ram Mohan Roy to later "liberals" like Vidyasagar and Srinivas Iyengar. Their general approach was in part also shared by other outspoken critics of Indian society like Justice M.G. Ranade, Gopal Krishna Gokhale, a follower of

Ranade, founder of the Servants of India Society, and one of India's great liberals, was to lead the moderate wing in the Indian National Congress. Gokhale himself, preferred to follow a political line.

A third group of reformers struck a more traditional note, although they were no less concerned with change, and in fact made a deeper impact. Foremost among these was Dayananda Saraswati who founded the Arya Samaj in Bombay in 1875. Dayananda Saraswati exerted a great influence on Indian nationalists, many of whom joined the Arya Samaj, a militant organization with branches all over the country, advocating the purification and revival of Hinduism, drawing its chief inspiration from the Vedas, but nonetheless engaging in reforming the evils of Hindu society, giving shelter to the aggrieved, and training young men and women in the course of national uplift and regeneration. The various missions established by the followers of Ramakrishna Paramhansa and Swami Vivekananda also engaged in educational and social work activities while still holding to the main currents of Hindu thought. More secular leaders in the Congress movement at a later date also saw value in not rejecting the religious basis of nationalism and in drawing inspiration from tradition for present action. Chief among these were Tilak and Gandhi.

POLITICAL RESPONSE

The social reformers of the late eighteenth and nineteenth centuries were without doubt the great pioneers of Indian nationalism. The awakening they brought among urbanized and educated Indians soon created a political response which, in turn, led the movement in another direction. By the time the generation of Ranade was replaced by the generation of Gokhale, the main leaders of social reform were found functioning in the broad framework of political agitation. Even during Ranade's time, Dadabhai Naoroji, the great Parsi leader from Bombay who later rose to great eminence and was the first Indian to be elected to the English Parliament, was highly critical of the British regime which, he thought, was draining the Indian economy through "exploitation." He advocated a political approach to the Indian problem. (Ranade himself was not an exponent of pure social reform but rather emphasized the larger dimension of social regeneration and awakening as preconditions of self-government). Then there were the extremist groups, springing up in Bengal and elsewhere, which wanted an end to foreign rule. Altogether, a current of discontent was seething in the country and called for an outlet.

The outlet was provided by an historic act in modern Indian politics, the founding of the Indian National Congress in 1885. Standing in a casual way—almost in a fit of absent-mindedness—and blessed by Englishmen and the local authorities, the Congress was ultimately to grow into a mammoth organization, supplying a unified leadership to the nationalist movement. The Congress, however, was (and still is) a compromise between two contradictory characteristics of Indian nationalism: conservatism and radicalism. The former manifested itself in the form of constitutionalism, moderation in the choice of political techniques, and adjustments with the Raj. The latter took various forms, ranging from non-violent agitation for British withdrawal from India to frank espousal of violent and terrorist action. In following the line of constitutionalism, the moderate leadership of the Congress worked hand in hand with the exponents of British constitutionalism both in India and in England. When the Congress turned away from strictly constitutional lines, it got into a direct tussle with the colonial authority. By following both approaches alternately, the Congress achieved its aim. In the process, it both acquired experience in the working of parliamentary institutions and built powerful organizational structures and cadres, a pluralist structure of support, and a mass base.

The development of self-governing institutions in India is a joint product of British rule and Indian response. Undoubtedly, a more obstinate imperial power—one without experience in operating democratic institutions and techniques of political bargaining—would have changed the course of Indian nationalism. Certainly, too, the sophisticated intellectual and cultural background brought by the Indians, as revealed in the response that English education brought in administrative and political recruitment, enabled the British to rule the country with such an economy of effort.

Almost from the beginning of the consolidation of British power in India, men of vision, sympathy, and understanding of the Indian people were among those who wielded power in India. These men thought of the days when Indians would govern themselves and the steps by which such a goal could be achieved. Until almost the end of the nineteenth century, however, little concrete thought had been given to the steps that should be taken for giving power to the "natives." (The only steps that were taken were at the local level in the direction of local self-government, and even these were without great success.)[6]

DEMAND FOR SELF-GOVERNMENT

Several factors joined in determining the first steps in the development towards parliamentary government in India in this century. First, the Congress grew more critical of the failure of the government to respond to the gestures of friendship and cooperation that its leaders had been making. There also emerged within the Congress, alongside the moderate leadership led by Gokhale, a powerful group of militants led by Bal Gangadhar Tilak, Lajpat Rai, and Bipin Chandra Pal. This group emphasized political struggle and the building of a strong nation-wide movement. Tilak made *Swaraj* (self-rule) itself the goal of political agitation. "Swaraj is my birthright and I will have it," he thundered. The new group put pressure on the moderate leadership of the Congress to ask for more and immediate reforms. Second, the partition of Bengal by the colonial power in 1905 gave rise to a fury of protest against the government.

Third, the mild measure of reform introduced by the British and known as the Indian Councils Act of 1909, by which for the first time some elected members were taken in the Viceroy's and the Governor's Councils, led to a demand for more representation and greater power to the elected elements who, as yet, were greatly outnumbered by the official and nominated members of the Councils. The demand for "Home Rule" became more intense after Tilak, imprisoned by the British from 1908 to 1914, returned home as a hero, joined the Home Rule League started by Annie Besant, and soon (with the death of Gokhale in 1915) rose to a position of dominance in the Congress. There followed a consolidation of nationalist forces among the moderates, the former extremists, and the Muslims (under an agreement of cooperation between the Congress and the Muslims League known as the Lucknow Pact). From this united front, a demand for "a large measure of self-government" was made. Fourth, and above all, World War I forced the British to seek the active cooperation of Indians in the war effort, and, in return, to assure them of a greater measure of self-government.

The result, known as the Government of India Act of 1919, established a moderate form of parliamentary government under foreign tutelage. A Central Legislature was constituted with two chambers, both of which included nominated members as before, but also a substantial number of representatives elected on the basis of general and "special" electorates. At the provincial level, there were further concessions in the direction of self-Government. There came into being a system of "dyarchy" according to which certain regulative and extractive functions of government were reserved for the governor and others were transferred to ministers who were to be responsible to the provincial Legislative Council, a majority of whose members were elected. The approach was first to allow a measure of responsible government in the provinces before trying the same at the national level. Although still retaining the overall control of the British, the Act was an important step in the direction of parliamentary self-government.

It is interesting to note, however, that the Act as with all subsequent british attempts at conciliation, received a cold response in the country. The Indian National Congress in considering the Act of 1919 passed a resolution saying that the Act was "disappointing" and calling upon the Parliament in Great Britain to establish "full responsible government" in India "in accordance with the principles of self-determination." The Congress, in effect, declined to cooperate on the basis of the Act.

GROWTH IN DISCONTENT

It is important to realize the change that had taken place in the political climate of India during the first two decades of this century. The urge for social and political reform was transformed into a desire for independence. Cooperative attitudes towards the British underwent a drastic change; the British began to be looked upon as foreign impostors who ruled arbitrarily and autocratically, without taking the wishes of the people into account. The partition of Bengal disturbed even the moderately inclined leadership and led to charges of exploitation. Dadabhai Naoroji theory of economic drain caught the imagination of the middle class intelligentsia and became a powerful weapon in the political armory of the nationalists. There followed the campaign for *Swadeshi,* a movement to prevent people from buying foreign goods and to substitute indigenous goods instead. Tilak's imaginative leadership of this movement generated great enthusiasm, created a boom in the local textile industry, and thus enlisted the support of the merchant class in India. The remark that Indians had to undergo a period of training before they were given responsible power, which had appeared to be a sensible approach to many in the past, now seemed humiliating. Indian nationalism had turned radical and took on a more assertive tone. The Congress, which started on a note of "responsive cooperation," now turned into a platform for the struggle towards self-government.

All this was natural. The spread of education and ideas, and the discontent with the existing state of affairs, was bound to articulate the natural cleavage between Indian and British interests. Actually, more fundamental changes were at work, changes that brought on the surface entirely new forces which were soon to change the nature of politics in India. First, a centralized national elite emerged for the first time, and discussed the problems of the country at a general and national level. In place of enlightened and outstanding individuals working for social and political reform in various places and through various associations, there was now a national leadership and a national association. The availability of a forum in the Congress played a critical role in this development. This was the great transformation of Indian history, the growth of a national consciousness and identity, and an organization to sustain it. Whereas British rule, through administrative integration and stability, had laid the physical basis for an all-India identity, the foundation of the Indian nation was not laid until the local response to foreign rule also took a national form and acquired prestige and an institutional base.

Second, with the development of such an elitist thinking and functioning in the context of a national organization, a realization of the political dimension of the nationalist movement also grew, slowly but unmistakably. The leadership realized that not reform and education alone were involved, but also a long and substantial struggle. It was seen that the nationalists were dealing with a powerful Empire and that it was foolhardy to expect that the Empire would liquidate itself. This is why Tilak said that Swaraj would have to be fought for. The experience with trying to wrest political reforms from the colonial authority had been frustrating.

NEW CLEAVAGES

Third, with the growth of awareness of the size of the problem, there grew divergent views on the best strategy to solve it, and this led to a cleavage within the ranks of the nationalists. Dissatisfied with the cautious constitutionalism of the moderates, the radical group led by Tilak sought control of the movement. Although defeated in their first attempt to gain control at the momentous Surat Congress of 1907, they continued to enjoy considerable support among the politically conscious sections of the people. After the return of Tilak from jail and the death of Gokhale in 1915, they gained a clear ascendancy. Tilak also, during this period, underwent a marked change in approach, from that of a dynamic agitator to that of a shrewed manager of power. This further consolidated the new forces in the nationalist movement and contributed to the righteous rejection by the Congress of the Government of India Act of 1919.

Thus the period after the partition of Bengal saw a hardening of relationships between the Indian leadership and the British authorities, notwithstanding the concessions offered by the British in 1909 and 1919 and the annulment of the partition itself in 1911. The political temperature in the country had changed; there was ferment in the ranks of the nationalist movement. The British themselves contributed to the alienation of Indian opinion, not so much by imprisoning and deporting important leaders as by more provocative measures such as the passing of the repressive Rowlatt Acts and the massacre of hundreds of Indians through mass shooting at Jallianwala Bag in Amritsar in 1919. Tension in the country was matched by tension within the Congress. With Tilak and his followers gaining dominance in the organization, the liberals went out and formed the Liberal Federation, just as earlier in 1907 the assertion of the strength of the moderates had forced out the group led by Tilak.

Such a changing of forces between the moderates and the radicals did not, however, materially affect the result of the Congress' efforts. The situation in which the Congress was placed was, in fact, far from satisfactory; it seemed that neither the moderates nor the radicals had any real solution to offer. The Congress had turned into a debating society. There was little that could be done if the authorities did not agree to grant greater concessions. Experience with trying to gain political reforms from the government—a line consistently and persuasively followed by the moderates—proved to be frustrating. On the other hand, the militants had also failed to take the country anywhere near the goal of self-government by emphasizing struggle and exhibiting a posture of militancy. Throwing a few bombs in the cities, killing a few Englishmen, or burning imported textiles was not leading to anything other than further repression at the hands of the authorities. The extremists, too, seemed to have reached a dead end. The fact was that the Congress had no substantial organizational base in the country from which to mobilize strength. Drawn largely from the narrow base of urbanized and educated middle classes, and agitating through an idiom of communication wholly unfamiliar to the people at large, the leadership of the Congress lacked any widespread following or organized support. Both liberal constitutionalism and extremist militancy had failed to provide the necessary leadership. In their failure to provide leadership, they created a void in the country.

CHARISMA AND RECONSTRUCTION

This void was filled by the rise of a remarkable man on the Indian political scene, Mohandas Karamchand Gandhi. Gandhi brought to Indian politics what it had long lacked, namely depth and an indigenous base. Returning in 1915 from South Africa where he had developed his technique of *satyagraha* (moral persuasion) in dealing with the race issue,[7] he toured widely to observe the Indian scene and drew his own conclusions concerning the nature of the problem that faced the country. Gandhi saw that a long struggle lay ahead, struggle not only with a foreign power, but also with the Indian people themselves. He realized clearly what few before him did, that the urbanized middle class alone did not provide a sufficient basis for national awakening. The task was to penetrate the masses, to arouse them from their state of apathy and isolation, to provide them with self-confidence and a positive elan in place of both the defensive postures of the moderates and the inferiority complex of the "anti-Western" radicals, and to confront the authorities with proof that they were dealing not with a small group of agitators, but with tens of thousands of people organized and disciplined into a great movement, drawn from all over the country. Gandhi also realized that he was dealing with an adversary who was not to be deterred by physical force and who, on the other hand, was not immune to moral persuasion, if backed by sufficient power and organization from below. The immediate task was to build this power and organization from below on the basis of a new self-awareness and sense of purpose.

Gandhi, himself driven by uncommon moral energy, proved remarkably successful in giving to the Congress a new direction, a powerful organizational base, and a mass following. He adopted unorthodox techniques to focus the attention of men and women from all segments of society on a common program of action. He appealed to them on the basis of "sacrifice" and morality. He led powerful campaigns of "non-violent non-cooperation" with the government in 1921, 1930, and 1932. Essentially movements of civil disobedience and challenge to authority, Gandhi insisted on keeping them non-violent and disciplined, and launched them in the form of moral resistance to injustice rather than as mass agitations. This was the essence of satyagraha. He himself undertook several fasts including "fasts unto death" to persuade the government into (or out of) some step. In this he often, though not always, succeeded, in the process also generating deep feeling in the country and gaining attention from other parts of the world.

But he was also a great builder and pragmatist. Between campaigns, he provided his followers with a comprehensive program of "constructive work." This included work among the "untouchables," the spinning of *khadi* (hand-spun cloth), tribal and village uplift, social work among the underprivileged, educational work, and work in various ancillary organizations of the Congress dealing with women, youth, labor, and the backward classes. Gandhi emphasized that political work should not be dissociated from social work, that they were not alternatives but were parts of the same program, thus ending the dichotomy that had for so long divided the exponents of alternative courses of action. At the same time such a program of "constructive work" proved to be an intelligent strategy for keeping the "army" of Congress workers constantly mobilized so that when the next campaign of civil disobedience came, a country-wide force already was available to join it.

NEW SYMBOLS

Gandhi imparted a powerful symbolism and great depth and diffusion to the nationalist movement. Known by his followers as *Mahatma* (a great soul), he provided both a concentration of charisma and its dispersal by resorting to powerful symbols of identity that forced all the sections of the Congress rank and file to fall in line. He did this in three ways. First he developed a model of "exemplary" life by making his own life—including its most intimate aspects—a museum of national learning and a pacesetter. The "demonstration effect" that resulted was powerful. Second, he converted large and unresolved issues of Indian society into charismatic symbols: he gave to the vast masses of "untouchables" the name of "Harijans" (children of God) and launched a nation-wide movement for their amelioration as part of the Congress program; he developed a massive program for the propagation of Hindustani (a combination of Hindi and Urdu) as a language of national unity; he championed the cause of women and spoke of their equality with men almost in the style of feminism; he turned the symbolism of Hindu-Muslim unity into a general platform of national cohesion. He created the powerful symbol of the spinning wheel and made indigenous home-spun khadi, which provided employment to the masses, into a prescribed uniform for all those who claimed to be nationalists; he turned the trivial issue of a tax on salt into a symbol of defiance and mobilized tens of thousands of people into a "salt march"; he used the full symbolism of individual "player" as a public institution of the nation, held every evening wherever he was, during which his solutions to the problems of politics were highlighted and publicized. The daily press gave to the prayer meeting a greater coverage than most other news items. Gandhi characterized his struggle against the British as "Experiments in the realization of truth."

Third, Gandhi turned all this symbolism of a pacifist, saintly Indian into a militant organizational style and indeed into a well-knit organizational structure of the Congress with a program of action and a powerful identity and discipline. This enabled him to include in the Congress men of diverse skills and intellectual backgrounds, representing nearly all streams of ideological thought and all the more important social interests and sectional groups. Gandhi valued the cohesion and unity of the movement above any doctrinal considerations, or even considerations of pride. Such an approach gave rise to a high tolerance of ambiguity and eclecticism in the organization of the national movement. It allowed both dissent and conformism to become integral parts of the overall consensual style of the Congress, and it gave to the national Congress great flexibility and freedom of maneuver. Such an approach prevented the growth of hard and fast cleavages in the nationalist movement which have afflicted freedom struggles in many other countries. (Gandhi also tried very hard to prevent the Hindu-Muslim cleavage but in that he ultimately failed.)

MULTI-DIMENSIONALITY

By thus providing mutually reinforcing symbols of great potency which had the sanction of tradition and were at the same time highly functional, Gandhi built bridges all over the place. He had the great gift of multi-dimensionality: of translating dimensions of time (the bridging of several centuries) into concrete dimensions of space (bridging the gap between town and country), converting both into a program of the present, and providing them with an idiom of modernization that had indigenous meaning, simplicity of communication, and a potency that was at the same time both organizational and personal. He constantly reinterpreted traditional concepts of authority and hierarchy, social obligation and self- realization, consensus and unity, grafted them onto the modern setting, and furnished them with a meaning that proved functional in the development of a distinctive national identity and affect. He sent thousands of Congress workers into the villages and asked them to "serve the people." They were to follow a strict code of conduct, deny themselves all sensual pleasures, live at a minimum cost, thus improving their own life and character while serving the poor and the lowly. They were implored by him to set the highest standards in public life, to "demonstrate" the need in a poor country to limit one's wants and the size of one's family, as well as the need for discipline and sacrifice for the common good. He used the traditional concepts of trusteeship, personal thrift, and fulfilling one's religion by attending to earthly obligations in mobilizing the business community and their resources for his various programs: along with building temples in the neighborhood they were asked to contribute to the great temple that was modern India. Gandhi constantly emphasized the moral aspect of social and political action, thereby drawing support from the traditional sectors of Indian society which he penetrated with great effect. Gandhi's great contribution as a nation-builder lies in bridging this enormous gap between town and country and between traditional India and modern India.

Reinterpretation of tradition for modernist purposes was only one aspect of Gandhi's political style. He was also a powerful iconoclast and rejected tradition where it was redundant for national purpose. Gandhi was as much a creator of new traditions as an interpreter of old ones; underlying both was a desire to shift and reconstruct given situations for the fulfillment of new purposes. Thus, while he utilized the traditional notions of trusteeship and self-restraint, he similarly rejected any special prerogatives of birth and status or even of knowledge and intellect. He doggedly resisted any belief in fatalist acceptance of social roles and repudiated the erosive individualism of traditional Hindu thought. Above all he made good the greatest deficiency of Hindu thought, namely, its lack of collective ethics and an organized civic sense. This was a greater achievement of Gandhi's than all his emphasis on self control and personal morality. His stress on institution-building and organizational discipline proved to be a far greater legacy for the future than his various commentaries on personal religiosity.

INSTITUTION-BUILDING

Gandhi produced a band of outstanding leaders all over the country and assigned to them special duties and functions in the Congress. These were the men who later provided a unified leadership for independent India at various levels in government and party organizations. He took a number of imaginative steps in the institutional development of the Congress. He instituted the Congress Working Committee, turning it into a powerful and august body. Popularly known as the "Congress High Command," it represented the national consensus and commanded authority. It developed as an instrument of collective leadership and overshadowed the larger representative body, the AICC (All India Congress Committee). While the latter often could be moved by deviant forces, it was the former which ultimately asserted authority.

Again and again Gandhi used the High Command (of which he was never a formal member) as an instrument for disciplining one and all. Whenever he suddenly suspended a mass campaign and provoked criticism and protests from the more militant sections, he would get his decision confirmed by the High Command. In 1939 when Subhash Bose was elected president of the Congress by the AICC against Gandhi's wishes, Bose was forced to resign the office even after he had been duly elected, as the traditional leadership of the High Command refused to cooperate with him. This was considered authoritarian on the part of

Gandhi and was bitterly criticized in the rank and file, but it was Gandhi who prevailed. As he had said years ago to the Congress, it had every right to change its leader, but if the Congress chose him as leader, it is he who would take decisions. His insistence on discipline and singularity of action was overwhelming; it drove him to demand from his disciples unquestioned obedience. But he chose not to act as a dictator, but rather to rely on the authority of the High Command. In the process, the High Command and its leadership acquired great prestige and legitimacy among the people. Its word was law and was respected. For the first time in Indian history, an all-Indian institution representing the national will and acting with full authority was created. It was Gandhi's great contribution to the institutionalization of the Indian nation.

Gandhi strove to give the Congress a broad-based organization. He established throughout the country district units known as the District Congress Committees (DCC) and made them the base of mass organization and membership. Gandhi always considered the DCC the chief vanguard of the people at the lower levels. He also established various other mobilization agencies for "constructive work" in special sectors, such as in labor, the Harijans, women, youth, and the tribal people. He realized early in the movement the need for organizations in which the Congress could keep its cadres engaged when it was not involved in non-cooperation movements. He also appreciated the role of continuous communications and discussion of ideas. Through *Young India* and *Harijan* he reached his followers in the various regions and prepared them on the minutiae of various facets of the movement. He did all this in order to give organizational shape and perspective to the nationalist movement. He was himself temperamentally against the notion of a party bureaucracy, but by taking these steps he instituted a powerful and coordinated movement with a hierarchy that penetrated deep into the country. After independence, the Congress set up many more units of organization and agencies of mobilization, but it was the pattern established by Gandhi that provided it with starting points. It is a pattern that still dominates the Congress organization and has been emulated by almost all other democratic parties.[8]

NEGATIVE LEGACY

Such an overwhelming role of one man had its undoubted costs. Gandhi's unique style of leadership and communications also had its costs. Significantly, the costs were not in terms of leaving the country "leaderless" after him as has happened in many other new nations; India's greatest resource at the time of independence was the availability of outstanding leaders at all levels and throughout the country. Gandhi's negative legacy lay in quite other directions. Chief among these was his tendency to moralize and to paint the ethical content of politics in such bold strokes. Consequently, he set unrealizable standards, so that sermonizing often took the place of attending to the details of statecraft; his overemphasis on the moral dimension of politics also meant that there persisted a style and an idiom that was wholly at odds with the reality of democratic politics. Gandhi combined a high sense of realism for the present with a thorough-going messianism for the future, his greatest failure being to have made no allowances for mortal men. In a peculiar way Gandhi missed the essence of democratic politics, and many of his followers (the Gandhians) even today exhibit this weakness. That Nehru could transcend this shortcoming is a tribute to his entirely different intellectual background and to his ability to preserve this despite the magnetic influence of his master.

Even during his own time Gandhi's style and methods created many problems. His concern at turning immediate issues of the movement to the larger strategy of national mobilization and institution-building produced serious gaps in communication, placed a premium on faith rather than tactical reason, and led to much impatience in his own ranks and not a little bewilderment outside. His tendency to combine both moral and strategic issues in his political style and pedagogy alienated other political groups. And both his followers and his adversaries—the British as well as competing political groups—were often left guessing as to his next move. All this created a climate of suspense and uncertainty, led to some tactical errors—"Himalayan blunders" as he once himself described them—and sharp reversals of strategy. More importantly, his style of mobilization failed to prevent cleavages within the movement and in some measure accentuated them. His role in consolidating the unity of India and resisting all attempts at weakening it was very great. But he appeared to be less than adequately sensitive to subtler issues of political cohesion and accommodation. In his attempt to resolve the communal problems, for instance, he invested heavily in symbol manipulation—as in the Khilafat movement or the development of Hindustani—but much less in the tasks of coalition-making. He often adopted an inflexible attitude, alienated leaders of other groups by invoking traditionalist symbols, and created suspicion regarding the real intentions of the Congress. All this does not, of course, add up to a categorical criticism of the Gandhian approach, for many of the issues were dilemmas inherent in the situation. Some of them emerged precisely in the course of forcing the pace of national awakening, in which Gandhi's role was simply phenomenal. He also showed a great deal of intuitive genius in sorting out some of the dilemmas that emerged, especially those that had implications for the building of a political community, but failed in others. His greatness lay in accepting defeat where he had failed and yet pushing ahead with the central tasks.

OTHER POLITICAL GROUPS

Gandhi's approach to the nationalist cause was, of course, not the only one, nor was his leadership unquestionably accepted. Thus while he was concentrating on training the people in non-violent non-cooperation, a group of prominent Congressmen formed the Swaraj Party to press the directly political approach for the achievement of dominion status, and passed a resolution in the 1927 Congress session held at Madras declaring independence as the goal of the Congress. This group organized an All- Parties Conference in 1928 and appointed a subcommittee which recommended full responsible government and dominion status for India. Gandhi was not a party to any of this. A younger group led by Jawaharlal Nehru and Subhash Chandra Bose sought a more radical approach and demanded complete independence. They succeeded in securing their objective at the 1929 session of the Congress held at Lahore where Gandhi himself moved a resolution defining swaraj as "complete independence". A still more left- oriented group formed the Congress Socialist Party. Meanwhile in some of the provinces other groups had emerged outside the Congress, some of them participating in the governmental system under the British. Chief among these were the Justice Party in Madras, a precursor of the later DK and DMK, and the Unionist Party in Punjab. Finally, there was the leadership of the Indian Muslims, a majority of which found it difficult to reconcile with Gandhi and the Congress. These were divided between the traditionalists whose sense of a basic schism between Hindus and Muslims made them hostile to the Congress and the progressives under Jinnah who had no sympathy for Gandhi's seemingly obscurantist techniques. Despite many efforts, Gandhi failed to dissolve the antipathies of these groups.

Gandhi himself was not adverse to the adoption of diverse means to the goal of freedom. Thus alongside organizational activity and the campaigns of civil disobedience, he also remained closely interested in constitutional development and entered into negotiations with the British authorities from time to time. Indeed, in spite of his concentration on mass satyagraha as against the Swarajists who emphasized constitutional development, he never gave up efforts at arriving at some understanding with the British at various stages of the movement. He always combined in his strategy instruments of resistance with the device of careful negotiation, often leading to compromise solutions that would allow the movement a breathing spell. Furthermore, Gandhi was himself an intensely orderly being. Although leading campaigns of civil disobedience, and often choosing a particular regulation or event for defiance, he never desired a breakdown of civil authority, whether British or Indian, and was always careful to call off a campaign when it appeared to get out of hand. On various occasions he entered into some sort of a "deal" and came out with a peaceful compromise in spite of the powerful opinion of his own supporters against such conciliation.

Thus in the civil disobedience campaign of 1922, when he found that some of his followers had resorted to violence, he called off the whole campaign, much to the chagrin of his loyal disciples, including Jawaharlal Nehru who protested from jail. Again, on his own release from prison in 1931, and responding to the declaration of the British prime minister favoring the advance of India to "full responsibility for her own government," he reached an agreement with the viceroy, Lord Irwin, known as the Gandhi-Irwin pact. Under the agreement, he suspended the non-cooperation campaign and attended the second Round Table Conference in England as the representative of the Congress.[9] Greatly dissatisfied with the Conference, where Gandhi found it impossible to work out an agreement among the Indians and saw that the British were making capital out of India's communal problem (which we will discuss at some length later in this chapter), he returned to India only to find that the government had put behind bars all the important leaders and thousands of others.

THE ISSUE OF SECULARISM

But while Gandhi was aware that eventually an understanding would have to be evolved with the British, he was not prepared to make compromises on fundamentals, least of all on issues-bearing on national unity. When he saw that British were reluctant to agree to a truly secular compromise, and would not give up their approach of "representing" the nation through several communal groups having separate electorates he entered upon another fast unto death, protesting the decision to create separate electorates for the Harijans. Greatly troubled by the "Communal Award" which threatened to destroy the unity of Indian society, Gandhi fought to preserve it from falling apart. The fast succeeded in forcing the authorities to withdraw their decision.

On the other hand, it is clear that after his unhappy experience with the Round Table Conference and his conviction that the conservatives in Britain were playing a dangerous game by exploiting the communal problem, both Gandhi and his followers were greatly intrigued as to the next step in the struggle. The Congress did not respond favorably to the Government of India Act of 1935, despite major concessions on the part of the British, including an increased electorate. The Act was singularly lacking in any conception of national cohesion. Or rather, the British conception of the Indian nation differed markedly from the Congress conception. (The Act provided for close to complete autonomy in the provinces and a federal structure of government which would have included the princely states.) From the point of view of the Congress leadership this inability to keep the cohesion of the nation in the forefront made the Act unacceptable as a political formula. However, as substantial powers were being transferred to popular ministries in the provinces, the Congress decided to participate in the elections to the provincial legislatures held in 1937 under the Act. It formed the government in eight provinces.

After two years in office, however, the Congress governments in the provinces resigned in 1939, protesting against the viceroy's action in declaring India's participation in World War II without consulting the Congress leaders. While Nehru and others were in favor of supporting the British war effort, and other "antifascists" talked of suspending the nationalist movement for the period of the war, Gandhi insisted that the Congress would not cooperate with the British except on the basis of immediate freedom. The British tried their best to win Indian support for the war and deputed Sir Stafford Cripps, a friend of the Indian cause, to persuade Gandhi and his associates to cooperate with the British in return for an assurance to convene a Constituent Assembly after the war. With the failure of the Cripps Mission, the demand for complete and immediate freedom was reiterated. With the British not responding Gandhi led a massive campaign in August, 1942, following the passage by the Congress of a "Quit India" resolution calling upon the British to leave the country. The entire leadership was imprisoned, but thousands of people offered satyagraha and courted imprisonment. There followed a long struggle all over the country, challenging the authority of the British to rule the country. Once again Gandhi undertook a fast in prison which nearly killed him. Upon release from jail of the main leaders in 1945, with the Labour Government in power in Great Britain and a totally changed climate of opinion in the world at the end of the war, negotiations for complete independence were undertaken but once again reached a deadlock. Before we consider these, however, there is need to discuss at some length the principal impediment in the road to independence and national unity.

THE COMMUNAL PROBLEM AND NATIONAL INTEGRATION

The issue that paralyzed the nationalist struggle under Gandhi was the so- called "communal problem" of India. As the struggle proceeded and conditions in the world as a whole changed, the issue was no longer whether India would gain independence but rather to whom power was to be transferred. What was the constitutional formula on the basis of which the Parliament of Great Britain was to relinquish its sovereignty in India? It was the communal problem—and the demand for a separate state for the Muslims—that became the critical issue of the negotiations on Indian independence. It is necessary to consider in some detail the background to this problem.

The roots of the problem are deep and can be historically traced back to the Muslim period. During the last few centuries, however, the Hindus and Muslims in India had learned to live together and had shared in the development of social and cultural traditions. Like ethnic groups everywhere, they would have developed as part of the same national community. Indeed, deep and subtle bonds had developed between the Hindus and the Muslims in India which endure today even after the partition of the country into two—bonds of language and region, of temporal and cultural values, of literature, history, and traditions. In spite of differing philosophies of religion, the Islamic doctrine of "brotherhood of all men" and the Hindu doctrine of "different roads to the same truth" had been subtly drawn together into an amorphous ideal of mutual tolerance and generosity that was peculiarly and characteristically Indian.[10]

The political evolution of India under the British, while it made great advances in other directions, led to certain developments in Hindu-Muslim relationships that brought old animosities to the surface and gave rise to alienation and hostility. The British government, the Congress, and the political leadership of the Muslims all contributed to this. Strangely enough, the very representative and secular notions of government that contributed to the political modernization of India aggravated the communal problem in India.

UNEQUAL DEVELOPMENT

The British had initially adopted policies that appeared to discriminate against the Muslims. Still conscious of the fact that they had come to dominate this vast subcontinent largely through subduing and undermining the authority of the Moghuls, they followed a policy of keeping the Muslims out of reach of advantageous positions in the new Empire, or of neutralizing or counterweighting their power in places where they still continued to be dominant. (They had followed a similar policy in regard to the Rajputs where the latter had challenged the advance of British power.) There were also other, less intentional, effects of the rise of British power which favored the Hindus. Whereas the Brahmins and other caste Hindus quickly availed themselves of the opportunities and jobs opened by English education, the Muslims, by tradition more closeknit and circumscribed in their learning and socialization habits, lagged behind. Economically, too, with the decline of traditional crafts, the slow encroachment of the Hindu merchant and money-lending classes, and the consolidation of new patterns of land settlement, the Muslims began to experience hardship. Having not yet forgotten the great days of the Moghul Empire, they experienced difficulty in adjusting to a minority status among a subject population.

It would also be remembered that an important component of the political and cultural renaissance of modern India came from a revival of Hinduism and indigenous Sanskritic culture after the colonial regime had restored law and order. Hindu society, for long in defense against the Muslim power, began to reassert its identity. Essential to this revival was access to the English language, the universities, and administrative and intellectual positions. A consequence of this was that the leadership of the nationalist movement for the first few decades was also mainly provided by the Hindus, many of whom drew inspiration from traditional Hindu scriptures and legends as a means of establishing the identity of Indianness.

MUSLIM REACTION

On the other hand, the impact of British education and nationalist opinion touched none but a fringe of Muslim intellectuals.[11] To the latter, the domination of the Hindus in administration and politics appeared to threaten the position of the Muslims in the new India. One of these was Sir Syed Ahmed Khan who led the attack on Hindu domination and asked the Muslims not to identify themselves with the Hindus, to keep aloof from the Congress movement, and instead to seek their salvation through cooperation with the British and through modern education. Sir Syed strove hard to remove mutual suspicions between the British ruling class and Muslim leadership, and led the foundation of a new educational movement for the Muslims from Aligarh where he established the Anglo-Oriental College in 1877 (which later grew into the Aligarh Muslim University). He also organized the Muslim Educational Conference which held annual sessions.

Such an intellectual reaction against the decline of Muslim power, coming as it did in the latter part of the nineteenth century, did not have much effect on political thinking since it had not yet been articulated on any clear programmatic lines. The Muslims had no serious feeling of hostility or resistance. On the contrary, with the decline in the government's suspicion for the Muslims, there was a greater acceptance of the latter, and the Aligarh movement, if anything, contributed to the participation of an increasing number of educated Muslims in the mainstream of modern India. With urbanization and the new education, traditional centers of culture and social distinction like Lucknow, Allahabad, Patna, Aligarh, and Hyderabad once again were booming with activity in which both Muslims and Hindus participated and mixed freely. The traditional distinctions between communities, sexes, and generations were still respected but there was a fine sense of decorum and honor in this and little evidence of animosity and hatred.

SEEDS OF DISINTEGRATION

All the same, the unequal development of the two communities, the fact that for a long time the nationalist and social reform movements were dominated by Hindus including the symbols of Hindu revivalism, and the discriminatory and often non-secular approach of the British—all sowed the seeds of the later problem of national integration. Contrary to general impression, modernization—especially education and urbanization—leads to an awareness of distinctive identities, breaks downs traditional modes of recognition and mobility, and emphasizes numerical strength and organized competition as means of finding a place in the system. Historical animosities get revived; at the same time new opportunities open up; and the principal challenge is one of efficient coalition-making. In the Indian case contrary tendencies developed, integrative as well as disintegrative. The latter ultimately prevailed, due to a combination of factors. Let us briefly review these.

APPROACH TO "REPRESENTATION"

The politicization of communal feelings in India was in part a consequence of the introduction of representative institutions, and owed not a little to the traditional British approach to the principle of representation. The british tends to think of representation as representation of groups, estates interests, territories, associations, communities. Their own background of a homogenous society in which national integration had preceded the growth of representative institutions made them take the former for granted. Thus they saw the problem of a plural society such as India as essentially a problem of the identification of natural groups and their mutual conciliation, and thought that the only solution lay in group representation.

Accordingly, in India, they evolved the system of "communal" and "special" representation. Quite early in their rule they recognized chambers of commerce and municipalities, for example, for representation in the Councils. In 1909, they introduced other classes for representation in the Councils: landowners and Muslims. In 1919, "communal" and "special" constituencies were created over and above the "general" constituencies. In 1933, separate electorates for untouchables also were to be introduced, but the decision was later reversed as a result of Gandhi's "fast unto death" against the proposal. Thereafter, in the Act of 1935, and in the negotiations for Indian independence that followed World War II, communal representation and the principle of "weightage"— that is, the principle that in allocating seats to minority communities, they should be "weighted" more than their numbers called for—were the chief instruments through which the British tried to solve the communal problem. The principle of communal representation remained the chief bone of contention between the British and the Congress, although the Congress, too, ultimately was forced to accept it as a basis of negotiation.

The growth of political consciousness among the Muslims need not necessarily have led to the division of the country. The logic of communal representation lay in the accommodation of the minority by the majority community in the framework of a single nation. There were continuous efforts on both sides to agree upon a solution. Thus, soon after the formation of the Muslim League in 1906 for the avowed purpose of promoting "among the Musalmans of India a feeling of loyalty to the British Government,"[12] a new leadership emerged in the League which reacted to such an attitude of servility and demanded that the League should take a full part in the struggle for national freedom. Led by enlightened intellectuals like Mohammad Ali Jinnah and the Ali brothers (Maulana Mohammad Ali and his brother Shaukat Ali), the League in 1913 adopted as its objectives the attainment of self-government under the British, the promotion of national unity, and cooperation with other communities for "the said purposes". To this the Congress warmly responded in its session held in December of the same year. Upon this followed a period of courtship between the two, leading to the famous "Lucknow Pact" of 1916. Responding to the League's loyalty to the nationalist cause, the Congress agreed to accept separate electorates which it had resisted for so long, weightage for the minorities, and even the right of the minorities to veto legislation affecting its interests and to which it was opposed.

The Congress went further. It supported the "Khilafat Movement" after World War I, a movement in support of the Sultan of Turkey and the integrity of his Empire and his *Caliphate* (spiritual headship of the Muslims). Gandhi used the opportunity to unite Hindus and Muslims in India. The result was that when the first major non-cooperation movement against the British (1920-22) was started, Gandhi had the full support of the Muslims who had grown bitter against the British. Many of the prominent Muslim leaders participated in the movement, including the Ali brothers, Maulana Abul Kalam Azad, and Dr. Ansari. Although Jinnah did not join the civil disobedience movement of Gandhi whom he considered too traditionalist, he continued to be a nationalist and strove to lead the League along modern "secular" lines.

GROWING CLEAVAGE

Events conspired against the continuation of the Congress League entente and the secular policy of Jinnah. By 1922 the morale of the nationalists in India was at a low ebb. At the height of the non-cooperation movement when public feelings ran high, Gandhi, provoked by an act of violence by his followers against 22 policemen in Chauri Chaura in UP, called off the movement. The Mahatma's decision caused bitterness. When the government arrested him (most other leaders being already in jail), there was widespread frustration. Moreover as Gandhi's termination of the movement coincided with the end of the Khilafat agitation, the period of joint Hindu-Muslim militancy also came to an end. The liberals and the moderates had already left the Congress, which had yet to acquire its new organizational identity. In this political vacuum, communal violence between Hindus and Muslims broke out at a number of places and worsened the situation. When the Simon Commission (charged with the task of making a first-hand study of the Indian situation and recommending new steps in constitutional reform) arrived in India in 1927 the Muslim League was found split in two: one section led by Mr. Jinnah who had advocated joint electorates for Hindus and Muslims and who joined with the Congress in boycotting the Commission; the other section led by Sir Mohammad Shafi who stood for separate electorates and was determined to co-operate with the work of the Commission. The Jinnah group also attended the All-Parties Conference convened by the Swarajists in 1928 and cooperated with its subcommittee on drafting a constitution. The Shafi group in the League rejected the report of the subcommittee, as did the All-Muslim Parties Conference held in Delhi under the chairmanship of the Aga Khan. The trend of Muslim opinion thus was turning against Jinnah and the nationalists who had left the League. Jinnah, in disgust, left the country and went to England.

The communal problem had by now reached an impasse. It had turned from a simple problem in group accommodation to a major issue of political integration. Several factors contributed to the worsening of the situation. The British government of the day, in part genuinely sensitive to the "minorities problem" but also manipulating it for stalling large political concessions, contributed to the deterioration of relationships. Being in a position of authority, their attitude proved to be almost decisive. At the same time the sudden suspension of the 1922 Satyagraha meant a virtual demise of the Khilafat movement (which was already weakening) and consequent disillusionment with the Congress leadership. Gandhi's overwhelming personality and his insistence on "moral means" and use of traditional symbols (often based on Hindu religious ideals) alienated the more rational among the Muslim leadership. The dilemma was that whereas the traditionalists among the Muslims were basically anti-secular, the modernists like Jinnah had no sympathy for Gandhi's political style and no patience for the larger goals of social regeneration that Gandhi so strenuously sought to achieve. The result was a perfect stalemate produced by British equivocation, the intransigence of the Muslim militants, and the incapacity of the Congress to break new ground. As it turned out, it was the frustrated but ambitious Jinnah who broke new ground.

COMMUNAL AWARD

The volte-face in India's communal politics came in 1928 when Jinnah returned to India a changed man. He accepted the communal approach he had fought so long, and presented the League with a radical fourteen-point program which, apart from communal representation and schemes of weightage and Muslim veto on certain kinds of legislation, asked for a declaration of certain provinces as "Muslim-majority areas" for all time to come. The program became the basis of Muslim demands at the first and second Round Table Conferences after which the British prime minister declared a "Communal Award" which conceded to the Muslims almost all they had asked.

The emergence of Jinnah in the new role changed the nature of communal politics in India. The League, for all its appeal, was not yet a force from the point of view of mass organization. In the 1937 elections, although it got a few seats in Bengal and U.P., it was in fact routed, had to concede a good deal to the Congress, and failed to win a majority in any of the four "Muslim-majority" provinces, namely Bengal, Punjab, Sind, and the Northwest Frontier Provinces. Against this position of the League, there was on the one hand the "mass contact movement" among the Muslims started by the Congress with quite some success, and on the other hand the hold of other Muslim or predominantly Muslim parties such as the Unionists in Punjab and the Khudai Khidmatgars led by the two Khan brothers (both outstanding nationalist Muslims, the younger of the two known as the "Frontier Gandhi") in the NWFP. It seemed as if the Congress and other parties (in Punjab, NWFP, and Bengal) might be able to challenge the League in its claim to represent the Muslims of India. To Jinnah's credit, he saved the League from such a plight, raised it to power, and when the next elections were held in 1945–46 swept the polls, capturing 446 Muslim seats out of 496.

ELECTORAL FRUSTRATION

In retrospect, it appears that the electoral disappointment of the League, by producing a crisis of confidence, transformed its whole approach to the communal problem—from separate electorates within India to a separate State for the Muslims of India. At this point, Congress statesmanship also became inflexible. When the question of accommodating the Muslims in the provincial governments arose on the assumption of office in 1937, Jinnah himself declaring the League to be in favour of the idea, the Congress leadership, perhaps "drunk with power" as Jinnah described it, rejected the plea. In attaching such conditions as the subjection of

League legislators to the Congress legislative whip, the Congress leadership only succeeded in further alienating Jinnah and his group. It is true that the claim of the Muslim League to be the sole representative of the Muslims lacked a basis in electoral support, even in the seats reserved for the Muslims, but it was a claim that the Congress had recognized as early as 1916, and that had been implicitly and explicitly recognized ever since. Its denial now was a denial of the Muslims' right to organize themselves politically.[13]

The conception of a separate state for Muslims in place of demands for special protection was the result of a radical reappraisal of the political situation on the part of the League leaders and altered the whole context of Hindu-Muslim relations in India. There is little doubt that the League's frustration with democratic politics contributed to the new militancy and extremism. Henceforth, Jinnah became the fervent supporter of the "two- nation theory" and the exponent of India's partition into two. The hesitancy and confusion that had kept the League in the doldrums for more than twenty years were straightened out under the dynamic impact of a single idea, steered to its logical culmination under the trained intellect of Jinnah.

THE DEMAND FOR PAKISTAN

The idea of Pakistan was first conceived in 1930 by Dr. Mohamad Iqbal who, in his presidential address to the Muslim League convention held in Allhabad, pleaded for a separate Muslim State made out of northwest India and consisting of the Punjab, the NWFP, Sind, and Baluchistan. But for a long time "Pakistan" remained no more than a vague idea conceived by a speculative mind. With the change in the political situation, the increasing power of the Congress and the humiliation of the League leadership on the electoral front, and the latter's desperate need to look for a new program, the idea was revived and made the basis of a new movement. Meanwhile, the currents of modernization—education, concentration in urban areas, development of indigenous literature—had influenced the Muslims, raised their self-awareness as a community, and, frustrated as they became with democratic politics, accentuated their sense of isolation and separate identity. In 1940, the Muslim League officially adopted a resolution favoring a separate and independent state, and Jinnah categorically denied the possibility of Hindus and Muslims being part of a common nationality. The Hindus and the Muslims, he said, were not only different as communities and religions, but also as social and historical systems, as civilizations, as nations. "The Musalmans," he demanded, "must have their homeland, their territory and their State." This, in short, was the two-nation theory on which the demand for the partition of India, and later the partition itself, was based.

It is, of course, by no means clear that the change in League strategy between 1937 and 1940 determined the future course of events. In terms of sheer size of support in the country and its distribution in various communities and groups, the Indian National Congress was the dominant force in the subcontinent. On the other hand, the timing of the League's new militancy proved significant. Events moved fast and the Congress Leadership could not attend to the task of dealing with the new turn taken by Muslim nationalism in the country. In 1939 World War II broke out and the Congress ministries resigned in protest against the British government's direct involvement of India in the war. There followed a showdown between the British and the Congress, the unsuccessful mission of Sir Stafford Cripps, the "Quit India" resolution of 1942 and the mass movement that followed it, and the imprisonment of the entire Congress leadership for the period of the war.

The Congress attitude towards the problem of participation in World War II did not so much affect the British response to the Indian struggle as alter the balance of political forces within India. The resignation of Congress ministries from power in 1939 and the "Quit India" agitation of 1942 resulted in a disorganization of the Congress throughout the country. With most of the Congress leaders behind bars, the Muslim League found an ideal chance for organizing itself. It came out of the war—during which it participated in several provincial governments—greatly improved in its organization and mass appeal. When the negotiations with the British took place after the war, the position and bargaining power of the Muslim League had improved considerably.

Many have since felt that, tactically speaking, the Congress decision to drop out from power in 1939 was a mistake. The point was forcefully stated by V.P. Menon in his *The Transfer of Power in India*, in which he argued that if the Congress had not resigned from the provinces, "the course of Indian history might have been very different. By resigning, it showed a lamentable lack of foresight and political wisdom."[14] Continuance in power, and presence in the constituencies instead of jails, might have also proved favorable when the next round of elections came, including perhaps in Bengal and Punjab in whose assemblies the substantive outcome of the partition plan was decided. All of this has some relevance, but the issues that really decided the course of events were of a different order.

THE BRITISH APPROACH

The real issues were two: the British attitude to the Congress and the Congress's own conception of the future Indian nation. The matter became increasingly clear as the negotiations for the country's independence were resumed after the war. In June 1945, Lord Wavell, the viceroy, invited the major political groups in the country to a political conference at Simla. The conference resulted in a deadlock between the Congress and the Muslim League and ended in failure. A mood of pessimism swept over the country. In January, 1946, a British Parliamentary delegation came to India; the British Cabinet Mission followed in March. Finding that the division between the Congress and the Muslim League could not be bridged easily, the Mission decided to issue its own plan for the country's independence. It rejected the demand for partition and instead evolved the formula of a loose federation, to be called the Union of India, to which certain limited functions (defense, foreign affairs, and communication) were to be "ceded." All other powers and all residuary powers were to be vested in provincial legislatures, with the further provision that after a period of ten years any province could, by a simple majority in the legislature, ask for a reconsideration of the terms of the constitution; and, in addition, provinces were free to form "groups" with legislatures and executives. A Constituent Assembly, consisting of representatives of each community from each province, was to convene in three sections corresponding to the main regions to draft the future constitution of the provinces and of the country. The "plan" was very much in line with the 1935 Act (which was never put into effect) and had all the limitations of a weak center and all the potentials of a national breakdown. For it was clear that what would have emerged out of the Constituent Assembly under such auspices would have been a virtual confederation, not a federation. Once again the British and the Congress conception of the future Indian nation conflicted sharply. This also meant that the real issues were not faced but simply passed on to the Constituent Assembly, which was liable to become an arena of violent conflict and disintegration. Although the Congress accepted the Plan "in principle," this did not mean much. For as it turned out later, if faced by the grim logic of a choice between division of the subcontinent and a weak and truncated nation, the Congress would choose the former. Actually, the League's withdrawal from its earlier acceptance of the Plan, its resolve to press the demand for partition, and its decision not to participate in the Constituent Assembly which was convened in December, 1946 (though it agreed to participate in the "Interim Government" under Jawaharlal Nehru) saved the country from the kind of constitutional wrangles that have elsewhere led to chaos and coup d'etat. At the same time the British refusal to hand over power to a Congress-controlled center determined the division of the country into two.

The final period was one of great tension. The British forced the pace of events. Prime Minister Attlee announced in the British Parliament on February 20, 1947, that his government had decided to transfer power into Indian hands at the latest by June 1948. The manner in which the transfer was to be made was to be decided during the next few months. Attlee also announced that Lord Mountbatten would go to India as viceroy, with a mandate to implement the government's decision on the transfer of power. Thus the onus of responsibility shifted to the Indian leaders. On the other hand, it is now clear that whatever the original intentions of the Attlee government, the announcement served to underwrite the changed balance of advantage in Indian politics and to boost the morale of the Muslim League. In effect it meant that the British were prepared to divide the country if the rival Indian groups failed to arrive expeditiously at a compromise. Such an approach considerably hardened the League's intention to press the demand for a separate state. Lord Wavell at the time had opposed the decision to set a date for British withdrawal. Many years later, Maulana Azad, the famous nationalist Muslim of India, wrote, "Perhaps history will decide that the wiser policy would have been to follow Lord Wavell's advice."[15]

Attlee's determination to force the pace of events was reinforced by Lord Mountbatten's ruthless dynamism as the new viceroy went about performing his historic task. Exhibiting a rare capacity for confounding rival parties to a negotiation and forcing decisions out of them, and possessing incomparable personal charm, Mountbatten performed the surgical operation of dividing the Indian subcontinent without loss of either time or sentiment. Moving like a dynamo, the new viceroy collapsed every obstacle that came in his way, succeeded in isolating Mahatma Gandhi from the stream of national decision-making—this being Mountbatten's biggest and most stupefying achievement—and drew together the pragmatic elements in the Indian leadership for administering a political operation unparalleled in modern history.

MOB VIOLENCE

The approach of the Attlee government to the Indian negotiations and the insensitive dynamism of Mountbatten may still not have resolved the issue in favour of the country's division into two had it not been for yet another overpowering fact. In different parts of the country (first in Bengal, then in Punjab, and then spreading to other regions) unprecedented communal violence, mass killing, and lawlessness succeeded in paralyzing the will of the Congress leadership to resist the ultimate triumph of the "two nation theory." Gandhi protested with all his might but it seemed as if the cause he was espousing had long been lost. His most important followers parted company with him—Nehru with a sense of tragedy, Patel with a tough-minded pragmatism.[16] The Mahatma answered by another series of heroic acts, a *padyatra* (pilgrimage on foot) across riot-stricken Noakhali in Bengal, converting Hindus and Muslims to ways of peace, undertaking yet another fast against the government of Nehru and Patel on behalf of refugee Muslims, and finally being shot to death by a fanatic Hindu for his espousal of the Muslim cause. His assassination created a trauma in the country and resulted in a dramatic cessation of communal riots throughout the country.[17]

In sum, on the one hand the British approach which combined a sense of urgency for withdrawal with a reluctance to hand over power to a Congress-controlled center, and on the other hand the breakout of mass violence forced the pace of events and the partition of the country. The alternatives were perhaps even more difficult to work out. A confederative (or nearly confederative) solution would have produced a more total disintegration of the subcontinent while a more ruthless policy of subjugating Muslim nationalism would have had lasting consequences for the nature of the Indian state. In either case the kind of nation-building that India has been able to effect since 1947 would not have been possible.[18] But the point still remains that events were rushed, and rushed in a particular direction.

The end came quickly. Votes in the provisional assemblies and referenda in disputed areas decided the territorial boundaries between India and Pakistan. The armed forces, the administrative services, and various financial assets and liabilities were to be divided between the two inheritors of British power in the Indian subcontinent. All this was decided in record time. The Indian Independence Bill, introduced in the House of Commons on July 4, 1947, was hurried through both Houses in twelve days. On August 14, the India (Provisional Constitution) Order, 1947, was passed and the next day Pakistan and India were declared the two new Dominions to which power was transferred. The British who had built the Indian Empire "in a fit a absent-mindedness" dissolved it in an incredible rush. They behaved as if they were afraid lest the Indians might once again ask them to stay on!

TWO NATIONS

The full story of the final stage of negotiations on the solution of the "Indian problem" is not yet known and some of the more crucial decisions are still guarded in secrecy. The general bearing of these decisions, however, is clear. The Partition of the subcontinent, while in some ways it cleared the air, left behind a legacy of communal hatred and unsolved political problems. Both India and Pakistan, and the mixed Hindu-Muslim populations of both, still live with this legacy and will perhaps have to live with it for a very long time to come. On the other hand, the manner in which the Labour government liquidated the great Indian Empire left behind a legacy of goodwill and friendship between Great Britain and India, which was symbolized in the decision to continue India's association with the British Commonwealth. The latter was later renamed the Commonwealth of Nations when India decided to continue its association as a republic while still recognizing the Queen as the head of the Commonwealth, this being a special contribution of Jawaharlal Nehru to the development of the Commonwealth idea.

Thus came into being the modern states of India and Pakistan, carved out of the same subcontinent, and sharing in many cultural and historical traditions. In the Indian part of the subcontinent, the Indian National Congress inherited power and formed the government of the country. The British Raj was followed by a long period of Congress Raj.

Notes

1 We have devoted the bulk of Chapter VI to this transformation in the nature of caste under the impact of democratic politics. Such a utilization of the varna model by low-placed castes for social mobility was noticed even in the nineteenth century by census superintendents and gazetteers, and it must have existed long before. See, especially, *Census of India*, 1911, Report on Bengal, Bihar, Orissa, and Sikkim, for a picturesque account of the "hundreds of petitions ... received from different castes... requesting that they might be known by different names, be placed higher in the order of precedence, be recognized as Kshatriyas, Vaisyas, etc."

2. Authors as different in style and mental attitudes as Irawati Karve and Nirad Chaudhari have commented at length on this propensity of the Hindus. See Irawati Karve, *Hindu Society— An Interpretation* (Poona, 1961); Nirad C. Chaudhari, *The Continent of Circe* (New York, 1966).

3. There are important exceptions to this statement. Thus in northwest India, where the Sanskritic tradition had not penetrated deeply enough and where Islam was able to destroy Hindu civilization more thoroughly than else-

where, the influence of Islamic customs and traditions is marked even today. See D.R. Chanana, "Sanskritisation, Westernisation and India's North-West," *Economic Weekly*, XIII, No.9, March 4, 1961.

4. The widely held image of colonial rule in India being essentially a "law and order" state is most misleading. The British initiated a number of measures in a variety of fields— economic, social, cultural—and investigated a large cross-section of Indian life. Many of the developments since independence, while they went much beyond what the British had ever conceived, built upon these beginnings.

5. For an historical account of the development of the different segments of this class, see B.B. Misra, *The Indian Middle Classes: Their Growth in Modern Times* (London, 1961).

6. Lord Rippon, a great liberal and a passionate if naive advocate of local self-government "as an instrument of political and popular education," drafted the famous resolution of 1882 for the establishment of autonomous local boards. The recommendation was repeated by the *Report of the Royal Commission on Decentralization* in 1909. Nothing much happened, however, although the "movement," as it was called, had a greater success in urban than in rural areas. Lord Rippon did, however, leave a kind image behind. Thus in the Naik Report on which one of the most far-reaching of the *panchayati raj* measures, that of Maharashtra, is based, there is an express acknowledgment to Rippon's ideals.

7. The issue was mainly of discrimination against Indians in South Africa. It is interesting that the Gandhian tools of non-violent resistance should have attracted the attention of some of the civil rights leaders in the United States. The impact, however, seems to have been superflucus.

8. For a study of these various organizational steps, see Gopal Krishna, "The Development of the Indian National Congress as a Mass Organization," *Journal of Asian Studies*, May, 1966, 25, No.3.

9. The first Round Table Conference was held in November, 1930, when Gandhi and several other Congress leaders were in jail, following the famous "salt march" of Gandhi and the massive movement of civil disobedience that followed it.

10. For an insightful account of the distinctive characteristics of Islam in India, see Wilfred Cantwell Smith, *Modern Islam in India*: A *Social Analysis* (London, 1946).

11. Actually the impact differed between regions. Where the Muslim community was predominantly agrarian or lower class, English education made little impact. This was the case in Bengal. Where it was more urban and upper class, as in Uttar Pradesh and the Bombay Presidency, the Muslims more readily took to English, though not as rapidly as caste Hindus.

12. Quoted from the petition presented by Aga Khan and other prominent Muslims at the time of founding the League.

13. For an analysis on these lines by an important Muslim leader of the Congress, see Maulana Abul Kalam Azad, *India Wins Freedom* (Calcutta, 1959).

14. V.P. Menon, *The Transfer of Power in India* (Calcutta, 1957).
15. Maulana Azad, *op.cit.*
16. For the laments of a leading nationalist Muslim at the reversal in attitudes of the Congress leaders, see the controversial book of Maulana Azad, *op.cit.*
17. The last six months of Gandhi's life showed his tremendous capacity for moral action and the true nature of his charisma. Stirred by the agony of violence all around him, the saint decided to attack the problem on his own. There was no fear in the man. Reminiscent of the "salt march" through which he had sought to challenge the "mighty empire", it was, however, more Olympic in its dimensions, informed by a poignant and tragic sense of human destiny. The peculiar energy and drama of Gandhi's personality will continue to pose an enigma for the analyst. In the words of Albet Einstein. "Generations to come may find it hard to believe that such a man as this ever in flesh and blood walked upon this earth."
18. On this aspect of the partition, as contributing to the evolution of a dominant center and a determined process of state and nation building, see Chapter VIII under "The Demands of Diversity."

3

Approach to Modernization

OUR CONSIDERATION of the historical antecedents of contemporary India provides us with a setting for this case study in political development. Before coming to the substantive aspects of the contemporary political system, it is necessary to grasp the significance of these antecedents for India's peculiar design for its present and its future. As already indicated, India has chosen to adopt an open and eclectic model of development, one that involves a simultaneity of goals and a mix between traditionality and modernity. What are its chief configurative characteristics that provide us with some specific leads on such a general "design for development"?

SIGNIFICANCE OF THE ANTECEDENTS

Foremost among these characteristics is the length, as well as depth, of the nationalist movement that preceded the coming of independence in 1947. In this respect India stands apart from all the other new nations of Asia and Africa. The Indian National Congress, Which was itself an outgrowth of considerable intellectual awakening, social "renaissance," and reformist activity throughout the nineteenth century, and indirectly of the systems of administration, education, law, and communications developed under a long and powerful imperial rule, was established in 1885.

More than sixty years after that, Indians were still engaged in a "movement" for independence which, as it progressed and was led by a succession of outstanding individuals, also provided a forum and training ground for social and economic reform, ideological articulation, and organizational action. It had time enough to pass through a series of phases and develop various facets of mobilizational activity. In its early phases the Congress passed through a prolonged period of intellectual agitation when its modernist goals were articulated through long and strenuous debates over almost thirty years. The movement was essentially urban middle class to begin with, then extended itself into the vast hinterlands of India, and developed organizational depth, intensity of allegiance around unified symbols, a homogeneity of ideas and outlook among thousands of cadres spread all over the subcontinent, and concrete experience in political and governmental management. We discussed in the last chapter the powerful symbolism that men like Tilak and Gandhi provided to the movement, a symbolism that self-consciously connected the nationalist movement with India's great past, and thus succeeded in mobilizing both the modernist and the traditionalist segments of Indian society. Such a penetration of the movement into the hinterlands of India became possible through the induction into the movement of several smaller Gandhis, Tilaks, Patels, and Nehrus in the various regions and at levels close to the grass roots of Indian society. All this made the program of the movement concrete and vivid in the eyes of the relevant public, as it was closely associated with the exemplary life histories of these leaders who gave up everything to become part of the movement. The legitimacy of the movement was thus almost never questioned and resulted in a massive consensus on both ideological goals and the means employed to achieve them. Gandhi's shrewd handling of the masses as well as of the colonial power, by establishing the self-evident "purity" of the means he employed, endowed the movement with a degree of power and conformity which made it very difficult to challenge its elan and authority. Much of this would not have been possible if the time afforded to the movement was either short or confined to the metropolitan areas as was the case with most other nationalist movements.

It is possible to overemphasize the "depth" of the movement.

Even after all the effort of the Congress to penetrate into the rural areas, large masses still were unaffected; their apolitical existence continued as ever. The Success of the Congress was only relative—relative to the failures of earlier efforts at politicization. Neither the great Hindu empires nor the great periods of Muslim rule had gone as deep into the hinterlands of India as the Congress movement succeeded in doing. And there lies its peculiarity. It was no doubt greatly helped by the unprecedented administrative unification and penetration of the subcontinent achieved by the British colonial regime, the law and order that prevailed throughout the land, the communication network made possible through the laying of railroads and modern transportation, the peculiar structure of district government, and, not least, the schools and colleges that grew up all over the land under the British Raj. Indeed here lay another great product of a long exposure to the colonial administration which again was longest among all the new nations. The authority of the Raj had been fairly stabilized and consolidated throughout the length and breadth of the vast subcontinent before the end of the eighteenth century. Then followed a period of continuous rule, territorial and administrative organization, land settlements and distribution of revenue functions, slow involvement of the "natives" in the system of government, the new education and the socialization of elite groups in a new scheme of secular order, and, during the last few decades of the Raj, active participation by Indians in governmental office, in elections at various levels, in higher education, industry, and the arts. The response to all this, whether positive or negative, took on much of its style and direction from the structure that the British had already evolved. The articulation of both the colonial administration and the political and cultural response had thus reached a point of maturity that greatly contributed to the quickening and maturity of the nationalist movement itself. Again time helped. Not many ex-colonial countries have been as fortunate as India in this respect.

The long duration of the movement led to other gains. The consolidation of all the major strands of political awakening in the Congress organization generated a unity of allegiance of both organization and personalities, of loyalty to a program of action and to an ideology. We have seen how Gandhi transferred his personal charisma to a wide variety of symbols; these were essentially symbols of action. "Constructive work" among the villagers, the tribals, and the Harijans, propagation of labour-intensive industries which brought jobs to the poor, literary and educational activity designed to develop distinctive linguistic traditions and identities—all were involved in the Congress approach to the building of a nation, alongside the typically political and propagandist symbols. In one sense the Congress was a highly amorphous and electric organization with a pragmatic leadership that accommodated various strands of thought and commitment. In another sense, however, the Congress had a distinctive ideology, an ideology that went much beyond the winning of independence, and involved almost a blueprint for the future. Anticolonialism and a solidarity with other colonial nations, a participant democracy, equality and social justice (especially toward the rural masses and the underprivileged castes), communal harmony (especially Hindu-Muslim), tolerance of minorities and respect for diversity, linguistic states, planned economic development and rejection of violence as a legitimate means for solving disputes (both domestic and international) were the main programmatic planks of this ideology. Each of these statements of intent had been incorporated in one or more resolutions of the Congress and was widely discussed and disseminated through the organizational, literary, and pedagogic organs of the Congress, and by the band of white-clad, Gandhi-capped volunteers who reached far and wide, in tens of thousands. Gandhi's great emphasis on discipline and selflessness meant that these maxims, though widely discussed, took on the character of an "established" doctrine that everybody accepted.

Such a consensus on the basis of a relatively well defined and comprehensive "ideology" was also directed to establish a continuity with the past and into the future. We have spoken of Gandhi's constant reinterpretation of tradition in order to legitimize his program and to "build bridges" over both time and space, and of how he succeeded, where his predecessors had failed, in involving and actively committing both the traditionalist and the modernist segments of Indian society to the Congress movement. This was his link with the past, and made the Congress appear as part of the unfolding story of the great Indian people. At the same time, the Congress reached out into the future by creating a widespread organizational network that penetrated vast areas at many levels, by recruiting local political elites whose authority at the local level provided the Congress with immeasurable strength, and by articulating a program of "action" which would take decades of work. It is this sense of continuity, of what Nehru called a "continuing revolution," that gave to the Congress in India the quality of an historic force. It rejected nothing, neither tradition nor the future. It created a pervasive symbolism of identity and effect, and a structure of institutional and personal loyalties, that would survive the coming of independence. In this it followed the great Indian tradition of assimilation and eclecticism. The Congress included all streams of ideological thought and all the most important social interests. It displayed a high tolerance of ambiguity in the concerns of the national movement, allowed dissent to become part of the overall consensual style of the Congress, and imparted to the organization great flexibility and freedom to maneuver. Again much of this came not so much from Gandhi alone but from long traditions of multi- ethnic, multi-national existence. Gandhi's genius lay in mobilizing such a past for changing the directions of the present.

Contributing to all this has been another distinctiveness of the Indian case. The long duration of the nationalist movement and its considerable depth in space and continuity backward and forward discussed in the preceding pages were, in turn, facilitated by what may be called the pre-history of the Congress movement. This pre-history is the solid bedrock of Hindu civilization within which the Congress sought to function and from which it took on part of its impetus and character. We have already noted some of the features of Hindu society and culture. We shall return to them in some depth in the chapter on political culture. Here we shall only touch upon points that have relevance to our consideration of the distinctiveness of the Indian experience with development: what aspects of Hindu civilization have contributed to the Indian model of political modernization?

The first point is, once again, the long duration and continuity of India's civilization, and the resulting sense of overriding unity that has characterized Indian society over the centuries. This unity has cut across political divisions, ethnic and linguistic diversity, and secular movements in religion, technology, and ideology. Indians have always had the feeling of "Indianness" in the sense of a cultural identity, which has imparted to the subcontinent a feeling of continuity and durability.

The converse of this unity is diversity. Indian unity is essentially polycentric, based on a continuing accommodation of diverse peoples and their diverse life-styles, and resulting in a remarkable capability for assimilation and "agglomeration." The consequence of such an approach to social aggregation—an approach that emphasized agglomeration more than segmentation, accommodation more than segregation, consensus more than confrontation—was that when the national movement and still later the nation-state came to be organized it was possible for the new elite to incorporate all the more important segments of Indian society and culture in the framework of the Congress.

Third, there was in Indian tradition a strong emphasis on a "civilizing elite"—the Brahmins—whose role was to integrate local cultures with the mainstream of Indian civilization (the "little traditions" with the "great tradition"), to mediate in conflicts arising out of ambiguity of status and locality, and to function as the custodians of tradition and the agents of adjustment and adaptation whenever the latter became necessary for the continuity of the former. The sanctity and legitimacy of such an elite, whose engagement in endless disputation over fine points enabled them to be the pedagogic priesthood of society, gave to Hindu society a unifying apparatus. Such a traditional intellectual class enabled India, when it entered the modern period, to be endowed with an ongoing leadership which was quick to pick up the new tools of civilization—the English language, legal expertise, and cultural prowess—and thus continue in its unchallenged authority. This also led to a kind of elitism which overlaid the heterogeneity and amorphousness of Indian social life with a dominant style and authority. In later times the authority of this elite was challenged and new classes emerged on the political scene. In the meanwhile, new channels of integration and identity grew and India moved from an elitist to a participant phase of political development. In the first few decades of Indian awakening, however, the availability of such an elite provided the new nation with a unifying framework that enabled change to take place without breaking the continuity of Indian civilization.

Other features of India's tradition may briefly be mentioned. There was in the caste system a specificity of roles and functions, including the function of the ruler. It was considered the legitimate business of those endowed with authority to rule, and that of others to obey them in secular matters. This gave to the national elite—manned essentially from the upper strata of society, educated, and urban—an authority that could not be easily challenged. Furthermore, there has been in Indian thought a strong emphasis on limitation of wants, on man's salvation being essentially an *individual* effort, both resulting in relatively few demands and pressures on the governmental system. There has also been, all along, a considerable deference to educational attainments (a Brahminic tradition) and a continuing conditioning of status hierarchy by the ability of groups to have access to political and administrative power. All this further consolidated the authority of the national elite. Finally, the lack of a theology and great ambiguity of moral and religious doctrines meant that the elite could interpret tradition in a selective and creative fashion, picking those elements that were relevant and functional to modern needs, and allowing the rest to grow or decay in isolation. This further enabled the new elite to impose its own ideology on the masses without great resistance from any custodians of "sacred truth." Change and adaptation was thus constantly possible, and new and modern elements continuously added to the flow of civilization, without any consciousness of break or disruption.

In sum, then, the length and continuity of both the nationalist movement and of Hindu civilization contributed considerably to the unity of the new India, and imparted to its modernist design depth, flexibility, and maneuverability. The upshot was a continuous interaction and interplay between a rich and pliable tradition on the one hand and the new framework of democratic institutions and values on the other. The behavioral and attitudinal underpinnings of both—tolerance of diversity and dissent, legitimacy of the new elite committed to free institutions, and assimilation of all major strands of social structure and thought—appeared to mix rather well and gave rise to a synthesis that was at the same time "traditional" and "modern." Had the nationalist movement been short in duration or shallow in its penetration, such a synthesis in depth would not have been there when independence came.

On the other hand, the very length of the movement had its disadvantages. The delay in the achievement of independent nationhood meant that India entered its era of planned economic change and political mobilization in a period of world history when both internal and external pressures began to mount in a simultaneous and spiralling manner. The challenges and crises that the country faced, latecomer as it was to economic and political modernization, presented themselves one upon another, acutely taxing the material and human resources of the new nation. The absence of gradual and incremental phasing of the modernization sequence, as was the case with the more developed nations, made it difficult to develop any coherent scheme of priorities, and launched the country to face all the crises of development at the same time. Such simultaneous changes also meant that the economic problem dominated all other problems at a time when even the economic problem could not be adequately handled without attention to the other problems of development. This led to a long period of goal ambiguity and considerable ambivalence in regard to the most efficient strategy of development. Eventually, of course, a distinctive approach to development was worked out (including a new model of economic development), and some sort of phasing did occur, but not without considerable loss of efficiency and morale, and only in the fashion of drift and muddling through in which time was lost, the confidence of the aspiring strata was somewhat shaken, and a new balance of elite-mass relationships became necessary, which led to considerable instability in the governmental structure. We shall discuss a little later the ultimate model that did emerge.

In a similar manner it can be said that the long duration and institutionalization of colonial rule before the coming of independence, while it laid the physical and administrative foundations for later political integration and economic development, also created certain rigidities, vested interests, and legacies in the overall framework of nation-building that proved difficult to shake when the new nation undertook new tasks and tried to implement massive programs of change. The most important institutional rigidities were in the structure and orientations of the administrative bureaucracy, in the educational system, and in the attitudes towards law, legislation, and implementation. The excessive formalism of problem solving, issue perception, and policy-making in India owes not a little to the habits of thought, educational techniques, and administrative framework developed during the colonial period.

Along the same lines one may argue that the long duration and institutionalization of an ancient civilization, which has been characterized above as facilitating India's peculiar model of development in which traditional and modernist orientations have been welded together, has also had its disadvantages. An intellectual tradition that emphasizes excessive formalism of the spoken world (and the revealed truth), a rigid social structure, a low collectivist ethos, a low salience of "organization" in the articulation of secular interests, absence of aggregation of interests towards the national level, and an approach to consensus that is based on avoiding rather than confronting issues have all contributed to the weakness of a national secular culture.

Many of these characteristics of the Hindu tradition, the colonial past, and the nationalist movement have been carried over into India's contemporary history since independence and have further interacted with modernist institutions, values, and commitments. We shall try to examine such an interaction, both before and since independence, with a view to considering India's modernization as a *response* to the *challenge of systemic change against the canvas of a continuing civilization.* The analysis will be presented in broad theoretical terms, mainly with a view to grasping India's general approach to modernization.

APPROACH TO MODERNIZATION

The Indian approach to development may be characterized as one in which the exposure to modernity led to a renewed awareness and quickening of traditional identity, it reinterpretation and rejuvenation, and its consolidation in the framework of new institutions and ideas. The Indian response to modern stimuli consisted of asserting the Indianness of India, reformulating this Indianness, and giving it a modern character. The model of those who conceive of modernization as a rejection of traditionality and a "transformation" on modern lines does not apply to India. Nor does the opposite model of those who deny potency to modern institutions and values and simply assert the durability and resilience of traditionalism.[1] Even the proponents of a middle course, in which certain parts of tradition are maintained and certain parts of modernity are added, suggest too simplistic a model. Still others have viewed modernization in India as essentially a restructuring of tradition along democratic lines.[2] Their attempt tends to emphasize rather exclusively the role of traditional institutions and norms in the processes of change. But they tend to under emphasize the stimulus that modern institutions and values have provided in awakening ancient identities and giving them a contemporary meaning. It was not as if the traditional institutions regenerated themselves *sui generis*. In what follows, instead of emphasizing either traditionalism or modernity at the expense of the other, or viewing them in disjointed fragments, we seek to examine the *relationship* in which they enter, the *processes* that engender this relationship, and the *functionality* of each to the other. For the need is to discern the peculiar "mix" that emerges when an ancient society comes to terms with the demands of a new age, seeks its continuity essentially through change, and achieves a new unity and a new identity without destroying either its rich diversity or its other, antecedent identities.

It is always difficult to seek the roots of change in history, especially in a complex society like India where stagnation of some parts and dynamism of others have characterized its long history. Anyone who draws the picture of a stagnant civilization that suddenly began to stir under an impact such as colonialism is likely to meet with justifiable ridicule. We have seen that the Muslim invasions and the consolidation of the Moghul empire shattered the complacency of the traditional order. Upon this came the period of colonialism which provided law and order, integrated the subcontinent under one rule, and stimulated certain large-scale changes in society and its intellectual bearings, including the momentous reaction to alien rule which provided the framework of the new nation. Viewed in this light there is little doubt that the major stimulus for change came from the diffusion of technological, institutional, and ideational influences from the West, of which British colonialism was an important bearer.

We have noted that India's response to the diffusion of world culture was not of one type, and ranged from a highly Westernized (liberal and socialist) ideology to a radical anti-Westernism. But the general outcome of these competing intellectual strands can be seen. It consisted of a pattern of response that accepted the changes that were needed for India to find its place in the modern world, used this challenge for its survival by reasserting the Indian identity, gave it a new meaning and endowed it with a new content. The indigenous agents of change—the new elite—thus sought to ensure continuity with the past by effecting important changes in the present, as well as constructing a utopia for the future. The new identity that they discovered was not simply revealed by finding out what they had been but also, and more particularly, what they were to become.[3]

The new elite that emerged was essentially a "national" elite for the first time in India. Such a transfer of leadership initiative from the localities to a center, such a centralization of elite roles, was the first major change in the Indian scene. In place of either local notables resolving local disputes which was a characteristic of traditional society, or of enlightened individuals scattered at various places and working for much needed reform which was a characteristic of the early phase of Westernization, there now emerged a body of men who thought in national terms, talked of a national consciousness, and of India's future as a nation. These were also men who talked in the language of purpose, of goals, of ideology. All this was new.

At the same time such a commitment to national goals, and concern for developing a nation-wide organization and support, led the new elite to devise strategies of penetration into the hinterland of India and mobilization of the people at large. Here, after a long period of essentially urbanized agitation and of experimentation with political forms, the leadership confronted the essential problem of modernizing an ancient society: the vast masses of the people were involved in their own preoccupations, did not understand the strange idiom of modern communication, and could be effectively mobilized only through indigenous symbols and channels which they could understand. We have already indicated the powerful symbolism that Gandhi developed in dealing with these issues, and how he turned old and familiar symbols to new purposes; how he linked the traditional notions of duty, charity, and personal salvation to the pursuit of public purpose. Here was a battery of catalytic slogans drawn from a continuing folklore which was characteristically Indian. Here is one major instance where a radical change in the structure of power in society—the rise of a centralizing elite—is consolidated and legitimized through a medium of communication and a style of mobilization that are drawn from a continuing structure of tradition.

This is one kind of relationship of continuity and change. But there are other kinds too. It is not as if modernity is as a whole legitimized by some kind of an instrumental use of tradition. Where tradition represents the consciousness of a long civilization, it tends to be selective. Thus a whole array of ideological goals were spelled out for the Indian people. The diffusion of new ideas and institutions included many overlapping and often conflicting approaches and goals: an authoritarian political system maintaining order and disciplined development versus a representative democracy based on individual rights and the right to dissent; a centralized state fostering uniformities in political conduct versus a loose federation maintaining the autonomy of local units; participation based on majority rule and party competition versus that based on interest group representation of minorities; state ownership of economic institutions versus private capitalism; production and export of primary goods in return for preferential treatment by industrial powers versus a strategy of all-out industrialization; an educational system devised for producing a gentlemanly elite versus the ideal of egalitarianism through educational opportunity and social mobility. The British administers and educators had conflicting opinions about the capacities of Indians to operate the complicated system of parliamentary democracy, and Indian leaders echoed both points of view. What is important is the pattern of response that finally took place, the choices that were made, and the resulting syndrome of ideology and consensus that emerged.

The choices that emerged were informed both by strength of tradition and conscious deliberation in regard to the structure of goals and authoritative allocations. Both the Brahminic attraction to liberal thought and the long tradition of tolerance of diversity and dissent contributed to the political choices that were made. There was genuine novelty in some of these choices because they went against some of the "evils" of the old order (its rigid hierarchy, its gross disparities and inequalities, and its intense parochialism). But there also existed a mind that was prepared, there was confidence that the peoples of India were capable of being the heirs of the enlightenment, and there was agreement that the best means of maintaining the richness of Indian civilization was to adopt a system of government that would respect the freedom and individuality of its diverse components. Modern authoritarianism—and that was the only form of authoritarianism possible in a nation-state—was unsuited both to maintain the unity of such a continental nation and to preserve its rich diversity of culture, language, and religion.

The choices were not always made in an either-or fashion, nor decided once and for all. To illustrate, the modernist elite was much attracted to (and still favors) the idea of a centralized nation-state through which the authority of the national leadership is consolidated and firmly maintained over against the divisiveness of the "centrifugal" tendencies inherent in the Indian situation. The partition of India which removed the chief rationale of a loose federation (an earlier idea under which the Hindu and Muslim majority regions would enjoy considerable autonomy) further reinforced the preference for a "strong center." Such a preference, however, went against the strong tradition of a decentralized policy and the great role that local politicians and notables had played in giving the nationalist movement its nation-wide character. It also went against the semi-populist Gandhian tradition which had glorified the people, asserted that the village must be the basis of the Indian nation, and believed in giving the underprivileged and exploited villagers their due share in the fruits of independence. Both strands were strongly expressed in the Constituent Assembly. Faced by these contrary pulls the constitution-makers chose an ambivalent federalism which gave to the center much scope and initiative, a major share in resources and all residual functions, but simultaneously gave to the states considerable powers and scope for maneuver. Still later occurred another Indian innovation, which came from the center but actually further consolidated the federal character of the Indian polity. This innovation, based on an ancient Indian institution and the Gandhian ideology but for which the main credit should go to Nehru, was a peculiar system of local government from the district downward, known as panchayati raj (alternatively as "democratic decentralization"). We shall deal at some length with this system and with the general character of Indian federalism in later chapters. Here we shall show how political choice, in regard to this crucial dimension of center and periphery, involved the force of tradition, the stimulus of modernity, the blending of those two in the ideology of the movement, pragmatic consideration, and the vision and commitment of the chief actors.

Not only was there this process of selectivity in which continuity of older traditions interacted with strategies of change. Traditional skills and orientations, and the structure of diversity in which they had flourished, contributed to the articulation and operation of the new system. Thus the most crucial link in the structure of political integration turned out to be not the national elite which sought to penetrate downward, nor the local elite at the village level which was gradually drawn upward towards the system, but the emergence of an intermediate elite between these two levels and its operation both downward and upward, mediating between the decision-makers and support-seekers on the one hand and the masses and their immediate leaders on the other. Labeled as "middlemen" or "link men," these intermediate leaders have shown a remarkable capacity for commuting between tradition and modernity and in bringing about a pragmatic relationship between the two. With this the traditional image of politicians as mediators and arbitrators between contending and bargaining parties has come into its own. They represent a peculiar culture of bargaining in India, lack of perception of which has led commentators to argue for an absence of bargaining culture in India.[4] The bargaining that takes place is often not direct between the parties involved in the bargain; it is brought about by agreeing upon a middleman who would set the terms of the bargain. Moreover, the intermediate elite that has emerged in

India at district and constituency levels does not simply bargain like "brokers"; they also make the parties in such a relationship aware of the opportunities that are being made available at each level, and the symbols and artifacts of each level that the other should know. In doing this, they also prove to be the system's mobilizers *par excellence.*

The articulation of such linkages in the system has also led to a model of integration which is different from either the model of aggregation of interests all the way upward characteristic of Western democracies, or the model of segmentation of interests and loyalties characteristic of "traditional" political systems. It is a model in which a dispersed structure of power is brought together in terms of intermediate "networks" which take the from of autonomous subsystems in the larger political system. These subsystems both aggregate local interests, and protect their identity and potency by acting as intermediate buffers in the system. Sharing some of the features of patron-client networks in traditional society, they at the same time facilitate the performance of modern political functions. It may be called a model of *intermediate aggregation.* We shall examine the institutionalization of such networks in the governmental and party systems in later chapters. It is sufficient here to note that the center-periphery dimension of nation-building in an old and plural society finds its significant crystallization through the emergence of intermediate subsystems that act as linkages between the center and the periphery; between "modernity" and "tradition."[5] And in this crystallization traditions of mediation and arbitration and of "bargaining through a third party" play an important role.

Consideration of these various aspects of the relationship between tradition and change also throws light on other themes of political development. How far really, in such a dualist system of traditional-modern relationships, can the central symbols of the polity penetrate? The old universals are being shaken by a new technology and a new kind of polity, making this a crucial question. Second, to what extent can a genuinely national identity be fostered in such a pluralist society? Third, if new identities do emerge, what is the nature of differentiations and cleavages that lend structure to these identities, or make for their dissipation? Fourth, in what way, in such a Janus-like model (backward-looking) and forward-looking at the same time), can a futuristic outlook be developed so that problems can be anticipated and handled and not left to the capriciousness of events and the whims of personalities?

We hope to deal with these themes in the course of this book and shall return explicitly to them in the chapters on political culture and system performance. Here, we offer certain summary clues.

ISSUES OF CENTER AND PERIPHERY

First, as regards the "central symbols" of the system: in any civilization there must exist central symbols which lend unity to the system. In India this was so traditionally when a complex structure of tradition had developed which dominated the processes of value crystallization in various local communities and regions.[6] These have been adequately described in the rich technological and anthropological literature on India. Peculiar to the Indian case was the fact that the central symbols involved in such a structure of tradition were not tied to a given political system.[7] Upon such a structure came the impact of modernization, involving a new system of institutional relationships, values, and symbols. Without destroying the old universals, the new symbols penetrated into the hinterland, gave new meaning to old identities and symbols, helped the traditional order to come to terms with the modern age, and in the process created intermediate subsystems and elites which forged linkages between local communities and the national political order. These intermediate elites became the transmitters of the new central symbols of the polity. As already mentioned, the new symbols were not wholly new; they took on a great deal from the continuing structure of tradition and because this structure was complex and variegated, a process of selectivity and creativity occurred, by which the prevailing diversity of interests and affiliations was made part of the new order. The process is still going on; its essential duality cannot be ignored; and the new central symbols become meaningful only as they operate in and through the ongoing diversity of the system and the structure of traditions inherent in this diversity. Traditions, however, need not always be old. New traditions have been emerging, and emerging rather fast. It is important to grasp that in a continuing civilization modernity can survive only by becoming part of tradition, by "traditionalizing" itself.[8] Through assimilation of these new traditions into the ongoing structure of tradition, the new central symbols of the system penetrate the whole of society. It is the only way they can become "central."

These comments on the central symbols of the system also apply to the problem of national identity. Much is presupposed in the Western literature on national identity. The Indian experience tends to reject the need for any single or even uniform pattern of identities for a nation-state to take effect. Indeed it is arguable that if the national elite in India had sought to impose one kind of identity on the whole people of India, it would most likely have failed, and if it had succeeded it would only have torn the country into pieces. It is not only the case that the existence of various primordial and parochial identities and loyalties reduces the tensions and loads on the national system. It is also the case that for national identity to take root in a systemic form it is necessary for it to be structured and mediated through various sub-systems of allegiance and affect. The model of an amorphous and abstract identity with the "nation" is unworkable in any society, let alone a large and complex one like India. The independence movement did indeed lay the foundation of a national identity and we have already argued that the length and depth of the nationalist movement account for India's relative success as a nation-state. But even the nationalist movement was essentially a means of penetration in which traditional identities and symbols were continuously mobilized and given a new meaning. The process has continued since independence. And a crucial concomitant of identity formation in both was a linkage between the restructuring of old and the formation of new differentiations.

The relationship between tradition and change becomes concrete and manifest when we turn to the nature of differentiations underlying such a structure of identities. It is often said that traditional societies lack differentiation of roles and functions and that modernization consists of their increasing differentiation and complexity. Consideration of the Indian case throws doubt on such a bland assertion. We shall deal at some length with this problem in Chapter VI, where we shall see that not only was there a high degree of differentiation and complexity in the traditional order in India but also that these differentiations have displayed flexibility and adaptability in the face of new changes. In the modern period this has happened in two important ways. Older differentiations of caste, religion, language, and region have taken on new organizational forms, such as the caste, tribal and linguistic associations, and federations. Along with such a reorganization of traditional differentiations new kinds of differentiations have come up all over the country and are made part of the ongoing structure of status and power. Professional, occupational, cultural, business, and purely political groupings are not only very active but have come to find a status in the traditional order. Very often the members of these groups are sons or relatives of members of the more traditional groups: thus in many parts of the country Brahmins were the first to find access to the new professions; sons of business families of the older type have organized industrial houses and chambers of commerce; members of the martial castes are prominent in the armed forces. Where there is no such continuity, the newly educated and the new politicians are incorporated into the ongoing social system by being coopted, often in high places, in the elite structure of the communities in which they reside, including in caste councils and associations.

An important feature of this pattern of organizational mobilization is the ability of the peripheral groups to seek new opportunities and bargain for positions in the new political structure. Ideological factors have further contributed to this process: there is reservation of jobs, educational openings, and legislative seats for backward castes, and there are large enough constraints on political parties to give a balanced representation to various caste groups. Such a strategy of mobilization tends to resolve an important dilemma of traditional societies: the dilemma of one or two ethnic groups getting all important rewards and others being relegated to a subject category and virtual non-membership in the nation, leading to a deep schism in society, and to violence and anomie. Even advanced political systems like the United States were not able to resolve this inherent cleavage in the process of political development sufficiently early in their history as a nation-state. Undoubtedly the nature of the caste system, whose multiple plurality prevents sharp and polarized cleavages, facilitates such a process of involvement and cooptation of peripheral groups in the political structure. More important than the uniqueness of the caste system is what may be called the assimilative capability of Indian elites, a capability that has resulted from a long history of incorporating all newcomers in the framework of Hindu civilization. Of equal importance is the very low salience of any sharp cleavage between traditional and modern or between parochial and secular forces as a result of the continuities that operate in India's search for modernity. Gandhi's role in this regard was crucial, and only slightly less important was Nehru's eclectic approach to political mobilization and his great sensitivity to the impact of representative processes of the fabric of democracy.

It would be wrong to ascribe the low salience of cleavages and the functional role of multiple identities and differentiations wholly or even mainly to continuities from tradition. For there were conscious attempts made by the national elite, very soon after independence, to deal with actual and potential sources of cleavage and disaffection in the country. Which brings us to the question of future-oriented thinking and action. Thus the legal removal of feudal rights, far-reaching labor legislation, conferment of special rights and privileges on the "backward" sections and on Harijans, the removal of inequities through the Hindu Civil Code, constitutional amendments to deal with archaic interpretation of property rights, a massive reorganization of the states with a view to removing linguistic tensions, and legislative constraints on secessionist movements have all, alongside a firm suppression of violence and anti-national agitations, gone a long way in neutralizing areas of tension and hostility. All these were done fairly early in the nation's life and, looking back, they appear like a series of anticipatory acts that have minimized the loads on the national political system. In reality they may not all be part of any intended plan of action. But they did arise from a certain ideology of the movement and of the national elite. The futuristic ideology of this elite (which was not necessarily in conflict with its approach to tradition) had as much to do with the mobilizational potential of the system as the antecedent capabilities that it had inherited. And even the latter were put to work by the new elite.

FACTORS OF CHANGE

Before concluding our discussion of tradition and change we would like to recapitulate and stress four points. First, the major stimulus for the far-reaching changes in India's social and political structure and the consequent reordering of traditional identities has come from its exposure to modernist impacts in ideas, communications, institutions, and technology. In stressing the strength and flexibility of tradition it would be misleading to think that the sources of change (as distinct from support for it) came from tradition itself. The few who have stressed the role of tradition in modernization have sometimes given such an impression;[9] we would like to explicitly deny such a romantic view of tradition. Tradition comes in at the stage of responding to the new stimuli, not as their source. There is, of course, evidence that changes were already taking place in antecedent relationships when the colonial impact came, but there is little doubt that in its volume and intensity it was Westernization that became the principal source of change.[10] To this impact, Indian society with its rich history and tradition responded in a manner we have described in this chapter.

Second, such a response to the modernist impacts was itself brought about not by local society but by the emergence of a new elite which represented a new "center" of society, more central than all the prevailing centers. This centralizing elite, as we have characterized it earlier in this chapter, became the dynamic agent of change, reproduced itself at lower and intermediate levels, built channels of communication throughout the nation, became the bearers of a new ideology, and mobilized traditional society towards new directions and purposes. The "input-output model" operates during these earlier phases of development in an inverted fashion: the major inputs come from the modernist elite in the form of penetration of new institutions, new values, and new resources and the "outputs" from the masses and local notables in the form of mobilization of political support and institutional allegiances.[11] Of course such a process of penetration was facilitated by certain continuities of values and traditions, of structures, and above all, of elites themselves. Western education drew the most enthusiastic response from the old literati, in large part from the Brahminic and other highly placed castes. (The response to Western education also exhibited the characteristics of Sanskritic and Vedic learning.) Thus it happened that the custodians of tradition also became the custodians of modernity which accounts for the smooth transition of the process of modernization. All the same, it was the emergence of a modernist, urban, professional, and English-educated elite, drawn from different regions but acting as representatives of the "nation," that proved to be the major integrative force of modernization. It was somewhat later that new kinds of modernizers emerged at intermediate and local levels and brought about a more comprehensive and structured modernization of the country.

Third, such a process of mobilizing traditional identities and structures was galvanized not by a loosely organized elite stratum but by the emergence of exceptional individuals who wielded charismatic authority and who continued to wield this authority over long stretches of time. India was fortunate in having such men at its helm; it was even more fortunate in their not being removed prematurely by death or disease as has been the case with some other new nations. Gandhi's enormous authority continued from the early 1920s to 1948; Nehru's from 1947 to 1964; Patel's from the early 1930s to 1950. There is no need to repeat here the great qualities of imagination, commitment, persuasion, and inspiration that these men brought to bear upon the whole development process. Many others, both at the national level and in the regions, ensured continuity of approach and a concrete heritage. Gandhi had the great quality of reproducing himself and the movement gave rise to scores of local charismatic figures who became powerful catalysts in the process of modernization and were able to draw even the more traditional elements in society into the political framework. Alongside the length and duration of the movement it is necessary to emphasize this personal dimension of the process of history. Not many new nations have been endowed with such an array of towering men for such a length of time.

Finally there was the great organizational *tour de force*: the Indian National Congress. We shall examine it as a system of power in a later chapter. Here we stress that, in keeping with earlier great periods in Indian history, not only was the country's modernist phase endowed with charismatic personalities but also with a charismatic organization whose authority and legitimacy was not questioned over more than eighty years. Very often Nehru and the other leaders have been credited with achievements which, in reality, they could not have had without the powerful organizational base from which they operated. Again the Congress was an eclectic organization with a non-doctrinaire though not inarticulate ideology, in which traditionality got meshed with modernity. It thus possessed, like its towering men, the power of charisma and a capacity for its outward dispersal.[12] It became the greatest historic force of India's road to modernity. Again India was more fortunate than most other new nations.

In sum, it is not simply a pliable tradition that has facilitated the process of change and reorientation of India's ancient civilization along a modernist path. Unprecedented intensity and concentration of modernist impacts brought about by one of the longest colonial thrusts in history, a long nationalist movement, the emergence of a centralizing elite steeped in the modernist ideology which penetrated deep into the regions, an array of charismatic personalities, and an all-encompassing organization have all helped steer India's peculiar reconciliation between tradition and change. Lack or recognition of these factors would result in too romantic a view of tradition; neglect of the role of tradition in such a process of politicization would give us too romantic a view of change. An adequate interpretation of India's approach to modernization requires a due acknowledgment of both.

Notes

1. I have discussed these opposite schools of thought in my "Tradition and Modernity Revisited," *Government and Opposition*, 3, No.3 Summer, 1968.
2. See, for example, Lloyd I. Rudolph and Susanne H. Rudolph, *Modernity of Tradition* (Chicago, 1967). In general, however, while disagreeing somewhat with this particular emphasis of the book, we find many grounds of agreement, especially in the authors' treatment of caste and leadership. On the whole, it is a welcome departure from the dichotomous models of tradition and modernity. Perhaps the case is over-stated, though.
3. Milton Singer, in Milton Singer, ed., *Traditional India: Structure and Change* (Philadelphia, 1959).

4. Myron Weiner, *The Politics of Scarcity: Public Pressure and Political Response in India* (Chicago, 1962). Gabriel Almond, in summarizing the import of the book in an introduction, says that India appears to lack a bargaining culture. Weiner's own emphasis seems to be the lack of a culture of direct confrontation. And there he has a point. We have discussed the matter more fully in Chapter V. For evidence of a slow emergence of direct bargaining among elite strata, see Chapter VIII, the section dealing with political successions.
5. The importance of intermediate groups and subsystems is well recognized in the literature, especially in the works of Burke, Durkheim, Tocqueville, and Tönnies. More recently, Edward Shils and Robert A. Dahl have dealt with this theme. In India R. Bhaskaran has written at length on this subject. Most others, however, have been preoccupied with what Clifford Geertz calls the "integrative revolution" of our times, and with the theory of mass society. For a recent review and critique of the Western literature, see Maurice Pinard, "Mass Society and Political Movements: A New Formulation." *The American Journal of Sociology*, LXXIII, No.6, May, 1968. See also R. Bhaskaran, *Sociology of Politics* (Bombay, 1967).
6. Robert Redfield originated the concept of "structure of tradition." See his "Civilizations as Cultural Structures?," a lecture delivered at the Center for Advanced Study in the Behavioral Sciences, Stanford. See also Bernard S. Cohn and McKim Marriott, 'Networks and Centers in the Integration of Indian Civilization', *Journal of Social Research* (Ranchi, India), I, 1 September, 1958.
7. This aspect of dissociation between culture and politics has been discussed at some length in Chapter VII.
8. The concept of traditionalization of modernity has been discussed in my "Tradition and Modernity Revisited," *op.cit.*
9. Rudolph and Rudolph, op.cit. and the various studies in Singer, ed., op.cit.
10. For an anthropological discussion of Westernization, see M.N. Srinivas, *Social Change in Modern India* (Berkeley, 1966), Chapter 2.
11. See my "Implications of Nation-Building for the Typology of Political System," paper presented at *Seventh World Congress of the International Political Science Association*, Brussels, 1967.
12. For a leading conceptual discussion of the theme, see Edward Shils, "The Concentration and Dispersion of Charisma," *World Politics*, XI, No.1, October, 1958. For a more detailed discussion of the Congress on these lines, see my "Nation-Making and Consensus: The Case of the Indian National Congress," paper presented at the *Seventh World Congress op.cit*

4

Institutional Strategy

THE ACHIEVEMENT OF INDEPENDENCE, while it proclaimed a period of change and reconstruction, did not constitute any sharp discontinuity in the development of political traditions in India. The close interaction between Hindu tradition, Western political thought, and the ideology of reconstructive nationalism had already led to a process of transformation which, while it did not shatter the foundations of Indian society, without doubt put it along a new path. The coming of independence further emphasized the new path and its futuristic orientation. "Long years ago we made a tryst with destiny," said Jawaharlal Nehru on the eve of independence, " and now the time comes when we shall redeem our pledge." In reality, however, there was greater continuity. In August, 1947, a transfer of power to an identifiable and legitimized elite took place. The Congress, which had provided the leadership of the nationalist movement, now turned itself into the ruling political party, and formed the government of the country.[1] The new elite shared in ideas and experiences many of the characteristics of the outgoing elite. Noteworthy in the changeover was this continuity in personnel, institutions, and ideas, despite the end of the British epoch in Indian history. The years that immediately followed were dominated by these ideas which were now incorporated into a legal document and translated into concrete institutional terms.

DECISION-MAKING ON THE CONSTITUTION

The making of a constitution and its institutionalization into concrete structures and rules of the game have proved to be matters of incalculable difficulty for the new nations of Asia and Africa.[2] India presents a striking contrast. Not only was an elaborate constitution made with speed,[3] but the democratic structure it established has been institutionalized in considerable detail and has functioned without interruption so far. This has been possible because of both antecedent agreements on fundamentals and continuing diffusion of these agreements in the generation that followed independence. We have already indicated how the long time span of the movement and its various phases allowed detailed discussion on goals and their incorporation in concrete resolutions and reports. The Motilal Nehru Committee, appointed by the All Parties Conference convened by the Congress,[4] spelled out in a comprehensive manner the features of free India's polity as early as 1928. It recommended, among other things, a parliamentary and federal structure of government and an exhaustive list of fundamental rights. Thirteen of the nineteen rights enumerated in the Nehru Report were included without any material alteration in the chapters on Fundamental Rights and Directive Principles of the 1950 Constitution. Jawaharlal, son of Motilal, moved another famous resolution in 1931, known as the Karachi resolution, which again attempted a comprehensive statement of objectives. A historian of the Congress, commenting on this resolution, brought out the significance of all such statements of intent: "Jawaharlal was rather keen on these matters, not because of the rival groups bent on criticizing the Congress, but because these were matters on which the Nation should be clear in its own mind and should carry on education and propaganda among the masses. This was the genesis of the resolutions."[5]

The existence of such prior agreement on the character of the new polity rendered elaborate discussion unnecessary when India's constitution-makers assembled from 1947 to 1949. The issue was sharply stated when, as a prominent member of the Constituent Assembly began to deliver a lengthy discourse on a familiar point, he was interrupted by another member who asked

"... whether we are to be allowed to discuss the things we have discussed for years again here on the floor of this house?"

Despite this background of discussion on vital issues, the achievement of independence did provide a moment of choice to the Indian leadership with regard to the institutional strategy it would like to adopt for the new republic. During its deliberations on the draft constitution, the Constituent Assembly considered alternative political choices available to the country. Some argued that the Indian polity should take as its model its own ancient institutions with suitable modifications in accordance with modern conditions. Some said that adult franchise and rule by the ballot box were not suited to the poor and illiterate masses of India. Nor were they necessary as India had better traditions to fall back on. Opponents of this view, who greatly outnumbered the traditionalists, pointed out, however, that the only relevant experience India had of systematic political organization as a nation was that of parliamentary democracy. Earlier experience was far too vague and fragmentary to draw upon. They said that more ancient systems were not relevant to the needs and values of modern society, which sought to achieve social and economic justice on the basis of the active participation of large masses of the people. Those who thought of poverty and illiteracy as impediments to the realization of democratic citizenship smacked of the kind of authoritarianism and intellectual snobbery that characterized English administrators who, while they cherished free institutions for their own people, thought Indians unfit for self-government.[6]

As the debate went on, the important point emerged that democratic institutions should not necessarily be considered as importations from abroad, that for nearly a generation the country had had a moderate experience of representative institutions, that it was the British government that had begrudged the people of India a greater measure of democracy and self rule which had been repeatedly demanded by the leadership, and that it was the Congress movement that had all along stood for parliamentary government and adult franchise. No one was to take away the ancient heritage of the country. At the same time, India had its own unique contribution to make to the growth of free institutions, and to peace and prosperity in the world. It was not only that parliamentary traditions were no monopoly of any country, but as one member of the Assembly put it, the adoption of democratic institutions "in no way compromises our Indianness," and the country ought to "adopt every technique the modern world can offer to keep itself Indian." Modern man is the inhabitant of a world society, and in constructing a national community he ought to use all available concepts and techniques. These arguments found overwhelming support among the members. Thus, when Jawaharlal Nehru moved clause ten of the Union Constitution Committee Report calling upon the Constituent Assembly to make India a parliamentary democracy under a cabinet form of government, he encountered little opposition to his recommendation. What amounted to a historic decision was taken quietly and without furor.[7]

Decision-making on India's institutional strategy was not, however, wholly a product of agreements reached during the movement. While such agreements indeed facilitated the smooth and rapid conduct of constitution-making, it could not, by itself, have made this possible. The agreements that existed were at a very general level; the deliberations of the Constituent Assembly had to be far more precise. When they tried to translate the general into the concrete, the key decision makers ran into serious disagreements and were forced to work out viable compromises. These included the rights of the states vis-a-vis the center, the importance of the judiciary in interpreting the constitution and the role of the "due process," the whole question of a proper balance between personal liberties of the citizen and the integrity of the nation and between the right to property and the goal of social and economic development, the extent of decentralization to lower levels of the polity, and the question of special rights and privileges of minorities, the depressed sections of society like the Harijans, and the tribals as against the simple principle of one man, one vote.

This was one aspect: the need for translating an ideological consensus into concrete institutional details. The other aspect of such rethinking was that the circumstances in which prior agreements had been reached and various constitutional formulae discussed no longer held true. The earlier emphasis on both unqualified individual rights and provincial autonomy was based on the assumption that the Indian subcontinent would remain united, and that to keep united, concessions would have to be made to win the confidence of the religious minorities, especially the Muslims. With the partition of the country and the traumatic experience of the violence that followed, the idealism of earlier intentions underwent drastic change. Faced with the reality of establishing effective central authority and preventing the country from falling to pieces, the need to arm the central government with effective powers against the states was widely felt. Similarly, preventive detention to strengthen the government's hands came to be accepted as a necessary evil, despite its restrictions on the most fundamental rights of a democratic citizen.[8] Again, while defining the relationship between Parliament and the courts, due consideration had to be given to the need to arm the state with powers to reduce social and economic disparities; consequently the "due process" draft clause was modified to suit Indian conditions. None of these changes was made without a great deal of discussion and consultation—and often prolonged differences—among the leaders, as well as on the floor of the Constituent Assembly.[9]

Acutely conscious of the need for agreement on the constitution if it were to survive, the national leadership not only tried to work on the basis of the existing consensus, but attempted also to create agreement where it did not exist, and to win over the allegiance of different sections of the citizenry. Efforts in this direction were reflected in the composition of the Constituent Assembly and the manner by which its proceedings were conducted and its decisions reached. Although, with the partition of the country, the Congress was left as the overwhelming majority party in the Assembly, it tried to give to the Aeembly as broad-based a membership as possible by nominating and supporting the election of representatives from all the major communities and from all shades of political opinion. It selected caste Hindus, Harijans, Muslims, Sikhs, Christians, Anglo-Indians, Parsis, and others. Of the thirty-one Harijan members in the Assembly, twenty-nine were nominees of the Congress. Likewise, it selected men who had never served the Congress in the past, such as Sarvepalli Radhakrishnan and N. Gopalaswamy Ayyangar, and men who had actively opposed it during the movement for independence, such as S.P. Mukerjee, the founder of the Jan Sangh, and B.R. Ambedkar, the leader of the Harijans. Dr. Ambedkar was elected chairman of the Drafting Committee and is often known as the architect of the Indian Constitution. The Congress leadership associated non-Congressmen, Including their former opponents, with all the committees of the Assembly. In fact, the Drafting Committee had only one Congressman of standing (K.M. Munshi) among its nine members. In constituting a Minorities Subcommittee of the Advisory Committee, the leadership not only gave adequate representation to all communities. but even associated individuals who were not members of the Assembly, such as P.K. Salve (Christian), Rup Nath Brahma (Tribal), M. Ruthnaswamy (Hindu), and M.V.H. Collins (Anglo-Indian). The Congress went further in its policy of accommodation. Three members who were elected to the Assembly League tickets (the elections to the Assembly had been held before the Partition) were nominated to the Minorities Subcommittee. Nor was all this done in the form of paying lip service to secular principles. It is significant that the Congress leadership went out of its way to include non-party men in the inner circle which consisted of senior persons who guided the work of the Assembly.[10]

In the Constituent Assembly itself no attempt was made to force decisions, the accent being on unanimity. Nehru himself stressed this point when he asked the members of the Assembly to frame the constitution "in the proper time and with as great a respect for unanimity as possible." In the same spirit, Dr. Rajendra Prasad, president of the Constituent Assembly, preferred to postpone debate and allow time to work out an agreed solution rather than to take a vote that might, as he feared, result in "something not wanted by anybody." The leaders were alive to the fact that a constitution adopted on the principle of majority vote alone would not last long. Thus when the Assembly was discussing one of those few issues that evoked great controversy, namely the question of national language. Dr. Prasad reminded the members that it will not do to carry a point by debate alone, for a decision on this issue, if not acceptable to the whole country, will be most difficult to implement.[11] This feeling pervaded the making of the constitution. The leaders were aware that the task with which they were engaged was not just the drafting of a document; they were constructing a nation. They bent their resources to create a strong foundation.

We have considered the making of the Indian Constitution in some detail as it brings out the factors that influence decision-making at a vital phase in institution-building in a new nation. As has been shown, the leadership developed an approach directed at eliciting the maximum consensus—both from the past and from the present—in a basic document that was to guide India's "tryst with destiny." What emerged was a federal structure of parliamentary government with a cabinet form of executive at the national and state levels, "directed" to liberal democratic goals of individual freedom and social justice in the fulfillment of which government was assigned a positive role.[12] The institutional structure that emerged was essentially modernist in character but with important departures from the Western model designed to facilitate national integration and social assimilation. The president of India, although meant to be a titular head, was given vast emergency powers to deal with breakdown of law and order in the states.[13] He appoints the governors of the states, rather than the people or the legislatures of the respective states. The central government, which advises the president in the exercise of his appointing and emergency powers, was given a major share in the nation's revenues and administrative and "directive" powers over the states. The central Parliament has precedence over the states in several matters including the exercise of "concurrent" rights between the center and the states and the abrogation of a State's legislative and executive functions in the event of a "breakdown of constitutional government." All this is designed to strengthen the authority of the center which also enjoys all residual powers. On the other hand, by undertaking the growth of local self-government at the lower levels and accepting village panchayats as an integral part of the political framework, and by agreeing to delegate major administrative tasks to the states, the Constitution adopted a structure of government that in its day-to-day workings, would become increasingly federal and participatory.

Another major innovation was the grant of special privileges to the peripheral groups in society—the "scheduled" castes and tribes and the "backward classes"—in terms of reserved seats and jobs in the various legislatures and in the administrative services. Although the Constitution envisages withdrawal of these privileges after a stipulated date, it is flexible enough to allow them to continue as long as the disparities between the "twice-born" and others continue to be substantial. Similarly the linguistic diversity of the country was accepted in the Constitution through adoption of all the major regional languages as having a national status. Although Hindi was assigned a special role as the eventual medium of administration and communication, this has not been enforced because it has run into serious objections from non-Hindi states. (See Chapter VIII.) Finally, the Constitution provides for flexible methods of adaptation to changing social demands. Constitutional amendments are relatively easy to effect; autonomous commissions, like the periodically constituted Finance Commission and the Election Commission, have powers to recommend major revisions in procedures: the Parliament can restrain the powers of the judiciary if the latter does not keep up with the times; and the mechanism of special conferences and commissions, often endowed with important powers, helps to bridge major differences between the center and the states.[14]

Despite all this, questions can still be raised as to the viability of certain provisions—or even basic arrangements—for an underdeveloped and heterogeneous nation like India. We shall turn to these questions more concretely in the chapters on political performance. For the purpose of this chapter it is enough to indicate the kind of institutional set-up that the country wilfully adopted for its development.

ISSUES OF CONSOLIDATION AND CHANGE

The making of the Constitution and the inauguration of the Indian Republic in January of 1950 were only part of a continuous process of institutionalization and consensus-making in this vast new nation. The growth of further consensus has involved new developments in the institutional layout of the country, important modifications of the formal structure of authority as found in the constitution, and a continuing debate on the "reconstruction of the Indian polity."[15] The introduction and working of a formal structure of institutions gives rise to distinctive pattern of behavior, evokes new allegiances and new traditions, creates new networks of power, and leads to a substantive change in the social structure of politics. Such a network of communications and power has been channeled along two main structures in India. One is the administrative hierarchy evolved in the Moghul and the British colonial periods and further developed under the impact of planned change. The other is the hierarchy of the Congress Party developed during the nationalist movement and greatly extended after independence with the help of governmental power, patronage, and elections. Together and mutually interacting with each other, these two account for the crystallization of the present Indian polity. During such an interaction, the institutional structure adopted in the Constitution has not remained static. Changes have taken place, some in the nature of filling in and adaptation of the formal apparatus; others are based on new ideas of social purpose and representative government.

Independence brought numerous problems and created new challenges for the country. There was pressure on the internal law and order situation, arising mainly from communal riots and violent disturbances on a large scale, and the task of rehabilitating refugees who were arriving by thousands from Pakistan. A Communist-led peasant insurrection had to be dealt with in Telangana, and a "police action" taken against the unyielding Nizam of Hyderabad. The government needed to gain the support of the administrative services and the armed forces left behind by the British, since the leading cadres in both were not sure of their new status, and were apprehensive about the manner in which their new masters would handle their interests. The leadership also faced the task of dealing firmly with extremist communal organizations that had gained strength as a result of the petition, and of pacifying the leaders of political and regional groups that had been alienated during the later phases of the nationalist struggle. Above all, the country's leaders had to accomplish the mammoth organizational and strategic task of integrating a wide array of former princely states into the Union.[16] In short those at the helm of affairs in independent India faced the job of keeping the country intact and of creating out of its disparate parts and varied elements a nation whose existence they previously had assumed.

It is a tribute to the broad vision and sense of realism of India's leaders that most of these problems were sorted out in a relatively short period and solved in definitive ways. Under the firm and determined leadership of the late Vallabhabhai Patel, who was put in charge of the States Ministry, and who was also the first home minister of India, the job of securing the accession of the princely states to the Indian Union, and later their merger and consolidation, was accomplished in a remarkably smooth and thorough manner. Even more striking was Patel's success in gaining control of the law and order situation and in securing the loyalty of the administrative and armed services, the minorities, and the many refugees from Pakistan. During the independence movement the Indian members of the bureaucracy had often been reviled for their arrogance and their "betrayal" of the nationalist cause, which had created a sense of insecurity in the public services. One of Patel's first steps was not only to assure the civil service that its position in the new government would remain the same as in the outgoing one, but to tell the politicians not to interfere with its functioning. Indeed he used the proven talents and capacities of the Indian civil service in the immediate tasks of consolidation with great effectiveness. The same applies to his approach to the armed forces.

The leadership's success in solving these problems was due largely to the approach it adopted of moderating firmness and determination on larger issues by the politics of accommodation, an approach that was to characterize most of its actions, particularly in the first decade after independence. On the level of issues and a program for action, too, it followed a conscious policy of avoiding conflict. Nehru himself put it thus in 1952: "... speaking for myself, I have been over-burdened with the thought that we must give the top-most priority to the development of a sense of unity in India because these are critical days. Any decision that might come in the way of that unity should be delayed till we have laid a strong foundation for it."[17]

This desire for national unity and consolidation was paralleled by a concern for the country's development and progress in social and economic spheres. Soon after the earlier problems were solved and the Constitution came into force, the government undertook comprehensive measures for economic planning. In 1950, the year the new Constitution was adopted, the government of India set up a Planning Commission which was entrusted with the task of formulating five-year plans, enunciating economic and social priorities of the nation and a general model of economic development, and recommending ways and means of mobilizing resources for implementing such a model. In a very short time a sophisticated framework of centralized planning, enquiry, and consultation was developed.[18]

It is important that the Planning Commission is not even mentioned in the Constitution and came up as a result of Nehru's firm belief that for political consolidation to become effective a strategy of economic development should be established fairly early in the nation's career. At the same time the government urged the Parliament to pass a number of reform and welfare law which included the Untouchability (Offences) Act. Likewise the governments in the states were encouraged to take action toward the abolition of landlordism, and to guarantee special privileges to the depressed sections of the community. To overcome the difficulty arising out of the vetoing of such actions by the law courts and sometimes even to forestall the courts from doing so, the central Parliament amended the Constitution. Thus, although the leadership was concerned with the preservation of unity in the country, their concern did not lead them to inaction. They realized sufficiently that national consolidation was not a function of conflict avoidance alone; it called for positive action that eventually would strengthen the forces of integration.

To a considerable extent, integration was achieved through some of the measures that were taken in this early period. Although most of the measures taken were aimed at securing social and economic development, in the process they neutralized some of the important cleavages that could have developed into major sources of instability in the country. Labor's potential for trouble, for instance, was greatly reduced by the host of labor laws that were passed, as well as by the direct interest taken by Congressmen in trade union activity. In the same way, measures enacted to give concessions to the scheduled castes and tribes and the backward classes in matters of admission to educational institutions and employment, along with other measures to raise their social status, prevented bitterness against the high castes from taking an ugly form. The abolition of feudalism and the redistribution of land rights in the rural areas removed another important root of social cleavage.

During the first decade after independence, the leadership undertook another major transformation, the territorial reorganization of India on the basis of language. Colonial rule had created administrative units known as provinces without worrying much about the social and cultural viability of these entities.[19] The nationalists regarded this condition as unsatisfactory. Consequently, several times in the course of the movement the Congress had declared that it would reorganize the provinces on a linguistic and cultural basis once India became free. The Congress based its own organization, following its constitution of 1921, on linguistically homogeneous units known as Pradesh Committees. However, faced with the numerous problems referred to earlier, shaken by the events following partition, and needing to consolidate national unity, the leadership was at first not inclined to implement this decision and was, in fact, having second thoughts. Although Nehru accepted the linguistic principle on the floor of the Constituent Assembly in November, 1947, when the Linguistic Provinces Commission (known as the Dhar Commission) appointed by the Assembly came out strongly against the idea, both the Congress government and the constitution-makers decided to lie low on the issue. Consequently the Constitution adopted a scheme of territorial organization which did not follow the linguistic principle.

But the demand for linguistic states continued to be pressed. Particularly insistent was the demand for the creation of an Andhra state by separating the Telugu-speaking districts from the Tamil-speaking parts of Madras. The pressure was so great that the Congress Working Committee itself endorsed the demand and recommended in 1949 the creation of the new state. The central government was still reluctant as it feared that the creation of Andhra would encourage demands from other linguistic groups in the various multi-lingual states. The government also felt, rather unrealistically, that a division of the country on these lines would promote linguistic nationalism and weaken the already fragile basis of unity in the country. This led to a split in the ranks of the Congress; a directive from the party's High Command asking Congressmen not to join any linguistic agitation carried little weight in the various regions, and almost all other political parties joined the agitation. The government's indecision was finally resolved when a leading advocate of the linguistic campaign in Andhra undertook a fast unto death, and died. Under such mounting pressure, a separate Andhra state for the Telugu-speaking people was created in october, 1953. With the creation of Andhra, the demand for linguistic reorganization of the states gained momentum. The government finally appointed a States Reorganization Commission to examine the various demands. The Commission, appointed in December, 1953, undertook extensive investigation, and submitted its report in October, 1955. It accepted the linguistic principle and recommended drastic revisions of state boundaries. With certain modifications its recommendations were accepted, and were rapidly implemented during 1956. Still later, following a further demonstration of public feeling, the exceptions that had been made were undone: in 1960 the states of Maharashtra and Gujarat were created out of the bilingual state of Bombay; and in 1966 the states of Punjab and Haryana were created out of the former composite Punjab state.

In spite of the leadership's earlier reservations and ominous forebodings by sympathetic observers,[20] the reorganization resulted in rationalizing the political map of India[21] without seriously weakening its unity. If anything, its result had been functional, inasmuch as it removed what had been a major source of discord, and created homogenous political units which could be administered through a medium that the vast majority of the population understood. Indeed it can be said with the benefit of hindsight that language, rather than being a force for division, has proved a cementing and integrating influence.[22] If there be any reservation it is that the states were not further split into smaller cultural units within each linguistic zone.[23]

Thus during the first decade after independence the constitutional, territorial, and developmental framework for the consolidation of India as a nation was laid. Where modifications in the structure adopted by the Constitution were required, such as the territorial reorganization of the country, the setting up of a planning commission, and the amendment of the Constitution to effect changes in land rights and property relations, they were made. Important legislation designed to remove the glaring inequalities of the system inherited from the British was also effected. The process of economic development through planned change had also been started: the First Five Year Plan was successfully completed in 1956 and a more ambitious Second Five Year Plan launched. The Congress Party committed itself at the Avadi session in 1955 to the establishment of a "socialistic pattern of society." The first policy statement on industrial strategy was made in 1948 and a more comprehensive and realistic announcement was made in the Industrial Policy Resolution of 1956. At the same time steps designed to promote political education and developmental penetration of the rural areas were taken: a comprehensive program of community development, covering the whole country with developmental blocks, was started in 1952 and was later integrated into a new system of panchayati raj also known as "democratic decentralization." The report of the study team appointed for this purpose had already been submitted in 1957.[24] By this time (1947-1957) two general elections and scores of local elections had already taken place and the Congress Party's structure of dominance was fairly well established.

Much was thus accomplished during the first decade in terms of political integration and institutional consensus, which enabled India to weather even more trying developments in the next decade. Throughout this period, despite numerous stresses and strains, a degree of stability and development was maintained, and the institutions established by the Constitution were able to strike roots and flourish. The further developments that have taken place since have been largely among the structures established in the first decade; their significance lies in their provision of operational content to such a structure and in opening up channels of communication between the institutional centers and the outlying areas where the masses of the people reside. We shall now examine the main substance of these developments.

CENTER AND PERIPHERY

There are many ways in which the political system has been institutionalized between the center and the periphery. Through the federal structure of government established by the Constitution, there has taken place a crystallization of relationship between national, state, and district levels. The organization of government at the national and state levels is more or less similar (with the exception that while the president of India is indirectly elected by the various state legislatures and the central Parliament, the state governor is appointed by the president). Past experience with constitutional government, British traditions, public opinion, and more than all this, the understanding of the developing political situation brought by powerful leaders at both levels have conditioned the relationship between New Delhi and the state capitals. They have been conditioned by specific political pressures, personalities, and the organization of various interests. Above all they have been conditioned by the most relevant fact of the first two decades since independence— continuous rule by the same political party at the national level as well as in almost all the states.

The general trend is for the states, which happen to be in control of a very large part of the country's administration, to consolidate their power and, while no doubt depending upon the center for such things as financial resources and planned coordination, to assert their rights and have an increasing say in running the country. The most important fact here is the critical position occupied by the office of the chief minister (the state counterpart of the prime minister) in the organization of the Indian nation. The chief minister is not only the most powerful person in his state, which accounts for the acute competition for this office in so many states; he is also slowly becoming an important figures in national affairs. In important political decisions such as the succession to the office of the prime minister or the appointment of the Congress president, the chief ministers have been consulted as if they were national leaders.[25] This is a right for which some of the chief ministers have themselves fought and acquired: for they are powerful men in powerful positions.

A parallel process has taken place in the distribution of power within the ruling party. The state Congress Committee and the state Election Committee have been gaining in importance, the president of the state Congress (or in some cases the state Congress boss if the president is a dummy)[26] is a powerful person with often a great pull at the center, and the state party tends to assert its strength and at times even force the national High Command to sign the dotted line. We shall examine this development in greater detail when we come to discuss the party system in the next chapter. Meanwhile, let us also note here that this trend of state units of political parties having their own way is also a growing feature of the non Congress parties.

Other factors have consolidated this power of state leaders. An important aspect of India's governmental system is that the actual machinery of carrying out governmental decisions and planned programs is in the hands of state governments and their lower echelons. Here the formal provisions in the Constitution are misleading. The Constitution lists in considerable detail the distribution of governmental functions between the center and the states, including functions that are held "concurrently." Schedule VII of the Constitution provides three lists of functions: (1) the Union list, (2) the state list, and (3) the concurrent list. The roots of ambiguity are to be found in the schedule itself. There is considerable overlapping between the three lists, especially between the concurrent list and the state list. The Constitution provides that the central Parliament may, under certain conditions, pass legislation on any subject on the concurrent list and, further, that the Rajya Sabha (the upper house of the Parliament) may resolve by a two-thirds majority to empower the central legislature to pass laws on subject that was originally included on the state list. There also is a provision for the central government to issue "directives" to the state governments on a variety of subjects, many of which form part of the state list of subjects. Then there are the various powers of the president which enable the latter to interfere in the affairs of the states under certain conditions. The president can dissolve a state legislature, take over the government of a state by proclamation, or request the governor of a state to report to the president on particular bills being considered by a state legislature. All these provisions empower the center to encroach upon the powers of the states, leading some observers to conclude that India is a federation more in name than in substance.[27]

A review of the government and administration of India since independence dispels such views. Frequently the state governments have been able to exercise considerable influence and to extract a number of concessions from the center on a variety of issues. Also in areas reserved strictly for the center, the states have asserted themselves, even entering into trade discussions with foreign countries.[28] There are powerful chief ministers in certain states; not even the prime minister can take these men for granted, or deal with them in a light-hearted fashion. Moreover, as the late Paul Appleby persistently pointed out, the nature of Indian administration is such as to give all the more important functions to the state governments, with the center considerably dependent on the states to carry out the center's programs of development. The central government, he pointed out, is "all staff and no line," which means that the functions of government are actually carried out in the field by administrations that are under the control of state governments. Over the years the states have developed a tendency to take for granted financial support from the center, including special help in cases of shortages and deficiencies. This has in practice served to counteract the control and reviewing powers of the central government as a result of grants-in-aid. Appleby concluded that the central government in India tends to be at the mercy of the state governments, thus expressing a somewhat extreme view on India's federal character.[29]

It is arguable that both extreme positions are a result more of logical reasoning than of investigation into the realities of the situation. The tradition of reducing the issues of federalism into questions of states' rights or the absence thereof have impeded a more realistic appraisal of the Indian case. In reality, constitutional patterns of federal action have depended upon the developing political situation in the country.[30]

A new feature in the distribution of political power in India is the growing importance of the democratic element in the political system, namely the voters in the constituencies and local elites. The has led to an increasing decentralization of political initiative and administrative decision-making. It has led to increased powers for leaders at state and district' levels, and a growing need for central leaders to consult them. The working of the Planning Commission itself, a body which is assigned the role of centralized planning and coordination of plan administration, reveals such a balance of interests. At both the formulation and implementation stages of planned programs, in the deliberations of the National Development Council of the Planning Commission of which all the state chief ministers are members, as well as in more informal consultations between the Commission and the states, politicians from the states have been able to influence the outcome of the discussions considerably.

State (and district) leaders also control a good part of the election machinery of the Congress Party. This is partly due to the size of the country which keeps the central leadership remote from the bulk of the population, and partly to the increasing importance of rural patronage and influence in the outcome of the election. This has raised the importance of the state Congress committees just as planning and development have raised the importance of state ministries. Furthermore, the new leadership that is recruited into the political system is also coming from the states, which is, of course, inevitable. Induction and socialization in politics and changes in political alignments have mainly taken place in the states and this has had its impact on political recruitment at the national level.

Alongside this is to be found another tendency. The national leadership continuously mediates and arbitrates in disputes that develop from time to time in the states. The Congress Working Committee (the High Command) and the key leaders in the central government have taken an active part in the resolution of disputes and the formulation of a consensus solution at the state level, including the determination of new leadership, whenever the situation demands it. It is here that the real power of the central High Command has been revealed. A close examination of party interactions in the Congress shows that political struggle at the state level has been either accentuated or modified due to the active interest of the national leadership. State leaders often complain bitterly that but for encouragement from above, the disputes with the states would not have been as sharp as they are. In fact, this is an important technique of political control that the central leadership in India has cultivated which, in turn, has determined the relative power of national and state leaders. The general approach of the High Command has been to keep a nearly even balance of forces, to allow disputes to seek their own level, to enforce arbitration when a serious imbalance takes place, to watch carefully where the wind blows and adjust the strategy accordingly, but in any case to hold a margin of discretion in the hands of the High Command. The entry of other political parties into position of power in the states and their relative instability have further increased the mediative role of the central leadership, including constitutional intervention by the president and the Parliament.

It used to be argued that the fact of the same party being in power at the center and in the states maintains the authority of the central government, but once this situation disappears, party rivalries will lead to a diminution of this authority. A closer examination of the party system as a variable in center-state relations, however, points to the opposite conclusion. While the Congress continued to be the main force, state chief ministers were found to carry considerable weight with the center; this still happens to be the case for leaders of the states where the Congress is in power. On the other hand, where the state government is run by another party or coalition, its leaders are found to be much more dependent on the central government as the chief minister of the state is no more than a chief minister, and the facts of the state's dependence on the center in respect to financial and planning matters, or even the allocation of food supplies, become more glaring. The central leadership is found to enjoy greater discretion with respect to non-Congress than to Congress chief ministers who are not just chief ministers, but also part of the Congress power structure.

PATTERNS OF STATE POLITICS

We shall return to a more detailed consideration of state politics and center-state relationships in the next chapter in the context of party system developments, for it is the differences in political party interactions that largely account for differential developments in the states. Meanwhile, let us examine some of the more important contrasts in state political profiles and the resulting "patterning" of federal politics. While the focus of this book is on the characteristic patterns and interrelationships that inform the operation of the Indian political system as a whole, and we do not intend to get lost in the esoteric details of its many constituents, it would be useful to briefly capture the alternative patterns of regional politics with which the national political system has had to deal.[31]

Four main factors have affected particular developments in the states: pre-independence political configuration, the nature and strength of "opposition" to the Congress, kinds of intra-state diversities that have informed the politics of the Congress Party in each state, and the differences in the social structure of various regions.

Thus it is important to bear in mind that, despite the "mass" character of the Congress movement, it had not penetrated a large number of regions. In some of these other parties or groups of parties had held the fort. Chief among these were Bengal, Punjab, and Madras. In others the preponderance of princely states had given rise to weak and fragmented "states peoples' movements" but these had not aggregated into clear-cut party patterns. Chief among these were Kerala, Mysore, Rajasthan, large parts of present- day Madhya Pradesh, the Pepsu part of Punjab, and Saurashtra (now part of Gujarat). To these may be added Orissa and Assam with their large concentrations of tribal population. The post-1947 political development of these regions displayed great variations and presented very different issues for the center. In West Bengal and Punjab the partition left behind a confused state of affairs, but the availability of outstanding political managers in the persons of B.C. Roy and Pratap Singh Kairon led to both a high level of political consolidation under the Congress and major strides in economic development. In Madras (now known as Tamil Nadu), on the other hand, the predominance of a non-Brahmin movement under the Justice Party provided a major challenge to the Congress Party until the latter itself moved away from Brahmin dominance under another outstanding political manager, Kamaraj Nadar. Similarly, among the former princely state areas, Rajasthan, Saurashtra, and Mysore had had states peoples' movements that had maintained close links with the

Congress. Consequently, despite some early challenges from the princes, the Congress Party consolidated its position very soon after independence, and these regions continued to provide stable bases of allegiance to the center. Madhya Pradesh, Orissa, and Assam, on the other hand, have continued to be areas of instability, considerable factionalism within the Congress Party, and large pockets of tribal and feudal resistance. In Kerala the cultural renaissance and political mobilization had been dominated by left-oriented politicians, with the result that the Congress failed to strike a firm root at any time.

Another important antecedent variable in shaping these differences was the availability, or lack, of a strong and competent bureaucracy. In Madras and West Bengal, both of which had been under British rule for a long time, a strong bureaucratic tradition contributed to political consolidation and economic development, and even princely states like Mysore and Baroda in Gujarat had established enlightened administrative traditions; but in areas like Madhya Pradesh, Uttar Pradesh, and Orissa lack of such a tradition, and administrative heterogeneity, contributed to their fragmented politics and economic underdevelopment.

In the regions where the Congress movement had penetrated more effectively—Maharashtra, Gujarat, the Andhra parts of Andhra Pradesh—the Congress struck immediate roots, provided continuous rule, managed to incorporate new regions—Saurashtra in Bombay State and later in Gujarat, Hyderabad and Telangana in Andhra Pradesh—and led to considerable planned development. The strains in state politics that continue in these regions, however, owe not a little to these pre- independence differences: Saurashtra and Telangana even today continue to be sources of strain in the politics of Gujarat and Andhra pradesh respectively. Other areas of fragmented political organization and administrative development are Bihar and UP. Though no effective challenge to Congress rule emerged until recently in these areas, political fragmentation and a feudal tradition have made for a large incidence of party factionalism and personalized networks of influence, with consequent instability and continuous changes in governmental personnel.

Of equal importance is the kind of social structure that has obtained in the different regions. Thus the consolidation of non-

Brahmin movements in Madras and Maharashtra and the political mobilization of the "middle castes" in Gujarat and Andhra Pradesh, as well as the existence of distinct dominant castes in these regions, and in Mysore, have led to stable patterns of state level political coalitions. On the other hand, a fragmented caste situation, as in Bihar and UP in the north and Kerala in the south, has resulted in an exaggerated role of caste in state politics, and consequent instability of political coalitions. In West Bengal the preponderant role of Calcutta after the partition has led to characteristically urban patterns of politics, with the great vogue of "united front" politics and an anti-establishment ethos. In contrast the predominantly agricultural character of Andhra Pradesh has led to the domination of the land-holding castes and the cooptation of lower peasant castes in some kind of a patron-client network. And the politics of tribalism have dominated the ups and downs of Congress and anti-Congress coalitions in Orissa, Assam, and MP.

We shall discuss the detailed implications of different kinds of caste interaction for political coalition-makeup in Chapter VI. Suffice it to note here that the differences in the antecedent conditions and the social structure of politics noted above have resulted in different patterns of "opposition" in the states and hence in differential pressures on center- state relationships. Thus, despite the consolidation of Congress power in West Bengal, there has all along been a strong tradition of "united front" opposition dominated by urban movements of protest in which progressive left parties have played a major role. For quite different reasons, the same happened in Kerala—the role of the Communists in the political mobilization of the depressed Ezhava caste, the parallel growth of educated unemployment, and the peculiar structure of rural-urban continuities. In both states the result has been a politics of polarization between the Congress on the one hand and the communist-led united front on the other. In Andhra Pradesh, by contrast, despite the earlier importance of the Communists based on the antagonism between two dominant castes—the Reddis and the Kammas—all over the state, slowly the politics of Congress coalition-making incorporated both Reddi and Kamma elements, and the opposition that now emerged was from areas not fully integrated in the state, namely Hyderabad and the Telangana region. A third pattern has been in Madras and Punjab where earlier movements of substantial opposition—the non-Brahmins in Madras and the Akalis in Punjab—have re- emerged and shaped the party politics of the two states. Finally in both the tribal regions— Orissa, Assam, MP—and the feudal areas of the north—eastern UP and Bihar—the political pressures have been essentially those of personalized rivalries and shifting factionalism, no matter which party or coalition is in power.

All these pressures have informed federal and intra-state political relationships. The issues of political coalition-making have been manifold; their integrative and disintegrative potential quite substantial. We shall analyze these, and their impact on post-1967 developments, in the next chapter. Enough has been described here to indicate the growing importance of state political patterns for federal politics. Two points follow. The role of the center and in particular of the Indian National Congress in mediating the various coalitional strains in the states has been profound in weaving together the heterogeneity of Indian society into a common *national* political framework. At the same time, the consolidation of state power in the framework of an increasing formalization of the federal constitution has made for typical patterns of institutional diffusion and decentralization. The result is a "mix" of center peripheral relationships. In the next chapter we shall see how, in the changed context of an effective multi-party system, such a mix is getting further institutionalized and how it is concurrently facing the political strains of multi-regional and multi-ethnic politics.

PROCESS OF DECENTRALIZATION

Such an articulation of relationships between the national and state levels is only part of the developing institutional structure that has taken place in the country since independence. On the whole, the process of diffusion has gone further down and has crystallized at lower levels. Let us consider the elements in such a process.

Four factors account for the diffusion of political power within the states. First, the administration of planned programs has increasingly come to depend upon implementation at lower levels, corresponding respectively to the functions to be performed and their technical requirements. The administration at the state level does more no more than break up large policy decisions of the state and national government into specific measures, and then pass them of for implementation as the district and lower levels, corresponding respectively to the functions to be performed and the technical requirements. The administration at the state level does no more than break up large policy decisions of then state and national governments into specific measures, and then pass them on for implementation at the district and lower levels. This was a pattern that was set up by the British who made the district the focal unit of Indian administration. Other measures of decentralization since independence, such as the strengthening of district development boards and the establishment of new local authorities of planned change like community development blocks, extension agencies, credit cooperatives, and statutory panchayats, have all further institutionalized the process of administrative and political diffusion with the states.[32]

Second, an elaborate network of patronage has developed, extending deep into the countryside. Much of this is controlled and directed from levels lower than the state. Availability of new kinds of jobs, distribution of loans and benefits, control of institutions dealing with credit and scarce materials, establishment of new positions of prestige and authority, the penetration of educational institutions and voluntary organizations with new resources, and above all a known and intelligible pattern of influence and corruption—all these have brought life and significance to the governmental machine, endowed it with political meaning, and led to an increasing communication between traditional society and the new structure of institutions.

Leaders at the state level initiated the process. In order to make itself secure in office, the ruling group in the state has increasingly relied on the rural vote, spreading its patronage far and wide controlling local authorities, educational institutions and other developmental agencies, including important voluntary organizations. Concomitantly, institutional power shifted downward and a different set of men emerged who took charge of these networks, captured positions in the party organization, and slowly acquired considerable strength and power. The new organization men that emerged are to be found away from the urban centers of state power in small towns and district capitals, closer to the traditional social order, and exhibiting a new style in Indian politics. They are pragmatic men, less oriented to the modernist idiom but modernizers in their own way, men who understand the subtleties and nuances of local society, powerful persons who have taken time in coming up, and who are therefore confident of their own strength. When the elections come, the state leaders have to rely increasingly upon these men who happen both to occupy positions of influence in the institutions of planned change and to be in close communication with socially entrenched and economically powerful local elites. Some of them are popular leaders, others ruthless managers, but they control the vote. The focus of power has shifted.[33]

Third, there is the great complexity of the electoral system. There are many levels of elected bodies in India—the national Parliament, the state legislatures, the district, the block and the village panchayats, and the town municipalities. Other very important elected bodies controlling vast economic power include the district cooperative banks, the producing and marketing cooperatives in important cash crops, and the various economic committees of the district panchayats.[34] Some of these are directly elected by the people, some are indirectly elected by representatives from the lower levels, and others by just the members who, however, represent varied strata of the people. There is considerable overlap in the men who control these various institutions. The general trend is for those who aspire to be elected to the state legislature to depend on the elites at the lower levels.

Fourth, underlying all this, and largely as a result of the operation of adult franchise, considerable shifts have occurred in the social base of politics. Sections of the people who had been hitherto denied access to political power and who had considered politics to be the legitimate concern of the martial and the learned classes have been exposed to the new ideology, have realized the power of numbers, and have started organizing themselves through their own associations and leaders. This is the rise of the "newly enfranchised" in politics. As a result of both political competition and the impact of programs of development and welfare on the leaders of society, there has arisen a mutual awareness between party politicians and community leaders anxious to have a greater say in the allocation of economic and political resources. Such a closing of the gap between political organization and the social structure of rural India, along with the downward shift of power within the government and the ruling party discussed above, underlines a tremendous transformation in the power relations of Indian society.

On the other hand, such diffusion has not led to any fulfillment of the idyllic vision of a self-contained village community. Both in terms of political sufficiency and as a unit of administration and citizen participation, the village is fast ceasing to be a focal point of attention. Even the more ambitious programs of "rural uplift" have had to settle at some level higher than the village, like the development block. Different influences have been trickling down to the village from higher levels - through the new uses to which traditional trade routes are being put, through education and new channels of communication, transport, and mass media, through extended kinship frameworks and caste associations, and above all through new types of administration and politics. Barring the traditional local feuds and village factionalism, political life in the village is increasingly drawn into the politics of a wider area. In leadership also, what matters is not the position of a village leader in the local community but the links he maintains outside that community. The only exceptions are where the village is many times larger than the average statistical village of India, as for instance in Kerala. In the few instances where the small village retains its complete autonomy owing to either an idyllic antagonism to politics or the instance by its elite on maintaining the integrity of traditional society, its relevance for organized politics is only marginal.

ROLE OF THE DISTRICT

At the district, the developments from various levels tend to crystallize. There are many reasons for this. Over the decades, the district has achieved a clear identity and administrative importance. In terms of size, too, with an average population of a million and a half, the district appears to be an optimum unit. The area covered by the district is neither too large nor too small to enable it to enjoy competence and autonomy, to draw the resources and the technical know-how that are needed for efficient administration, and to maintain the right balance between homogeneity and diversity that is needed for sustaining an active elite group. It is the first level in the country where officials try to implement planned programs. The traditional power wielded by the district collector has also succeeded in creating an image of authority which makes for certainty and dependability in the minds of the people. Any structure of authority, when it gains stability over a long period, articulates many other structures after its own image. Thus, it has happened that owing to its continuity from Moghul to British to post-independence times, the district has become a level at which not only the administration but also political and social communications have crystallized.

The most important lever of local power in Indian politics is the District Congress Committee. The support provided by leaders from different districts determines the composition of state ministries and state Congress committees. This is so important that recent innovations in public relations have taken the district as their basis. Thus in some states, such as Maharashtra and Gujarat, districts have been formally distributed among the state ministers for considering the grievances of the people, receiving representations, and being generally responsible for the welfare of the district and its coordination with the state. The districts are also beginning to claim "representation" in ministry formation at the state level. They do not all succeed, and several other factors are involved in ministry formation, but the district is nonetheless emerging as a distinct configuration in state politics.

Even the economic and social structure seems to have adjusted over a period of time to the conditions of district existence. Individuals identity themselves as coming from this or that district. Associations of various castes, other primordial systems of social communication, community alignments between elite groups, and social factions in state politics all get articulated at the district level. The fact that important urban centers, trade routes of justice, educational institutions, and commercial centers have also developed around the district headquarters has conditioned the social and cultural activities in the surrounding area. The establishment of resourceful agencies such as the district cooperative bank, the land mortgage bank, various licensing authorities, agricultural and forestry departments, police headquarters, school authorities, and above all the headquarters of the district panchayat and the district collectorate have all tended to bring various interests to the district capital. In this, the offices of the district collector and the Congress Party boss have played key roles.

The office of the collector in India is in many ways unique and its supposed stature and authority have engendered a sort of institutionalized charisma that is in some ways unparalleled in modern administrative development. Despite all attempts to disparage such an image under new ideologies of development, sometimes crudely described as "de-collectorization" of the district, this is one legacy of British administration which it would be hard to break. Recent developments in some states have given rise to another officer in the district in the same rank as the collector and armed with widespread developmental functions and powers. While this may affect the status and functions of the collector and possibly polarize and weaken the administration, it will further confirm the importance of the administrative district in the Indian system.

More than all this, of course, is the importance of the district in the development of political institutions and leadership. The district has been the scene of much recent change. Institutional development is of a high order. It started with a large number of developmental and "semi-official" agencies, institutions of credit and economic development, health facilities, and schools and colleges which together provided a network of nonofficial patronage. Over this structure came the rapid extension of community development and panchayati raj, thus further spreading the networks of influence. Although community development established a new unit of administration in the development block, which is much smaller than the district, it was from the district level that technical know-how and resources for the blocks were made available. Important functions and resources were transferred to the district and the block levels and a rationalization of both official and non-official administrative structures occurred, which further augmented the power wielded by the district leaders. The emergence of elected heads of the districts, paid and provided for from the public exchequer, further consolidated these developments. These are men who have also brought a new style to the management of politics. Generally coming from the well-to-do class of peasant proprietors, they are men of some means, skilled in the art of managing men and running institutions, and very knowledgeable concerning local conditions. They exhibit greater self-confidence in dealing with not only the members of the public but also those in the bureaucracy, both locally and at higher levels. Thus the introduction of the new agencies has not only made for decentralization of functions and resources; it has also led to a remarkable concentration of social, economic, and political power in the hands of a few men, the growth of party machines, and an articulated system of tension management.

In less than a generation since independence, government and politics in India have started functioning at various levels. They have permeated local society with multifarious agencies of development and political mobilization, have brought into being an elaborate machinery of consultation, investigation, and decision-making, and are drawing all of this together into a common national hierarchy. With this, the so-called "gap" between tradition and modernity, between one political culture and another, is giving place to a common synthesis.[35]

SIGNIFICANCE OF PANCHAYATI RAJ

The institutionalization of this synthesis deserves special attention. One of the more imaginative institutional innovations made by the national leadership—in the long run more imaginative than the linguistic reorganization of the states or the setting up of the Planning Commission—is the introduction of panchayati raj. It it a step that simultaneously is decentralizing the Indian polity and integrating it into a common framework of institutional allegiances. The leadership may not have fully perceived its consequences; indeed the administrative and intellectual circles received the proposal with considerable doubt and cynicism.[36] The credit for wholeheartedly supporting the decision goes to Nehru, whose uncommon faith in the efficacy of democratic processes made him defend the new institution against all criticism. He had equally de fended the community development program, the forerunner of panchayati raj.[37]

The community development (CD) program, started in 1952 and exhibiting considerable bureaucratic expansion as well as a great deal of rhetoric and romanticism, nevertheless failed to fulfill the essential goal of bridging the hiatus that divided rural society from the governmental structure.[38] There were many reasons for this failure. For one thing, the whole program was conceived in administrative terms, with the result that rapid administrative coverage became a substitute for intensive development.[39] The ambivalences arising from a centralized missionary approach, trying to "transform the masses," resulted from expecting everything from the government rather than instilling the objectives of mass mobilization and voluntary self-help.[40]

Second, the human and material resources placed at the disposal of the movement, since these had to come almost entirely from a government committed to assigning top priority to rapid industrialization, proved woefully inadequate. Third, such a combination of a bureaucratic approach and meagre resources distorted the priorities of the movement; while block headquarters were easily constructed and official ranks filled, the essential targets of agricultural development activities recorded insufficient progress.[41] Fourth, there was inherent gap between the overall strategy of economic development and the movement's ideology of revolutionizing villages—a gap that was filled by incessant rhetorical appeals for greater public cooperation. After much effort was expended on the movement and high expectations were aroused, an authoritative inquiry was commissioned which told the government that the movement lacked something very basic, namely the political involvement of the people. The report of the inquiry as well as other investigations into the shortcomings of the movement stressed that not until power and initiative were transferred to the local elites could the government expect to fulfill developmental, much less political, objectives enunciated in the directive principles of the Indian Constitution.[42]

The result has been panchayati raj, an integrated system of local self-government with the twin objectives of democratic decentralization and local participation in planned programs. Although there are important state variations in implementing these new institutions, giving rise to alternative models of political mobilization,[43] there are some basic features which can be briefly stated. First, panchayati raj exists at three levels, the village level panchayat, the block level *panchayat samiti*, and the district level *zilla parishad* (district panchayat), drawn into a coordinated network of developmental personnel, functioning from the state downward and the village upward. One generally notices a combination of local initiative and control and mediation from above, displaying the same characteristics as are found in the relationship between the center and the states. Second, Unlike community development, which was essentially conceived in bureaucratic terms, these are elected bodies, manned by politicians entrusted with developmental tasks and under whose guidance the appointed officials are supposed to work.[44] Third, there is a greater devolution of functions of resource mobilization and public cooperation to these bodies, functions that were formerly very inadequately carried out by bureaucrats from the state and the district. The result is a greater filling in of the administrative and political hierarchy, and the growth of something like a national continuum stretching from the village to the central government. The hierarchy is not yet fully filled in, nor is the continuum operating smoothly. We still deal here with a transitional state of institutional development. But the trends are clear and provide further filling of the space between the center and the periphery.

The new institutions of panchayati raj may draw part of their legitimacy from ancient traditions and folklore, but they have been mainly crystallized by acquiring new meaning in their operation, by a considerable devolution of functions, resources, and powers. They are essentially new institutions under an old name.[45] Moreover, they are part of a larger phenomenon. Operating through these institutions, a new kind of political functionary has emerged at the local level who may, in the course of time, become more powerful than the elected representatives at the state and national levels. Politicians in the Congress—and gradually in other parties as well—are beginning to realize the potentialities of the new institutions. They often prefer positions in panchayat samitis and zilla parishads, or in associated organizations like the district transport authorities and the district cooperative banks, to being elected to the state legislature. In the former, they are acquiring considerable administrative and managerial skills. Known in the Indian political vocabulary as the "non-officials"—as against the appointed officials who held the center of the stage so far[46]—the politicians are playing an increasing role in bridging the gap between local society and political authority. It is difficult to see how the national-building activities conceived at higher levels could have made their impact without the active and interested participation of this new representative element in Indian politics. The incentives that are driving the non-officials into sustained administrative activity far outweigh the capacities and motivations of the bureaucrat and the traditional administrator from above: but for the private enterprise of the former, the public functions of the latter would be difficult to perform. Moreover, it is not simply by manning administrative and distributive agencies that the non-official exercises his power. His real power comes out of his ability to take into confidence socially entrenched interests and groups. And as this happens, traditional interests come to terms with the new order.

THE GROWTH OF INTERMEDIARIES

Such a patterning of linkages between traditional and modern sectors of the nation still underscores a fluid state in institutional development. Whereas a loose continuum has been established between the people and the government, direct identifications with the new system of institutions are yet nascent. Meanwhile such a process of political mobilization has led to the crystallization of "intermediate systems" at various levels. The political non-official, who does so much to lubricate the country's institutional structure, can hope to do so only on the basis of creating for himself further structures of support in local society. He has to establish rapport with the "influentials" at several vantage points, with caste and religious leaders institutional leaders, opinion leaders consisting of educated and professional men in the locality, new upstarts who have made political haggling their full-time vocation, and, not the least important, the local bullies who can intimidate and cajole the people, who normally keep faith, and who in their crude way maintain peace in the locality. One or more of these middlemen may be present in a particular situation, and the network of support may range from being unifocal, with one man controlling the full coalition of local interests, or multi-focal, with specialized and competing networks in the same area. But in either case, the mediative role of such intermediaries is found to be important in most places.[47]

All these various networks of relationship—the ascriptive and influence networks of indigenous society, the patronage network provided by bureaucracy and planning, and the network of parties and factions brought into play through the electoral system—get enveloped in an ongoing structure of participation in which the various publics and their specialized elites are drawn together. Elections to state and national legislatures, of course, provide the biggest opportunity for political participation. Local elections to the system of panchayati raj, the selection of Congress candidates for different elections, and organizational elections within the Congress Party provide further opportunities. There are many other opportunities. Consultation over distribution of development grants, decisions on cooperative credit and agricultural loans, allocation of scarce commodities, decisions on construction of schools, libraries, dispensaries, link-roads, and tube wells, negotiations on matching grants for specific projects—all these have increasingly become objects of discussion, "influence," and pressure, and have, over the years acquired the status of public events. The coming of panchayati raj at the district and lower levels has without doubt introduced a new and powerful factor in the consolidation of all this, one that will both simplify the diffused participation structure described above and integrate it with higher levels of political and economic decision making, thus adding greatly to the competitive potential of the rural social structure. Such a process of governmental penetration and political mobilization of the nation's traditional sectors, which lie in the logic of India's model of development, here finds its further extension and consummation.

A distinction can be made here between "modernists" and "modernizers." The modernists are to be found mostly in metropolitan urban areas, in both intellectual and political circles. They initiate change and articulate the ideals of modern India and the goals of development. But they do this more often than not in abstract and a priori terms, and are often found to be insensitive to the aspirations and demands of the population. The modernizers, on the other hand, operate at lower levels, are given less to debate and more to application penetrate the traditional sector, and mobilize support from it for modernist ends. At the same time, they perform the feedback functions by being the principal communicators of "removement and dynamism to the whole process of nation-building and integration. With time, the modernizers are also found to replace the modernists at higher levels. The usual assertion of a "shift of power" from urban to rural areas is an oversimplification of this more comprehensive process of democratization.

BUREAUCRACY AND POLITICAL DEVELOPMENT

We should like to make a few general points. First, our discussion of the massive steps taken by the Indian government to penetrate into the periphery and evolve an operating national hierarchy shows that for all its "mass appeal" the nationalist movement had not really reached far into the indigenous structure of Indian society. It was Gandhi's great achievement to take the movement beyond the narrow confines of the urban middle classes and, what is more, to provide an ideology of reconstruction in which the village became the principal focus of national attention. But the major operational tasks were undertaken only after independence.

Second, even what has been accomplished since independence should not lead us to any conclusion in favor of a model of an integrated political community, as is commonly understood in discussing more developed political systems. India is far from being a "mas society"; there are still great distances and wide disparities. Both the institutional strategy of penetration from above and the diversified political culture of India tend to underemphasize its mass character and the country is likely to continue for a long time to be a pluralistic order, in which differentiations take on the character of autonomous and frequently isolated "subsystems." What we have discussed so far should emphasize more the dimension of structural integration than the dimension of mass participation.

Third, although our general emphasis so far in this chapter has been on the processes of *political* penetration, we have also indicated the role of administration and economic planning in crystallizing these processes. Without the latter, the former could not have gone very far; the two are coordinate parts of the country's institutional strategy. It would be useful to give a little more consideration to this aspect, namely the relevance of administrative structure and economic planning to political institutionalization.

CONTINUITIES FROM THE PAST

Public administration in India reflects the same characteristics of continuity and change found in the development of political institutions discussed above. The British left behind an administrative network that was designed to serve the purpose of a regime trying to rule a vast subcontinent through the device of a unified district administration informed by common principles of government and disciplined by a structure of authority invested in an "all-India" civil service.[48] Such a system still dominates India's administrative arrangements. Similarly, the early features of the system in which important political and developmental decisions were cast in an administrative mold also continue to dominate the style and approach of the Indian leadership to problem-solving and implementation. Such a system has been called upon to absorb four major transformations: an enormous expansion in the functions of government, important changes in the structure of decision-making following the introduction of political masters at each level of government, the influx of democratic decentralization at district and lower levels, and the new institutions of economic planning, coordination, and control, including a phenomenal growth of the public sector.

We have already seen how, despite the earlier history of bitterness and estrangememt between the nationalist leadership and the public services, the Congress succeeded in winning over the confidence and loyalty of the services by maintaining their position in the new system of government. In fact, however, the concessions went further. The leadership did not simply incorporate the administrative services in the new system; rather they turned over the initiative for future reconstruction to the entrenched bureaucracy. Consequently almost all the changes necessary for political and economic development have been administered through the structure of the public bureaucracy. Thus the countrywise organization of elections held every few years, the entire program of community development, the whole network of credit and service cooperatives, the sponsorship of a plethora of "voluntary organizations" initiated and aided by government support, large scale public corporations and public sector undertakings, projects involving huge outlays and technological know-how, large tasks of "research and development," even the formulation and implementation of political innovations such as the establishment of panchayati raj bodies, and above all the full burden of control and allocation of commodities in short supply—all this and much more has been handled through the extension and elaboration of the pre-independence administrative framework.

Nowhere are the disadvantages of continuity in change so manifest as in India's administrative sphere. And yet what is surprising is that this has been done without total breakdown. When it is remembered that the Indian administration is rather pithily manned in its higher echelons (there are just about 3,000 members of the IAS who control and run the greater part of the national and state administrate structures), that it is essentially decentralized in character (for it is only at the district level that the main tasks of implementing decisions begin), and that the chief administrators are generalists moving from one job to another rather than specialists in continuous control of public undertakings, the salience of adopting an inherited administrative structure rather than thoroughly reorganizing it becomes clear.[49] India has largely avoided both the alternatives of developing a parallel political machine as found in the socialist countries and leaving the bulk of the initiative for economic development to market forces as in some of the Western countries. It has, similarly, fought shy of going fully in the direction of separating local from national development administration, and has chosen to make do with a complicated meshing of vertical and horizontal controls, characteristic of its eclectic approach to social engineering.

NEW DEVELOPMENTS

Important institutional developments have appeared in the structure of public undertakings. Soon after independence, various proposals for establishing agencies of economic coordination all the way down from the Cabinet Secretariat were implemented. The Planning Commission and its many committees and organs of investigation, on the one hand, and various developmental ministries, on the other, spearheaded a whole network of departmental enterprises, public companies and corporations, a machinery of consultation between the center and the states, an array of assessing and reviewing functions, and new organs of decision-making with regard to mobilization and dispersal of economic and human resources. Several developmental ministries have come to be headed by politicians who are in fact technocrats,[50] and a body of specialized know-how and technical functionaries has been created in the departments. The same is taking place in the states. While still operating in the framework of the administrative services and their relatively small numbers, there is an increasing tendency to keep the most seasoned civil servants in central departments and as heads of economic and top decision-making functions in the states (the chief secretaries and the development commissioners). These men bear the main burden of development—together with their immediate political masters who tend to stay on in the same jobs for long stretches of time—resulting in a common outlook and in a surprising mastery over technical detail. The burden on these over-worked men is far more than a rational system of institutionalization would demand, but given the complexity of tasks and the constant fear of fragmentation of initiative, the system is not without its advantages.[51]

At the local levels these developments have caused two structural changes. One is a dual system of power, one under the traditional district collector for carrying out traditional functions of rule maintenance and the general progress of the district, and the other under a development officer of the same rank as the collector, who presides over various developmental agencies at the district, block, and village levels.[52] The other development is the duplication of political-administrative relationships of the central and state levels at the district and block levels under the new system of panchayati raj. While the officials still carry the burden of development administration, they are now subordinate to the elected non-officials who in turn are responsible to elected (block) councils or (district) assemblies. As we have seen, the initiative for such development came from the central government, the Planning Commission, and its National Development Council who were concerned with the low state of response from lower levels of the administration. These bodies also assume many spontaneous and autonomous functions, thus making administration more responsive to pressing local needs. There is an increasing interplay between local government and the centralized bureaucracies of state and national governments, in part through the dyarchal structures described here but largely through consultation and bargaining on developmental decision-making. The content of this bargaining is becoming increasingly economic and gets structured according to competing perceptions of priorities.

Of all the advantages of such a system, the most important is the ability of higher levels of government to make an impact on lower levels—to come to the aid of the people in time of acute need or scarcity, to spread new ideas and new schemes of agricultural development, and to influence local decision-making through promise of funds and other levers of patronage. Conversely, the system has led to continuous feedback in the peculiarities of the local situation, including political pressures that must be taken into account in higher-level decision-making.[53] Alongside the functioning of political intermediaries discussed above, such a crystallization of administrative channels has facilitated communication between government and local society.

THE IDEOLOGICAL IMPEDIMENT

However, any strategy of institutionalization involves more than adaptation of old and establishment of new structures of decision-making and channels of communication; it also involves putting these structures to use and making the policy process responsive to the needs of the situation. An important dilemma of a new nation is that the confrontation between a "dynamic" elite and a "stagnant" society leads to policies that lack realism and operational relevance. The elite tend to view the development process with doctrinaire complacency, to invest heavily in generalized platitudes in line with the official doctrines, and to think of the relationship between an institutional step and its intended consequences in unidimensional terms. It is only when serious setbacks bring the elite face to face with reality and new interpretations of the situation steadily gain ground that the policy process undergoes the necessary changes. An examination of the Indian case confirms this.

After the impressive success of the modest-sized First Five Year Plan, a bold strategy of heavy industrialization as a general formula of rapid development was adopted. On the rural side a "comprehensive" program of community development, proposals for sweeping land legislation to be undertaken by the state governments, and an ambitious plan for cooperative farming were conceived in a highly doctrinaire fashion.[54] In concrete terms, however, the effort to industrialize at a rapid pace consumed the bulk of India's scarce resource while agricultural development, the crux of the rural problem, was dealt with in a rather fragmentary manner.[55] And yet without the development of this key sector of the country, 80 per cent of whose population lived in the rural areas, not much headway was possible. The results were full of frustration. Plan shortcomings, refusal of state governments (who happened to be more in touch with operative social structures than the intellectuals of the Planning Commission) to fall in line on land legislation and cooperative farming, and the unresponsiveness of the people to the romantic exhortations of community development made it clear that implementing a program of development implied more than just the planning of targets.

The gap between expectations and realization was filled by pious declarations, a continuous flow of new ideas which were never implemented,[56] and a snobbish attitude on the part of the planners and the administrators who shifted the blame to the low motivation of the farmers and the rural people. Foreign as well as indigenous social scientists lent support to such diagnoses by their theories of lack of innovative behavior and the general fatalism of the Indian masses.[57] The crucial point was lost that lacking the essential inputs in agriculture and in the face of a wooden and self-indulgent bureaucracy, the farmers had good reason not to take the risks involved in adopting innovations that were being preached to them in monotonous repetition.

Meanwhile, the democratic process brought forth its own dynamics. The active functioning of the federal structure, the local elite groups, and the party system produced new kinds of leaders at the top, leaders who were both more vote-conscious and more sensitive to the primary needs of the people, and who therefore wanted rethinking on the country's development strategy. The chief ministers, Congress President Kamaraj, Prime Minister Shastri, and after him, Indira Gandhi and other pragmatists in the Congress contributed to this rethinking; sensitive administrators like Food Minister C. Subramaniam and his devoted band of civil servants worked out the details in terms of a "new economic strategy"; and the serious circumstances of two successive famines and the continuing humiliation of depending on foreign countries for the basic necessity of food finally clinched the issue.[58] The plan schedules were disturbed, a whole series of liberalization of economic controls was undertaken, the Planning Commission was reorganized (in effect it was reduced to its proper status from its earlier exaggerated role), administrative structures were made specific and problem-oriented, and a considerable revaluation of priorities was effected.

At the same time as economic policy became the focus of political controversy, and gradually an instrument of rival groups in the Congress Party, political confrontations tended to be couched in the language of economic and social issues. Thus while the agricultural crisis led to a host of policy changes in the direction of a more pragmatic approach to issues of growth, a political tug-of-war between the organizational leadership of the Congress Party and Mrs. Gandhi led, in 1969, to a frontal decision on her part to nationalize the major banks and assign to the government a predominant role in credit and investment policies. Whereas the crucial question for the future is whether such steps will become operational instruments in the drive toward rapid growth or simply turn into an ideological substitute for such a drive, there is little doubt that a process of closer approximation between political cleavages and conflicts over policy has begun. This is likely to bring about, during the next few years, a series of clarifications in the country's vague declarations of "objectives." The precise modifications and policy priorities that will come from such a confrontation of rival groups will determine the political character of India's model of growth.

We shall consider these issues in much greater detail in Chapter IX. It is enough to note here that the institutional structure adopted by the country and the political dynamics that it has generated have demanded a resolution of system ambivalences, and that the gap between a centralized bureaucracy and local society is now being bridged by adequate modifications in the country's utopia. The system is still full of inadequacies and discontinuities; the communication between the center and the periphery is riddled with many ambiguities; the complacent attitudes with regard to the effect of well meant intentions and pious resolutions still persist: and the deadweight of inherited structures and entrenched interests continues to lend inertia and rigidity to the functioning of key national institutions. Institutionalization of India's political consensus is yet in a fluid stage and the leadership seems to be only dimly aware of the institutional imperatives of the development process. But there is also a trend toward confrontation with the hard issues of growth and the remodelling of both policies and administrative structures in the direction of problem-solving capabilities. Its distinctiveness from the earlier period of amorphous goal-hunting and its shift from grand strategy to specificity of decision-making suggest a new phase in the country's political and administrative development. After considering other dimensions of political development, we propose to return to an evaluation of the system's performance on various issues (in Chapters VIII to XI).

INSTITUTIONALIZATION AND LEGITIMACY

It has been argued that an important reason for India's political stability despite the strains and stresses involved in the development process is its "early institutionalization."[59] Our consideration of the institutionalization of Indian democracy both before and since independence tends to support this generalization. But it is necessary to go beyond such a general statement and look into the constituents of what we have called the "institutional strategy" of the Indian political elite. As we do so, we can see that the dichotomy between "institutionalization" on the one hand and "participation" on the other, or between "institutionalization" and "ideology," begins to break down. The pertinent questions are: Institutionalization of what? What are the main stimuli and response that have structured the institutional dimension? And what is the role of ideas and processes (participation, mobilization) in the evolution of institutional structures and their legitimization?[60]

Four peculiarities of the Indian case emerge from this chapter. First, India has been fortunate in the length and continuity of its process of institutionalization. A long colonial rule during which the broad lines of its territorial and administrative structures were laid, a fairly long nationalist movement when its goals were articulated and a broad consensus on them achieved, and the unhampered rule of the Congress Party over two decades when the structures and procedures adopted by the Constitution were allowed to penetrate and strike roots have all consolidated the institutional framework of democracy. A corollary of this point is that there was never a sharp break in this effort; length of experience was buttressed by continuity in political and administrative traditions. The "machine" was not "smashed". Both tradition and a special kind of leadership contributed to such an approach.

Alongside length of experience, however, was the depth of the process. Both the nationalist movement and the "nation-building" movement which took off from it deliberately sought sanctions from the countryside and, with that in mind, penetrated toward the periphery of the nation. This involved processes of mobilization and participation which may theoretically sound risky and which indeed increase the "loads" on the system, but without whose relative success the institutional framework would have been without its necessary legitimacy. The main feature here has been a spiraling between institutionalization and participation. Each state of crystallization of institutional structures was followed by a fresh influx of participation roles which in turn needed to be woven into the ongoing institutional pattern. The leadership did not fight shy of involving more and more groups in the mainstream of national politics and affording them opportunities in return for their agreeing to play the rules of the game. Such an approach has led to much openness and fluidity, and the growth of intermediate structures and styles, with the result that institutionalization has become an ongoing process, not just the establishment and maintenance of a set of given structures.

Third is the role of ideology. It is difficult to see how the kind of consensus and integration that the country has been able to develop would have been possible without firm ideological convictions on the part of the leadership, its readiness to disseminate these convictions and translate them in institutional terms, and the slow percolation of the ruling ideas of the "tall men" of the movement into rank and file and beyond to the politically relevant masses. To read the voluminous collection of Gandhi's writings and speeches is to go through a monotonous ratiocination of basically a very few maxims and convictions. By constantly repeating them he made them part of the national vocabulary and symbol system. Nehru did the same. Harping constantly and in an almost tiresome manner on the themes of democracy, socialism, planning, non-involvement in power blocs, and related ideas, he created a framework of discourse which laid the semantic and symbolic basis of national unity. We have seen how for a time such semantics became a substitute for action. At the same time without their *prior* dissemination, the pragmatic phase of Indian politics would have led to a scramble for power uninformed by any prescriptions or limits. Without such interplay between ideology and issue confrontation, political institutionalization would have soon petrified and dissolved itself in the morass of party politics. With their prior legitimization, on the other hand, as we shall see in the next chapter, party politics became the great vehicle of national integration.

Finally, there is the point of *institutional change*. We have seen how, starting from the structure adopted by the constitution-makers, the Indian leadership had had to constantly improvise and develop the structure further. This is most important for any successful institutional strategy: the institutional structures should not simply be legitimized once and for all; their legitimacy has to be constantly renewed when confronted by new issues and problems. It is important to realize that the problem of institutionalization and integration of a new nation becomes essentially one of re-institutionalization and re-integration. It has to move from the old universals and their institutional forms—caste structure, local polities, regional organization—to new institutions and often to new universals. And this again is not done at one point in time but goes on for several decades, and in a sense never stops. Any static view of institutionalization which contraposes "stable institutions" against "unstable processes" fails to take account of the realities in which new nations like India find themselves.

Before we conclude we should like to sound a note of caution, as we did in the last chapter, against reading too much deliberation and rational calculation into the process. Our expression "institutional strategy" has to be read more in post hoc terms, as surmising from a given process of development, than in the sense of an intended plan in detail. The broad features of the institutional framework, of course, grew out of a certain intent and purpose—and we have already indicated the role of ideology in India's institution-making—but even where they were intended, the consequences were not always foreseen. Indeed there is reason to believe that if all the consequences were foreseen—it should not be forgotten that there were a great many tensions and frustrations and not a few failures in the process—the leadership might not have taken the steps that it did; and the kind of experience through which the country has lived might not have come about.[61] Modern India's history— like the history of most nations—is full of vague intentions, dim perceptions of reality, and a lack of clear anticipations even while thinking in terms of a "strategy" of progress. What is relevant for us is not the intent but the content of the strategy.

Notes

1. Gandhi himself was against this. He advised the Congress to disband as a political entity and to form instead a non-political social service organization. Although consistent with his moral approach to politics and his great

concern with the loss of idealism once power was achieved, this was a piece of advice that showed a surprising lack of political realism. As was to be expected, no one paid heed to his advice.

2. Edward Shils, "The Fortunes of Constitutional Government in the Political Development of the New States," in John H. Hallowell, ed., *Development: For What?* (Durham, 1946); Samuel P. Huntington, "Political Development and Political Decay," *World Politics*, XVII, No.3, April, 1965.
3. The Constituent Assembly met for 165 days between December, 1946 and November, 1949, dividing its time between constitution-making and law-making as the Provisional Parliament. On January 26, 1950, the new constitution was adopted, when India declared itself as a "sovereign, democratic republic."
4. The conference was attended by representatives of thirty-four political groups. See Granville Austin, *The Indian Constitution: Cornerstone of a Nation* (London, 1966).
5. B. Pattabhi Sitaramayya, *The History of the Indian National Congress* (Bombay, 1946), I,p.463.
6. E. Stokes, in *The English Utilitarians and India* (Oxford, 1959), shows how the utilitarian instinct of British administrators took an authoritarian form in India.
7. For a more detailed summary of the discussion on alternative courses in the Constituent Assembly, see W.H. Morris-Jones. *Parliament in India* (London, 1957).
8. See David H. Bayley, *Public Liberties in the New States* (Chicago, 1964), pp.26-35. For a more extensive treatment of the Indian Act, see David H. Bayley, *Preventive Detention in India*: A Case Study in *Democratic Social Control* (Calcutta, 1962).
9. For a definitive and extremely well-documented account of such decision-making, see Austin, op.cit. Those interested in constitutional history may also consult B. Shiva Rao's five-volume study, *The Framing of India's Constitution* (New Delhi, 1966-1968). On this theme of consensus-making in the Constituent Assembly I have benefited from discussions with Bashiruddin Ahmed.
10. Austin, op.cit., pp. 18-19, lists the names of eleven members of the Assembly who constituted the "inner circle." Seven of these, Rajendra Prasad, Azad, Patel, Nehru, Pant, Sitaramayya, and Satyanarayan Sinha, were leading Congressmen. B.R. Ambedkar, A.K. Ayyar, and N.G. Ayyangar were non-Congressmen, Ambedkar being a vehement opponent of the Congress. K.M. Munshi was once an active Congressman, but had subsequently withdrawn from Congress activities. (He later joined the Swatantra Party.)
11. A myth has gained currency that Hindi became the official language of the Indian Union by a majority of only one vote. That this is no more than a "legend," based on a controversial vote at one stage in the discussion in the Congress Assembly Party on what numerals to use in Hindi, has been established beyond doubt by Austin, op.cit., pp. 299-300. The major

decisions on the language issue were a result of a long process of bargaining and compromise.

12. These are set up in a chapter on "directive principles" in the form of a statement of ideals and commitments—almost a utopia—which takes India's constitutional document far beyond a charter of strictly constitutional arrangements.

13. The views of the framers of the Constitution on this point were expressed by Mr. T.T, Krishnamachari, a member of the Drafting Committee: "So far as the relationship of the President with the Cabinet is concerned, I must say that we have so to say completely copied the system of responsible government that is functioning in Britain today; we have made no deviation from it...except when necessary because our Constitution is federal in structure..." *Constituent Assembly Debates*, X, p.956. This interpretation has, however, been contested, most notably by the first president of India, Dr. Rajendra prasad, himself.

14. On all of this, see Austin, *op.cit.* Even those not interested in formal details should read his concluding chapter, "Comments on a Successful Constitution," pp. 308-330.

15. This is the title of a major document of dissent on the country's institutional set-up from one of India's foremost political leaders, Jayaprakash Narayan. We shall consider his arguments in the chapter on coalition-making.

16. The British Empire in India had a dual nature. While a large part of the Indian subcontinent was administered directly by the colonial regime and was known as British India, some 500 princely states of all sizes continued to be run by native states. The princely states were not sovereign by any means for they had accepted the "paramountcy" of the British monarch. However, when the British withdrew, the new states of India and Pakistan did not automatically acquire sovereignty over the princely states as they did over their respective parts of the former British India. Both India and Pakistan, therefore, were faced with the problem of enforcing the merger of the princely states into the main territory, a task that was not by any means easy.

17. Government of India, *Speeches of Jawaharlal Nehru*, 1949-53 (Delhi, 1954). Jitendra Singh has discussed this earlier approach of the leadership towards conflict in "A New legitimacy," *Seminar* (New Delhi), 63. November, 1964.

18. For earlier evaluations of the planning and intelligence machinery of the government, see Wilfred Mandelbaum, "Who Does the Planning?" and Merrill R. Goodall, "Organization of Administrative Leadership in the Five Year Plans," in Richard L. Park and Irene Tinker, eds., *Leadership and Political Institutions in India* (Princeton, 1959), pp.301-328. For a full-length study of planning as a political process, see A.H. Hanson. *The Process of Planning* (London, 1966).

19. During the present century, however, the British showed realization of the strength of linguistic and cultural factors in territorial organization. The new provinces of Bihar, Orissa, Assam, and Sind (now part of Pakistan) bore

closer resemblance to cultural regions. Both the Montagu-Chelmsford Report of 1918 and the Simon Commission Report of 1930 had recommended the establishment of linguistic units.

20. Even as realistic an observer as W.H. Morris-Jones, writing at that time, expressed misgivings on the issue of states reorganization. He took a particularly dim view of Andhra where he found "sub-regional tensions" and "deep caste divisions and a delicate balance among the political parties" producing "an intricate tangle." See his *Parliament in India* (London, 1957). In reality Andhra has been one of the better governed states in which the Congress Party's dominance, which cuts across regional divisions and tensions, is still marked. It is also a state where the use of Telugu has brought forward indigenous elite groups from the peasant castes into the forefront of politics. Such an emergence of linguistic elites has, of course, alarmed those who think of the English-educated ruling class as the principal basis for national unity. The most extreme exponent of this view is Selig S. Harrison, *India: The Most Dangerous Decades* (Princeton, 1960).

21. The Constitution of India provided for three types of states: class "A," which included the provinces that were formerly part of British India; class "B," the former princely states that were merged on a contiguous basis; and class "C," which were centrally administered Union territories. As a result of the States Reorganization Act, all areas have been put into two categories: states and Union territories.

22. Other aspects of the language issue still threaten the country's unity. Most important among these is the question of national versus regional languages, and the place of English. For an analysis of the whole issue, see Chapter VIII.

23. The States Reorganization Commission, while no doubt in keeping with the nationalist sentiment and the general demand for linguistic autonomy, went further by giving its verdict in favor of single-language states (other than the Hindi-speaking states). In fact there was no reason why more than one state within each language area should not have been set up. Subsequent experience has shown that there are factors other than language which contribute to political cohesion, administrative efficiency, and economic development. On this see M.N. Srinivas, "The Future of Fission," *The Times of India*, November 16, 1967, and Rajni Kothari, "National Unity in Danger: Case for Smaller Units," *The Times of India*, February 10, 1968. We shall deal with this question of "size and democracy" in Chapter VIII.

24. Planning Commission, Committee on Plan Projects, *Report of the Team for the Study of Community Projects and National Extension Service*, popularly known as the Balwantrai mehta Committee Report (New Delhi, 1957). The report has had considerable impact on Indian thinking on rural democracy and development.

25. Ever since Nehru gave up his twin responsibilities of prime ministership and Congress presidentship in 1955, with the exception of one year when Indira Gandhi filled the position, it has always been a chief minister from one of the states who became the Congress president. On the role of the

chief ministers in the various "successions" to the prime ministership see Chapter VIII.

26. The most notable case is that of the Bengal Congress which was dominated for more than a decade (until 1969) by Atulya Ghosh, the classic figure of a "boss," who occupied no formal position in the state Congress or the state government but carried great authority with the central leadership.

27. K.C. Wheare, the Constitutional expert, described the Indian Constitution as a "quasi-federation." *Federal Government* (London, 1953). For an extreme view on the center having usurped the rights of the states, see K.V. Rao, "Centre-State Relations in Theory and practice," *The Indian Journal of Political Science*, October-December 1953.

28. The matter came to light when B.C. Roy, West Bengal's powerful chief minister, entered into a trade agreement with a foreign concern on behalf of his state. Because of his standing in the Congress and particularly with Nehru, his action was considered an eccentricity and ignored. More recently, however, when a minister of Kerala and the chief minister of Madras explored trade opportunities with Japan and some Western countries, Finance Minister Morarji Desai himself said that there was nothing wrong in state governments trying to develop their own areas.

29. Paul H. Appleby, *Public Administration in India; Report of a Survey* (Delhi, 1953).

30. For a critical evaluation of opposite interpretations of center-state relations on the above lines, see the first article in my "Form and Substance in Indian Politics," *The Economic Weekly*, XIII, Nos, 17 and 18, April 29 and May 6, 1961. A more recent survey in the formal tradition of Wheare but viewing federalism as an equilibrium between unifying tendencies and pressures for diversity is R.L. Watts, *New Federations: Experiments in the Commonwealth* (Oxford, 1966). Watts examines the Indian case in detail.

31. For those who are interested in state politics from the state rather than national perspective, a number of studies can be cited. Myron Weiner, ed., *State Politics in India* (Princeton, 1967); Iqbal Narain, ed., *State Politics in India* (Meerut, 1967); Paul R. Brass, *Factional Politics in an Indian State: The Congress Party in Uttar Pradesh* (Berkeley and Los Angeles, 1965); Baldev Raj Nayar, *Minority Politics in the Punjab* (Princeton, 1966); F.G. Bailey, *Political and Social Change: Orissa in* 1959 (Berkeley and Los Angeles, 1963); Selig S. Harrison, "Caste and the Andhra Communists," *American Political Science Review*, 50, No.2, July, 1956.

32. District local boards and cooperatives existed even before independence and were especially active in the more developed regions such as Bombay and Madras presidencies. Those who describe the British administration as essentially restricted to law and order and revenue functions greatly distort the matter. Of course, these steps were rudimentary, depended greatly upon ad hoc initiative, and generally excluded popular participation. On this, see K.B. Naik, "Initial State of Organization (1904-1912)," in the Bombay Cooperative Institute, *Fifty Years of Cooperation* (Bombay, 1954). On the

general development of local self- governing institutions, see Hugh Tinker, *The Foundations of Local Self- Government in India, Pakistan and Burma* (London, 1954).

33. I have described the factors contributing to this shift from national and state to local leaders in "India's Political Take-off," *The Economic Weekly*, XIV, Special Number, July, 1962.
34. On the importance of cooperative institutions in state politics, see B.S. Baviskar, "Cooperatives and Politics," *Economic and Political Weekly*, XIII, No.12, March 23, 1968.
35. The most important statement of this gap is contained in W.H. Morris-Jones, "India's Political Idioms," in C.H. Philips, ed., *Politics and Society in India* (New York, 1963). See also his *Parliament in India*, op.cit., pp- 37–40, where the first interesting discussion of different levels of politics is to be found. Also, Myron Weiner, "India's Two Political Cultures," in Lucian W. Pye and Sidney Verba, eds., *Political Culture and Political Development* (Princeton, 1965).
36. The present author shared some of these doubts at the time. See the second article in my "Form and Substance ...," *op.cit.* The article also contains a review of the achievements of the program and a brief documentation on the subject.
37. "... authority and power must be given to the people in the villages. let them function and let them make a million mistakes. Do not be afraid about it. We are restricted in our thinking and in our movement because of the way of our thinking. Let us give power to the Panchayats." Jawaharlal Nehru in *Kurukshetra: A Symposium* (Delhi, 1961).
38. This combination of simpler administrative expansion and verbal rhetoric, exhibiting high-minded conviction at the top unrelated to the realities on the scene, was the biggest weakness of the CD movement. The rhetoric itself was highly ambivalent. It spoke of the innate capacities of the rural masses but decried their apathy; it wanted the people to come forward but also believed that only government action could produce results. The ambivalent rhetoric was supported by an ambivalent policy under which an administered program from above was meant to generate local enthusiasm. For an astute discussion of the problem. See Reinhard Bendix, *Nation-Building and Citizenship* (New York, 1964), pp.266-83.
39. The speed at which the CD blocks and national extension agencies were established was staggering and underlined the bureaucratization of the program. In 1953 the decision for an eventual nationwide coverage was taken and by 1956, 1,200 blocks covering a fourth of the rural population had already been established. By 1963 almost the whole country had been covered. The fact that such an extensive coverage went against intensive development was brought out in the report of a United Nations mission. U.N. Commissioner for Technical Assistance, *Report of a Community Development Evaluation Mission in India*, 1958-59 (Delhi, 1961).
40. Even the development of the "voluntary sector" was undertaken under

government auspices and given a peculiarly bureaucratic orientation. Under the program sponsored by the Committee for Public Cooperation of the Planning Commission and stimulated by the ideological pre-dilections of Deputy Chairman Gulzarilal Nanda, grants were given to the Bharat Sevak Samaj, a nonofficial body which had Nehru and Nanda as its patrons, to open Lok Karya Kshetras ("People's Work Areas") in various parts of the country with a view to mobilizing voluntary labor and people's participation. For an illuminating evaluation of the program, see Planning Commission, *A Study of the Lok Karya Kshetras of the Bharat Sevak Samaj* (New Delhi, 1960).

41. Mehta Committee Report, *op.cit.*, I, p.4, *passim*, Planning Commission, Programme Evaluation Organisation (PEO), *Evaluation Report on Working of Community Projects* & NES Blocks (Delhi. 1956).

42. See the various PEO Evaluation Reports published by the Planning Commission in New Delhi. The Planning Commission had indicated its dissatisfaction with the performance of the CD movement and had called upon the National Development Council to sponsor a "special investigation" in the matter. Accordingly the Mehta Committee was appointed, which got to work immediately and produced a mammoth report in December, 1957. Its principal recommendation was to "discover or create a representative and democratic institution" which will "evoke local interest and excite local initiative in the field of development."

43. For a handy summary of the system and its variations in three states, see Centre for the Study of Developing Societies, *A brief Description of Local Self-Government System in Gujarat, Maharashtra and Uttar Pradesh* (Mimeo. 1966).

44. Some may be indirectly elected. The block level panchayat samiti in most states consists of representatives, or just the elected heads, of the constituent panchayats. The district panchayat (or zilla parishad) is similarly, in a majority of states, indirectly elected by the samitis. later developments, however (as in Maharashtra and Gujarat), have been in the direction of direct elections to the district bodies. There are also variations in the presence or participation of officials in the deliberations of these bodies. For full particulars, see the CSDS monograph, *ibid.*

45. Planning Commission, "The Village Panchayat and the Pattern of Village Development, July 1954-October 1955," by Tarlok Singh (mimeo.). But there was ambiguity in regard to the functions of the new institutions. Official thinking seemed to oscillate between the instrumental view of panchayats as agencies of centralized planning and the view that they should be developed as institutions of genuine local self-government. See, for instance, Mehta Committee Report, *op.cit.* The opposite views were found among visiting experts too as, for instance, between Daniel Thorner, the instrumentalist, and Albert Mayer, the decentralist. For an examination of the opposite viewpoints, see John T. Hitchcock, "Centrally Planned Rural Development in India," *Economic Weekly*, XIII, March, 1961.

46. In fact the term was first coined in the British days when non-officials were

mere adjuncts to the officials. The situation is now reversed, though much still depends on personality equations in specific situations.

47. Such a state of political articulation represents a transitional state in institutional development. There is evidence that in some of the Indian states, like Kerala Madras, Maharashtra, and Gujarat, where political parties and government agencies have penetrated to the lowest levels, the need for such middlemen is declining. Citizens tend to interact directly with officials and party politicians. In less developed states, however, the mediating structures continue to dominate the bargaining process. See R. Chandidas, "The Fourth General Elections: Madhya Pradesh, A Case Study," in *Economic and Political Weekly*, II, Nos.33-35, Special Number, August, 1967. On the general theme see Jayant Lele, "Local Brokers and national Leaders: A Study of Support-Linkages in a Developing Policy," a paper prepared for the annual meetings of the American Political Science Association, September, 1968 (mimeo.).

48. We have already discussed the Indian Civil Service (ICS) in Chapter II. The successor to the ICS, some of whose members still occupy senior positions in the government of India and the state governments, is the Indian Administrative Service (IAS), which retains most of the features of the ICS.

49. There is continuous talk of a thoroughgoing reorganization. Several investigations have been commissioned by the government from time to time. See especially Paul Appleby, *op.cit.*, and *Re-Examination of India's Administrative System* (Delhi, 1956); and A.D. Gorwala, *Report on Public Administration* (Delhi, 1951). At this writing, a very comprehensive inquiry is under way by the Administrative Reforms Commission, a high-powered body appointed by the government of India, with wide terms of reference. Judging from some of the reports and studies sponsored by the Commission, we should have a wealth of information on all aspect of Indian administration, as well as some far-reaching recommendations for change. Whether the recommendations will be implemented or left on paper is another matter. The experience of the past is not reassuring in this respect.

50. Important examples are C.D. Deshmukh, K.L. Rao, M.C. Chagla, V.K.R.V. Rao, S. Chandrashekhar, and Triguna Sen. Asoka Mehta would also fall in this category. Even C. Subramaniam, While he was in the government, behaved more like a technocrat devoting himself to the intricacies of his specialized ministry (at first steel and then food and agriculture) than like a general politician.

51. For the criticism that in Indian administration too few men are trying to do too many things at the top, see Paul Appleby, *Public Administration, op.cit.* On the importance of a coherent and unified elite in the new nations if democratic stability is to be maintained, see Edward Shils, "Political Development in the New States," *Comparative Studies in Society and History*, II, 1960.

52. The line between administrative and developmental functions is hard to draw, however. The collector retains many functions, such as development

of new industries or preservation of forests and mineral resources, which are "developmental."

53. This was not immediately apparent. Nor is there an effective feedback everywhere, even now. Very often the panchayats function in a proforma manner and class and caste dominance does not permit interests to be aggregated, and the right type of leadership is not forthcoming. Meanwhile the introduction of the elected element reduces the morale of the hitherto powerful civil servants. With all this, however, the trends are clear: elections are forcing upper-class leaders to seek support of lower classes; the integration of the panchayats in a vertical hierarchy tends to discipline them; and above all the "wooden bureaucracy" is being challenged out of its complacency. On a sympathetic survey of the criticisms against the system, see A.H. Hanson, op.cit. On the possibilities of the system and an empirical report on the role of elections and representations upward, see S.C. Jain, *Community Development and Panchayati Raj in India* (Calcutta and Bombay, 1967).

54. In all this, resolutions and rhetoric took the place of much-needed resources and political drive. We have already seen this in the community development program. The land legislation program suffered similarly from an incongruence between radical policy and political reality. On cooperative farming, the leadership took an equally doctrinaire attitude. In the well-known Nagpur Resolution, the Congress Party decided to establish, as if by the stroke of a pen, a "cooperative commonwealth" based on pooling of land and joint farming. The resolution resulted in a sharp reaction in the country, including the formation of the right wing Swatantra Party, and the proposal was quietly shelved. The chief victim of all this romanticism was real agricultural development.

55. ·On the absence of an integrated approach to the planning of agricultural development (and other similar shortcomings in the planning process as a whole), see D.R. Gadgil, *Planning and Economic Policy in India* (Poona, 1961).

56. The boldest of these ideas is "planning from below," basing state and national plans on the structure of "village plans." The idea has never been seriously implemented but, despite greater awareness of the logic of planned development, it has not been given up either. A provocative treatment on the whole subject is in Hanson, *op.cit.*, in the chapter on "Grass Roots," which also provides details on the steps that were taken to implement the idea.

57. Speeches and writings of India's intellectual leaders are full of references to the apathy and lack of motivation of the Indian farmer. The UN Mission report, *op.cit.*, alludes to a series of "causes of stagnation" in village India. A popular Indian writer on these lines, popular especially among foreigners, is Kusum Nair, Blossoms in the Dust (London, 1961). Among works of social scientists that have played some role in spreading the theme of low motivation and lack of innovative behavior is David C. McClelland. *The Achieving Society* (New Jersey, 1961). There have been a host of researches

on innovative behavior in India, a majority of them sponsored by American academics.

58. It would be wrong to ascribe the change to the new strategy entirely to pressures from below. Realization of the inadequacies of the earlier model and of the need to give priority to agricultural development was continuously growing even at the top. Nor should the international angle be lost sight of. There was continuous pressure and hard bargaining from the World Bank and the United States government and AID mission. But as an AID report states, the biggest factor in favor of the improved climate for agriculture is the political support for it within India.

59. See Samuel H. Huntington, "Political Development and Political Decay," *op.cit.*, where he has argued that participation, if not preceded or accompanied by institutionalization of the system, leads to "decay and that India has been fortunate in this respect." Others, however, think that if institutionalization of democratic structures comes too early, it leads to exacerbation of conflict and consequent instability and "breakdown." A firm basis of national identity must be established before launching on any institutionalization of democracy. See Dankwart A. Rustow, *A World of Nations (Washington*, D.C., 1967). pp. 120-132.

60. I have dealt with these issues generally in "tradition and Modernity Revisited," *Government and Opposition*, IV, No.3, Summer, 1968.

61. On the general theme of "unintended consequences," see Albert O. Hirschman, *Development Projects Observed* (Washington, D.C., 1967), Ch.I.

5

Party System and Coalition-Making

SO FAR WE HAVE EXAMINED the historical legacies with which the new Indian nation started, the peculiar mix of tradition and change that informed its approach to modernization, and the institutionalization of this approach in terms of the adoption and development of constitutional structures and their application to social and economic policy-making. In pursuing such a line of analysis we have seen how through the penetration of institutions and ideas and the diffusion of certain symbols and procedures, the political system is achieving an identity of its own.

The question now is: To what extent has society responded to such penetration, and the political system been legitimized, for the elites as well as for the politically relevant publics? An attempt to answer this question should take us into those subsystems of the polity which account for its dynamics. In the Indian context, there are three major subsystems that call for somewhat detailed investigation: the party system and its handling of the major institutional issues of coalition-making and consensus; the caste system and its development as the social infrastructure of politics; and the system of attitudes and orientations that fill in the political culture underlying the operation of both the institutional system and its infrastructure. This and the next two chapters are given to a consideration of these three topics and themes related to them.[1]

COMPETITIVE DOMINANCE

It should have been clear by now that the dynamic core of India's operating institutional system, its centerpiece as it were, is the Congress Party. We have already seen how by long duration and through sustained organizational penetration the Congress for the first time gave to the country a coherent and unified leadership which could speak for the nation as a whole, acquired a powerful identity of its own, and came to possess authority and legitimacy over the subcontinent. It is equally important not to lose sight of the fact that historically the Congress had developed as a movement of protest, not only against the colonial regime but also against some of the most stubborn features of traditional society: social regeneration was as much at the heart of its program as was national independence.[2] Indeed it was constantly reiterated that the latter was only a means to the former. This dual inheritance from the movement—of being an authoritative spokesman of the nation as well as its affirmed agent of criticism and change—continued to characterize the Congress even after its presumed change from a freedom movement to a ruling party. Such role ambivalence underscores the fact that the achievement of independence in modern times is only the beginning of the nation-making process: continuing the voice of dissent against the status quo is as relevant for this process as rule maintenance. Failure to live with this ambivalence in its internal structure has disrupted many a ruling party in the new nations of Asia and Africa. And yet this may be the only condition of developing a viable party system in the context of the simultaneous tasks of unification and mobilization. At any rate that has been the orientation with which the party system started in India and it has provided the setting for its development since.

It is a party system with a difference, oriented towards building an authoritative structure of political affiliations downward to the base, assimilating new and divergent interests upward to the center, and weaving all these into a framework of organization that was originally designed as an oppositional movement, rather than an extension into the constituencies by two or more parliamentary groups in the wake of a widening franchise as happened in many of the Western countries. The consequence of directing political mobilization through the movement's organizational network (which now assumed the role of the ruling party while permitting dissenting elements to organize themselves into oppositional and factional pressures) gave rise to a pattern of dominance and dissent that gave considerable legitimacy and resources to the new inheritors of power, but subjected them to continuous criticism and scrutiny from a variety of social and political sites. The system was differentiated and crystallized through a confident implementation of universal adult franchise which, by allowing for an open confrontation between competing elements at various levels, made acceptance of the authority of the governing party legitimate and mandatory. The elections confirmed the dominance of the Congress at the national level, led to political consolidation at various other levels, provided substantial cushioning through the mobilization of rural support, and, together with the penetration of planned programs, for the first time enabled a national government to reach out to the villages of India. As this happened, oppositional strata became more organized and self-confident, and ultimately challenged the Congress at various levels.

PREVAILING PERCEPTIONS

This, in a nutshell, has been the point of departure of the development of the party system in India, which we shall consider in greater detail in a moment. Meanwhile let us note again that the chief architects of the Indian nation seemed to be largely unaware of the logic of the system as delineated above; namely, the continuing role of the Congress as a broad-based movement, involving within itself both dominant and dissident groups, and functioning alongside government as an agency of political penetration. Discussion of the organizational strategy that the National Congress should adopt after independence, and the steps that were taken in the first few years, show this unawareness quite clearly. Gandhi himself showed the least insight in the power dimensions of national consolidation. Just before his death in 1948 he proposed a virtual dissolution of the Congress as a political machine. He argued for converting the Congress into a

Lok Sevak Sangh, a nonpolitical institution devoted to social service and "constructive work" among the people. Those who aspired to political office and wished to pursue parliamentary or governmental careers should leave the Congress and set up political parties of their own persuasions. The Congress itself "must be kept out of unhealthy competition" for power. The proposal was an extreme form of the idea that "the movement has not ceased and must be carried on," but in wishing away the political dimension, it was highly unrealistic, and was duly ignored.[3]

A diametrically opposed stand was taken by Patel, the organization man of the Congress, who wanted to purge the Congress of other political groups and sought to make of it a cohesive and disciplined political party. He persuaded the Working Committee in 1948 to amend the Congress constitution, forbidding the existence, within the organization, of other parties which had "a separate membership, constitution and programme."[4]

The chief result of the amendment was to oblige the Congress Socialist Party (CSP) to pull out of the parent organization. But the implication of Patel's approach went beyond this: it sought to take the Congress away from its all-embracing character and turn it into a close-knit party of disciplined cadres.[5] Being a hard-headed "realist" he looked more for discipline than for comprehension. While Gandhi took too romantic a view of "carrying on the movement," Patel's idea of transforming the Congress into strictly a political party with a single ideology and tight discipline showed an equal lack of understanding of the eclectic role that the Congress, as a government, was to be called upon to perform in the decades to follow.[6]

The fact that the Congress, it its new role as a government party, had to combine the functions of a continuing movement and a political party was better understood by Nehru, who was also less apprehensive about ideological differences within the party. This was partly because he was confident of imposing his own views as to the lines along which the Congress should take the nation, and partly because he was averse to open expression of conflict within the party so long as it could be avoided.[7] As we saw in the last chapter, very early in his role as leader of the new nation, Nehru had expressed himself as in favor of postponing an issue rather than precipitating it if it proved divisive. Although operating more on the intuition of a pragmatic politician than on any intellectual grasp of the logic of the system, Nehru's understanding of the consensus framework represented by the Congress was better than that of most of his contemporaries. He failed, however, in his appreciation of the role of the party organization in the new system. While the main focus of attention after independence had to turn from the organization to the government and while the government was also to take on new functions of mobilization, the role of the organization as an articulator of interests and opinions and as a transmission belt between the government and the people was still very important. In the absence of well-developed opposition parties and before Parliament itself developed its instruments for the ventilation of grievances and the crystallization of dissident opinion, the Congress party had to perform these functions. Nehru's concern for consensus and for his own supremacy prevented him from consciously allowing the national organization this role. Following an early confrontation with his opponents in the organization, he came down firmly against them and prevented the organization from assuming an autonomous role. While in state politics he understood the importance of party organization as a rival faction to the governmental group, and in fact turned the rivalry to good effect in his role as the principal operator of the system, at the national level he insisted on unified control. Only toward the end of his life, with the return of party stalwarts of their prior role in the system, did the party organization come back into its own, although the role of the government as the principal catalyst of social and political change was by then well established.

Aside from the role of the Congress after independence and the position of the party organization vis-a-vis the government, there was also the question of the role of opposition parties in a system in which one party was to assume such a dominant position. Again there was in general a lack of any serious thought on the problem. In the beginning there was hope of "ousting" the Congress from power. After the first, and still more after the second general elections this turned into frustration on all sides and an incessant search for closing the ranks and confronting the Congress with a united opposition. The model of a two-party system was the most popular among intellectual circles; time after tine, important Congressmen too, hoped for the emergence of such a system. The theme still continues in Indian discussion of the party system. Meanwhile some of the more promising opposition politicians, notably Jayaprakash Narayan, withdrew from political activities altogether, saying that party politics was unsuited to Indian conditions.[8] One other reaction to Congress dominance was that of Asoka Mehta, the socialist leader, who said that given the compulsions of economic backwardness and the great need to mobilize all talent to the tasks of development, the role of the opposition parties was not to oppose in the traditional sense but to cooperate with the ruling party in a critical spirit; it was a "corrective" rather than a competitive role that they had to perform.[9] The sermon fell on deaf ears, as a counsel of despair, and as making a virtue out of necessity. But the essential function of opposition parties as part of the regional structure of power, acting as a thermostat for maintaining the competitive nature of the Congress itself, was generally lost on the leadership. It was only in the mid-sixties, following the fragmentation in the Congress ranks, and taunted by the sparking ridicule of the dynamic Ram Manohar Lohia, that the various non-Congress parties began to evolve a recognizable strategy of "opposition".

APPROACH TO PARTY SYSTEM ANALYSIS

Thus, as in many other countries, the operators of the system did not fully anticipate the nationships between different parts of the political system. Part of the responsibility goes to prevailing scholarly preconceptions on the functions of political parties. Based on the interest group approach to politics, parties are looked upon as discrete organizational entities, apart from governmental institutions, and operating on the basis of articulated "support structures" and "identities." They are conceived as simply part of the representational structure of parliamentary government, contesting votes and seats, articulating and aggregating prevailing divisions in society, as part of the input processes of modern politics.

Such an approach fails to grasp the systemic relationships of dominant and dissident structures in the articulation of which government and party are inextricably intertwined. It ignores the linkages through which authority networks, mobilizational roles, and pro- and anti-government responses by various constituencies at various levels are institutionalized. It also misses the point that parties perform aggregative as well as non- aggregative functions, operate through various intermediate structures of interaction which manage to localize conflicts and contain pressures from building up, and crystallize a dispersed structure of identities as part of the ongoing process of governmental penetration. And yet the real contribution of the party system to political development lies in its role of being a catalyst of governmental performance at various levels; parties do not simply compete and represent but also turn competitive arenas and representational processes into resources for and against government.

Once this is perceived it will also be seen that a two-party system does not necessarily provide an adequate framework for coalition-making and the assimilation of diverse identities that characterize a plural society. Evidence of mounting frustration and anomie in some Western nations suggests that even there a two-party system often fails to provide efficient means of political choice and interaction, especially for minority and dissident groups, and that a more dispersed organization of parties, with linkages at different levels of government, may perhaps do this better. And yet the two-party norm is still widely prevalent, even in the new states. In what follows, we look at the party system in India not so much in terms of discrete organizational entities known as parties in the fashion of the interest aggregation theory, but rather as part of an interacting process of governmental penetration, performance at various levels, and society's response to such penetration and performance.[10]

SALIENT CHARACTERISTICS

We may first lay out the general context from which the party system has evolved and the patterning of consensus and dissent in its functioning.

1. The party system evolved from an identifiable political "center" that emerged in the country in the decades before inde-

pendence. The institutional expression of this center was the Indian National Congress, crystallized through its nation-wide organization, and identifiable in terms of its elite.

2. It was a small elite, homogenous in social background, mainly upper caste, English-educated, and constituting almost a "one class" ensemble.[11]

3. Opposition groups also emerged from this class. Even before independence the Congress had contained quite a degree of factional differentiation. After independence both factionalism within the Congress and the crystallization of opposition outside it went further. Most of the dissenting elites, however, had at one time belonged to the Congress and shared much of the social and intellectual background of Congressmen.

4. Political dissent was thus a function of fragmentation of the *Political* center of society rather than a projection of autonomous interests in the social and economic spheres. Such dissent was largely articulated through the new institutions of parliamentary democracy and adult franchise at different levels of governmental and developmental activity. It was not from the diversity of social interests but the fragmentation of political groups themselves that oppositional activity found its stimulus.

5. Such an observation on the *process of dissent* also throws light on another peculiarity of Indian politics: the vague and overlapping differentiations between government, dissident factions within the government party, opposition parties, and dissident factions within the opposition parties. Both the structure of authority and the structure of opposition are found to be amorphous and fragmented; consequently there are no clear lines between government and opposition and both seem to dissolve into the "ruling class." This also makes the line between "government" and "party" difficult to draw.

6. The factor that disciplines and structures such a loose continuum of elites is governmental power and the authority of the government party at various levels. There is not only a sharing of outlook and ideological consensus because of common socialization in the past; there is also the compulsion to maintain links with the governmental framework as it exists in the present. This necessitates the maintenance of factional and party identities: only so is it possible to have entree into the system. Those who have failed

to mobilize a clear identity have more often than not gone into the wilderness, no matter how influential they were at one time. This accounts for the persistence of party identities despite the overall amorphousness of party structures. This also accounts for the seeming paradox that Indian parties are able to enforce a greater measure of discipline on their members than is the case with American parties despite a higher incidence of mobility between parties in India. Government being a center of almost everything political, only those who maintain channels with it—for or against—happen to survive.[12]

7. Such a structuring of political communications has led to a very open system. Not only is there freedom to form new parties and frequent movement between parties, but there is another kind of openness which is somewhat peculiar to India: the continuous interaction between opposition parties and factions within the government party. Whenever a government party has ruled for a length of time as has the Congress Party, it develops an internal, identifiable structure of factions. Once this happens the maneuverability of the opposition parties increases. They are able to influence policy and decision-making not only by providing a complete alternative to the government party, as is happening in recent years, but also by influencing factions within the latter, either by criticism in the constituencies and legislatures or by the sheer personal weight of some opposition leaders (who have often continued to command respect even after they have departed from the parent organization). In the absence of a sufficient challenge from outside, as was the case until 1967, factions within the government party assumed the role of opposition parties, often quite openly, and reflected the policy positions and ideological stands of opposition parties. The continuum between government and opposition was structured by such factions, which made for a considerable openness of political communications.[13]

8. Such a role of opposition parties in influencing decision-making has been found to be more effective where the authority of the government party is stable and continuous due to a comfortable majority than where its margin of preponderance is either thin or unstable. This is due to two main reasons. Where governmental authority is stable, factional competition within the party is both possible and permitted. Second, a stable margin of

differentiation between the government and the opposition leads to a smooth working of the "rules of the game" of democratic politics, more so than would be the case when the margin is unstable and the temptation to flout conventions and somehow topple the government from power becomes irresistible. Insecure majorities, instead of fostering cohesion, under conditions of weak institutionalization, often lead to increased dissidence and an erosion of the system's consensus. Both kinds of opposition are to be found in India.

9. The openness of the system is not, however, limited to the functioning of parties. In most modern polities that subscribe to some ideology of participation, elements that fail to find access to the institutional channels register their protest through so-called extra-constitutional means. Such protests have always been important in India and, what is more significant, they have enjoyed a certain measure of legitimacy. The nationalist movement itself left behind a legacy of legitimate protest; there has since been much innovation in the armory of protest as we shall see later in this chapter. The ambivalent concept of democracy also lends justification to political protest which is normally waged in the name of the masses. On the whole, barring a section of legalist opinion, there is acceptance of the value of such protests, and governments have learned to be sensitive to them and to deal gently with them. Where a government lacks such sensitivity, it has found it hard to uphold its authority.[14]

10. Generally speaking, both dissident movements within a government party and protest movements outside the framework of political parties are, barring some extremist fringe movements, directed not so much toward upsetting the old order as to finding an entry into it. This is why, unlike their counterparts in the affluent nations, such movements tends to be sporadic and unaggregated, and as the normal run of politics assumes its course, their cause tends to be laid aside. In their agitational phase, of course, such movements adopt the pedagogy of "confrontation."

11. Notwithstanding assertions to the contrary, the goals of dissenting and oppositional elements tend to be limited. Again barring a few exceptions, they do not challenge the basic institu-

tions of the system or the values that sustain them. Rather by pushing toward the center of power, they share in the overall consensus of the system: more often than not they base their appeal on the values declared by the ruling elite but which were not implemented so far. Such an approach is in part due to the common socialization of the main actors in the movement, and later on under Congress rule. Thus it is significant that, although after the fourth general elections non-Congress governments were formed in half the states, in the beginning the task was entrusted, in six cases out of eight, to former Congressmen. It was only later that a more distinctive anti-Congress style emerged. This has permitted a continuity not only in personnel but also in ideological and pragmatic commitments, and even in the style of politics, as we shall see below. As a result, because conflict is accepted as legitimate, its institutionalization takes place largely within the permissive boundaries of the system.

12. The central role of government lends an anchor to the system. Much of the party system functions through the government: the government party itself spreads its network through the leverage that the structure of patronage and development resources provides; the dissident factions aim at acquiring positions in this resource structure; and opposition parties and protest movements make demands on the same structure. Furthermore the bureaucratic routine of government—is responsible for such a large part of the political system that periods of instability in party alignments do not seriously jeopardize the normal functioning of the system. There are not only constitutional devices to tide over such periods but also administrative structures and traditions that were developed at a time when parties did not exist, and which endure even when the latter get out of their normal gear. Furthermore, the creative role of government in the integration of society sets the stage in which parties function. The Congress Party and its national elite were largely responsible for crystallizing such a focus which has since continued despite major changes in the party system. The Congress, when it came to power, assigned a positive and overwhelming role to government and politics in the development of society. Second, it made the power of central authority the chief condition of national survival. This power was

not only consolidated but greatly augmented. Third, it made legitimacy the principal issue of politics and gave to the government and the government party an importance of great symbolic value. The political system got legitimized through identification with a particular leadership, and its agents and heirs. Later, when the forces of dissent gained ground, they acquired the symbolism of "anti-government." Thus both the orientation of local elites and the role of electoral confirmation and reprisal have crystallized around the central symbolism of government.

13. All this does not mean that there is no challenge to the system on a more fundamental level. In fact the striking thing about the ideological dimension of Indian politics is the frequency with which intellectual doubts about the system are expressed, sometimes by leading members of Indian society, which, however, does not seriously disturb the system's functioning. We shall discuss the deeper attitudinal aspects of this paradox in the chapter on political culture. Suffice it to note here that the legitimacy of the system has not yet acquired enough depth, that its performance on the economic front leaves much to be desired, that the problems it has been called upon to handle have been formidable, and that as issues have become crystallized, the general process of dissent has penetrated right into the center of the system. It is not surprising therefore, that the working of the system evokes cynical attitudes from certain quarters. However, since such criticism comes mainly from intellectual and urban elements who also seem to value freedom of opinion and expression of dissent, the "fundamental critique" seems to take place largely at a verbal level.

14. While the modern setting of government provides goals and structures, the styles they pursue often represent continuity of antecedent modes. One aspect of this is the importance of personalized networks, their shifting and amorphous character, and their lack of organized aggregation. A related aspect is isolation and fragmentation, even between parts of the same organization. National and state organs of the same party pull in opposite directions, coalesce with elements that are socially and ideologically incongruent, and invite the charge of opportunism. The great variance in social settings and problem clusters between regions compels regional organs to devise autonomous strategies of ac-

tion; this reinforces the fragmented character of political organization. The same party as government at one level and opposition at another also adds to this condition. Such variance in alignments results in failure to build a unified image and a low salience of policy orientation. Only the Congress, owing to its background and its nationwide scope, has been able to develop a composite image. The only other parties who have succeeded on this score are purely local parties like the Dravida Munnetra Kazhagam (DMK) in Madras, the Akali Dal in Punjab, and the tribal parties in Assam and Orrisa. Even the communists, generally regarded as more close-knit than others, have failed in India to present a unified image. Both in Kerala and in West Bengal, where the two communist parties are strongly entrenched, they still function as essentially state parties. As political mobilization has increased, the role of local parties and independents as well as the regionalization of "national" parties has increased rather than diminished.

15. This has led to an exaggerated emphasis on personalities in mediating political relationships. Although the role of charismatic individuals is on the decline, from time to time powerful personalities have enjoyed an almost arbitrary role in crystallizing political relationships. In a very real sense a "succession crisis" recurs in the functioning of political organizations in India. The decline in the SSP following the death of Ram Manohar Lohia is an example. Although party loyalty is supposed to be high in the Communist Party the successive dislodging of men like P.C. Joshi, Ranadive, and S.A. Dange has led to a continuous splintering of the party. The Swatantra Party did not even start as a united party and may not survive its brilliant founder, C. Rajagopalachari, even in its present form. The Jan Sangh, in its attempt to acquire a national image, is losing support in the regions. And in the Congress Party itself sharp cleavages have appeared, following the disappearance, in quick succession, of its "tall men." During 1969 this led to serious and open divisions in the party at the highest level and a long period of confusion in the party's ranks throughout the country. On the other hand, the Congress has shown greater resilience than others, and its ever-present collegiate character has been mobilized to preserve its morale and integrity. Access to governmental power has also, of course,

added to its capacity to survive major crises in its leadership; and it is not unlikely that the relative coherence of the Marxist Communist Party in Kerala and West bengal is owned also to its proximity to power.[15]

16. Despite considerable fragmentation in the ranks of non-Congress parties, their access to governmental power following the diminution of the Congress party's degree of dominance since 1967 has increased their sense of efficacy. Although not many of them have been able to maintain themselves in power for any length of time, the possibility of regaining power does not seem as remote as it used to be for the first two decades of independence. Also the Congress is no longer that monolithic a power; its dominance does not have to be accepted fatalistically. This has led to two important consequences for other parties. On the one hand, there is a greater sense of participation and involvement, an increased stake in the system, and a chastening of extremist positions and doctrinaire orientations. On the other hand, such an ascendancy of parties with diverse backgrounds of interests and ideological positions and the contraction of the Congress Party's margin of preponderance are both leading to a greater issue confrontation in Indian politics. It is leading to an increase in political controversy on specific aspects of policy, a closer examination of issues that were hitherto shelved, and thus a more problem-oriented style of politics. Such a change in style increasingly emphasizes governmental performance rather than simple access to its resource structure. Which means that the real tests of the system lie in the future.

EVOLUTION OF THE SYSTEM

We may now describe the main thresholds through which the system has passed since independence, the changes that have taken place in the structure of coalition-making as a result of the opening out of the political center, and the extent to which these changes have been institutionalized.

THE EARLY PHASE

Gandhi's death was followed by a coalition of two men, Nehru and Patel. It was in many ways a strange coalition. In their ideological positions, personalities, basic attitudes, and political appeal, the two men had differed all along. Nehru's intellectual orientation, great mass appeal, and penchant for progressivism sharply contrasted with Patel's cut-and-dried political style, organizational commitment, and non-ideological posture. Although both needed each other in these critical years, were mutually deferent and very discreet, and tried to avoid a showdown, the differences were so fundamental and the issues so pressing—the Congress had to make up its mind on so many policy problems—that the conflict had to be resolved before long. it came out in the open in the election for the Congress presidentship in 1950 when Purushottamdas Tandon, a conservative politician backed by Patel and his organization men, won against Kripalani, a progressive. Soon after this patel died and the national government, now dominated by Nehru, and the Congress Party organization drifted in opposite directions. The party executive took actions that prejudiced the cause of the progressives in the Congress: it forced Kripalani and his Congress Democratic Front to leave the party, showed signs of considerable independence, and was even alleged by Nehru to have shown "undue interference" in the functioning of the national and state governments. Not only was the conflict between the governmental and organizational wings at the highest level intolerable for Nehru; he also wanted to see that in the coming first general elections in 1952 the right kinds of men were elected and brought into the government.

Nehru acted with determination in a bid to wrest control of the party. His first step was to remove Tandon from the stewardship of the party: by asking Tandon either to allow Nehru to reconstitute the Working Committee or to accept his resignation from it, he forced Tandon to resign. Nehru's second step was to become Congress president and be in change of both government and party, a position which continued for another four years.[16] Meanwhile he established himself in full control of the situation, led the party to victory in the crucial first general elections which established the dominance of "Congress under Nehru," and took the major decisions on domestic and foreign policy which set the framework for the future. After this he allowed others to succeed him as Congress president; he was in sufficient mastery of the situation to allow diversification of political authority.[17]

It is important to understand this early conflict in the Congress Party. Our emphasis in this book on the amorphousness and eclectic character of political organization in India, and particularly of the Congress, should not lead us to ignore the importance of conflict in the articulation of an authoritative "consensus". In most newly independent nations a struggle for ascendancy takes place within the ruling coalition soon after independence as the leadership begins to turn governmental power to policy ends. Only those that have managed to resolve this conflict to a quick and orderly end have succeeded in passing from the phase of consolidation to that of purposive development and orderly change. India under Nehru succeeded in doing just this after 1950. The next ten years were the peak of Nehru's political career and he proceeded with great confidence and energy to put the country along the road to self-realization in terms of the two great passions of his life and thought: democracy and economic development. Much of the "institutional strategy" described in detail in the last chapter was put into effect during these years.

THE ELECTORAL ARTICULATION

The chief direction of this strategy lay in opening out from the modernist elite to the people at large: the significant constituency was not just the delegates to the All India Congress Committee who confirmed Nehru and Nehru's men in power every so often, but the nation as a whole. Only a few months after Nehru forced a struggle for political ascendancy between the progressives and the "machine men" within the Congress and resolved in favor of his own leadership, the country had its first general elections based on universal adult franchise. The elections, held in February 1952, took place under conditions of much suspense and anxiety. The politically alive public was as yet essentially urban where the challenge to the Congress appeared to be fairly well articulated. No one was sure how the rural and illiterate masses would respond to this wholly new "ceremony" in the relationship between government and society. The elections provided an opportunity to political parties to stretch their efforts downward, but to almost all of them it was a "leap in the dark." The administrative task was colossal; there was fear of violence spreading out as a result of the daring introduction of open conflict in local society; and the feeling of threat to democratic procedures from the communalists on the one hand and the communists on the other was, in 1952, fairly widespread. The Congress Party itself was still bruised and anguished over its internal trials and it was not yet clear if it would be able to put up a united front. Above all no one knew how nearly 173 million voters spread over 196,000 polling booths would respond to the appeal of 192 political parties and over 17,000 candidates to be elected to more than 3,700 legislative seats.

In actuality the elections "confounded all those skeptics who thought the introduction of adult franchise was too risky an experiment."[18] The Congress Party emerged as the principal political force in the country, with an overwhelming majority of seats at the center and in most of the states.[19] Thus in the Lok Sabha it secured 364 out of 489 seats of 74.4 per cent of all seats. In the state assemblies it won 2,246 out of 3,283 seats or 68.4 per cent of all seats. And with slight fluctuations it held this position for the next fifteen years through three general elections and a number of "mid-term" elections in the states. Even after 1967, when in the fourth general elections other parties and coalitions displaced the Congress as the governing party in several states, the Congress has continued to be the dominant political force in the country and is the only party with a nationwide following (see Tables V.I, V.2, and V.3).

It would, however, be wrong to conclude that the Congress has held a "monopoly of power" in India. Even before 1967 this was not true. For one thing there has always been a multiplicity of political parties opposing the Congress and some of these have succeeded in dislodging the Congress from power. In votes the combined strength of the non-Congress parties and candidates has always been more than that of the Congress, as can be seen from the tables. Even in seats the Congress has never commanded an absolute majority in all the assemblies. And except for two brief

TABLE 5.1 **Indian Electoral Trends—1962–67. Party Returns to Lok Sabha from Each State**

States	Congress		Communist		Socialist		Swatantra		Jan Sangh		Regional		Independents	
A.P.	34	35	7	1	—	—	1	3	—	—	—	—	1	2
Assam	9	10	—	1	2	2	—	—	—	—	1	1	—	—
Bihar	39	34	1	5	3	8	7	—	—	1	3	1	—	4
Gujarat	16	11	—	—	1	—	4	12	—	—	1	—	—	1
Haryana	3	7	—	—	1	—	—	—	3	1	1	—	—	1
J & K	—	5	—	—	—	—	—	—	—	—	—	1	—	—
Kerala	6	1	6	12	—	3	—	—	—	—	3	2	3	1
M.P.	24	24	—	—	4	—	—	1	3	10	1	—	4	2
Madras	31	3	2	4	—	—	—	6	—	—	8	25	—	1
Maharashtra	41	37	—	2	1	3	—	—	—	—	—	2	2	1
Mysore	25	18	—	—	—	3	—	5	—	—	1	—	—	1
Nagaland	—	1	—	—	—	—	—	—	—	—	—	—	—	—
Orissa	14	6	—	—	2	5	—	8	—	—	4	—	—	1
Punjab	10	9	—	—	—	—	—	—	—	1	3	3	—	—
Rajasthan	14	10	—	—	—	—	3	8	1	3	1	—	3	2
U.P.	62	47	2	6	3	1	3	1	7	12	4	1	5	8
W. Bengal	22	14	9	10	—	2	—	—	—	—	3	7	2	7
U.T.s	11	12	2	1	1	—	—	—	—	7	—	1	—	3
TOTAL	361	284	29	42	18	36	18	44	14	35	34	44	20	35

Notes: 'Communist' includes both CPI and CPI(M). 'Socialist' includes both SSP and PSP. 'Regional' includes other parties. The state electoral boundaries are as of 1967. *Source*: Election Commission, Reports on Third and Fourth General Elections.

TABLE 5.2 **Indian Electoral Trends—1962–67. Party Returns to Lok Sabha from Each State**

States	Congress		Communist		Socialist		Swatantra		Jan Sangh		Regional		Independents	
A.P.	177	165	51	20	2	1	19	29	—	3	—	1	51	68
Assam	79	73	—	7	6	9	—	2	—	—	12	9	8	25
Bihar	189	128	12	28	36	86	50	3	3	26	20	14	12	33
Gujarat	113	93	—	—	7	3	26	66	—	1	1	1	7	5
Haryana	31	48	—	—	4	—	3	3	4	12	3	2	9	16
J & K	—	61	—	—	—	—	—	—	—	3	73	8	2	3
Kerala	63	9	29	71	20	19	—	—	—	—	11	19	3	15
M.P.	142	167	1	1	47	19	2	7	41	78	16	2	39	22
Madras	139	50	2	13	1	6	6	20	—	—	53	138	5	7
Maharashtra	215	203	6	11	10	12	—	—	—	4	18	24	15	16
Mysore	138	126	3	2	21	26	9	16	—	4	10	1	27	41
Orissa	82	31	4	8	10	23	—	49	—	—	37	26	7	3
Punjab	49	47	9	8	—	1	—	—	4	9	19	29	5	10
Rajasthan	88	89	5	1	7	8	36	48	15	22	3	—	22	16
U.P.	249	199	14	14	62	55	15	12	49	98	10	10	31	37
W. Bengal	157	127	50	59	5	14	—	1	—	1	29	47	11	31
U.T.s	31	77	—	6	—	4	—	1	—	7	4	28	8	27
TOTAL	1938	1693	186	249	238	286	166	257	116	268	319	359	262	375

Notes: 'Communist' and Socialist as in Table 5.1. 1962 returns for Kerala and Orissa pertain to 1960 and 1961 mid-term elections respectively. No elections were held in these states in 1962. Regionl includes important parties like the DMK in Madras, Akali Dal in Punjab, and the National Conference in J&K. *Source:* As for Taable 5.1 (Reference was also made to Government of India, Fourth General Election: An Analysis—1967.)

TABLE 5.3 Electoral Trends in India—Percentages of Votes and Seats of the Congress Party in State Assemblies and the Lok Sabha

State Assemblies (as of 1967)	1952		1957		1962		1967	
	Votes	Seats	Votes	Seats	Votes	Seats	Votes	Seats
A.P.	31.51	34.33	41.72	61.75	47.25	59.00	45.42	57.49
Assam	43.91	72.38	52.35	67.62	48.25	75.24	43.60	57.94
Bihar	41.92	74.13	41.91	66.04	41.35	58.18	33.09	40.25
Gujarat	55.93	90.38	56.40	74.24	50.84	73.38	45.96	55.36
Haryana	40.31	83.60	45.85	70.91	40.42	57.41	41.33	59.26
Kerala	35.75	38.28	37.85	34.13	34.42	50.00	35.43	6.77
M.P.	44.53	76.56	49.83	80.56	38.54	49.31	40.67	56.42
Madras	38.41	47.83	45.34	73.66	46.14	67.48	41.38	21.37
Maharashtra	47.14	80.79	45.31	51.52	51.23	81.44	47.03	75.19
Mysore	51.28	77.10	52.08	72.60	50.22	66.35	48.43	58.33
Orissa	38.85	47.86	38.26	40.00	43.28	58.57	30.62	22.14
Punjab	30.73	53.64	48.51	82.56	45.74	56.98	37.74	45.19
Rajasthan	39.71	53.68	45.13	67.61	39.98	50.00	41.42	48.37
U.P.	47.93	90.70	42.42	66.52	36.33	57.90	32.20	46.82
W.Bengal	38.42	61.75	46.14	60.32	47.29	62.30	41.13	45.36
Lok Sabha	44.99	74.44	47.78	75.10	44.72	73.08	40.78	54.62

Notes: The comparative figures have been worked out keeping the present states in mind, and redistributing earlier election areas accordingly.

1957 returns for AP include 1955 elections to the former Andhra state, too; 1962 returns for Kerala and Orissa assemblies pertain to 1960 and 1961 midterm elections, respectively.

Source: Election Commission, Reports on First, Second, Third, and Fourth General Elections. Computations were made at the Data Unit of the Centre for the Study of Developing Societies, Delhi.

spells in 1952-53 and 1963-64 the Congress alone has not ruled the entire country. In 1952 it failed to get an absolute majority in four states: Madras, PEPSU, Orissa, and Travancore-Cochin, and managed a bare majority in Rajasthan. Its position in Madras was saved by the separation of the new state of Andhra where, however, the Communist Party of India (CPI) brought down the Congress government in November, 1954 and president's rule had to be imposed. Its failure to maintain a working majority led to fresh elections in PEPSU (1954), Tranvancore-Cochin (1954), and Andhra (1955). Although in PEPSU the Congress got a clear majority and in Andhra its excellent electoral organization succeeded in truncating the strength of the Communists, in Tranvancore-Cochin it failed to do so and had, in order to keep the Communists out, to agree to a minority government being formed by the PSP. The latter continued in office until 1956 after which the state—renamed Kerala after the states' reorganization—was put under president's rule until the second general elections in 1957.

The linguistic reorganization of the states in 1956 strengthened the position of the Congress, which emerged very strong after the second general elections held in 1957. With the formation of Andhra Pradesh by combining the Telugu-speaking areas of Madras with the former Hyderabad state, and with the separation of Communist-dominated Malabar from Madras, the Congress achieved a position of dominance in both Andhra Pradesh and Madras. On the other hand it failed to obtain a majority in Kerala and Orissa. In Orissa it was forced to enter into a coalition with its principal opponent, the Gantantra Prishad, a local party.[20] In Kerala the Congress finally lost to the CPI which formed the government and remained in power until 1959 when combined anti-communist forces brought it down. In another mid-term election, in 1960, a "democratic front" composed of the Congress, the PSP, and the Muslim League defeated the CPI and formed the government. Soon after, however, strong pressures from within the Congress led to its forcing first the Muslim League and then the PSP out of the Kerala government, and the Congress itself fell from power in 1964. After a prolonged period of president's rule and two further elections (1965 and 1967), a Communist-led coalition reduced the size of the Congress to a bare nine from its former 63 seats in the assembly and came to power in Kerala.

By this time (1967) the Congress had lost power in five other states and was toppled from power in three more states, owing to internal defections. The Congress has since regained some of its lost position in the states, rules comfortably at the center, and is still the only truly national party in the country, and a force for cohesion in an otherwise fragmented situation. Even so, it was never, and is not now, more than the most plural among a plurality of parties.[21]

It is necessary to emphasize the importance of continuing pressures from other political parties upon the Congress. For one thing they suggest that 1967 does not represent such a sharp break or turning point in Indian politics as it might appear. The polarized view of the time sequence according to which Congress was everything before 1967 and is since 1967 no more than one among so many parties is a gross oversimplification of reality. While there is little doubt that 1967 represents a major step in the direction of an increasingly competitive policy, it should not be forgotten that even before 1967 the Congress had to contend with very significant and often conclusive challenges to its authority; and even since 1967 it is still the dominant factor in Indian politics. Second, the above presentation puts the Congress where it belongs: at the center of Indian politics. It is the center in two senses, one according to which most other parties and factions have developed out of the Congress center and articulate their policies and factional strategies around it, and second in the sense of occupying the center of the ideological spectrum in Indian politics, as a center party on both sides of which are to be found other parties and factions. There is only one center party in India and that is the Congress Party.

Third, such a view of continuity and change brings out the essential role of the Congress Party: as socializing agency and norm-setter for all other factions and parties rather than just a dominant party in any mechanistic sense as found in the analysis of Maurice Duverger and others. Fourth, this explains why the intraparty competition and dissidence within the Congress are at least as important as the competition from outside; the two are closely intertwined. Finally, such a way of looking at the Congress also brings into relief the meaning of the 1967-69 change which is based on a polarization that is peculiar to India: Congress versus anti-Congress; government versus anti-government. It is a polarization that has, on the one hand, led to a very efficacious organization of dissenting elements. On the other hand, however, it continues to place the burden of all responsibility on the central leadership and symbols of government under the Congress Party even now that the Congress does not control the channels of decision-making in so many states. This has, among other things, led to a growing emphasis on governmental performance and an increasing scale of demands on the center. The close identification of the political system and its consensus with a "dominant" party has led to this highly problematic phase in India's political development. Before we turn to the emerging trends in the party system, let us look briefly at the patterns of competition before 1967.

THE SIGNIFICANT OPPOSITION BEFORE 1967

The opening out of the party system first began through the internal processes of dissidence within the Congress Party. The Congress has been more a framework of consensus than a discrete political party. As it operated both through the government, which gave it command over different kinds of resources at various levels, and through its organization, which enabled it to recruit various kinds of elites and mobilize intermediaries and the people at large to support these elites, the Congress soon became an arena of bargaining, conflict, and arbitration. Responding to such a system, a wide variety of social and political organizations emerged at all levels—party factions, caste associations, regional and tribal parties, and specialized clientele—pressing upon the government and the Congress for participation, resources, recognition, and ventilation of specific grievances. Representing the major interests in society, such a structure of pressures aggregated through dissident groups within the Congress and opposition groups outside. Here it should be noted that given the overall strategy of institutional penetration from the center downward, the more significant interests are institutional and intra-elite interests which, in turn, articulate the latent cleavages and interest configurations in society.

The internal group structure of the Congress became institutionalized at district and state levels, often resulting in keen competition and rivalry between the "ministerial" and "or-ganizational" wings of the government party, the organizational wing performing the representative role of opposition, often acting as "anti-government," and in some cases leading to a displacement of the governmental elite. As early as 1953 the state Congress president of Madras, Mr. Kamaraj, displaced the eminent C. Rajagopalachari as chief minister and brought his own team into the government. C.B. Gupta in UP, B. Patnaik in Orissa, Nijalingappa in Mysore and the anti-ministerial group in Gujarat all first emerged in control of the Congress organization, mobilized sufficient support in the legislatures, and finally toppled the ministerial group from power. In every state, despite the continued rule of the Congress (except in Kerala), there was a high turnover of elites including chief ministers and cabinet ministers, as shown in Table 5.4. The differences often arose on points of policy or political strategy, and sometimes represented generational or ideological cleavages, but soon were enmeshed in the politics of coalition-making. In each case the central High Command intervened and in some cases it succeeded in influencing the precise choice; but in general its mediation had to take into account the prevailing balance of power in the state, and its task was often simply to facilitate the change-over.[22]

ELITE TURNOVER

A dramatic instance of the pressure of opinion and institutional power represented by the organizational wing upon the governmental wing of the Congress Party was provided by a unique formula of elite turnover that emerged during the early sixties. The formula was first enunciated by Congress president Sanjiva Reddy in his presidential address in 1961 in the form of a "ten year's rule" according to which those who had been in office for ten years continuously should step down from power and devote themselves to organizational work. But its real impact came with the highly publicized "Kamaraj Plan" (named after the then Madras chief minister and later Congress president, Mr. Kamaraj), under which some of the most important central cabinet ministers and state chief ministers were made to resign, with a mandate to devote themselves to organizational work. The Plan, on the one hand, gave to Prime Minister Nehru an unprecedented opportunity to carry out a massive reshuffle of officeholders, but on the other hand asserted the principle of equal status of the party organization with the government.

TABLE 5.4
Ministerial Turnover under Congress Dominanace (1952 to 1966)

States	*Chief ministers*[a]	*Cabinet ministers*	*Other ministers*
AP	3	26	1
Assam	1	9	10
Bihar	2	15	21
Gujarat	5	19	26
Jammu &Kashmir	3	16	12
Kerala[b]	4	26	—[c]
Madhya Pradesh	3	17	22
Madras	2	12	—[c]
Maharahstra	3	29	30
Mysore	2	30	8
Orissa	4	20	5
Punjab	2	18	24
Rajasthan	1	18	18
UP	3	15	33
W.Bengal	1	16	34

[a] A chief minister or minister who was returned to the same position after being replaced for some time is not counted as a change.

[b] The turnover in Kerala includes other parties as well as the Congress.

[c] No such position in these states.

Source:: Times of India Yearbooks, 1952-1966

The effects of the Plan in some ways proved very costly to the Congress Party by provoking a messy struggle for power at the highest level from the time when Nehru's health was declining until 1969, when Indira Gandhi finally revived the position of the prime minister and her government over party bosses. In the interim period, however, the Plan served to stress the role of both the party organization and the state leaders in national affairs, especially in times of crisis, as in the coming struggle for succession. (We shall discuss the succession issue in detail in Chapter VIII). Here was another, and perhaps the most important, instance of the explicit and implicit process of the turnover of elites even while the same party was in continuous power.

ROLE OF OTHER PARTIES

In this process of elite turnover opposition parties performed their role from the outside; but it was a role that was critical for the operation of the system. Because the elaborate group structure within the Congress reflected almost all shades of opinion and interest, opposition politicians were able to affect the balance of dominant-dissident relations within the Congress. If the leftists mobilized more support outside, the leftists in the Congress improved their position too. This happened in the early days of socialist challenge to the Congress. Later, when the Swatantra Party mobilized support in favor of the landed classes and against certain Congress policies like cooperative farming, the rightists within the Congress could make themselves felt. The model here is one in which several "parties of pressure" operate upon a single "party of consensus" and influence the latter's internal balance.[23] Second, opposition parties have sometimes provided refuge to dissident elements from the Congress who have momentarily, from the outside, waged their battles with the ruling group inside the Congress, and have often returned to the Congress once the rival group in the party has lost power.[24] Third, new opposition parties have often emerged to focus attention on a neglected issue. These are temporary phenomena and once the issue, like the linguistic issue in Maharashtra and Gujarat, has been settled, the new recruits in politics are given a place in the Congress Party itself.[25] Finally, there has been, over the whole period, a slow trickling of defectors from the Congress, who have lost hope of operation effectively from within the Congress; these have swelled the ranks of the opposition. Defections out of the party of prominent Congressmen as well as important sectional groups have gone on for a long time: prominent leaders like J.B. Kripalani, C.D. Deshmukh, C. Rajagopalachari, and krishna Menon have left the Congress for good; so have large sections of regional groups like the Kshatriyas of Gujarat, the Jats of Rajasthan, and the Ahirs of Haryana.

These defections from the Congress gained momentum between 1962 and 1966, years of acute political strain due to the convergence of a series of crises: two wars that drained the country's resources and shattered its self-confidence, the death of Nehru and Lal Bahadur Shastri in quick succession and the succession crises that followed each time (leading to intense politicking within the Congress, including its High Command), two severe droughts and mounting hardship for the common people in the form of high prices and scarcity of subsistence goods, a drastic devaluation of the currency and increasing external pressures from the aid-giving nations that proved embarrassing to the Congress leadership. In this setting of events the authority of the central Congress leadership, which was itself divided, declined and it became difficult to coalesce the multiplicity of pressures of the party's resources. The result was still more defections from the Congress Party.

THE 1967 CHANGE

The fourth general elections, held in February, 1967, became important in this process of further fragmentation of the party system, a process that turned dissidence and criticism within the party to defections outside the party. Such fragmentation continued even after the election; whereas the Congress lost power in five states in the elections, Congress governments were toppled from three more states after the election, following further defections from the legislature party in these states.[26] In these defections two institutional devices played key roles: the nomination of candidates for the party ticket before the elections, and the formation of ministries after the elections. Again these reasons for dissidence were not new; 1967 differed in the readiness with where Congressmen decided to leave the Congress, and in the diminished force of restraining factors within the Congress. Whereas nomination for party tickets and formation of ministries hitherto led the discontented factions to turn themselves into dissident groups within the party, the factional articulation now took the form of open defections from the party.[27] As indicated earlier in this chapter, a decline in the margin of preponderance of the ruling coalition, under conditions of a low salience of identities, may result in further defections and opportunism. it is not yet clear, however, whether the defectors who left the party everywhere in 1966-67 left it for good, or whether they are still waging the old battles from outside in the hope of influencing the system in terms of its older dynamics. The evidence so far suggests both kinds of factional movements from the Congress Party.[18]

The process of factionalism is not limited to the Congress; it has affected all other parties as well. Thus, rival Congress parties in some states are professedly parties of dissident Congressmen.[29] There are also two, and in some states three Communist parties. The Socialist Party has broken into two parties with the more numerous Samyukta Socialist Party (SSP) split into warring factions; the Jan Sangh is split between its extremist and moderate wings; and the Swatantra Party has been in a process of continuous internal rifts and quite a few defections. There are several fronts among the depressed sections, the scheduled castes, and the tribes, the tribal parties being especially prone to factionalism. Furthermore, as nearly as the non-Congress parties after 1967 have had to resort to coalition-making (among themselves and with Congress defectors of all kinds, without regard to whether such combinations were "coalitionable"), this resulted in a much more amorphous and heterogeneous assortment of groups than was ever found in the Congress Party. One result of this was that whereas the defection of dissident factions within the Congress Party first led to a defeat of Congress governments in the 1967 elections and soon thereafter, the inability of the anti-Congress united fronts to "hang together" led to a toppling of those governments in one state after another.[30]

An interesting aspect of both the Congress approach to power in the generation after independence and the approach of the anti-Congress united fronts between 1967 and 1969 has been the effort to develop an all-inclusive and catch-all strategy of coalition-making. The Congress was a characteristic catch-all party, trying to encompass all the more relevant segments of political reality, including a great many oppositional segments. It was like Hindu society in miniature, accommodative and agglomerative, given less to specificity and differentiation and more to consensus and catholicism. The Congress was a "grand coalition", with great historic antecedents, and itself representing the Indian-nation in most of its essentials. The opposition parties, while they played their "minority" roles in such a system saw clearly that they could not come into their own except by all the minorities coming together and challenging the hegemony of the government party which, anyway, at no time enjoyed more than 45 per cent of the votes in the country. The high priest of such a strategy was the late Ram Manohar Lohia, the charismatic socialist leader and founder of the SSP, himself a leader in the art of defecting from established parties but soon realizing the folly of such an enterprise, and assiduously devoting himself to the mission of destroying the Congress monopoly of power by uniting all anti-Congress forces in the country. Lohia was fairly successful in his mission, polarized the country along Congress versus anti-Congress lines, and in the process took on whoever was prepared to oppose the Congress. The immediate goal of dislodging the Congress from its dominant position was accomplished, but the results were hardly enduring, as Lohia was himself to admit shortly before his death in 1967.

FRAGMENTATION AND REALIGNMENT: 1967-69

When the all-inclusive style of the opposition confronted the hitherto all-inclusive style of the Congress, both sides had to make amends. The period 1967 to 1969 has been one of considerable "learning" in India. The very fluidity of political alignments and the rampant opportunism that characterized the "politics of defection" in this period soon led to a general discrediting of such politics, and produced a more discerning approach to coalition-making. Electoral politics contributed considerably to such a stock-taking on all sides. Since 1967 the Congress has allowed the dissidents to leave the party, has developed a more cohesive character, and is talking of developing a more disciplined party.[31] The approach brought handsome rewards in the 1968 mid-term elections in Haryana and in part in the 1969 mid-term elections in UP where the warring factions were brought together in a Congress version of the united front.

On the other hand, it also became clear that the only non-Congress parties that proved coalitionable after 1967 were the Marxist Communists in Kerala, the DMK in Madras, and the Swatantra-Jana Congress coalition in Orissa, all of which shared the characteristic of being a cohesive regional force in the respective state, with considerable local support,[32] rather than an ad hoc alliance of various parties and defecting Congress men who happened together to win more seats than the official Congress, as elsewhere. When a fresh trial of strength took place in four state mid-term elections in 1969 (known in India as the "little election"), the former kind of cohesive regional party or coalition emerged as a viable alternative to the Congress as in West Bengal and Punjab, while the latter kind failed to do so, as in UP and Bihar. See Table 5.5.

The results have been considerable for coalitional politics. In West Bengal, where the anti-Congress United Front (UF) made the most dramatic comeback in 1969, what took place was an almost total closing of the ranks within the UF, an intelligent process of bargaining before the elections, and hence a sharp polarization of political alternatives. The Congress had at no time in West Bengal—and this has been true of several other states—polled a majority of votes. By confronting it with a cohesive alternative, its electoral weakness was exposed and a large majority obtained for the UF. Significantly, in 1969 the popular vote for the Congress did not decline at all and yet it lost heavily in terms of seats. The West Bengal midterm elections of 1969 have thus become a model for united fronts everywhere, although it is doubtful if it could be reproduced as easily in other places.[33] In a somewhat different fashion however, this was also achieved in Punjab where the dominance of the Akali Dal and the closing of the ranks of its various factions forced its traditional opponent, the Jan Sangh, to fall in line. The Communists in Kerala already had achieved this in 1967.

The picture of state politics in 1969 (at the moment of writing) suggests some important developments since 1967. For one thing the disparate united fronts no longer rule in a majority of the

TABLE 5.5
Midterm Elections in Five States — 1967 and 1968–69

States	Congress 1967	Congress 1969	Communist 1967	Communist 1969	Socialist 1967	Socialist 1969	Jan Sangh 1967	Jan Sangh 1969	Other parties 1967	Other parties 1969	Independents 1967	Independents 1969
Haryana												
Seats	48	48	—	—	—	—	12	7	5	20[i]	16	6
Percentage of votes	41.33	43.88	1.44	0.46	3.79	0.97	14.39	10.45	6.08	27.14	32.97	17.10
U.P.												
Seats	199	211	14	5	55	36	98	49	22[e]	107[d]	37	17
Percentage of votes	32.20	33.98	4.50	3.55	14.07	9.58	21.67	17.26	8.87	25.93	18.9	9.70
Bihar												
Seats	128	118	28	28	86	70	26	34	17[f]	49[b]	33	19
Percentage of votes	33.09	30.30	8.19	11.31	24.58	19.21	10.41	15.91	5.84	2.16	17.88	21.11
W. Bengal												
Seats	127	55	59	110	14	14	1	—	48[g]	78[c]	31	23[j]
Percentage of votes	41.13	41.31	24.64	26.96	4.01	3.17	1.33	0.83	15.41	12.97	13.49	14.76
Punjab												
Seats	47	38	8	6	1	3	9	8	29[h]	45[a]	10	4
Percentage of votes	37.74	39.19	8.46	7.91	1.23	1.33	9.84	9.02	26.98	32.34	15.76	10.21

Notes: In Haryana the midterm elections were held in 1968; in all other states in 1969. For the sake of simplicity, however, we compare 1967 and 1969. 'Communist' includes Communist Party of India and Communist Party of India (Marxist); and 'Socialist' includes Samyukta Socialist Party and Praja Socialist Party.

a) Akali Dal: 43 seats and 29.59 votes.
b) Janata Party: 14 seats and 0.28 votes.
c) Bangla Congress: 33 seats and 8.01 votes; and Forward Bloc: 21 seats and 4.89 votes.
d) Bharatiya Kranti Dal: 99 seats and 21.22 votes.
e) Swatantra: 12 seats and 4.73 votes; and Republican Party of India: 10 seats and 4.14 votes.
f) Jana Kranti Dal: 13 seats and 3.33 votes.
g) Forward Bloc: 13 seats and 4.43 votes; and Bangla Congress: 34 seats and 10.16 votes.
h) Akali Dal: 26 seats and 24.68 votes.
i) Vishal Haryana Party: 16 seats and 14.86 votes.
j) Revolutionary Socialist Party: 12 seats (percentage of votes polled is not available).

Sources: (1) Report on the Fourth General Elections in India 1967 (Vol. II), New Delhi: Election Commission, India, 1967. (2) Press Information Bureau, Government of India, releases on midterm elections, 1969.

states. In Madras there is a single party government while in Kerala, West Bengal, Orissa, and Punjab there are fairly stable coalitions in power. Nowhere else is a united front any longer in power. Indeed the unstable states are now in the Congress domain: M.P., Bihar, and U.P. (In Bihar in a matter of four months after the 1969 election two coalition governments, one led by the Congress and another by dissident Congress groups, came into being and collapsed, and president's rule was imposed in July, 1969.) These have been factionridden states from the beginning, in part due to their sprawling size and disparate populations, and in part due to their feudal background and socio-economic backwardness. They may continue to be areas of instability for a long time but may also, at least in relative terms, witness an increasing polarization between the Congress and a coalition of regional parties like the BKD and the state units of "national" parties like the Jan Sangh. here again, as began to be apparent in the 1969 elections, and as has been clearly demonstrated in West Bengal and Kerala, Haryana and Punjab, an appeal to the electorate may force a more clear realignment of political forces.[34] The Indian electorate is showing a large degree of political awareness and sophistication and has severely punished both the Congress and the anti-Congress parties, like the Jan Sangh and SSP in UP and Bihar in 1969, when they failed to provide stable and purposive government.

A crucial link in this process of realignment is the ability of contending parties to convert votes into seats. Here is an interesting contrast in the relationship between multiple contests and Congress performance. A state-by-state correlational anayasis between number of candidates, Congress vote, and non-Congress vote revealed in a majority of a states a negative correlation between the first and the third.[35] it seems that the non-Congress candidates take away more from the Congress than from each other. Thus while it is true that a multi-cornered contest enables the Congress, the most plural among all parties in a large majority of constituencies, to win the seat, it is also significant that its total vote drops as the number of candidates increases Contrariwise, where there is a more polarized context, the Congress vote goes up, or at least remains steady, though this may not always give it the seat. Thus in Kerala in 1967 and West Bengal in 1969 where the Congress lost heavily in seats, its vote did not fall, and in fact went up slightly in Kerala. Remarkable in Indian electoral politics is the ability of the Congress to maintain a steady 35 to 40 per cent base. The vote of various non-Congress parties is unsteady, with the exception of the communists in West Bengal and Kerala, and the DMK in Madras. And it is in this respect that further elections and electoral alignments will determine both the composition of state governments and their ability to provide orderly government and a record of performance.

FUTURE TRENDS

On the other hand, it is also clear that the 40 per cent steady base of the Congress Party, while it confirms it as the preponderant political force in the country, will increasingly prove to be inadequate for winning and maintaining state power. Nor is its majority at the center that secure on the basis of a 40 per cent support base. For just as the other parties have now a much better grasp of the kind of electoral organization needed for winning power at the state level, so they are also likely to realize before long that it is necessary to put up simultaneous candidates for the Parliament and take advantage of the present electoral system under which state and parliamentary elections are held at the same time. What enabled the Congress to retain power at the center even while it lost in half of the state assembly constituencies in 1967 was the considerable incidence of "split voting" arising from the fact that most of the non-Congress parties were content to operate at the state level. (On the basis of a national sample study to be presently reported, as many as 33 per cent of the voters voted differently at the parliamentary than at the assembly level.) But the experience of the DMK in Madras, where it won all the Lok Sabha seats it contested, and the Swatantra elsewhere, which managed to do almost as well in Lok Sabha as in assembly constancies, shows that the Congress is no less vulnerable in parliamentary constituencies.

To be sure, many factors seem to favor the Congress at the national level. One, which we have already mentioned, is the non-aggregation of state patterns at the national level, partly because there are different parties in different states, and partly because several small parties and a plethora of independents are both not interested in the national level and incapable of managing the campaign for a large parliamentary constituency. Second, in many of the states, especially in the north, regional parties are gaining at the expense of "national" parties; thus the Jan Sangh in UP has been replaced as the second largest party after the Congress by Charan Singh's party of dissident Congressmen. The SSP also lost quite a number of seats in both Bihar and UP. While the two communist parties have consolidated their position in West Bengal and Kerala, they have lost in other states, like Punjab and UP. Such a regionalization of party politics is likely to confirm the dominant position of the Congress for some time to come. Third, there is considerable overlap and mutual competition between different non-Congress parties in the states with the exception of West Bengal and Kerala, a situation that favors the Congress Party. Finally, many of the non-Congress state parties are willing to grant to the Congress Party its position at the center and its role in influencing coalition politics at the state level in return for a recognition of their status in state politics. This is understandable, as in the Indian federal set-up there is so much initiative and resources that the center commands.

All the same, it is becoming more and more clear that the Congress Party's firm and continuing hold on 40 per cent of the electorate is proving an inadequate base for stable political power. This point goes beyond the mere arithmetic of electoral politics and raises questions of policy and ideology. Over the years the Congress has turned from a party of change to a party of status quo. It is getting too closely identified with entrenched interests in both rural and urban areas and is found to be lacking in the policy drive and reconstructive elan that characterized it in the first generation of independence. Unless it regains at least some of that approach which had underlined its position as the nation's principal political force, there is less and less likelihood that it will retain its present position in national politics. On the other hand, given the historical character of the Congress as a coalitional arena and the absence of a viable alternative, any well thought out policy drive must be fostered by an equally well thought out coalitional strategy which aims at reconstructing the elements of

India's federal and polycentric system. To wish away the integrative dimension of political performance would be as fatal to the country's future as to neglect the policy imperatives of planned change. The task is by no means easy and, because of a lack of the necessary historical insight, may well lead to either prolonged instability and stagnation or an ideological polarization that would lead to chaos.

It is against these considerations that the trends towards the future acquire meaning. A cohesive political center presiding over a diverse structure of political affiliations is vital to the efficient performance of the Indian political system, including performance in the economic sphere. There is little doubt that at least for the next decade only the Congress party can provide such a center. The challenge before the Congress is to launch a simultaneous drive on two fronts: a policy drive that will win the allegiance of the new and growing periphery of the hitherto deprived masses in urban and rural areas; and an organizational drive by which party organs penetrate into the constituencies and mobilize support instead of relying on "vote banks" manipulated by "influentials."[36] The former is the task of the central governmental leadership, the latter of the organizational leadership. In sum, the challenge before the Congress is to "perform" on both the policy front and the institution-building front. And the essential condition of both is cohesion and unity at the center.

Short of such a determined push forward in the next couple of years in both governmental performance and performance in institution-building, all the trends points in the opposite direction. First, as discussed above, the translation of regional support of non-Congress parties into parliamentary seats will mean that the Congress will lose its majority at the center. Second, a number of non-Congress parties on the left and the right are likely to consolidate their legislative strength in the states: on the left, Communist-led united fronts in West Bengal and Kerala and the DMK in Madras; on the right, the Jan Sangh in the northern states, the Swatantra in Orissa, and the Akalis in Punjab. An unstable center facing left and right consolidations in the states is a far more dangerous proposition than a stable center facing a conglomeration of non-coalitionable entities in the states as was the case after 1967. Third, as such a confrontation develops and politics becomes more issue oriented, the chances are that the factional network of the Congress Party will itself get polarized and lead to an eventual split. The serious divisions within the Congress High Command in mid-1969 over the nationalization of the major banks and the elections of the president of India following the death of Dr. Zakir Hussain suggest that such a split between the "young turks" led by Prime Minister Mrs. Gandhi and the older generation of leadership controlling the party organization was very much within the realm of possibility. It is this divorce between those who want to reassert the party's role in social and economic development and those whose main eye is in maintaining the hegemony of the Congress machine that is likely to make all political calculations self-defeating at a time when the masses on the periphery are getting increasingly politicized. Meanwhile, an examination of electoral trends shows that a substantial part of this periphery—which includes both the new literates and the growing mass of small peasantry and agricultural workers—is being mobilized by parties other than the Congress.[37] The challenge for the Congress is how to prevent these trends and re-establish its "left of center" position.

If these trends continue, and the Congress is not able to penetrate classes hitherto not associated with it, what are the prospects for the future? It seems that the country is set on a period of coalitional government, not only in the states but also at the center. Indeed, it may even be that in some of the states single-party governments—or united fronts dominated by a single party as in West Bengal—will be in office, while at the center a coalition government will become the rule. There is little doubt that the Congress (whichever group dominates its coalitional structure) will be the chief partner in the central coalition for a long time to come; the other parties are too restricted in their national coverage to be able to send a sizeable group to the Lok Sabha. At the same time, however, the dominant party in several coalitions may be some party other than the Congress, such as the Communist Marxists in West Bengal and Kerala, the Jan Sangh in M.P. or U.P. of both, and the dominant regional party in Madras, Punjab, and Orissa. In terms of nationwide following, of course, the Congress is likely to continue as the dominant political force in the country, but without necessarily transforming its numerical dominance into effective political power at all levels. If it succeeds in closing its ranks and re-establishing its lost momentum, its role will be still more central.

A PERIOD OF COALITIONS

On the other hand, coalitional governments need not necessarily be less effective or purposive than single-party governments; the government of Kerala is not any less effective than the government of Andhra Pradesh, Orissa less than Assam, or Punjab less than Haryana. Much depends on the nature of factional coalition that any government represents, whether single-party or multi-party. In a way, the "Congress system" has always been a system of coalition, multi-group in character, and informed by a continuous process of internal bargaining and mobility, as we have already seen. Moreover, it seems that continuous power without threat from the outside lowers the responsive sensitivity of a government, and that an increase of competitive pressure and fear of electoral reprisal may increase governmental responsiveness. Also, in a situation where government and governmental resources are the principal object of identity and alienation, and where so much has to be done in terms of basic material needs, as in India, the different coalitions must feel pressed to respond in the same manner and to find a place in the ongoing consensus of the system.

It will not be surprising, therefore, if after an initial period of learning and the working out of appropriate conventions of coalitional politics, the governmental process in India shows a greater approximation to what needs to be done—a greater sensitivity to indigenous opinion in place of borrowed models, and a larger stress on implementation and performance. Despite vague impressions to the contrary, the fact is that the striking shifts in policy and greater emphasis on implementation have come more in the post-Nehru era of strains and stresses than during Nehru's dominance and virtual monopoly of political power. Similarly, while the first experience of coalitional governments produced an atmosphere of instability and amorphousness, it is likely that as the new rules of the game evolve, the growing proximity of the new governments to the distribution of social needs and interests will lead to a yet greater emphasis on governmental performance. It has been the thesis of this book that the politics of adult franchise and participation, and diffusion and decentralization of political power that it entails, would lead to both a more responsive and a more integrated polity. It follows that the elections of 1967 and 1969 represent steps in the direction of such a realization.

GOVERNMENT THE FOCUS

The point made above, that the integrating element in India's increasing political diversity is the growing focus of identity and alienation on the government, is central to this analysis. The government provides the arena around which both consensual and dissident orientations are taking shape. "Opposition" is essentially opposition to the government; it may take place from within the government party or from without, against the Congress as well as against other government parties. Such an orientation of oppositional trends has been there for a long time; it is now becoming more pronounced and cumulative. Thus the various challenges from within the Congress Party from 1954 to 1967 were directed against the "governmental wing" while the anti-Communist movement in Kerala in 1959 was directed against the incumbent Communist government. Since 1967 the opposition to a government party has not only been directed against the Congress but also against other parties in government, as against the Communist-dominated United Front in the Kerala municipal elections in 1968, the Jan Sangh in UP and Haryana in mid-term elections, and the SSP and its allies in Bihar.[38] The point that orientations towards the government play a critical role in the articulation of both elite orientations and electoral confirmation or reprisal is borne out by the changes that have taken place since 1967 vis- a-vis both Congress and non-Congress parties. Although it is a little early to advance a confident generalization, it seems that the role of voter reprisal is going to play a major part in future elections. Governmental performance, the ability of alternative alignments to provide cohesive and coalitionable teams, and the institutionalization of party support and identities are going to be critical in the years to come.

Meanwhile the Congress it still both the ruling party and the overwhelming political force at the national level, and controls various avenues for influencing state politics. Whenever a state coalition has failed to hold a majority, the Congress leadership at the center has intervened through the instruments of president's rule, the Lok Sabha, and the state governors. It has also maintained good working relationships with a majority of non-Congress state governments, almost as well and sometimes better than with the Congress governments in the states.

THE FEDERAL CONSENSUS

The last point indicates the positive thrust of the regionalization of the party system, namely the widening base of the basic institutional consensus which was so far represented by the Congress alone but is now spreading to other parties as well. For one thing almost every major party has access to governmental power somewhere. As we have already seen, even while the Congress Party held power everywhere its factional structure permitted other parties to influence decision-making in the Congress and to that extent they were not entirely cut off from the mainstream of national and state politics. But it is one thing to have an indirect role in decision-making through factions within a ruling party and quite another to occupy positions of office if this was in a small area and as part of a wider coalition. With all its possibilities, the former role inevitably led to frustration; will all its limitations, the latter role leads to direct participation and a sense of efficacy. Participation in government also leads to a heightened sense of responsibility, awareness of the problems of government and hence a degree of realism, and, more than anything, a chastening of hostile and negativistic attitudes held for long as a result of being continuously in a "minority" position.

Second, control of governmental power by different parties at different levels has led to greater accommodation and appreciation of opposite points of view. An important development since 1967 is the emergence of a consensus system between the center and the states which cuts across party loyalties and identities, around common problems of government and common issues of political management. Soon after the formation of Congress and non-Congress governments in the different states in 1967, the prime minister, Mrs. Indira Gandhi, and her close associates like Mr. Chavan, the home minister, were able to develop a working relationship with non-Congress chief ministers in the states. Indeed it was found that managing some of the non-Congress chief ministers, each belonging to a separate party, was easier than managing Congress chief ministers who tended to be more than mere chief ministers and often assumed national roles in the affairs of the Congress Party and the national government. Mrs. Gandhi and Mr. Chavan were able to win the confidence of several non-Congress chief ministers like the late C.N. Annadurai of Madras, R.N. Singh Deo of Orissa, Charan Singh of UP, and Gurnam Singh of Punjab. The mutual confidence seems to have developed so well that when many of these governments experienced internal crises and found it difficult to hold the ruling coalition together, the chief ministers discussed their problems with the Congress leadership at the center and not infrequently sought their advice, often to the embarrassment of both their colleagues and their Congress opponents in the respective states. Those who had predicted a breakdown in the party system after the emergence to state power of parties other than the Congress, seem largely to have ignored both the common background of the leadership at the two levels and the flexibility of the party system to absorb changes in personnel and party levels.

Such a sharing of background and flexible relationships—in good part owing to having worked in the past in the same movement and often in the Congress Party as well—it meant that the "institutional consensus" went beyond a peaceful circulation of elites. In terms of programs and policies, too, there was not much difference between the outgoing Congress government and its successor, including in states where the Communists and the Swatanatra—seemingly at opposite ideological poles—came to power. Every succeeding government seemed willing to carry on essentially the same "centrist" policies initiated by the Congress. Some of them, like the Communists in Kerala and the DMK in Madras, have boasted that they are implementing the Congress program better than the Congress.[39] The various united fronts and their "coordination committees" have worked out minimum programs which turned out to be similar to the programs that opposing factions within the Congress had agreed upon. Even in the styles and idioms of politics the successors of the Congress Party seem to have exhibited the same political nuances and coalitional approaches as their Congress counterparts. On the whole, the 1967 shift involved much greater continuity than change, so that when the new coalitions gave way and Congressmen came back to power the latter found things very much the same as when they were removed from power.

Still the structure of consensus has undergone a marked change. It is no longer the Nehruvian consensus which had mainly crystallized in the broad framework of the Congress Party, not is it the Lal Bahadur Shastri kind of consensus in which opposition parties were consulted before any major decision was taken. The consensus that is being worked out under Nehru's daughter is more broad-based and in many way Congress Party needs to be standardized more fluid, involving various state governments of different political complexions, state party leaders in the Congress, an articulate parliament, and—not the least important—the experienced voice of top civil servants.[40] The various elements of the political system seem to play more direct and continuously interacting roles.

SUBSTANCE OF THE CONSENSUS

On the other hand, the substantive consensus on specific issues is still fluid and only gradually evolving. We have seen how the traditional Congress consensus, while it was characterized by an over-all "left of center" position,[41] was always prone to be swayed through the sensitivity of its internal factional structure, by pressure from the left or the right. More lately, however, both the fact that the only national parties that have been consistently growing in strength are the two Communist parties and the fact that the various regional parties have a "non-position" on so many national issues are likely to strengthen the hands of the new generation in the Congress keen to revive a left of center consensus in the country. And as this happens, the emerging consensus is likely to be less tentative and less open to momentary fluctuations.

Two other factors would seem to contribute to such an articulation. The "rightist" parties are ceasing to press an alternative ideological position: the Jan Sangh, in its search for a national and secular identity, is shedding a great many of its earlier extremist positions on issues like language and religion (e.g., the holy cow), while the Swatantra is either declining as a political force as in Bihar, Rajasthan, and Gujarat, or being drawn towards the national consensus through governmental participation as in Orissa. Second, in a society so ridden with basic developmental problems and in which government plays such a dominant role, a left of center consensus is the only natural one to be articulated and institutionalized.

We remark here that such an articulation is not the consequence of interest aggregation or even aggregation of party structures. On the contrary, an important element in this articulation is the regional and local crystallization of the system, and the growing role of "intermediate systems". It is precisely the increasing dispersal of the political system and its symbols that is bringing about a mobilization of the periphery and its consequent integration into national politics. Here it is worth repeating that since 1967, state and regional parties are playing an increasing role, and even independents are on the increase. The DMK in Madras, the Akali Dal in Punjab, the BKD in UP, the erstwhile Ganatantra Parishad in Orissa and the regionalised groupings of the Left Communists in Kerala and West Bengal all provide viable and relatively cohesive party groupings; they are likely to play an increasing role in the institutionalization of India's party system. While such a development is likely to leave the Congress in a dominant position at the national level owing to the non-aggregation of opposition to it from state to national politics, it is at the same time endowing the federal political system with an efficient network of linkages backward and forward, thus filling in the formal "consensus" of the constitutional framework.

GAPS IN UNDERSTANDING

Some serious gaps must be filled in the development of new rules of the game of the emerging political system. The federal consensus has not always been easy to maintain, nor has the central leadership been always discreet and fair in its dealings with the states. It has often given in to partisan pressures from the states. In imposing central rule on Kerala in 1959 by dismissing the lawfully constituted Communist government, as well as in aiding the anti-Communist elements in the West Bengal crisis of 1967, the central leadership laid itself open to the charge of prejudicial conduct. Generally speaking, there is not yet a proper understanding among some of the leaders of the implications of the very system they are operating. The Congress Party leaders do not yet seem to appreciate fully the point that it is through the active participation in the governmental system of parties and groups representing different shades of ideology and opinion, and even more through their sense of participation and fair game, that the political system can be consolidated. Not until this is fully appreciated, however, can the system's consensus be said to have been institutionalized.

On the other hand, encouraged by the divisions within the central leadership of the Congress Party since 1967, the Communists in Kerala and West Bengal have been tempted to raise the voice of confrontation with the center, and even some talk of undermining the system from within. It is one thing to seek entry into the constitutional system and make it more representative of people's aspirations, and even more radical. It is quite another thing to think that the latter can be accomplished only by a strategy of disruption of the political system as a whole. Here lies another source of challenge that will have to be contained in the course of expanding the system's consensus.

The significance of these points for party system perspectives is that India has been for some time now moving from a dominant party system to a system of *competitive dominance*.[42] One dimension of the system is articulated along the federal axis, between the Congress dominant center and the multi-party states with different parties and coalitions wielding governmental power in different states: it is the dimension of non-aggregation. A second dimension is found at the state level where either the Congress is still the dominant party as in Maharashtra, Mysore, Andhra Pradesh, and so forth, or some other party is dominant like the Communist Marxists in West Bengal and Kerala, the DMK in Madras, and the Akali Dal in Punjab.[43] A third dimension operates at the level of the electoral constituency where it is found that "the number of constituencies where one party enjoys a virtual monopoly over its competitors is on the decline .... Nevertheless, the modal constituency in India remains the dominant party constituency—typically, a constituency in which the winner gets a little over 45 per cent of the vote and the next-best trails about 12 to 16 percentage points behind.[44]

IDENTITY AND DISSENT

Inevitably such a process of consensus tends to be structured around the Congress Party, which has until recently been the pacesetter of Indian politics. As we said earlier, the Congress has been sustained in this position partly because of its position in the governmental and elite structures, but also by its penetration towards the population at large; its dominance owes both to its authority and its permeability. Party penetration in India has been more in terms of identity with the Congress, however loose and nominal, than with other parties which are only now making themselves felt, although identity for the latter is also beginning to show. In a national study conducted during the 1967 elections, it was found that as many as 70 per cent of the population showed preference for political parties (and 3.4 per cent for independents) and out of this, 43.1 per cent of responses were in favor of the Congress while the rest were distributed among other parties. The distribution of responses is given in Table 5.6.

Even allowing for some over-reporting for the government party and under-reporting for opposition parties, especially the left parties (as shown by the actual proportions given in the last row of Table 5.6), the Congress Party still emerges as the largest focus of awareness and expressed preference. It is well known that voting for parties is not as stable as expressed preferences and depends on several local and fortuitous conditions. Hence the discrepancy between indicators of preference and actual voting. On the other hand, it should be noticed that only 26.7 per cent of the respondents came out as having no preference at all or did not answer the question, whereas about 38 per cent of the electorate had not voted in the election: a substantial proportion of non-voters also have party preferences. It is also interesting that only 11.8 per cent reported that they did not vote. Even when you add

TABLE 5.6
Party Preference in India, 1967 (Percentages)

	Congress	Jan Sangh	Swatantra	Socialist (both parties)	Communist (both parties)	DMK	Other Parties	Inde-pendents	No part	DK, NA, refusals
Party fell closest to	43.1	7.1	5.1	4.9	4.1	3.0	2.5	3.4	26.2	0.5
Party reported to have voted for in 1967 (State Assemblies)	43.1	7.1	5.2	7.4	5.5	4.1	2.3	7.0	Did not vote 11.8	6.6
Actual party vote in 1967a (State Assemblies)	40.0	8.8	6.8	8.7	8.7	4.4	6.0	16.7	—[b]	—

a) The figures are percentages of valid votes polled, not of the total electorate.
b) As the rest of the percentage is of valid votes polled, the non-voter category is left blank here. Actually as many as 38 per cent of the electorate did not vote.

Source: Centre for the Study of Developing Societies, Delhi, "National Election Study, 1967," povisional tables.

the 6.6 per cent refusals to it, the confessed non-voters fall far short of actual non-voters; people are reluctant to say they did not fulfill their obligation to vote.[45] There is no space here to carry out more complex analyses of relationships between party preference, party vote, and other substantive measures of identification, which we hope to undertake elsewhere. There are also important limitations in interpreting survey data of this kind, which cannot all be explored here. But what is presented here is sufficient to show the character of party penetration and the role of party affiliations in the general process of politicization. If it is remembered that the questions asked in the survey were open-ended and the party names (or symbols) were expressed by the respondents themselves, at least the extent of awareness of the parties, if not any stronger articulation in their favor, seems remarkable. And among the various parties, the Congress Party receives the largest proportion of identification.

TABLE 5.7
Approval or Disapproval of Charges Against the Congress, 1967 (Percentages)

Charges	Strongly agree	Agree	Disagree	Strongly disagree	DK & NA
The Congress failed to keep prices down	61.0	23.4	6.8	1.7	7.1
The Congress failed to distribute food properly	51.8	23.7	13.4	3.1	8.0
The Congress failed to root out corruption	55.5	22.6	7.1	2.0	12.8
The Congress failed to keep law and order	36.9	28.5	15.7	4.5	14.4
The Congress failed to provide help for farmers	38.3	21.6	21.9	8.0	10.2
The Congress failed to provide strong leadership	35.4	27.5	13.7	3.7	19.7

Note: The data presented here are preliminary and unweighted (the sample was predominantly male) and the exact figures are likely to be corrected somewhat in later analyses.
Source: Centre for the Study of Developing Societies, Delhi, "National Election Study, '1967," provisional tables.

But while identification with the Congress Party is high, so is discontent with it. The Congress as the government party was the object of a great deal of censure, and, it would seem, of electoral reprisal too. In the national sample study of the 1967 elections reported above, the respondents were presented with a series of current charges against Congress rule and asked if they agreed or disagreed with these charges. The results are very significant. From 75 to 90 per cent of the respondents had an opinion, and a majority disapproved of the Congress record. (See Table 5.7.)

Once again it should be mentioned that there are important limitations on such questions; there are also problems of "response set" in as much as the questions were all framed in the negative. There is therefore the danger of exaggeration of negative opinion as evidenced from the fact that despite such critical attitudes the Congress vote did not significantly fall in 1967. Even so it is interesting that so many of the respondents had an opinion on these issues; the fact that they discriminated so well on the different items suggests that the questions did work. This combination of a high degree of identification with Congress as the government party and a marked expression of discontent with it shows the considerable intertwining of government and party in the crystallization of mass political attitudes, a point we have made at several points in this chapter.

The awareness of the existence and operation of parties among more than 60 per cent of the general population, given the low level of literacy and media exposure and the short history of electoral politics, is itself remarkable. Even so, a word of caution is in order. The symbols of party, government, or nation have not yet been anchored deeply enough in Indian awareness. The general level of politicization is low; the exposure to national symbols is mediated by intermediate structures and influences,[46] and the majority of the population is too busy with its own problems and still entrenched in primordial structures of family and caste to have any intense feelings of identity and affect for party and government. What is described in this and the foregoing chapter has to be seen in relative terms, as institutionalization of given structures at a certain level of political development.[47] Within this general limitation, however, there is no doubt that both government and the party system are emerging as dynamic agents of change, and at the same time as articulators of institutional and programmatic consensus, and also as objects of electoral discontent and reprisal.

SOCIAL COMPOSITION OF PARTIES

From where do the *dramatis personae* of these various parties come? Are there any significant differences in their background? And are there any differences in the social base from which they derive their support? We shall attempt to answer these questions in two stages, first in respect to the social composition of representatives, and then in respect to the social composition of their constituents.

MEMBERS OF PARLIAMENT

A recent review of the social characteristics of members of Parliament[48] shows that the traditional dominance of parties and legislatures by lawyers is declining and that their place is being taken over by farmers and agriculturists. The proportion of lawyers has been declining from 35 per cent in the first Lok Sabha to 30, 24.5, and 17.5 per cent in the second, third, and fourth Lok Sabhas respectively. In contrast, the corresponding figures for agriculturists are 22.4 per cent, 29.1 per cent, 27.4 per cent, and 31.1 per cent. The agriculturists, of course, encompass a wide range of rural groupings, from feudal lords to large and small peasant proprietors, but they do represent the rural interests as against the urban and professional interests which dominated both the national movement and the decade following independence.

As for the differences between parties, as must be expected, the Congress party encompasses a wide variety of occupational groups, while some of the other parties have a more cohesive, and therefore narrow, base. (See Table 5.8) This is especially true of the Swatantra Party and the two Communist parties, though in quite opposite ways. The Swatantra seems to be a coalition of landed interests and former princes on the once hand and businessmen and retired civil servants on the other. Here it should be noted that although land-based occupations figure in a number

TABLE 5.8

Distribution of MP's by Party and by Occupation—Fourth Lok Sabha (Percentages)

	Land-based	Politics, social and trade union work	Law	Medicine and engineering	Education and journalism	Trade and industry	Former rulers	Administrative service	Other
Congress	36.8	17.0	22.2	3.9	9.8	5.1	2.5	2.9	1.8
Swatantra	40.5	2.4	12.0	4.8	2.4	16.7	7.1	7.1	7.1
Jan Sangh	22.9	19.4	13.0	3.3	12.9	12.9	0.0	6.5	6.5
CPI	10.5	73.7	0.0	0.0	15.8	0.0	0.0	0.0	0.0
CPM	0.0	80.0	5.0	0.0	15.0	0.0	0.0	0.0	0.0
SSP	42.1	42.1	5.3	0.0	10.5	0.0	0.0	0.0	0.0
PSP	23.1	15.4	38.5	0.0	15.4	0.0	0.0	7.7	0.0
DMK	37.5	8.3	16.7	0.0	16.7	16.7	0.0	4.2	8.3
Other Parties	13.0	21.7	21.7	0.0	26.7	17.4	0.0	0.0	0.0
Independents	19.3	12.1	19.4	6.5	12.1	16.1	12.9	3.3	0.0
All Parties TOTAL	31.3	21.1	17.3	3.2	11.2	7.8	2.8	3.0	2.2

Sources: Ratna Dutta, "The Party Representative in Fourth Lok Sabha," *Economic and Political Weekly*, IV, Nos. 1-2, January, 1969

of parties, the Swatantra attracts the rest while landed aristocracy more than the middle peasantry which figures more in the ranks of the Congress, the Jan Sangh, the DMK, and the two socialist parties. Similarly, although "trade and industry" figures in the Jan Sangh and DMK as well as in the Swatantra, the latter represents large-scale industrial interests while the former consists of smaller traders and shopkeepers.[49] On the other hand, the two Communist parties draw overwhelmingly upon trade unionists and other "professional" politicians and journalists.

Among the non-Congress parties, the Jan Sangh and the DMK have, starting from a predominantly urban and lower middle class base, spread themselves into other groups, including the land-based interests. A closer examination of Jan Sangh reveals that whereas it still is an urban-based party in most states where it commands a following, in Uttar Pradesh it has managed to make a sizeable dent in the Congress Party's rural base. As UP gives to the Jan Sangh about half of its support in the country, this makes the Jan Sangh a party with a wider base than a few years ago. Similarly, the DMK, starting as a protest movement in the urban areas of Madras, has managed to become a statewide party, largely again by eroding the erstwhile solid base of the Congress in rural Madras. Indeed despite the diametrically opposite ideological stands of the Jan Sangh and the DMK, they both seem to appeal to the same issues—language and regionalism—and the same clientele—middle and lower middle classes—and are rooted in similar social groups, in the north and the south, respectively.[50]

The SSP and the PSP are two offshoots of the former Socialist Party, but are quite different in both ideological appeal and social background. The PSP has continued the "democratic socialist" and highly secular ideology of its predecessor, is manned largely by professional social workers, trade unionists, lawyers (which still constitutes its largest occupational grouping), and journalists, and continues to work in certain rural areas of Mysore, Maharashtra, UP, and Assam. The SSP, on the other hand, adopted a more radical program under the late Ram Manohar Lohia and sought to achieve a distinctive identity by penetrating into the masses, taking up the cause of the underprivileged in the rural areas, and in urban areas appealing to new themes of nationalist consciousness such as language. As a result, while the PSP continues to draw from a wider social base, the SSP has become a coalition of party professionals and small and medium peasantry. In many of its appeals, as well as in regional coverage, it is closer to the Jan Sangh than the PSP.

Finally, it should be noted that the large numbers of independents who lend both color and fluidity to the Indian Parliament come from a large variety of groupings. It is important to stress this because an impression prevails that the independents constitute a class of non-political privilege and wealth. While it is true that the land-based among them represent the privileged strata, almost 70 per cent of them are spread over a variety of other, and highly politicized, groupings.

PREVIOUS EXPERIENCE

An important background characteristic of a representative is the extent to which he has been socialized into politics before being recruited at the highest level of national politics. Table 5.9 provides us with information on this for the members of the Fourth Lok Sabha. It is reassuring that despite the rapid expansion of the social base of Indian politics, only 29.3 per cent of the members of Parliament are without previous legislative experience at any level. When one looks at differences between parties, however, it becomes clear that a major part of this aggregate picture derives from the dominance of the Congress Party in Parliament. For the differences are striking: whereas only 15.9 per cent of Congress representatives have had no previous legislative experience, the figures for PSP and DMK are 30.8 and 33.3 respectively, and they shoot up much higher for SSP (42.1 per cent), Communist Marxist (45.0 per cent), CPI (47.4 per cent), Jan Sangh (48.4 per cent), and Swatantra (64.3 per cent).

On the other hand, the representatives of the two Communist parties, and to a lesser extent the two socialist parties, have had a close association with the trade union movement; only 22.2 per cent of Congress representatives affiliate themselves with the movement. When one turns to the cooperative movement, again Congress seems to do better than others, though the movement as a whole is still weak in India, except in some areas like

TABLE 5.9
Distribution of MP's by Their Previous Experience—Fourth Lok Sabha (Percentage)

	Con-gress	Swa-tantra	Jan Sangh	CPI	CPI(M)	SSP	PSP	DMK	Other parties	Inde-pendents	All par-ties total
Previous legislative experience											
None	15.9	64.3	48.4	47.4	45.0	42.1	30.8	33.3	39.1	35.5	29.3
National level only	29.2	9.5	6.5	26.3	10.0	5.3	23.1	25.0	26.1	29.0	23.7
State and national levels only	20.6	7.1	19.4	15.8	40.0	31.6	23.1	8.3	13.1	29.0	20.1
Village, District/ municipality, state, and national levels	34.3	19.0	25.8	10.5	5.0	21.1	23.1	33.3	21.7	12.9	26.9
Trade union experience											
None	79.8	88.1	87.1	26.3	35.0	47.4	61.5	75.0	79.8	87.1	75.5
Yes	21.2	12.0	12.9	73.7	65.0	52.6	38.5	25.0	20.2	12.9	24.5
Experience in cooperatives											
None	79.4	83.3	90.3	94.7	95.0	84.2	100	87.5	100	93.6	84.7
Yes	20.6	16.7	9.7	5.3	5.0	15.8	0	12.5	0	6.5	25.3

Sources: Ratna Dutta, "The Party Representative in Fourth Lok Sabha," *Economic and Political Weekly*, IV, Nos. 1-2, January, 1969

Maharashtra. On the whole, although some members of Swatantra have had some experience with cooperatives and a number of Jan Sangh representatives have worked in village and district politics, the two rightist parties bring relatively less previous experience to the Parliament. In contrast both the Congress Party and the Communist and Socialist parties seem to do better, the latter parties especially at the state level. (Thus as many as 40 per cent of the Communist Marxists have had experience at the state level.) One would have expected the leftist parties to include more fresh and inexperienced recruits but it seems that, thanks to their longer history, intellectual background, and close involvement with other spheres of activity, they have managed to bring a substantial background of experience to their legislative tasks.

SUPPORT STRUCTURE OF PARTIES

It is well known that in the new nations party leaders and representatives come from a social background that is many levels above the masses they seek to represent. While it is important to know what social strata are found in the ranks of the elite and to what extent different parties represent the diversity of interests in society, it is even more interesting to know the nature and extent of the respective support in the constituencies. Here, of course, the first striking fact about India which has been mentioned is that while the Congress continues to be an all-India party with a fairly steady following around 40 per cent, the strength of the other parties is localized. Thus what is presented below in regard to the support bases of these different parties has to be viewed in the context of this general regionalization of all parties other than the Congress.

Even so, the patterns are noteworthy. Tables 5.10 and 5.11 provide data from the national election study reported earlier. Table 5.10 shows the distribution of the vote of different occupational groups by parties. Table 5.11 turns the same data around and shows the distribution of each party's vote by occupational groups. Given the large electoral base and all-India character of the Congress Party, it is not surprising that it has drawn a large percentage of each occupational group. Our general statement of a steady 40 per cent base of the Congress in the various regions holds true, with some exceptions, for various economic groups too, once again confirming the broad-based character of the Congress. However, the Congress seems to be doing less well among white collar workers and is particularly weak among the unemployed stratum of the population. It is most strongly entrenched, of course, in the two agricultural categories and in the two categories of skilled and unskilled workers.

For a better grasp of how the vote for the other parties is distributed, we must turn to Table 5.11. Here again it is revealing, as in the analysis of the occupational background of representatives, that while the Jan Sangh has a fairly strong following among the white collar and other urban groups, it has also made a significant dent in the rural segment, mainly among the owner cultivators. It is still very weak among the working class in both urban and rural areas. The two communist and the two socialist parties seem to do much better in these strata of the population, but there are significant contrasts: the left communists seem to do much better than the right communists in the urban working class. The right communists receive the bulk of their support from the two agricultural classes, and predominantly from the owner cultivators. The same is true of the DMK.

The SSP seems to be the party of the underprivileged; more than 44 per cent of its support comes from agricultural workers, unskilled urban workers, and the unemployed. This is in keeping with the radical ideology of the party, which is known to have often embarrassed its various united front partners on the cause of the underprivileged.

A striking fact that comes out of these tables is the exceedingly narrow electoral base of the Swatantra Party. Its overwhelming support comes from the landed class and the only other group from which it draws any sizeable support are the agricultural laborers; it can be safely assumed that most of this is along traditional patron-client lines. Again, while all parties seem to draw a sizeable support from the rural areas, there are significant variations in the social class profiles of these parties, the Swatantra Party followed by the Jan Sangh drawing mainly from the landed aristocracy and the leftist parties drawing from smaller peasantry and the landless. But while the Jan Sangh has been spreading out

TABLE 5.10
1967 Party Vote, by Occupation (Percentages)

	Professional	Business	White collar	Skilled worker	Unskilled worker	Owner cultivator	Agricultural worker	Unemployed
Congress	1.8	6.6	5.3	10.9	9.3	49.2	13.4	3.6
Swatantra	0.0	2.0	2.0	2.0	3.9	73.5	11.8	3.9
Jan Sangh	3.5	6.3	12.0	7.7	6.3	50.7	7.0	6.3
CPI	1.7	1.7	6.7	6.7	10.0	53.3	15.0	5.0
CPM	4.3	4.3	8.5	25.5	14.9	25.5	10.6	6.4
SSP	4.2	6.3	5.6	12.5	14.9	25.0	20.8	9.7
PSP	1.4	5.6	6.9	26.4	6.9	34.7	15.3	2.8
DMK	1.2	3.7	1.2	15.0	6.2	55.0	15.0	2.5
Other parties	2.2	15.2	21.7	28.3	4.3	13.0	4.3	10.9
Independents	0.7	6.7	7.5	10.4	10.4	46.3	12.7	5.2
Did not vote	2.2	6.5	10.9	12.2	13.5	32.6	15.7	6.5
DK, NA, etc.	2.3	3.0	11.3	9.0	9.0	45.1	9.0	11.3

Source: Centre for the Study of Developing Societies Delhi "National Election Study 1967," provisional tables.

TABLE 5..11
1967 Party Vote, by Occupation by Party (Percentages)

	Congress	Swatantra	Jan Sangh	CPI	CPI(M)	SSP	PSP	DMK	Other Parties	Inde pendents	Did not vote	DK, NA, etc.
Professional	39.5	0.0	13.2	2.6	5.3	7.9	2.6	2.6	2.6	2.6	13.2	7.9
Business	47.0	1.7	7.7	0.9	1.7	5.1	3.4	2.6	6.0	7.7	12.8	3.4
White collar	31.2	1.4	12.1	2.8	2.8	2.8	2.8	3.5	0.7	7.1	7.1	17.7
Skilled worker	39.9	1.3	4.8	1.8	5.3	3.9	8.3	5.3	5.7	6.1	12.3	5.3
Unskilled worker	42.6	2.2	4.9	3.3	3.8	5.5	2.7	2.7	1.1	7.7	16.9	6.6
Owner cultivator	46.1	8.4	8.1	3.6	1.3	2.0	2.8	4.9	0.7	6.9	8.4	6.7
Agriculture worker	44.3	4.7	4.0	3.6	2.0	5.9	4.3	4.7	0.8	6.7	14.2	4.7
Unemployed	29.4	3.9	8.8	2.9	2.9	6.9	2.0	2.0	4.9	69	14.7	14.7

Source: Centre for the Study of Developing Societies, "National Election Study, 1967," provisional tables.

in its support, the Swatantra continues to have a very restricted base. (We have already noticed the narrow social base of Swatantra representatives too). One consequence of this narrow base has been a relationship of real tension between its national secular leadership represented by such people as M.R. Masani and N.G. Ranga and its ranks in the legislatures and the constituencies.

Finally, it may be noted that the independents are, just as in their own social background, fairly well spread out socially in their support, except among the professional class. In contrast, the various smaller parties seem to be largely restricted in their appeal to the urban areas. Rural support depends to a considerable extent on party organization over time. Most of the smaller parties being transitional in nature and basing their main appeal on immediate issues, their strength seems to be limited and ephemeral, even though in total volume they may draw a large percentage of the vote in a given election.

PARTY IDEOLOGY

When we look at the above analysis in some perspective, even while granting the extremely rough and approximate nature of the data, we begin to see that ideological and issue distances as revealed in party platforms and appeals are not without meaning. It is true that in a predominantly agricultural society the terms "left", "center", and "right" are not as relevant as in industrial societies. This is shown in the fact that the CPI draws so much of its support from the class of peasant proprietors whereas the SSP combines in its appeal radical social policies with an almost rightist posture on the language issue by its strong advocacy of the cause of Hindi. The fact that the DMK, a regional protest movement whose original platform was based on southern militancy, has nonetheless directed its social appeal along almost socialist lines, is an indication of the complex character of opposition movements in India. Also, as we have argued in the preceding pages, assumption of state and local power by most of these parties at some place or other has led to a convergence of views on issues and governmental programs, thus leading to a remarkable consensus between seemingly divergent groups. Granting all this, however, there are significant differences, in part simply because of important differences in their support base and in the social characteristics of their elites.

It appears from the data presented here that both in its ideological appeal and its support base the Swatantra Party is "rightist." Ideologically it is wedded to a free enterprise economy, a closer understanding with Western democracies, and in liberal political program. Its support is extremely narrow, limited as it is to the landed classes and private industry. In terms of its Hindu communal background and its traditional base among petty traders in small towns, the Jan Sangh appears to be more "rightist" but on the other hand its ambition to be an all-India party is driving it to cast a wider net. It is seeking support in the southern states and among the Muslims in north India, and it has been rather successful in finding a wide rural base in states like the UP. Eventually, the Jan Sangh promises to be a party not very right of the center, able to challenge the Congress on the basis of a Congress-like program, and emerging as a viable alternative to the Congress in a number of states. Finally, while the strength of the DMK, the Akali Dal, and the various regional parties in the northern states serve to detract from a left-right confrontation, it is nonetheless significant that the two Communist parties have been the most successful of all the non-Congress parties. They have been able to cultivate a steady base in the working class, the growing ranks of the lower middle class and the unemployed in the urban areas, and the small agriculturists and landless in the rural areas. The main problem of the Communist parties, of course, is their narrow regional base, limited as they are to West Bengal, Kerala, and the Andhra Pradesh, with some support in the industrial areas of Bihar. With growing industrialization, they well may pick up in a few other states, especially if they manage to close their own ranks, to gain wider acceptance and respectability, and to absorb large segments of other leftist parties. As they do this they are likely to move still closer to the Congress ideology and the emerging "left of center" consensus.[51]

INTEREST ARTICULATION

We may pause here to consider the importance of organized groups and associations in the kind of political articulation that we have noticed so far. We have rejected the approach to party system analysis which stems from prevailing theories of interest articulation and interest aggregation. When we turn to interest groups proper we find once again a situation that is distinctly different from the other democracies. The main features are as follows:

1. As was mentioned above, given the dominant role of government in political institutionalization and social and economic development, the most important interests are crystallized in the form of "institutional interest groups"—the major political parties, the bureaucracy, and the factional network that cuts across different levels of governmental functioning. Such a crystallization has been further informed by the highly pluralistic and non-aggregative character of interests in India; it is only through parties and factions and their regional allies that the vast heterogeneity of interests are in some measure ordered and articulated. Parties, in turn, may be narrow or broad in their interest coverage as we have already seen, but it is still through parties rather than autonomous associations that groups interact at the political level.

2. Another major feature that follows from such an articulation is that most interest configurations are "mixed" rather than discrete; they are part of the larger coalitional pattern that characterizes India's diffuse political system. Although there are a number of state and even national associations, their political relevance takes place only in terms of coalitional structures that are concurrently more fragmented and mixed. Any conceptual framework that treats interests as discrete organizational entities is not very helpful in such a context. The only national associations that exist are conceived in terms of "federations" of chambers of commerce, trade unions, teachers' associations, and so forth. Their real impact on politics are at levels much below the nation. The associational interest groups are thus dissolved in the structure of institutional interest groups.

3. Another aspect of the mixed character of interest groups is the role of traditional family and kinship structures in the or-

ganization of the modern sector. Thus an important differentiating fact about the development of business and industry in India is that, as distinct from most other new nations where the bulk of entrepreneurial activities are carried out by foreigners, in India the role of traditional trading and mercantile families in modern business and industry has been prominent. The antecedent skills and expertise are carried over in the modern sector with the result that "community" and "associational" interests get mixed up in the organization of the modern sector. It is the family interest—preserved through the modern device of the managing agency firm—that predominates the organization of business and industry, and prevents its articulation on typically Western lines.[52]

Similarly studies of trade union organizations have shown the considerable role that family, community, and caste loyalties have played in their actual operation. While their involvement in the modern sector has tended to individualize interest and "conflict of interest" perceptions, the notion of an aggregated interest articulation in class or associational terms characteristic of Western countries is not much in evidence. This is in line with the point that political parties too have not taken on a "class" character in India. The fact that, unlike in the West, adult franchise and political mobilization have taken place simultaneously with other developments has meant that all kinds of groups and interests have found entry into the political process, thus giving to the interest articulation of Indian politics a diffuse and multi-group character.

4. That brings us to our main point. The significant interest articulation in India is not in respect to social and economic interests in the modern sector but in respect to antecedent structures of caste and community in the large and pervasive traditional sector. Indeed the former is greatly influenced by the latter. Both the continuing sense of community between urban and rural sectors and the fact that the country's developmental strategy is oriented to the politicization of its vast hinterland have placed the major emphasis of interest articulation on the incorporation and co-optation of traditional elites and the structures and institutions that they command. We devote the whole of the next chapter to a consideration of this important dimension of society-polity interactions.

5. Finally, let us repeat that it is governmentalization of social and economic structures that provides the dominant framework of articulation in India. There are several features of this orientation. The first of these has already been noticed, namely the role of the party system and governmental penetration in the crystallization of interest identities and hence the fact that the most important modernist interest groups are institutional rather than associational. Second, there is in India a persistent tendency to accord a low salience of recognition and legitimacy to associational interest groups. Trade and business associations, farm lobbies, even trade unions are not considered legitimate bases for political bargaining. If they are to make themselves felt, they ought to operate in and through party and bureaucratic structures. Third, there is the context of a mixed economy: as government is the principal legitimate instrument for change and modernization, there is no place for "interest groups" except as they are mediated through agencies that have a claim to the government's attention, namely parties and factions. This does not mean that there is no place for intermediate structures; on the contrary there is a plethora of such structures. But these have to be more directly political rather than associational in the Western sense. (This is why whereas in the West political demands are often involved in economic strikes and the like, in India economic demands are ventilated and organized in the form of a political strike or demonstration.[53])

6. All this involves serious costs. The fact of non-recognition of organized interest groups except when they are politically organized leads to an emphasis on loudness of protest and violent outbursts. For those who find it difficult to find a political party or faction to champion their cause, the only recourse left is to indulge in street demonstrations and the like. We shall see in a moment that the system survives by being tolerant of such outbursts. But it is not clear whether this is a net gain; whether a more organized interest articulation would permanently increase loads on the political system which would be difficult to handle under conditions of scarcity, and thus it would be more economical to allow occasional outbursts of violence; or whether a more viable "bargaining culture" would come about if associational interests were made a strategic part of the operating system.[54] It seems that the prevailing Indian opinion has taken the former view.

ROLE OF PROTEST

As noted above, an important ingredient of political articulation in India is the role of the "politics of protest," which does not always take an institutionalized form. In any system of participation that claims to be open, what is sometimes called "extra-institutional" or "extra-constitutional" opposition must play a pivotal role. An important aspect of the crystallization of oppositional strength in India is the confident use made of protest demonstrations and strikes. To these are added new Indian versions of opposition against authority, often spontaneous, sometimes organized, and by and large endowed with legitimacy gained during the nationalist movement and since. These are hunger strikes and fasts, *bandhs* (general strikes in whole cities or states), *gheraos* (cordoning of men in authority), and *dharnas* (sit-in strikes before offices or homes of public figures). Such opposition is sometimes directed against state governments, sometimes against the central government, and sometimes against specific managements or officials. They usually center around specific grievances such as low receipt of food rations, low wages, or bad conditions of work in offices, colleges, or industries. They often begin in a spontaneous way but are then provided the auspices of organized groups like trade unions and student bodies, parties, and even local and state governments: the most dramatic dharna in recent years was the one staged by Communist ministers from Kerala in the compound of the prime minister's house in New Delhi. The overwhelming might of the Congress Party is the chief target of these agitations, although the Congress has also sponsored demonstrations against state governments where other parties are in power and important spokesmen of the Congress have defended them as legitimate instruments of democracy.[55]

Generally, the Indian attitude toward such agitations has been one of considerable tolerance and some legitimacy. Although the coercive power of the government is deployed against agitations whenever the latter threaten to be violent—and all parties in power have requested such help, including the Left Communist governments of West Bengal and Kerala—the police is expected to act with much restraint; whenever it fails to do so it has invited much public wrath and, in most cases, a public inquiry. By and large it is realized that angry demonstrations and even violence have a place in a free society and while the use of force to quell violence is considered legitimate, it is expected that those who employ such force will behave "responsibly."[56] There is also, apart from a few isolated and old-fashioned "liberals," a noticeable absence of a "backlash" sentiment in the country in the name of maintaining law and order.

The main limits on agitational politics are the size of the country and lack of very efficient communications (which make coordinated agitations difficult to achieve), the coercive power of state authority (which has always been adequate except where the government itself is reluctant to use it as it happened for a short time in West Bengal during 1967), and, above all, the general antipathy of the Indian people to violence and public expression of anger and hostility. This antipathy—coupled with the realization that agitations do not pay, are a double-edged weapon, and in the long run reduce the legitimacy of those who use them all the time—has been spreading among the leadership of most political parties. But, all the same, the instruments of gherao, bandh, and dharna will remain an important part of the armory of oppositional politics in India, and in their own way contribute to the openness of the system.

The increasing pressures on the Congress Party resulting from the access to power of dissident groups and other political parties as well as the growing role of agitations and demonstrations for the ventilation of specific grievances have led to another important consequence: the greater issue orientation of Indian politics. So long as the "Nehruvian consensus" lasted, personalities played a dominant role, party organization was of a rather eclectic kind, and political communications tended to be diffuse, sweeping, and often doctrinaire. The position was sustained by a mystique of planning that emphasized utopian goals rather than concrete performance, and a general apathy among the neglected sections of society. The growing articulation of oppositional forces both within and outside the Congress Party, and the lagging performance of the government in the economic and especially the agricultural sphere at a time when the hard-headed rural leadership is gaining power, have led to an open confrontation of "issues," and the pressure to develop concrete policies and put them into action. The last few years have found an increasing realism in the policy process, mounting demands for "delivering the goods," and a growing fear of reprisal at the hands of the electorate. The performance side of government is becoming a matter of increasing tension in Indian politics.[57]

INTELLECTUAL CRITIQUE

Before bringing this chapter to an end, mention must be made of one other kind of opposition. The increasing fragmentation of coalition-making and the tendency of politicians to engage in the "politics of defection," the increasing loads on the regulative and coercive structures of government, and the general gap between promise and performance have given rise to doubts among certain educated sections as regards the viability of an adult franchise democracy in solving the pressing problems of national integration and economic development. There are as yet only a few who talk of other alternatives such as a military takeover and there is much healthy skepticism that such a remedy would prove worse than the disease. But there is, among certain intellectual quarters, speculation on the desirability of some kind of "system change," such as adoption of a presidential form of government or some form of authoritarian interregnum. There is also another brand of such opposition in the form of a romantic disenchantment with any "Western type" political system, and with party politics as such. There has always been a small section in India, highly educated and generally greatly committed to the values of a free society, who have asked for a partyless democracy, for a government of merits at the top, or for a fully grass roots democracy of the people in tune with "populist" tendencies in other parts of the world. It is in essence a special idiom of dissent, a search for "clean politics," and conveys an exasperation with excessive professionalization and crude pragmatism of the run-of-the-mill politicians. By and large such critics are highly respected individually, perform important corrective roles, but are as a body uninfluential.[58] We shall return to the theme in the chapter on political culture.

There is a vast array—and multifarious sites—of oppositional politics in India. They are greatly fragmented, lack organized aggregation, and are often more in the spirit of a continuous comment on the operating system than an institutionalized alternative to it. The result is that although appearing like challenges to the system or its subsystems, they have in fact dissolved in the ongoing structure of authority and dissent and have lent resilience and continuity to the system's consensus. The disadvantage of the system is its large residue of uninstitutional behavior and the sporadic outbursts of instability at one point or another. Its advantages, on the other hand, are enormous flexibility, a low temperature of politics, and continuous assimilation of successive elements seeking recognition and entry into the system. The crucial question for the future is: As the system expands outward toward the periphery and tackles pressing issues of performance, will it be able to retain its incremental character as in the past, or will it give place to a long drawn out process of polarization?

Notes

1. This chapter is a further development of my earlier work on India's party system: "Party System," fifth article in "Form and Substance in Indian Politics," *The Economic Weekly*, XIII, June 3, 1961; "The Congress 'System' in India," *Asian Survey*, IV, No.12, December, 1964; "Party Politics and Political Development," *Economic and Political Weekly*, Annual Number, February, 1967; "Nation-Making and Consensus: The Case of the Indian National Congress," paper presented to the *Seventh World Congress of the International Political Science Association*, Brussels, September, 1967; and "Oppositions in India: Pervasive and Weak," in Robert A. Dahl, ed., *The Emergence of Oppositions* (New Haven, 1970). The article on "The Congress System in India" has been reprinted in *Party System and Election Studies*, Occasional Papers I of the Centre for the Study of Developing Societies (New Delhi, 1967). I have drawn heavily on these writings in the present chapter, although in both substance and conceptualization I have tried to go beyond them.
2. The Congress was an instrument of dissent in another sense too. Like any broad oppositional movement it contained within its fold several splinter groups ranged over a wide span of ideological and policy perspectives. Thus the Communist Party, the Hindu Mahasabha, and the Socialist Party were all at one time part of the Congress movement. Dissidents from the ruling leadership also often pulled out of the Congress, set up other parties, and often returned to the Congress when the situation had crystallized in their favor.
3. This final testament of Gandhi, written the day before he died, continues to

live as a symbol of the moral idiom of Indian politics. It is still cited on the one hand by ex-Congressmen who left the organization out of distaste for party politics and, on the other hand, by spokesmen of parties like the Jan Sangh and the Swatantra who think that if only Gandhi's advice had been followed, some kind of a two- or three-party system would have developed.

4. The Congress had already, in the thirties, expelled the Hindu Mahasabha which had a unit functioning within the Congress on grounds of "communalism," and the Communist Party during the war, following its support of the British war effort and opposition to the resolution of the Congress asking the British to "quit India." The main organized group that remained was the Congress Socialist Party. But other groups soon emerged, like the Congress Democratic Front and the Congress Socialist Forum.

5. Patel did not, of course, conceive of the change in such clear-cut terms; it appears that he was more adamant in forcing the "left-wingers" to leave the organization. Thus in 1949 he behaved quite differently. During one of Nehru's absences from the country, the Working Committee passed a resolution allowing individuals who were members of the Rashtriya Swayamsevak Sangh (RSS), a rightwing Hindu organization, to be members of the Congress. The decision was later reversed under pressure from Nehru.

6. It is interesting that it was a Gandhian, Shankarrao Deo, general secretary of the Congress in 1947, who showed a better grasp of the situation than either Gandhi and Patel. In a party circular at that time, he said that unity and stability in the coming years of trial, as well as the "unfulfilled tasks" of development in social and economic matters, required continued rule by one big political party, and that this was the role the Congress had to perform.

7. Nehru was reluctant to force the socialists out of the Congress. Although he did allow Patel to have his way (just as he had all along allowed Gandhi to have his way against the left-wingers during the movement), he often reopened negotiations with the socialists with a view to bringing them back to the Congress; and at different stages sections of the socialist ranks did return to the Congress, mainly due to the influence of Nehru who became the acknowledged leader of all progressive forces in the country. The differences between Nehru and Patel were primarily ideological but they also represented different conceptions of the Congress as party and as government.

8. Jayapakrash Narayan, *Socialism to Sarvodaya* (Varanasi, 1956), *Towards a New Society* (New Delhi, 1958). *A Plea for Reconstruction of Indian Polity* (Varanasi, 1959), *Swaraj for the People* (Varanasi, 1961).

9. Asoka Mehta, *Politics of Planned Economy* (Hyderabad, 1953); "The Opposition in the New States," *Papers on the Rhodes Seminar on Representative Government and Public Liberties in the New States* (New Delhi, 1958). Mehta presented his views to his own party in his report to a special convention entitled "Political Compulsions of Backward Economy." See Report of the *Special Convention of the Praja Socialist Party* (Betul, 1953.)

10. For a more detailed statement of this approach, see my "Introduction" to *Context of Electoral Change in India* (New Delhi, Centre for the Study of Developing Societies, 1969). Myron Weiner has dealt at length with the Indian parties as organizational variables. See his *Party Politics in India: Development of a Multi-Party System* (Princeton, 1957), and *Party-Building in a New nation: The Indian National Congress* (Chicago, 1967). For a criticism of Weiner's approach from the perspective of governmental performance, see Francine R. Frankel, "Democracy and Political Development: Perspectives from the Indian Experience," *World Politics*, XXI, No. 3, April, 1969.

11. Gopal Krishna, "One Party Dominance—Development and Trends," in *Party System and Election Studies*, Occasional Papers I of the Centre for the Study of Developing Societies (New Delhi, 1967).

12. Some of the most powerful politicians at one time have, once they left the Congress or some other important party, gone into wilderness. The Congress has been particularly hard on them and has generally succeeded in doing without them. Examples are C. Rajagopalachari, J.B. Kripalani, N.G. Ranga, and Harekrishna Mehtab. Krishna Menon and T.T. Krishnamachari are other prominent cases, although the latter has not officially left the Congress. On the other hand those who have succeeded in evolving new parties and establishing new institutional channels with the governmental system have gained in strength, as for example Ajoy Mukerjee, Charan Singh, and Gurnam Singh. Another evidence of the importance of party channels with government is that although, due to multi-cornered contests and local standing, a very large number of independents get elected to legislative bodies, with the exception of the few who wield influence with the government party, almost all of them are found to be politically irrelevant.

13. For an early formulation of this role of opposition parties, see my "Party System," *op. cit.* W.H. Morris-Jones has diagrammed this view in his "Dominance and Dissent," *Government and Opposition*, I, No. 4, August, 1966. For a conceptualization of "open" and "closed" systems of opposition, see Edward Shils, "Opposition in the New States of Asia and Africa," *Government and Opposition*, I, No. 2, February, 1966.

14. Parliament democracy is not always efficient in maintaining governmental sensitivity. I have developed the argument and applied it to a particular case of such opposition in "Direct Action: A Pattern of Political Behavior," *Quest* (Bombay), No. 24, January, 1960.

15. The coherence of the Marxist Communist Party is also due to the towering authority of its respective leaders in Kerala and West Bengal, E.M.S. Namboodiripad and Jyoti Basu. The same factors account for the integrity of its late leader, C. Annadurai. For a more detailed treatment of political succession and institutionalization of the rules of the game, see Chapter VIII of this book.

16. The need to control all avenues of power at an early stage of political development has been felt, for good reasons, by similar leaders in other new nations, such as Nkrumah in Ghana or Sukarno in Indonesia. The difference

was that Nehru's democratic sensitivities and the intellectual environment of India did not permit a total usurpation of power as happened in Ghana and Indonesia.

17. Although Nehru stepped down from the Congress presidentship in 1954 (finding the burden of both offices too much to handle alone), all future incumbents of the post until his death owed their position to Nehru's good will. On the other hand, as we shall see, he allowed considerable turnover in state politics, allowing the party organs to compete with Congress ministries both on policy issues and in the distribution of power.
18. *The Times of India*, February 6, 1952.
19. The Congress failed to get an absolute majority in the states of Madras, PEPSU (Patiala and East Punjab States Union), and Travancore-Cochin. However, as other parties fared even worse, after various coalition efforts and a brief spell of president's rule in PEPSU, the Congress formed the government in these states as well. Except in Kerala, the Congress continued to rule at the center and all the states till 1967. In Orissa the Congress entered into a coalition with the Ganatantra Parishad from 1957 to 1961 and in Kerala with the Praja Socialist Party (PSP) and the Muslim League from 1960 to 1964.
20. The arrangement continued until 1960-61 when the organizational faction in the Congress, led by the brilliant political manager Bijoyanand Patnaik, succeeded in bringing an end to the coalition and once again confronting the Ganatantra Parishad in a mid-term election (1961), defeating it, and forming a Congress government under a new leadership. Shortly thereafter the Parishad joined the Swatantra Party.
21. The strength of the opposition to the Congress in earlier elections is not properly brought out from the simple fact that the Congress succeeded in forming governments in the various states. Thus in 1957 the Congress was badly defeated in large parts of Maharashtra by a linguistic party that had become popular owing to the government's not inplementing the linguistics formula in the former Bombay state, although, thanks to Vidarbha and Gujarat regions, in the state as a whole the party returned with a majority. Again in 1962, in Rajasthan the Congress managed to win just half the seats (88 out of 176) and in Madhya Pradesh less than half (142 out of 288), but was able to form the government with the support of independent members in both legislatures.
22. Thus in the tussle between the old guard headed by Chief Minister Sampurnanand in UP and C.B. Gupta, the organizational tycoon of the state Congress, Nehru, who himself came from UP, took keen interest from the beginning. Although he succeeded for a while in supporting Sampurnanand, he had ultimately to recognize the situation, and in the end personally supported Gupta's rise to chief ministership. Similarly, in spite of great sympathy for Jivraj Mehta of Gujarat, the High Command had to agree to the replacement of him and his group by the organizational leaders of the Gujarat Congress. On the general theme, see Marcus Franda, "The Organizational Development of India's Congress Party," *Pacific Affairs*, 35,

Fall, 1962; and Stanley A. Kochanek, *The Congress Party of India: The Dynamics of One-Party Democracy* (Princeton, 1968).

23. Kothari, " The Congress 'System' in India," *op.cit.*
24. For a case study of such a role of opposition from the outside in the factional structuring of positions within the Congress, see Bashiruddin Ahmed, "Congress Defeat in Amroha: A Case Study in One Party Dominance," in *Party System and Election Studies, op. cit.*
25. Such oppositional "movements" for the amelioration of particular grievances also succeed in bringing new, and generally young and dynamic, elements into politics. Once the issue is resolved, however, these parties lose their appeal, but part of the new recruits stay on in politics. Quite often the Congress itself is able to absorb them as it did under the capable Mr. Chavan in Maharashtra.
26. In the elections the Congress lost power in Madras (where a single party, the DMK, came to power), West Bengal, Bihar, Punjab, and Orissa (in all of which "united fronts" composed of parties all the way from the Marxist Communists to the Jan Sangh came to power). After the elections defections from the Congress took place in three more states, mainly on the issue of ministry formation, and united front governments came to power. These were Haryana, UP, and MP.
27. The struggle over nomination in the Congress Party (known as the selection of candidates) is of crucial importance in the functioning of the party system, in some places even more important than the general elections. Also it provides a considerable framework of participation which involves a much larger "catchment area" of participation and socialization than is possible in electoral contests. Ramashray Roy and W.H. Morris-Jones have conducted full-scale inquiries in the selection of Congress candidates. See R. Roy, "Selection of Congress Candidates," *Economic and Political Weekly*, December 31, 1966, January 7 and 14, and February 11 and 18, 1967. Roy's work on nominations in 1967 elections is yet to be published. So is Morris-Jones' work. The phrase "catchment area" has been used by Morris-Jones.
28. Following the "toppling" of the anti-Congress fronts several ex-Congressmen negotiated their return to the Congress party or, to save face, to an ally of the Congress. This happened in West Bengal, Bihar, and Madhya Pradesh. In Madhya Pradesh, a section of the dissidents did come back in 1969 and enabled the Congress to return to power through a Coalition government. Most ex-Congress chief ministers were also found to be on excellent terms with the central government and the Congress High Command. On the other hand, the central leadership of the Congress Party has not shown any great readiness to take the defectors back, occasionally on grounds of principle but more often on pragmatic considerations such as unwillingness to upset the new coalition. Also, where there have been sharp differences, as in West Bengal, the break has been clearly more definitive, and all attempts at negotiation have failed.
29. This happened first in Kerala in 1964 when the dissidents founded a "Kerala

Congress" against the official Kerala Pradesh state Congress. This was followed in West Bengal by a "Bangla Congress" in 1966, a "Jan Congress" (people's Congress) in several northern states before the 1967 elections, and lately a Bharatiya Kranti Dal (BKD) in UP and Bihar and another Loktantrik Congress Dal in Bihar formed by a prominent faction of the Congress led by former chief minister, Mr. Binodananda Jha.

30. This happened in five states from December, 1967 to February, 1968. These were Haryana, West Bengal, Punjab, UP, and Bihar. In Bihar it happened twice. On the break of united fronts a short-lived attempt was made in Bihar and West Bengal to form minority governments of factions that left the united fronts with the backing of the Congress. In West Bengal the Congress itself officially joined the coalition. In both cases, as the coalition lacked the strength of a strong Congress legislature party the attempt failed. In March, 1969 the united front government in MP was brought down when the dissident Congress group deserted it and returned to the Congress. (We use "united front" as a generic term for all such coalitious. The exact nomenclatures differ from state to state, however.)

31. For a documented account of the Congress Party's thinking on its own internal structure and the steps it has taken to achieve greater cohesion, see W.H. Morris-Jones, "The Indian Congress Party: A Dilemma of Dominance," *Modern Asian Studies*, I, No. 2, 1967.

32. The Marxist Communists in Kerala under E.M.S. Namboodaripad and in West Bengal under Jyoti Basu are each a distinct regional force and operate differently than the all-India party or the party in other regions. Although they head a coalition in the respective states, they are the "dominant" group in the government. On the other hand, the Swatantra Party in Orissa is simply another name for the erstwhile tribal party in that state, the Ganatantra Parishad. In alliance with the local dissident faction from the Congress, the Jana Congress, it has been able to provide a fairly stable government. The alliance is in fact the same as the Congress Ganatantra Parishad coalition that ruled the state from 1957 to 1961, and was displaced by the new Congress leadership under Patnaik. The old group left the Congress and formed the Jana Congress, while the Parishad turned itself into the state Swatantra Party. The most stable of the three, of course, is the DMK in Madras, a regional movement-turned-political party, which is strong enough not to need any alliance. Although it is not yet clear, the Akali Dal in Punjab may also crystallize into a viable "dominant party."

33. Two factors were peculiar to West Bengal in 1969. In part due to the political geography of the state and in part due to the electoral alignments of 1967, the different parties in the UF had carved out distinctive spheres of influence in the constituencies, which facilitated the distribution of seats in 1969. Secondly, and this is perhaps even more important, the symbolism of "united front" is fairly old in West Bengal politics, has achieved legitimacy in popular appeal, and between 1967 and 1969 became a powerful "pressure from below," forcing the various constituents of the UF to fall in line. Somewhat similar, though perhaps less compelling, conditions obtained in

Kerala between 1965 and 1967. On the other hand, where there is either much of an overlap in the claims of different parties or a low salience of respectability for the united front concept, the West Bengal success story is likely to remain an aspiration hard to put into effect. Even in West Bengal and Kerala there is evidence of growing differences among the constituents of the UF.

34. See my "India's Political Transition," *Economic and Political Weekly*, II, Special Number, August, 1967, where I had argued for the role of mid-term elections in forcing such realignments.
35. The analysis was carried out at the Data Confrontation Seminar held in Ann Arbor, Michigan, in April, 1969 on the basis of data computed by the Centre for the Study of Developing Societies, Delhi. There is no space here to report the correlations. The same conclusion has been reached by W.H. Morris-Jones and B. Dasgupta, "India's Political Areas: Interim Report on an Ecoligical Electoral Investigation," *Asian Survey* IX, No. 6, June, 1969.
36. The point was tellingly brought out in the DMK campaign in Madras in 1967. One of DMK's slogans in the campaign was "The Congress has the vote-getters; we have the votes." On the general theme, see the articles by Ramashray Roy and R. Chandidas in *Context of Electoral Change* (Centre for the Study of Developing Societies), *op. cit.*
37. This finding has been suggested by two sets of data: correlation between population proportions and party vote in the four elections, and a comparison of party identification figures from two large-scale studies carried out by the Centre for the Study of Developing Societies, one in 1966 and the other in 1967. Both of these suggest that while the proportion of Congress supporters remains fairly steady, with a slight decline in 1967, the supporter of all other parties have increased markedly, and the latter has been largely accomplished by mobilizing the peripheral voter. Some of the 1967 data are presented later in this chapter but a more detailed analysis will be published later.
38. In some of these the Congress made a dramatic "comeback," owing not a little to the disarray of anti-Congress alliances and voter dissatisfaction with their record in office. Thus in the stronghold of the Communists, Kerala, it was a majority of municipal elections in 1968. This was followed by similar successes in UP and in Gujarat and in prestigious by-elections in Rajasthan (in the forte of the charismatic Maharani of Jaipur) and in West Bengal. On top of all this came the all-state mid-term elections in Haryana where the Congress returned with a comfortable majority. In the "little election" that followed in February, 1969, however, the results were mixed. In UP the Congress improved its position and formed the government while the Jan Sangh, its principal opponent, lost badly; in Bihar the Congress lost a few seats but was still able to form a coalition government, thanks largely to the fragmentation of non-Congress forces; but in West Bengal and Punjab, although it maintained and slightly improved its popular vote, in terms of seats it was all but routed in the former by the UF and decisively replaced in the latter by the Akali Dal-dominated coalition. (See take 5.5 for the results.)

39. Thus the DMK leader, C. Annadurai, replying to the Congress leader C. Subramaniam's comment that the DMK administration had no program of its own and was only continuing the policies of the Congress, retorted that instead of criticizing this the Congress should congratulate the DMK for successfully implementing Congress policies (*The Hindu Weekly Review*, July 22, 1968). E.M.S. Namboodaripad, the Marxist chief minister of Kerala, has all along made such a claim, and with some justification.

    Here we may note that in a national sample study of the 1967 general election, when asked about the important differences between party programs and policies, about 65 per cent of the respondents could answer the question and out of this 41 per cent thought there were no differences.

40. See Chapter VIII.

41. An empirical examination of elite and mass opinion on such issues as ceilings on land holdings and urban property, cooperative farming, and the policy of non-alignment led to such a conclusion. Between 60 and 80 per cent of members of Parliament in the Second Lok Sabha, and about the same proportion of supporters of different parties with the exception of the Swatantra Party, favored these policies. On the opinion of members of Parliament, see Surindar Suri, "Changing Face of Lok Sabha," *Link* (New Delhi, August 15, 1961), and Albert M. Cantril, *The Indian Perception of the Sino-Indian Border Clash: An Inquiry in Political Psychology* (Princeton, 1963). On mass opinion, see Indian Institute of Public Opinion, *Monthly Public Opinion Surveys* (New Delhi, January, 1964). For a useful analysis of the different surveys conducted by the IIPO see Samuel J. Eldersveld, " The Developing Pattern of Party Preferences," *Monthly Public Opinion Surveys* (January, 1964).

42. In some ways the process of change that came out so dramatically in 1967 had already begun in 1962: a close examination of electoral trends by constituencies shows this. For a characterization of 1962 as a critical election, see my "India's Political Take-off" and "The Take-Off Election" in *The Economic Weekly*, XIV, Annual Number, February, 1962 and XIV, Special Number, July, 1962, respectively.

43. On the other hand, the dominance of parties like the Communist Marxists in West Bengal depends on an accommodation of a large number of small and marginal parties, which in turn gives a lease on life to and consolidates these various parties. Again the continuity with the "Congress system" is interesting. The Congress system too was a system of a dominant core surrounded by a large number of small factions on all sides.

44. The quote is from the work of Peter McDonough on the measurement of party systems (University of Michigan dissertation, 1969).

45. The data reported here are based on a national study of the fourth general elections carried out under the auspices of the Centre for the Study of Developing Societies, based on a stratification of constituencies by types of party competition. The sample consisted of 2,287 respondents from 47 parliamentary and 94 assembly constituencies. (The data reported here are of the male respondents as the analysis of female respondents has not yet been

carried out.) The study is being currently analyzed and written up. Extensive analysis of the relationship between party identification, changing voter alignments, and party system perspectives, within the general conceptual framework of governmental penetration, will be presented in this study. Interested readers may look out for the publication.

46. In the survey mentioned above, whereas only 17.8 per cent of the respondents knew the name of the chief minister correctly, 24.1 per cent knew the same of the chief minister's party correctly. It may be safely inferred that identity with local potentates leads to identity with parties like the Congress, whereas state and national figures still seem remote.

47. For an analysis of performance on the different issues of institutionalization and coalition-making, and on likely trends in the future, see Chapter VIII.

48. Ratna Dutta, "The Party Representative in Fourth Lok Sabha," *Economic and Political Weekly*, IV, Nos. 1 and 2, January, 1969.

49. *Ibid.*

50. *Ibid.*

51. Talking of acceptance and respectability, the silliest charge that continues to be levelled against the Communists is that of "extra-territorial loyalty." The grounds for such an allegation are flimsy and full of bad taste. No doubt, by their futile and endless controversies on abstract issues of ideology, the Communists have themselves contributed to such criticism.

52. On this see Helen B. Lamb, " The Indian Business Communities and the Evolution of an Industrial Class," *Pacific Affairs*, XXVIII, No. 2, June 1955 and Bernard E. Brown, "Organised Business in Indian Politics," *The Indian Journal of Political Science*, XXIII, No. 2, April-June, 1962.

53. Ralph James, "Politics and Trade Unions in India," *Far Eastern Survey*, XXVII, No. 3, March, 1958.

54. On all this, see the documentation and interpretation of Myron Weiner, *The Politics of Scarcity: Public Pressure and Political Response in India* (Chicago, 1962). Weiner's work is the most systematic account of associational interest groups in India.

55. C. Subramaniam, president of the Tamil Nadu (Madras) Pradesh Congress Committee who led a "silent" demonstration of an estimated 100,000 people against the DMK government, defended such actions as intended to "educate the electorate to agitate for removal of grievances." He added that in advanced countries like the United Sates, propaganda was carried out through the medium of radio or television. But in the prevailing conditions in India processions and other forms of demonstrations were necessary to educate the electorate. Quoted in *The Hindu Weekly Review*, August 12, 1968.

56. The material conditions and training in civil responsibilities of the Indian police leave much to be desired, and the strains and abuse to which they are subjected by political groups and hooligan elements have often been exasperating. To this the police have often reacted by strikes and agitations.

A most notorious instance of this was provided in August 1969 when, provoked by certain actions of the state government, policemen in West Bengal mobbed the legislative assembly. The incident aroused instant indignation from all quarters. Whereas in handling riotous situations caused by other elements, the police in India have by and large shown a commendable record of patience and maturity, their own grievances have often turned them to protest behavior. For a pioneering study of the Indian Police, see David H. Bayley, *The Police and Political Development in India* (Princeton, 1969).

57. See Chapter IX.

58. The most influential among them is Jayaprakash Narayan, an ex-revolutionary and former socialist leader who has turned into an exponent of the *sarvodaya* view of politics which aims at eschewing party politics and building an "organic democracy" based on the village community. A man of enormous popularity and great personal integrity, and possessing a truly universalist outlook, Narayan has also tried to mediate in the problems of Nagaland, Kashmir, and Indo-Pakistan relations. His world view is best stated in his *Plea for Reconstruction of the Indian Polity, op. cit.*

6

Social Infrastructure

WE HAVE SEEN how the institutionalization of the Indian model of democracy has led to an expansion of the political center from its modernist citadel outward toward society and its diversities. The main theoretical issue is: How does such a system mobilize support and find bases in traditional society? We deal here with an ancient civilization, with a highly differentiated social structure, and with long standing traditions and collective orientations. Parliamentary government, parties, and opposition movements are essentially modernist impacts on such a society. How do the two meet? Are they simply a superstructure over a wholly alien culture, or is the communication between the two showing some signs of fusion and interaction? Of crucial relevance here is the caste system of India. The subject is so important, and so charged with preconceived notions, that it calls for a somewhat detailed analysis.[1]

PREVAILING PERCEPTIONS

Everyone recognizes that the social system in India is organized around caste structures and caste identities. In dealing with the relationship between caste and politics, however, the tendency is to start at the wrong end of the question: Is caste disappearing? In part such an approach comes from a widely held dichotomy between communal and associational forms of organization. In reality, however, no social system disappears. A more useful point of departure would be: What form is caste taking under the impact of politics, and what form is politics taking in a caste-oriented society? Those who complain of "casteism in politics" in India are really looking for a sort of politics which has no basis in society. They also probably lack any clear conception of either the nature of politics or the nature of the caste system. (Some of them would want to throw out both politics and the caste system.) The process of politics is one of identifying and manipulating existing structures in order to mobilize support and consolidate positions. Where the caste structure provides one of the most important organizational clusters in which the population is found to live, politics must strive to organize through such a structure. The alleged casteism in politics is thus no more and no less than *politicization of caste*. By drawing the caste system into its web of organization, politics finds material for its articulation and moulds it into its own design. In making politics their sphere of activity, caste and kin groups, on the other hand, get a chance to assert their identity and to strive for positions. Drawing upon both the interacting structures are the real actors, the new contestants for power. Politicians mobilize caste groupings and identities in order to organize their power. They find in it an extremely articulated and flexible basis for organization, something that may have been structured in terms of a status hierarchy, but something that is also available for political manipulation—and one that has a basis in consciousness. Where there are other types of groups and other bases of association, politicians approach them as well. And as they, everywhere, change the form of such organizations, they change the form of caste as well.

The few who are free from a dichotomous view of caste and politics and are prepared to look into precise empirical relations suffer from another preconception and often a contrary theoretical construct. Reflecting the style of much social science theorizing, these writers display an instrumental view of political activity.[2] Accordingly to them, the substance of political relationships can be analyzed by reference to the changes taking place in patterns of social and economic dominance; they tend to underemphasize the capacity of political actors to influence these patterns. Politics, in this view, is an instrument wielded by a particular stratum in society to consolidate or raise its position; its function is to reproduce, or modify, existing states of superior-subordinate relationships. Such an approach blurs understanding of the developmental reality which consists not in any approximation to a preconceived framework but in the changing interactions of the constituent elements in a dynamic situation. But in the particular case of caste and politics, even this is only partly relevant. Where caste itself becomes a political category, it is futile to argue as to whether caste uses politics or politics uses caste.

In the other extreme from the reductionist school are some political scientists who, fascinated as they are by the politicization of the caste system, cannot, however, escape the compulsion to reduce the interactions between caste and politics to a neat model. Although they have given up the traditional political scientist's aversion to caste, and have also mercifully given up the erstwhile dichotomy between voluntary associations as belonging to the "modern" secular order and caste organizations as belonging to the "traditional" order, they fall in the same trap again by imagining a total transformation of the caste system through its involvement in politics, "the democratic incarnation of caste" as an American author calls it.[3] Such analysts tend to go over to the other extreme and to rarefy caste as a political force in contemporary India as compared to other factors. Their basic approach is still essentially one of explaining empirical phenomena in terms of a unified conceptual model that enables neat generalizations to be imposed on a complex reality.

All these approaches are basically oriented towards an ideal type contradiction between caste and politics, and represent different variants of professional rigidity. What they all fail to see is that there never was a complete polarization between the caste system and the political system, and that what is involved in the contemporary process of change is neither a mechanistic projection of existing structures of dominance and dependence nor a total shift from one system to another, but really a change in the context and levels of political operation, a shift in social criteria and priorities, and the introduction of new institutional media of social integration. Thus a relative decline in the importance of pollution as a factor in determining caste hierarchy, and the diminishing emphasis on the summation of roles as involved in the *Jajmani* system, do not by themselves involve any basic destruction of the caste system, but only a shift in the critical criteria of social awareness and the structural differentiations through which such an awareness is mobilized and organized.

We shall examine the relationships between caste and politics as basically a relationship *for the specific purpose of organizing public activity*. Our focus is not so much on what happens to the caste system as a result of its involvement in the political process but rather what structures and networks of relationships enter into the political process and how. We can not wholly avoid the question of what politics does to the caste system, for certain forms adopted by the caste system in the wake of a wider secular ordering of relationships, such as the caste association or the caste federation, become very much the stuff of politics. But it is still by focussing on political structures and their pursuit of collective goods that we approach this subject.

POLITICAL DIMENSIONS OF CASTE

Keeping in mind the focus of our inquiry, there aspects of the caste system call for special attention. The first is what may be called the *secular dimension*. In emphasizing caste as a stratification system in which distances are rigidly maintained through endogamy, pollution, and the legitimacy of rituals, caste as a system of conflict and interaction has received sparse attention. Yet the fact is that factionalism and caste cleavages, patterns of alignment and realignment among the various strata, and a continuous striving for social mobility have always been prominent features of the caste system.

Traditionally there were two aspects to the secular organization of caste—the governmental aspect (caste and village councils and arbitration procedures) and the political aspect (intracaste and intercaste alignments and cleavages). These were buttressed or dissipated by the authority relationships of local elites with the center or centers of society. Religion, occupation, and territory provided the bases for secular mobility. These are still relevant for the generalized process of contemporary secularization; only the emphasis and proportions have changed. Instead of allegiance to a king through the rise of a new sect or the elevation of certain caste or territorial groupings, and instead of management of the civil aspects of society mainly at local levels, we now have more participatory and vertical modes of involvement. What has really changed is the context, following the rise of the nation-state and political democracy, and their organizational concomitants. But the change is still more incremental than sudden, as found in the gradual involvement and cooptation of more and more strata in the political structure.

Thus in many regions it was the Brahminic section that first responded to English education and were the first to benefit from political and administrative power; with the slow expansion of education and the franchise, others came in. In some other regions, especially, others came in. In some P other regions, especially where the Brahmins were never so powerful and certain agricultural upper castes wielded castes wielded positions of dominance, vertical intercaste ties provide an ongoing structure of political recruitment. Here it was by initiating these upper peasant castes into the new politics that almost the whole social structure was mobilized. This precluded any strong formation of horizontal solidarities.[4] In still other regions the spread of new religious sects and the financial power wielded by the communities that responded to these (such as the Jains and Vaishnavas of Gujarat and Marwar) made for a different model of sequence in regard to accession to political power.

New solidarities in the middle castes were evident in many regions even before the British came, and the phenomenon of hypergamy (the Hindu practice of marrying the daughter into a caste at least as high as, and preferably higher than, her own) was often a function of the influx of new and lower sections of society from pastoral and tribal ways of life into the agricultural mainstream of society. Here is an instance of occupational mobility giving rise to both a modification of kinship patterns and an expansion of the secular-associational base of traditional society. The process of secularization in recent decades owes considerably to these differentiations of antecedent society, its varna hierarchy, and polytheistic religions which preceded the onslaught of more contemporary modernizing forces. Yet another process was the breaking through of territorial restraints, thus widening the base of occupational mobilization. The pastoral castes of Saurashtra turned into the agricultural low caste of Kanbis in Gujarat which a later rose in status through their hypergamous affiliation with the regional dominant caste of Patidars. Similarly the shoemaker caste (Mochis) of Saurashtra turned into the tailor caste (Darjis) of Gujarat. Or again, to take another pattern in Maharashtra, a new subcaste of Deshmukhs became differentiated from other subcastes of the Marathas on their accession to special land rights, out of which developed a new hypergamous relationship which continued until the development of a non-Brahmin political movement and latter-day land legislation led to a re-identification of a common heritage. Thus the formation of new monogamous and hypergamous subcastes led to both greater differentiation and a blurring of the sharp traditional distinctions. Even the concept of man-woman relationship in terms of a superior-subordinate affair played its role in developing distinctive hierarchical relationship in the caste system, and enabled special types of mobility and differentiation which later proved instrumental in facilitating political identities and secular associational urges.

Second, there is the *integration dimension*. The caste system not only determines the individual's social station on the basis of the group to which he is born but also differentiates and assigns occupational and economic roles. It thus gives a place to every individual from the highest to the lowest and makes for a high degree of identification and integration. At the same time, it is an integration structure of a specific type, namely, one that is more intense in its small group orientation and particularistic loyalties, and where wider loyalties operate only when they are structured through the prevailing differentiations. This aspect is important in understanding the structural impact of democratic nation-building. For the competitive style of democratic politics involves not only distributive and conflictual aspects but also aspects of group action and cohesion; democratic politics is as much a process of fusion as of fission. The traditional emphasis in studies of the caste system on differentiation and affirmed segmentation has neglected the integrative dimension.[5] The political age, however, emphasizes both, strengthens the integrative dimension and at the same time links the conflict potential of aggregative processes onto a broader canvas. Differentiation has all along been an essential ingredient in the Indian approach to integration, and it has now become an important variable in the development of democratic politics.

We have seen in Chapter II that in actual operation caste affiliations take not the vertical homogeneous class and status form of varna but the horizontal and segmental form of jati. Yet a system that has survived for so long creates of powerful symbolism, rationale, and mythology of its own. The varna referent represents a "scale of values" which provides both a spur to integrative behavioral patterns and a symbol of competition that enables the aspiring and mobile groups to lay claim to high status while still affirming widely prevalent values. It "furnishes an all-India frame into which myriad jatis in any single linguistic area can be fitted." Furthermore, certain varnas also provide symbols of high status and at the same time symbols of opposition, as for example, the Kshatriyas against the Brahmins; "disputes as to relative status are an essential feature of the caste system." It thus enables the low placed castes to affirm widely prevalent values in Indian society at the same time that they claim high status. Thus varna aggregation and jati segmentation are intimately connected in the Indian system which has made for a high degree or integration and containment of structural and psychological strains inherent in the process of technological and political change.[6]

Third, there is the *dimension of consciousness*. Again, in their concern with stratification, sociologists have generally neglected the ideational underpinning that is inevitably associated with any social system. Thus the contest for positions between various jatis often follows some variation of varna either by approximating to the reality as in the case of the various layers of Brahminic status, or by invoking label as in the case of the claim of certain castes to be Kashatriya (a caste of warriors and rulers). Indeed the very fluidity and nebulousness of the concept of Kshatriya, and yet its historically compelling symbolism for social mobility, has been an important lever in structuring secular aspirations from time to time in the various regions, following real shifts in the social and economic positions of different groups. The same holds true though in a lesser degree for the Brahminic symbol as well as the symbol of certain middle range castes. Caste has several meanings, refers to varna at one level and to other meanings of segmentation at other levels. By shifting from one referent to another, it demonstrates the basic continuity between the various referents—doctrinal, ritual, economic and occupational, and associational-political. At the same time by being different things at different points in social interactions, it provides for immense flexibility, and produces tension management and assimilative capabilities. It follows that the system can also withstand the decline of certain features (considered essential at one time) such as the Jajmani system of role differentiation and summation; or the importance of pollution as a system of hierarchical determination. Both functions can now be performed by new elements in the secular setting of society.

This also brings out the importance of the manner in which traditional status urges such as "sanskritization" get intertwined with more modern urges like Westernization and secularization.[7] Under the impact of universalized aspirations (economic well-being; rationality urge; political integration) the Brahminized urges may be simply repudiated by the advance guard of a lower caste which, ironically, re-establishes its original (non- Brahminic) identity to foster solidarities and legitimize its contemporary strivings in the modernist sector. Alternatively, a caste may sometimes interpret its traditional status in society to buttress and mythologize its contemporary aspirations. Examples are to be found in the Patidars of Gujarat, Mahisyas of Bengal, and Jats of Rajathan. Still another approach is found in regions where the Brahmins did not dominate the modernizing process, which was led by powerful peasant castes who were in turn closely associated in vertical ties with other castes. This enabled a cutting short of both the sankritization phase and the phase of lower caste solidarity and led straight to multi-caste factional politics as an avenue of social mobility. Andhra Pradesh and Bihar provide good examples of a rapid succession of various caste groups into factional networks of politics which provided the new channels of mobility.

By itself the sanskritization urge produces some very basic psychological strains in the group that is trying to acquire a new identity in its search for status, as in the process its status becomes *subjectively* ambivalent and thus insecure; as with Jews, Negroes, and other minority groups elsewhere, it is a "negative assertion," a mood of "submitting yet opposing" the emulated group. Hence the tension, especially for the more conscious sections. Also, as long as they do not succeed in raising the status of the group, their infirm status necessarily creates an insecure and unsettled position in society, leading either to compensatory devices for social recognition or real withdrawal into something else. The status urge in Hindu society is an intensely frustrating and painful experience, as we shall see when we come to discuss political culture. To this is added a further edge by resorting to a mechanism of status raise which starts from negating the original existence and striving for something which may turn out to be a mirage and may possibly lead to reprisal at the hands of the higher castes (as in the case of the Smiths of South India).

It is a tribute to the subtle dynamics of Hindu society that in spite of this psychological cost, the adjustments of sanskritization go on all the time; and one of the many reasons is that the structural distance that a group tries to jump can often be related to the achievement of other indices of power and position in the modernist segments of society, thus facilitating the transition to a consensus on the new status of the striving group. Important in this respect is the crucial role that the distribution of secular power has always played in status ranking in Hindu society; and the consequent capacity of the system to keep adjusting to its changing hierarchical balance.

Altogether, then, the secular, integrative, and ideational dimensions of caste have provided a sophisticated and differentiated cultural background for receiving the modernist impacts and responding to them without either great disruption or any widespread feeling of dissonance and alienation.

STAGES OF ARTICULATION

Modernist influences penetrated Indian society slowly. There is no need here to repeat the details of recent history. Liberal education, governmental patronage, adult franchise, and an expanding market economy have been the influences that have penetrated the caste system and involved it by stages. The involvement resulted from a mutual give and take. The new institutions and the new leadership offered economic opportunity, administrative patronage, and positions of power which drew the articulate sections of society into the modernist network. In return, the political elite was provided with a basis of support that was already structured and endowed with symbols of identification and experiential meaning. By making concessions to local opinion, taking its cues from the consensus that existed as regards claims to power, and articulating political competition on traditional lines, the new elite was able to organize castes for economic and political purposes. With this came a new species of political organization, articulated around particularistic divisions, yet giving to these a secular and associational orientation. Politics and society began moving nearer and a new infrastructure started to be.

Three stages can be noted in this process. The struggle for power and benefits was at first limited to the entrenched castes in the social hierarchy.[8] Leadership and access to governmental patronage came from a limited group of individuals who were the first to respond to new educational opportunities and who were also traditionally endowed with pedagogic and sophistic skills that mattered most in the days of limited politics. This group consisted of individuals from certain "higher' castes, was not yet based on any militant caste consciousness, and was united more by a common social and intellectual endowment and idiom than through any organizational or political mobilization. However, wherever this took place mainly on the basis of one higher caste (or subcaste), it soon gave rise to a feeling of deprivation and antagonism in other high castes, especially among those that had earlier enjoyed social or economic power, and resulted in the emergence of another political group, still drawn largely from the higher castes. The domination of an *entrenched* caste thus produced a quick response in the form of an *ascendant* caste, one that was not satisfied simply to function in the context of interdependence and complementarity in the social sphere. Thus polarized in its first encounter with the new secularism, the caste structure occasioned a bilateral structure of caste politics.[9] Such a polarization was avoided either where the one entrenched caste was greatly separated in social power and ritual status from all others or where different castes or subcastes were entrenched at different power points, either regionally or institutionally, involving the points in a legitimized coalitional pattern.

This bilateralism was followed by a second stage in which power strivings and demands for benefits exceeded the availability of resources; competing groups had to develop more numerous bases of support; and competition began within the entrenched and more articulate sections of society. This may be termed the stage of caste fragmentation or of "factionalism."[10] Intercaste competition was now supplemented by intracaste competition and the process of politicization. Leadership cleavages were created; political attitudes began to condition symbols of solidarity and consensus; and there came into being multi-caste and multi-factional alignments that cut across antecedent boundaries. Mobilization of further support for each of the contending factions gave rise to a process of cooptation from other castes that were until now kept out of the power system. The power structure of the caste system now became more complex and entered into a more varied network of relationships, involving such other bases of support as economic patronage, patron-client loyalties, bond groups, and new organizational forms such as caste associations and caste federations.

Once again the process took a slightly different form in regions where vertical intercaste ties already existed by reason of agricultural and other economic bonds, traditional patron client and/or hypergamic relationships, or intraregional variation in dominant-dependent relationships. In such instances this stage saw a further articulation of vertical factional networks of mobilization and competition. Wherever vertical chains of relationships already existed, politics found readymade channels and the need for evoking new solidarities and forcing new alignments in the form of caste associations and caste federations was less pressing. The upper tiers of each of the rival chains simply were recruited into politics and carried the whole network with them. The process of further cooptation of elites from other castes became easy as traditions for such cooptation already existed. In other words, the expanding mobilization of politics either found an ongoing vertical network or created one through its aggregative propensities.

The new vertical framework of political organization brought about other forms of regrouping. It enabled different entrenched (or dominant) castes in different regions to confront each other at the higher levels such as district and state (as for example the Kammas and Reddis in Andhra, the Patidars and Annavals in Gujarat, the Lingayats and Okkalingas in Mysore, the various district and regional dominant castes of Madras, and entrenched castes of Bihar). And at each level within this hierarchy there grew a new mode of organization in which associational and federal forms of caste on the one hand and factional forms of politics on the other played an increasing part. With this the importance of individuals and of personalized networks increased and leadership took on a more positive role.

All this, however, was limited to the leading two or three castes—well-to-do, educated, and generally upper caste. The lower castes were still in a dependent relationship with either the entrenched or the dominant castes. However, during the second stage itself there started a process of mobilization of lower castes into politics for the purpose of adding to the factionalized support base of rival leaders. This was done simply by coopting leaders from hitherto dormant sections of society by providing them with junior positions and a part of the divisible benefits in return for electoral support; or, where it was not possible to tackle the problem on the basis of simple cooptation, by entering into a more organized mobilization through coalitions of subcaste groups, bargaining with "link men", and appealing to wider identities and animosities. Where the simple cooptation device worked, the task was to induce critical leaders into the power elite and not to worry about the backward "masses"; where it did not work and the situation was more differentiated, new schemes of mobilization were needed. It is also likely that in time the new entrants to politics may themselves be able to forge a coalition strong enough to pose a challenge to the leaders from the entrenched castes. This would depend upon their combined numerical strength, degree of economic independence, and the nature of leadership. It would also depend on the extent to which the consciousness of caste in these sections took on the form of a political class, self-assertive and indignant against exploitation from the upper castes, and eager to taste political power themselves.

It should also be stressed here that different stages in the social organization of politics call for somewhat different leadership and organizational skills, and the movement from one stage to another may entail displacement of one kind of leadership by another; consequently one social group endowed with one type of skills may be displaced by another endowed with another type of skills. Thus in the early stages of intellectual awakening and urban-style political organization, the need was for people able to deal with Western and Westernized administrators, well versed in fine points of debate and ideological disputation, possessing legal acumen, and capable of founding and sustaining small associations of public-minded persons that would agitate for specific causes. Such men were mainly provided by the Brahminic and traditional administrative classes who not only took to the new education but had also been endowed by a long tradition of scholastic knowledge and formal brilliance. With the movement into a more diversified and "mass" oriented politics, however, not only was there need for a wider base of support articulation but also for new types of managerial and organizational skills. With this shift in orientation, the Brahminic and administrative castes began to be outnumbered by men from commercial and peasant proprietor occupations, occupations that had always called for a high level of interpersonal skills, a pragmatic and bargaining approach to problems, and an ability to marshal a new type of solidarity among their own castes, often based on a reinterpretation of their traditional status and a populist and anti-elitist ideology.

These were the new entrepreneurs, the new innovators, of politics. They were less modern than the elites they replaced, less educated and more rural-based, and operated through an idiom that was decidedly more traditional. But more important than these statistical characteristics is the fact that the innovativeness with which they are credited— their ability to organize, to show a pragmatic evaluation, to take risks, and to utilize "modern" means of technology and organization—came more from inherited characteristics and early socialization in prevailing life styles than from any conscious adoption of a new culture. One such political and organizational skills came to the fore, and the corresponding displacement in the social base of politics took place, political activity not only achieved a new dimension but also got markedly differentiated from other social activities, and took on a life and character of its own. The full articulation of this change comes in the third stage (to be discussed presently), with the still greater diversification of the base of politics, and with factors other than caste entering into the picture.

The process of factionalism within the entrenched castes, a similar structuring of other ascendent castes, the system of cooptations and caste coalitions—all of these, though they brought about a fragmentation of the caste system, were in reality still very much caste-oriented even though they generated politicized values and impulses for personal power. We enter a third stage of development when the weakening of older identities and the introduction of politicized values coincide with other changes taking place in society through the impact of education, technology, changing status symbols, and urbanization, New and more expanded networks of relationships come into being; new criteria of self-fulfillment are created; the craving for material benefits becomes all-pervasive; and family migration systems undergo drastic changes. With these, the structure of particularistic loyalties becomes overlaid by a more sophisticated system of social and political participation, with cross-cutting allegiances, a greater awareness of individual self-interest, and forms of involvement and alienation that are pre-eminently the products of modern education and the modern system of social communications. It has been repeatedly observed that economic differences within the same castes, including the lower castes like the Ezhavas of Kerala or the Harijans, break their homogeneity and expose them to other modes of differentiation and cleavage patterns. An essential feature of modernization is the development of new and more clear-cut differentiations. Political, economic, educational, and communications functions, traditionally performed by the same social structure, are now differentiated and are established in terms of their own purposes, structures, and dynamics.

Politics, of course, is still a big enough influence but it is better understood as an active partner in the modernization process, more as providing schemes of integration and division to be developing social system than as either undermining or replacing caste as a secular social entity. A widening base of institutional organization now occurs in which, on the one hand, caste identities take on new forms of articulation, thus changing the very ethics of the social system and diminishing the importance of its ritualistic and ascriptive bases; and, on the other hand, more diverse forms of organization and interest identification enter the political system and give rise to a highly mobile and cross-cutting loyalty structure in politics. Caste on one side ceases to be an exclusive political support base and on the other side lends itself to increasing political manipulation, both of which contribute to its participation in a broader network of relationships. In its traditional form, the caste system integrated society through ordering primary identities along a legitimized hierarchy of status positions and occupational roles, including the "political" roles of arbitration and adjudication. By participating in the modern political system, it is at first exposed to divisive influences and later to a new form of integration resulting from a new scheme of universalist-particularist relationships.

Secular involvement in the modern period has not only fostered new attitudes and offered new rewards; it has also exposed caste and communal ties as by themselves patently inadequate and often prejudicial for the building of stable support. For one thing castes, where they are large, are not homogenous and where they are small, not enough of a numerical force. Second, too close an identification with one caste alienatsd other castes. Electoral politics lead to a multi-group structure of support, a structure that both "fragments" castes and "federates" them in a common organization. Third, political parties gain stability only by involving all the major sections of the community. Finally, the politicization of caste makes for outward-looking, upward-moving orientations and as this results in the phenomenon of multiple and overlapping identities, the emerging model of secularism is one in which caste is only one of many components entering into the political process. Meanwhile, the caste component itself undergoes a major organizational transformation and is subjected to new symbols of affiliation and identity.

NEW FORMS OF AGGREGATION

This development in depth of the system calls for closer analysis. Widespread confusion characterizes the discussion of "casteism" and "communalism" in politics, even among the sections of the leadership and the social scientists who should know better. An impression prevails that whereas things like education, urbanization, and industrialization were making inroads into traditional sectarian loyalties, electoral politics have resuscitated them and re-established their legitimacy, and that this has given rise to disintegrative tendencies that will disrupt the democratic and secular framework of the Indian polity. Evidence is cited from the behavior of political parties, all of which invoke primordial sentiments and organize their support on the basis of caste and communal identities. Now much of the evidence cited, though exaggerated, is often true; what is not true is the inference that is so often drawn from it. For in reality the consequences of caste-politics interactions are just the reverse of what is usually stated.[11] It is not politics that gets caste-ridden; it is caste that gets politicized. Dialectical as it might sound, it is precisely because the operation of competitive politics has drawn caste out of its apolitical context and given it a new status and identity that the "caste system" as hitherto known has begun to disintegrate. To put it in another way, it is precisely because the *legitimacy* of caste as the only basis of political power has been eroded that caste *calculations* have increased. Such things as respective numerical strength of different castes, choice of candidates, factions within castes, and economic ties between castes are calculated as variables in the situation. This is natural in any political system and applies equally to other types of social organization and ethnic groups. One must grasp that caste calculations were *not* needed when only persons belonging to some castes had a right to office; caste was irrelevant because it was omnipotent. Today with the breakdown of these barriers and the pragmatic pursuit of power, caste has turned into just another variable in politics along with many other variables. As Harold A. Gould has put it, it has come down from being a "determinant" of politics to an "ethnic variable."[12]

In fact, it is possible to argue that it is because "ethnic" identities are openly acknowledged, politically organized, and made explicit bases for bargaining that a more open process of institutional penetration and political integration has been possible in India. In societies where the prevailing secular ideology has frowned upon such open articulation of parochial identities, the process of assimilation has proved much more painful and often destructive of the antecedent culture. India too has learned through bitter experience the costs of overplaying secular claims and suppressing open organization of ethic identities as bases for bargaining and coalition-making (as did the Congress movement vis-a-vis the Muslims until it was too late). In regard to the caste system, however, despite the prejudices of the modernist leadership and the intelligentsia, a much more open process of group articulation and aggregation has been possible, and has resulted in important shifts and adjustments in the social base of political power.

We have tried to describe an extremely involved process of aggregation in this chapter. The process crystallizes in two distinct but related forms. First, a "dominant elite" emerges, which is drawn from different groups but shares a common secular orientation, which is structured into a diffuse network of relationships that stretches across social boundaries yet continues to induct leaders from each important segment, which is homogenous in terms of some of the values and rules of the game but is divided into many special groups and subelites. Such an elite structure articulates interest differentiations and meaningfully represents the more organized segments of society, while allowing the mass of society to have its own pace of change and make its own adjustments with the modern world.

Second, castes take on an openly secular form for new organizational purposes. Such forms include (a) associations of caste members ranging from simple hostels and recreational bodies to reform clubs and pressure groups, (b) caste institutions or conferences that are more broad-based and cover entire states or linguistic regions, and (c) caste federations composed of not one but several castes which may sometimes be socially homogenous but at other times may simply have some specific interest or political objective in common. It is this specificity of purpose that distinguishes these new organizational forms—caste associations and caste federations—from the more inclusive ascriptive groups traditionally known as castes.[13] They are organized to secure economic benefits or educational openings, or for the more clearly political purpose of uniting to fight the hegemony of the upper castes, but in all cases for one or more specific purposes. Once formed on the basis of caste identities the caste federation goes on to acquire non-caste functions, becomes more flexible in organization as time passes, begins to accept members and leaders from castes other than those with which it started, stretches out to new regions, and makes common cause with other voluntary organizations, interest groups, and political parties.

With time, the federation becomes a distinctly political group, wielding considerable bargaining strength and numerical power, still able to appeal to caste sentiments and consciousness by adopting a common label (such as "non-Brahmin" or "Kshatriya"), claiming high status in the past and fostering a sense of deprivation in the present, and out of all this forging a strong and cohesive political group. It has gone far beyond the earlier caste associations in performing the functions of political mobilization, articulation of group interests, and awareness of such interests.[14] The "dominant elite" talked of above either includes leaders drawn from such organizations or closely interacts with them.

The role of secular ideas in the development of these new organizational forms has been ambivalent. They encouraged movements of social reform and social amelioration of backward sections of society, presumably with a view to break their isolation and parochialism, to make them conscious of their opportunities, and to integrate them with the emerging centers of society. For the mobilization of existing identities towards new ends, associations were formed on the basis of existing caste labels, initiative for which came by and large from the urban educated and politically conscious members of the respective communities. Once the new associations became going concerns, however, controversy emerged over their involvement in politics. A combination of vested interests and a rather limited conception of secularism led one section of the leadership to reject the direct participation of caste organizations in politics.[15] Another section, generally rural-based and conscious of the growing power of numbers and the importance of group identities, pressed for the political role of caste and the need to move from single-caste associations formed for the limited goals of providing educational and job opportunities for their individual members to multi-caste federations, emphasizing numerical strength, bargaining for groups rather than individuals, and thus forming substantial political coalitions.[16] With the passage of time, the latter kind of leadership has gained in ascendancy, though not all the major caste groups in the country have been successfully organized for political participation. Clearly, castes that have not passed through this stage of political organization have remained weak in their bargaining strength and their individual members have had to resort to less organized and more anomic activities to gain political recognition or make themselves heard.[17] By and large, however, caste associations and caste federations have provided an important infrastructure of politics in India and, within the Indian context, perform a role comparable to interest groups in the West.

OTHER ETHNIC GROUPS

In considering the developing infrastructure of Indian politics, we have deliberately focussed on the caste system and its associational-federal articulation under democratic politics. This politicization of primordial structures has proved so central to the coalition-making style of Indian politics, encompasses so many strata and levels of society-polity interactions, and brings out so well the broader meaning of India's institutional strategy that it was useful to develop the main analysis in the framework of "caste and politics." Before bringing the chapter to an end, however, brief mention must be made of two other related issues: the position of those castes and tribes (the "scheduled" castes and tribes) that the makers of the Indian Constitution thought to deserve special political attention; and the position of religious minorities, especially the Muslims.

Although the economic and social condition of the Harijans and the scheduled tribes continues to be quite unsatisfactory as far as their position in the social structure goes, the process of their involvement in politics has not been very different from the other lower castes described above. If anything, the constitutional provision of certain special privileges including reservation of legislative seats and administrative positions[18] has acted as a special catalyst of political mobilization. It is noteworthy that through their special bargaining power in politics (even outside the constituencies reserved for them), the cooptation of their elites into competing coalition networks, and the need felt by higher caste leaders to solicit their support, the political position of the Harijans and the tribals is way ahead of either their social status or their economic competence: the advantages of the former counter the disparities of the latter.[19] In optimizing their opportunities, both groups are found to operate increasingly through associational and federal organizations as well as political parties and have often, as in the case of the Assam tribals, carved out a special position for themselves.[20] And because of their special constitutional status, membership in these organizations is not considered "communal" or "casteist." On the contrary, most of the major political parties have their own organizations for Harijan and tribal "welfare." Thus political recognition seems by itself to secularize particularist identities and lead to a substantive integration with the modern centers of society.

The same cannot be said of the position of religious minorities, especially of the Muslims. (The other non-Hindu religious groups are small in number and in areas where they are numerically significant, as are the Catholics in Kerala and the Sikhs in Punjab, they enjoy such political importance that they seem to fit very well with the general description of caste and politics give above.) We have seen in Chapter 2 how the nationalist ideology under the Congress frowned upon open expression of the Muslim identity in politics and still more upon separate political organization for the Muslims. In fighting the two-nation theory of the Muslim League and establishing the claim of the Congress to represent all communities, the movement failed to create a proper atmosphere for secular interaction between different communities through their own organizations, and left behind a poor legacy. The creation of Pakistan further strengthened this prejudice against "communal organizations". Consequently, when democratic politics led to an open articulation of the major groups in society, the Muslims felt highly ambivalent about whether or not they should also organize themselves politically. In time, two distinct groups emerged, one led by the Jamiat-ul-Ulema, which emphasized educational and religious activity at the expense of specifically Muslim organizations in politics, and the other led by the Jamate-Islami (and more recently the Majlis-e- Mushawarat), which has emphasized political action and has started making specific political demands and even fielding candidates in the elections.

The division between the two groups is not very different from what took place in many caste associations and federations as described above, although a long period of frustration has given rise to a sharper debate among the Muslims, and the proponents of the political line have not always used a "constitutional" language. By and large, however, political involvement, wherever it has taken place, has reduced the sense of isolation and particularism of the Muslims and has resulted in the same kind of factional adjustments as we have noted in our consideration of the various castes. Thus in Kerala, where the Muslim League has survived as a political party, it is not only much more secular in its outlook than is the case in other parts of the country but it has also achieved an important position in political coalition-making in that state, and has shown a greater sense of efficacy of politics. More recently, in the third and even more in the fourth general elections Muslim political organizations became active in many parts of the country and this is leading to a gradual, through still hesitant process of secular involvement. Although there are no reserved seats for the Muslims, by convention the Congress and other major parties allot a certain minimum of their party tickets to the Muslims. All this contributes to the growing assimilation of this important minority into national politics. Studies of electoral participation in constituencies with sizeable Muslim population also indicate a differentiated structure of support, factional identities within the community and coalition-making with other communities, participation in associational organizations, in general a process of "secularization" as defined above, and all without losing the distinctive Muslim identity.[21] Once again, while apprehension and mistrust still operate at the social and economic level, increasing evidence of accommodation and interaction is noticeable at the political level. The process of politicization, no doubt, creates its own tensions and even violent outbursts, as they do in the relationship between entrenched and newly enfranchized groups of other kinds. We shall discuss the "performance" aspect of these issues in Chapter 8. But the general analysis of caste and politics advanced in this chapter is also applicable, with obvious limitations of context and subculture, to the special cases of religious minorities as well as the scheduled castes and tribes.

CONCLUSION: PROCESS OF REINTEGRATION

The main theoretical point that emerges from our analysis of the political involvement of different kinds of social and ethnic groups is with regard to the relationship between social identity and political integration. Contrary to certain prevailing notions on the "identity crisis" in societies that have not developed an overriding national identity, we have found that it is through the political articulation of particularistic identities that a more stable pattern of integration becomes possible, and that it is in cases where such an open articulation has not been permitted that the outcome tends to be anomic and lacking in efficacious behavior. On the other hand, we have also seen that such articulation leads to a gradual but definite shift in organizational and symbolic affiliations, gives rise to intermediate structures that mediate between society and polity, and with time creates a cultural mix that provides anchor to the modernist political center.

We have seen how such a process of exposure on both sides leads to new forms of integration between society and politics. The process can be described as "secularization" of the social system and this process holds the key to the tremendous shift that politics has brought about in Indian society. Whereas sanskritization brought submerged caste groups out into the mainstream of society, and Westernization drew the sanskritized castes into the framework of modernization, it is secularization of both kinds of groups through their political involvement that is leading to an erosion of the old order and its reintegration on secular-associational grounds. The transition to the new order, which is by definition full of ambiguity and fluidity, highlights parochial symbolism as providing reference points of identity and cohesion.[22] But the reintegrative process gradually builds up new mixes of universalist-particularist orientations, renders the primordial basis of secular ties inefficient and often prejudicial to individual and group interests, initiates the formally illiterate masses into a slow awareness of the political community, and develops in them a stake in the latter.

On the other hand, for any political system to become stable, it is necessary that its procedures and symbols are both internalized and traditionalized; they should not be accepted just for their utility but should be valued as such, as intrinsically meritorious and valuable, endowed with inherent goodness; in other words, the new procedures and values must themselves be turned into "tradition," something that must be nurtured with care, developed further, and made strong. No society lives without traditions and the essential challenge of modernity is not the destruction of tradition but the traditionalization of modernity itself.[23] In the context of caste and politics, this means two things. First, those elements in the caste system that have a secular and integrative potential should be strengthened at the expense of the more obscurantist and dysfunctional elements. This, we have seen, is already happening. Second, the new modes of institutional articulation that secular democratic politics has provided to the social system must themselves become enduring parts of India's traditions. This has yet to take place. The essential test of India's strategy of political development lies in this criterion of "tradition of modernity." And the test of the great social system of India with its proverbial capabilities of assimilation and tolerance also lies in the same criterion. Will it prove pliable enough to imbibe the new system of values and institutions as vital traditions of Indian society? It is a criterion that replaces the dichotomy in which the old is sought to be wholly replaced by the new.

Notes

1. An earlier version of this chapter appeared as an introductory essay in Rajni Kothari, ed., *Caste in Indian Politics* (New Delhi, 1969).
2. This is not only true of the Marxologists in the West and in India. (Curiously, the Communists themselves in the Soviet Union, China, and eastern Europe do not suffer from such a misconception of the role of politics.) Some of the more creative among American social scientists are prone to such theorizing. See especially Barrington Moore, Jr., *Social Origins of Dictatorship and Democracy* (Boston, 1967). In India the most systematic exponent of politics

as a reflection of class positions is A.R. Desai. See his *Social Background of Indian Nationalism* (Bombay, 1959).

3. Lloyd I. Rudolph, "The Modernity of Tradition: The Democratic Incarnation of Caste in India," *The American Political Science Review*, LIX, No. 4, December, 1965. The dichotomy between voluntary and caste forms of organization alluded to in the text was also drawn by Lloyd I. Rudolph and Susanne Hoeber Rudolph in an earlier analysis, in "The Political Role of India's Caste Associations,"*Pacific Affairs*, XXXIII, No. 1, March, 1960. As in our comment on their *Modernity of Tradition in* Chapter III, however, we should state once again that the analysis provided by the Rudophs is a substantial improvement on earlier political scientists. Our only criticism is that they have overstated their case.

4. See Carolyn Elliott's study of Kammas and Reddis in Andhra Pradesh in Kothari, ed., *Caste in Indian Politics, op. cit.*

5. See, however, the illuminating essay of Irawati Karve, *Hindu Society—An Interpretation* (Poona: Deccan College, 1961) where she develops the concept of "agglomeration."

6. On the integrating role of varna, see M.N. Srinivas, *Religion and Society among the Coorgs of South India* (Bombay, 1962). The quotes are from Srinivas's work.

7. The concepts of "sanskritization" and "Westernization" have been made familiar by M.N. Srinivas. Sanskritization is an influence that leads lower castes to emulate the practices of the Brahminic castes in their search for status and recognition, while the Brahminic castes themselves are exposed to the influence of Westernization. For Srinivas's most recent statements on the subject, see his *Social Change in Modern India* (Berkeley, 1966) and " The Cohesive Role of Sanskritization" (mimeographed, University of Delhi, 1966). For an empirical treatment of secularization, and the submergence of sanskritization and Westernization under it, see the studies in *Caste in Indian Politics, op.cit.* Srinivas has also devoted a chapter of his book to secularization.

8. The term "entrenched caste" is to be distinguished from "dominant caste" as used by M.N. Srinivas. According to Srinivas's criteria, a dominant caste not only exercises preponderant influence economically and politically but is also "numerically the strongest in the village or local area." (" The Dominant Caste in Rampura," *American Anthropologist*, February, 1959). The entrenched caste, on the other hand, while it fulfills the chief criterion of economic and political power, and is usually "high" in terms of ritual status, may be numerically small, and it usually is. In regions where large peasant castes are found in "entrenched" positions, however, there may be considerable overlap between the two concepts although in such cases to talk of whole cases as being "entrenched," or even "dominant," may be misleading.

9. Examples are Brahmin versus non-Brahmin in Madras and Maharashtra. Rajput versus Jat in Rajasthan, Baniya-Brahmin versus Patidar in Gujarat,

Kayastha versus Rajput in Bihar, Kamma versus Reddi in Andhra, and Nair versus Ezhava in Kerala. Often in the development of this process, as one polarization is resolved in favor of one caste or caste category, new polarizations emerge, such as between Patidars and Kshatriyas in Gujarat or Marathas and Mahars in Maharashtra. At other times, however, more complicated and fragmented constellations of power have emerged.

10. This factionalism must be distinguished from the traditional factionalism prevalent in caste society, which is more on lines of kin-group and lineage. The factionalism discussed here is one that grows out of political competition in which more than one personalized network of support contend for secular power.

11. For a brief review of the opposite positions on this question and a general statement on the role of caste in social integration, see Surajit Sinha, "Caste in India: Its Essential Pattern of Socio-cultural Integration" in Anthony de Reuck, ed., *Caste and Race: Comparative Approaches* (London, 1967). For those interested in caste in a comparative perspective, the volume as a whole is recommended.

12. See his "Changing Political Behavior in Rural Indian Society," *Economic and Political Weekly*, II, Nos. 33-35. Special Number, August, 1967.

13. There is increasing literature on caste associations. Rudolph and Rudolph, "The Political Role of India's Caste Associations," *op. cit.*, is still the best treatment of the subject. On caste federations see Rajni Kothari and Rushikesh Maru, "Federating for Political Interests: The Kshatriyas of Gujarat," in *Caste in Indian Politics, op.cit.*; F.G. Bailey has talked of these formations as a "new *group*, a new corporate group with political interests but recruited not solely on the basis of political interest." See his "Two Villages in Orissa (India)," in Max Gluckman, ed., *Closed Systems and Open Minds: The Limits of Naivety in Social Anthropology* (Chicago, 1964). (Emphasis as in author's original.) See also Bailey's "Closed Social Stratification," *Archives Européennes de Sociologie*, IV, 1963.

14. See "Federating for Political Interests," *ibid.*, for the main differences between a caste association and a caste federation, and a documented case of the phases through which a caste federation achieves a distinctive political identity.

15. Such a view is expressed at various levels. Thus the Congress Party, at its historic session at Avadi in 1955 (when among other things it adopted the goal of a "socialistic pattern of society"), resolved that no active member of the Congress should hold simultaneous membership in any caste or communal organization. In effect, the Congress leadership ruled out the participation of caste organizations in the party. For an impact of the resolution on the internal decisions of a caste federation, see "Federating for Political Interests," *ibid.*

16. *Ibid.*

17. Thus it is not surprising that in urban metropolitan areas and in states like West Bengal that are overwhelmingly dominated by metropolitan areas

anomic political activity has had a greater play than in regions where organized group interaction on the basis of caste federations and rural political elites has created viable coalitions.

18. As mentioned in Chapter 4, the Constitution of India provides for a variety of special benefits for the scheduled castes and tribes; new government programs have added to these benefits and provided protection against discrimination. The most important of all provisions, of course, is the reservation of seats in the central and state legislatures and in all local institutions where the elective principle works. Sometimes the reservations exceed the proportional weight of these communities.
19. What Robert A. Dahl has characterized as "dispersed inequalities" seem to operate here. The traditional position of those groups was one of "cumulative inequalities." *Who Governs*? (New Haven, 1961).
20. Following prolonged agitations by the All Party Hill Leaders Conference (APHLC) the central government agreed to create an autonomous state for the tribals within the state of Assam (known as a "subfederation"), a political innovation in democratic participation. The Nagas have also carved out a separate state for themselves. In other states like Bihar and Orissa, important tribal parties have succeeded in forcing the successive political coalitions to accord to them a substantive voice in state politics. In other areas like Madhya Pradesh they have not been so successful. Also, despite the success of select groups, the tribals are on the whole still an underprivileged group in Indian politics. For further discussion, see Chapter 8.
21. Rajni Kothari and Tarun Sheth, "Extent and Limits of Community Voting: The Case of Baroda East" in Myron Weiner and Rajni Kothari, ed., *Indian Voting Behaviour* (Calcutta, 1965); Paul Brass, *Factional Politics in an Indian State:The Congress Party in Uttar Pradesh* (Berkeley 1965), Chs. VI & VII; Bashiruddin Ahmed, "Congress Defeat in Amroha: A Case Study in One Party Dominance" in *Party System and Election Studies*, Occasional Papers I of the Centre for the Study of Developing Societies (New Delhi, 1967). For a trend analysis on these points, see Gopal Krishna, "Electoral Participation and Political Integration" in *Context of Electoral Change in India* (New Delhi, Centre for the Study of Developing Societies, 1969).
22. For a theoretical treatment of the "reintegrative" process and the role of parochial identities in the same, see D.L. Sheth and Rajni Kothari, "Social Change, Political Integration and the Value Process," paper presented to the *International Roundtable on Values in Politics*, Dubrovnik, Yugoslavia (mimeo., 1965).
23. Rajni Kothari, "Tradition and Modernity Revisited," *Government and Opposition*, 3, No. 3 (Summer, 1968)

7

Political Culture and Socialization

IN THE PRECEDING CHAPTERS we have employed the method of comparative politics to interpret India's historical and institutional modernization, and the response of indigenous society to such modernization. But the concrete political experience of a nation is anchored in a specific cluster of traditions and orientations. By closely examining the interaction between enduring themes of its political culture and the changing realities of its politics, we are likely to find important clues to the seeming ambivalences of the country's developmental experience, to view its achievements and shortcomings in some kind of a perspective, and to refine our tools in assessing its future possibilities.

We may be able to ask: Are the modernist developments enabling the country to better handle some of its age - old issues? Are they filling in some of the crucial gaps in the capacity of this ancient society to find its place in the modern world? Or are the cultural and psychological conditions such as to pose serious handicaps in its way? The cultural and personality variables and the patterns of socialization of individuals and groups provide one dimension of political dynamics; the institutional and behavioral changes brought about by modern political and economic development and the pressing problems that call for solution in the ongoing system provide another. Neither can be considered in isolation. It is the purpose of this chapter to suggest hypotheses on the manner in which the two are interacting in contemporary India.

We shall try to provide an overview of the cultural and historical perspective of contemporary nation building in India, suggest a few propositions on the distinctive themes of its political culture, relate these to patterns of socialization and acculturation, and consider how the institutionalization of a new political center entails, on the one hand, a reinterpretation of tradition and, on the other hand, a basic shift in the very structure of antecedent consensus.

PERSPECTIVE OF HISTORY

India is perhaps the only great historical civilization that has maintained its cultural integrity without identifying itself with a particular political center. In contrast to the great historical empires, the unity of India owed itself not to the authority of a given political system but to the wide diffusion of the cultural symbols, the spiritual values, and the structure of roles and functions characteristic of a continuous civilization. The essential identity of India has not been political but cultural. To be sure, as we discussed in the last chapter, there always was a secular component to India's culture and it was through a constant interplay between the political and the cultural, the secular and the spiritual, that the system was able to adapt itself to changing situations. Still, there has all along been a marked disassociation between government and society, and the basic identities by which Indians have felt themselves to be Indian are not political but cultural.

It is not very clear which specific elements in India's historical development account for its cultural continuity despite the absence of identity with a strong political center, and indeed despite a chronic state of political instability and changeability.[1] What is clear, however, is the early dissociation between the spiritual and the secular components of Indian civilization, without at the same time giving rise to the ecclesiastical-temporal battles so characteristic of the West; and a constant interplay and cross-cutting between these two polarities. In part this was because the establishment of political centers was the work of "foreign" conquests, while the rest of society adapted to the changing fortunes of kings and conquerors. And, with the exception of a few barbaric ravages by passing invaders, the conquerors, in turn, respected the autonomy of society and its religious traditions.

This cross-cutting between the spiritual and the secular, institutionalized by alliances between the political and the priestly figures, has been the chief mechanism of Indian society's absorptive capacity. It has also permitted differential and segmented change, avoiding too much "aggregation," without at the same time eroding society's faith in certain basic elements of its culture. In the social and religious spheres, it permitted a concomitance of certain universalistic movements for change (Buddhism, Vaishnavism, Sikkhism) with traditionalist-militant movements for the preservation of antecedent forms and practices (à la Shankaracharya), while both kinds of movements continuously reformulated basic elements in India's cultural tradition. Hence, when in the nineteenth century elites from leading social strata led ideological or reformist movements, this appeared to a majority of Indians as more in line with earlier movements of ideological perfection and ejection of the "wrongs" that had crept into Hindu society, rather than as any revolutionary upsetting of the social order.

We stress these "traditions of change" in Indian society. The implicit contrast often drawn between the stability of traditional society and the upheavals that accompany the changes brought by modernization fails to account for a case like India where there has been this constant interplay between the forces of continuity and the forces of change which inform tradition's capacity for absorption and retentiveness. In the words of a perceptive observer from abroad, "... we will have to think of Indian modernity in terms of the continuity of India's ever changing tradition."[2] Even more important, it was because of the continuity of India's cultural identity that far-reaching changes in the secular sphere were easy to effect from time to time. Lack of a strong identification with a given political order, the presence of a retentive base in the cultural system, and the tendency to de-emphasize the importance of secular changes, were precisely the conditions that permitted a continuous adaptation to, rather than hostility toward, changes in the political sphere. There was little sense of a threat to the "essence" of Indianness for the essence was not really political. In historical societies with a more continuous secular tradition and in which the dominant identity was with the political order, such changes have given rise to both prolonged resistance and a considerable sense of humiliation and futility when they eventually did come about.[3] Viewed in this way, we also can see why in the most recent period, despite the nationalist creed, India's modernist elite showed no marked hostility to the adoption of apparently alien political institutions for the country's modernization.

To this point about the functional utility of an antecedent dissociation between cultural and secular traditions must also be added the point that both these traditions were embedded in a differentiated structure of identities, and in a world-view that was not only highly permissive and accommodative but also self-consciously pluralistic. While the dissociation permitted a wide range of changes in the political sphere, the pluralistic antecedents provided a hospitable ground for giving a "democratic" orientation to these changes. Indeed the democratic ideology fitted very nicely Indians' predilection for the autonomy of social and primordial institutions, the legitimacy of intermediate structures between state and society, the freedom to retain local identities, and the tolerance of cultural and religious diversities.

Such a structuring of identities explains why the usual observation that in the new nations participation in national political associations and voting serve to exacerbate "parochial" identities does not apply with great force to India. For the so-called parochial identities were not political in India for a considerable period of time. When ultimately a political system emerged at the national level, it assumed the characteristics of a new all-India cultural tradition rather than a mere juxtaposition of pre-existing tribal or territorial loyalties as has happened in some other new nations.[4] In time when the new political system was dispersed and decentralized, regional and linguistic identities did emerge and these have increasingly provided material for political conflict, but by that time the exchange equations of the new all-India frame had been well established. A clear distinction should, therefore, be drawn between segmentation based on new kinds of political identity (regional or linguistic) and the antecedent segmentation of caste and community. The former informs the political exchanges among the higher elites while the latter provides the stuff of mass politics. Commentators who see an identity crisis in India resulting from the difficulty of transferring from parochial to national identity draw their inferences mainly from the former.[5] They also seem to place too exclusive an emphasis on national identity, following the historical experience of the West, whereas the Indian model of identity formation is more likely to be structured through a series of intermediate identities.

On the other hand, the fact that the larger identities in India were essentially cultural meant also that the new political center had considerable freedom of maneuver, gave rise to a new and distinctive elite, and made it possible to effect a new kind of socialization for those who entered the modern sector. To be sure, the antecedent traditions of subsystem autonomy and tolerance of social and religious diversity contributed to the new crystallization. But it is also true that there was much that was novel in the new state and the political and social ideology to which it was committed. Largely due to the relative absence of encroachment from the other centers of society, the elite in the political and intellectual centers could be socialized along new lines, identifying with ideas and institutions that were alien to begin with, and undertaking an ambitious design for living for their people. Again, although it sounds paradoxical, the new political order could make its inroads into society in so short a time largely because of the lack of pre-existing political identities. On the other hand, India's great modernizers did not view their task as one of hostility to primordial and local traditions in the name of some total or unifying ideology. The dominant note of Gandhi's message to India's urban intellectuals was to go to the villages and "build bridges," a message which is still very much alive; adult franchise and economic development have only added to its significance.[6] Responding to such a style the traditional elites have adapted to the new dispensation and reordered the basis of their interaction with the political sphere, while still retaining the autonomy of the social and cultural spheres.

The transition from endogamous and restrictive caste panchayats to caste associations and caste federations is symptomatic of this continuing orientation towards a diffuse, assimilative and consensual cultural style. The general result of such an interplay has been the articulation of a secular order which is highly differentiated and segmental, and respectful of the autonomy of various subsystems. In this manner India has been able to avoid the convulsive experiences of societies with long-standing secular identities which started their new "revolutionary" careers by rejecting the legitimacy of other spheres in a self-righteous assertion of the supremacy of the political order.

Such an orientation has had its disadvantages. The absence of a compelling political identity overriding local and primordial identities has led to certain negative predispositions towards secular authority. For example, Indians lack an overriding sense of secular identity. Given a long tradition of dissociation between cultural and political spheres and of in-difference and passivity towards the political center, India has developed a value system that is strongly oriented to rural agricultural society (despite the existence of large urban areas for a long time). Absence of a strong and persisting political center meant that the aggregative demands on parochial identities were minimal. This produced a lack of a strong internalization of civic authority, a low level of commitment to political tasks, lack of any marked compulsion to provide active support to political elites, and in general an absence of predominant collective attachments beyond the primordial and local levels. To this must be added a certain sense of distrust and insecurity in dealing with large and impersonal collectivities, largely owing to a lack of intense experience and continuous participation in such collectivities. The problem is accentuated by a general lack of a sense of national history and of a cultivated national pride as found in the more secular political cultures. We shall see later how all this is embedded in patterns of socialization in Indian family and in spiritual and religious traditions.

Closely related to weak civic orientations is a low scale of expectations from secular authority. In stressing permissiveness and adaptability Indian culture has so far paid little attention to the performance aspects of collective behavior. The result is both a low scale of demands upon political authority—which may be desirable in the traditional period—and a weak supportive orientation toward authority—which may prolong the period of transition.

Another consequence of low levels of demands and supports

is that conflicts and cleavages in the periphery may keep mounting and lead to a state of chronic frustrations while political mechanisms for aggregating and resolving these cleavages may fail to develop. Here the emphasis on tolerating rather than resolving conflicts may prove highly dysfunctional. The rigidities of a caste system which are not made the target of purposive political action may further contribute to such a state of frustration and a pervasive cynicism in collective orientations.

Finally, when such a society enters the political age and is under pressure from national and international sources to stand up to the challenges of such an age, the problem of regulating the interrelationships among different segments that have had autonomous and relatively independent modes of development may become acute. In other words, whereas the need to develop a differentiated and plural framework of modern politics may be more easily met in India than in more centralized political cultures, by the same token the need to develop aggregative mechanisms and action orientations which come from overriding political commitments may provide the major challenge for India's political modernization.[7] There is reason to believe that the transformations taking place in the caste system, the growing role of the party system and other intermediate structures, and the striking autonomy of the political elites and their penetration in the manner of a new cultural tradition may ultimately create the proper conditions for the channeling of aggressive drives towards the new political center. And in the meantime the dissociation between primordial and secular structures and the low level of demands may perhaps prove functional. A more detailed analysis is needed before assessing the outcome of such an interaction between antecedent conditions and new impacts.

THEMES OF POLITICAL CULTURE

Much of what follows is in the form of analytical generalizations that are "unproved." While the identification of particular orientations of political culture can be a powerful aid in understanding, it is bound to be gross and may not hold true for all times or all sections of society, and certainly not for all individuals. In a country as vast and heterogeneous as India this should be obvious. On the other hand, we have already noted that what has imparted unity and homogeneity to India over the centuries is precisely this sharing of a common culture and socialization into its basic structure and orientations. We are mainly concerned here with those orientations that are politically significant. We shall present them as major themes in political culture, themes that appear of an enduring value, and are likely to influence political development in modern India.

1. TOLERANCE OF AMBIGUITY

India has a high tolerance of ambiguity. Historically and culturally Indian society has been eclectic, encompassing a great many differences and contradictions and used to much uncertainty and unpredictability. It has rationalized such experience by developing a concept of unity that is embedded in diversity and self-consciously admits contradictions in the scheme of things, and it has managed these uncertainties and contradictions through a highly formalized hierarchy of statuses and roles. Philosophically, the Indians are prone to think that everyone must work out his own self-identity and self-realization (salvation). Faced by a successive influx of different influences and challenges, Indian society has admitted considerable ideological flexibility and has tolerated different value premises and doctrinal positions. The various movements of ideological reform and continuous adaptation in an uncertain and changing political situation have led to a marked tolerance of cleavages and factional disputes, autonomy of individual and group ethics, and the cultivation of differentiated and overlapping identities. Both group values and individual morality are conceived as transient and situation-specific. Hence the legitimacy of ethical relativism and tolerance of dissent. Hence also a peculiar concept of morality "according to which there are as many moral codes as appointed stations in life, rather than one common ethical system for all men regardless of position and social function..."[8] This outlook has produced great ambiguity in the structuring of belief systems, and a propensity to learn to live with such ambiguity, manage it through doctrines of coexistence and ultimate synthesis of diverse positions, and order the moral dimension of life in the image of a necessary diversity and uncertainty of the real world.

This is linked to the Indian concept of reality and truth, which consists of a reconciliation of seeming opposites and a convergence of disparate and contradictory view towards an Ultimate (void) where all positions meet and in which all specificities dissolve. Truth is the ultimate reality (the Absolute), everything else is relative. Truth cannot be achieved as an abstraction outside of the self but comes as higher experience of the consciousness.[9] To the contention that truth in itself cannot provide a basis for morality since it does not tell one what is right and what is wrong, the answer is that one must do what one believes to be right through a process of self-realization and moral excellence.[10] As the ultimate Being (the Absolute, the Brahman) is impersonal, it needs to be experienced and declared by individual persons. Hence the notion of "myriad paths" to reality. Hence also the notion of synthesis. The modern expression of this life-style is the belief that Indians must work out a synthesis between tradition and modernity, which are not conceived as necessarily contradictory.[11]

One can see how the above fits with the Indian propensity for plural identities rather than a single overriding identity with central authority, as well as how it has been easy for Indians to be socialized in the democratic norms of individual freedom, ideological flexibility, and subsystem autonomy. However, it is necessary to make two other points in order to set the Indian emphasis on "tolerance" in a proper perspective.

The first point is with regard to the *ordering of ambiguity*. Any system that is wide open and flexible develops rigidities in some sphere, which imparts a sense of confidence and maneuverability. In India we find this in the social and institutional sphere. Ideologically Indian society has faced many challenges and this has produced a high degree of ideological tolerance and flexibility. Institutionally, however, Indian society has been traditionally very rigid, working out a precise and clearly identifiable hierarchy, formalized rules, and conventions, conformity with which was mandatory and defined by birth, and a system of substantive and symbolic distances which articulated the hierarchy in a definitive and predictable manner. Thus developed a peculiar combination of a high tolerance of ambiguity and diversity in thought and value patterns on the one hand and a deep concern with formal rituals and compliance with "rules of the system" on the other. By being institutionally rigid but ideologically tolerant, society became capable of integrating diverse subgroups and sects and cults. On the other hand, this led to a kind of tolerance which was only another name for intolerance, namely tolerance of injustice and disparities, and of humiliation and deprivation by superior individuals and groups. Such deprivation was considered part of the natural order of society: it was a function of one's station in life. To be sure, this tolerance of deprivation has allowed an easy acceptance of authority and its symbols, deference to higher-ups and the older generation, and has prevented rebelliousness and disorder. But it has also produced a low morale in collective orientations, too much submissiveness and a sense of futility, indirect rejection and withdrawal from the larger system without concomitant tension-building and an aggressive search for alternatives, and considerable cynicism regarding the use and abuse of authority. Such cynicism is most noticeable in times of change and uncertainty.

The second point relates to the social transformation of modern times. As just mentioned, traditionally Indian society has been ideologically tolerant but socially rigid. However, once social rigidity (in the form of a legitimized caste hierarchy) begins to break down and fluidity sets in under the impact of modern changes, ideological tolerance may in turn, at least during the transitional period, begin to break down, as it is no longer possible to integrate various groups in the model of a caste society. Such intolerance can be the consequence of a sense of strain and insecurity resulting from the disintegration of antecedent role distribution and summation systems. In contemporary India this is happening in those strata of the population which have been exposed to processes of politicization, urbanization, and modern education.

It appears, however, that despite this strain, the Indian tradition of tolerance of ambiguity and ideological flexibility will continue to inform the development of its new identity as a nation state. Already this is apparent in the approach to minorities, strategies of coalition-making, and tolerance of wide-ranging dissent and opposition. Indeed it may be that while the immediate impact of structural and institutional changes may lead to a sense of insecurity and consequently a propensity towards intolerance, this is not likely to affect the long-embedded traditions of tolerance and even less the community life style of plural identities and segmental autonomy which has enabled Indians to survive the continuous onslaughts that they have received as a civilization. On the contrary, contemporary processes of change and change absorption show that this lifestyle has provided Indian society with a mechanism for integrating the ambiguities generated by the process of political modernization. In the words of a valued colleague, the real point of interest is:

> ... how the people's historical experiences of politics and the links which these experiences have had with modal identities can be hitched to the needs of new political forms, how the primordial identities can be made to yield a culturally viable national political style, and how this new style on its part can be integrated within the community life style as a legitimate force of change. Political culture in such a case is mainly the evolving style of meeting a historical challenge.[12]

2. AUTHORITY AS FRAGMENTED

An important component of this lifestyle has been the notion of authority as fragmented, dispersed, and intermittent. This is true in the Indian family and kinship system, as we shall see when we discuss socialization. It is also true in the social system of caste and community and generally in village life. By and large Indian social structure is based on the culture of superior-subordinate relationships with a clear allocation of rights and duties across the boundaried which determine the legitimate social hierarchy. Only when ambiguity exists in regard to a particular issue across these boundaries is there need for a specified elite to arbitrate in the dispute. By its nature such an exercise of authority roles is intermittent and temporary.

This conception of authority as arbitration (which incidentally also implies that the judicial functions is the essence of politics) is also carried over in the wider political system. The chief political role of the king or his accredited representative was to arbitrate in disputes brought to him; for the rest, local society was to be left to its own ways of managing its affairs. The same was the function of a "leader,"[13] whether it was priest, teacher (*guru*), or the judicial-political head of a given unit. Given the "pervasive factionalism" of the Indian village and lineage systems as well as continuous bickering across village and territorial boundaries, this role was important, but its exercise was not continuous and not very institutionalized.[14] The internalization of the formal rules of the social system took care of the main mechanisms of conflict and consensus; authority was invoked only when things got out of hand and there was uncertainty with regard to the rules, especially in times of change and institutional fluidity.

Such a role of authority has been carried over in modern times, resulting in the great emphasis in Indian politics on consensus reached through the intervention of a higher level administrator (such as the district collector) or politician (such as the Congress Party functionary).[15] This was true under the British; it is true even now. Another result is the popularity of notions of arbitration in areas where disputes are likely to be recurrent, as in the legislation governing trade union disputes.[16]

With the penetration of the new political center, the nature of hierarchy has expanded upward. This has provided indigenous society with ways of transcending the capriciousness and oppression of local mechanisms of dispute resolution. But the notion of authority as essentially arbitrative has continued. Such an orientation partly explains why in modern times there is frequent recourse to government and government leaders in the settlement of issues which in other societies would be considered not the business of government.[17] As the concept of government is essentially a juridical concept, it is not considered improper to ask higher levels of authority to mediate in local disputes and their decisions are normally taken as binding. Thus in spite of the continuous factionalism in the Congress Party, what is remarkable is that there have been very few occasions when the verdict of the higher level arbitrator in a local dispute (and there is quite a machinery of dispute resolution along these lines) has not been considered binding. On the other hand, such a tradition has facilitated enlargement of local society toward the larger political community. The higher level leaders have also followed the antecedent style, have refrained from imposing a completely alien structure of rules, and have instead sought to arrive at a "consensus" through the processes of slow mediation and arbitration, sounding out opposite positions, and finding a middle course that would not greatly please any side but would have to be accepted by all. This, rather than the formal confrontation between organized interests, is what constitutes the "bargaining culture" of India.[18]

In the articulation of this bargaining culture there has been considerable fluidity as regards which disputes to take where. A low level of institutionalization of the bargaining process has been inherent in the notion of authority as dispersed and intermittent. But by the same token the governmental sphere achieves an inconspicuous growth, becomes an agent of considerable change, and yet does this through mediating in existing relationships rather than by imposing itself on them. Authority continues to be dispersed and through such dispersal encompasses more and more of social reality. The legitimacy of the larger political process and, contrariwise, the functional role of intermediate structures in the articulation of this process thus become mutually reinforcing owing to the prevailing orientations to authority. Here is another instance of the shaping of the new politics in the life-style of the culture of society.

3. IDEOLOGY AND POLITICS

Another subtle adaptation of an antecedent norm leading to a major transformation is found in the relationship between ideology and politics. Alongside the role of the elite in the resolution of conflicts, there has all along been another role perception of the elite in society. This is its role as morality-inducer, as exhorter and interpreter of the moral dimension of this-worldly existence. In more centralized secular cultures like China the state is considered to be the custodian of society's virtue and thus the natural socializer of citizens in things moral.[19] In India with its tradition of society's autonomy from the state, such a monopolizing stance of the rulers was not accepted (despite Kautilya[20]). Instead, the role of the elite as custodian of the moral standards of society and as a model of exemplary behavior was performed by a special class of literati, the Brahmins. At the same time the political rulers too were supposed to pursue "heroic" tasks that would bring great and unpredictable achievements to their credit — as through military conquests — and thus legitimize their claim to charisma and a place alongside the gods. And it was not uncommon for the secular heroes to partake of the charisma of the priestly class.

Now what is remarkable in this respect is the convergence of the traditional Brahminic and the modern secular images in the leaders of contemporary politics. The political elite constitutes the new priesthood of modern India, partly because of its revolutionary role in bringing about mammoth changes, partly because of the exemplary and saintly or the grand and heroic styles of men like Gandhi and Nehru, and partly because of the overriding importance of the politician in social life and his growing intimacy with society's life processes. One result of this convergence is the expectation of the politician as a moral man, the frequent resort to exhortation and sermonizing, and the pressure to make promises and assurances that almost everyone knows cannot be fulfilled. Indians value the leader's combining the qualities of a man of thought and a man of action: hence the great fascination for men like Nehru. Here, traditional role images both legitimize the new bearers of the culture's traditions and expect from them roles that do not belong to them *qua* politicians. On the other hand, there does not seem to be great anxiety as regards the inevitable gap between the ideal type and the actual embodiment of the ideal type, between the moral idiom of the politician and his actual behavior. Hence the verbal insistence on consensus in spite of rampant factionalism in almost every walk of life. Hence also the constant denunciation, even exaggeration, of corruption in public life without any great institutional attempt at its eradication.

In modern times this accent on verbalization has translated itself into an accent on ideology. It must be remembered—a point to which we shall return when we discuss patterns of socialization — that in Indian culture high ideals have always been stressed; its ideological stance has always been moral. But the general permissiveness of faults and imperfections have made for a high degree of tolerance of the gap between what is said and what is done. Hypocrisy in public life is understood and tolerated, indeed expected. It is part of the overall cynicism that Indians are known to display towards matters social or political. Even in the individual the aspiration is generally towards the cultural norm which is very high, but failure to reach the ideal does not cause great distress. All this also explains why one meets with so much exaggeration in Indian politics, with a tendency to set abstract goals but not to translate them into concrete demands, to make high-sounding resolutions but a correspondingly weak implementation of such resolutions, which, however, does not cause any great sense of shame or defeat.

4. TRUST AND DISTRUST

Our discussion of cultural orientations to the ideal and the real lead us to a consideration of perhaps the most crucial theme of political culture, namely the extent of institutionalization of social and political norms, consequent predictability in the behavior of one's fellow men, and the resulting patterns of trust and distrust in collective undertakings. In India there has been traditionally a rather weak institutionalization of objective checks against self-centered behavior (hence the great emphasis on exhortation on the part of the elite). The Indian view of the innate nature of man is unlike both the Christian notion of man's inherent sinfulness and the Confucian notion of his inherent goodness. Hence there is neither the belief that society should deliberately tame self-centered impulses nor the belief that proper socialization will bring out the natural goodness of man. Instead the stress is on one's own "deed," on the accumulation of credit or debit in accordance with what one has himself done, regulated by the impersonal law of *karma*. Morality, according to Indian thought, has its primary reference to the individual, and the aim of duty is to one's own self-realization. Morality is not principally "other-regarding" as in the Western conception but "self-regarding," to use Mill's famous dichotomy.[21] It is this ideal of the right deed as a path of self-redemption which is conveyed by the law of karma,"

... the law which apportions to each individual what he has himself earned by his own deeds.... There are thus no duties which are not strictly speaking duties to self, and duty in the sense of positive moral aid to others is self-contradictory in its very conception."[22]

An important aspect of moral orientation is the extent to which individuals and groups are able to trust each other in common pursuits. Here one is struck by the pervasive skepticism of the Indian mind, skepticism in regard to the possibilities of achieving something collectively, a basic suspicion of others, suspicion especially of authority and its intentions and a fear of underhanded and circuitous dealings by others.[23] Even among elite circles — professional as well as political — there is an absence of abiding trust in one's colleagues. It is found easier to work in superior-subordinate roles than as equals; there is anxiety about the stability and dependability of coalitions; and there is continuous concern as to whether the other person will fulfill his part of a contract. Lack of institutionalized checks against self-centered behavior makes life un-predictable especially in non-primordial and secular settings, and this aggravates the sense of suspicion of others. The usual way out of this predicament has been transcendentalism, submitting to a supposedly superior being.

Once again the pressures of modern life and the increasing involvement in large scale collective actions contribute to change in these orientations. Even so, it is interesting that so far trust and *camaraderie* have best come out in settings where it was possible to submit to a charismatic and transcendental authority rather than where people of the same stature had to work together. Gandhi provided this in a unique manner — and was himself remarkably free of any sense of threat from others — so did Nehru. But even Nehru was suspicious of leaders who rose to national stature and appeared to challenge his position in the country.[24] The post-Nehru period, which depends so much on the ability to forge a truly collective leadership, has time and again revealed the basic suspiciousness of Indian political life, even on the highest level. Indeed perhaps the principal challenge of the present leadership at the center is with regard to this ability of coalitional partners to trust each other as equals.

We shall return to the question of the growth of collective

orientations in contemporary India through the very ambiguity of its Janus-like self-image. But before we do that, we ought to deal briefly with the basic personality characteristics and moral beliefs that are a product of patterns of socialization peculiar to the Indian culture and which contribute to the orientations to politics that we have been discussing in the preceding pages. Having looked at the specifically political themes of political culture, we should now see how these are embedded in typical personality configurations (arising from childhood socialization) on the one hand, and in belief systems arising from the interpretation and reinterpretation of cultural and philosophical themes (adult learning) on the other.

POLITICAL SOCIALIZATION

There has been an increasing volume of specialized work on personality and learning components of moral orientations in Indian culture, including childhood socialization.[25] We will not even attempt to summarize this. Instead we will briefly present some of these findings which we think have implications for the analysis of India's political culture. We do this through a series of related comments.

1. Almost all students of Indian personality have been struck by the extreme indulgence of the Indian child, principally by the mother but also by other members of the family. This gives rise to a sense of omnipotence in the infant, a feeling that is fortified by nursing practices and physical proximity with the mother for an extended period of time. This has two important consequences. Lacking the frustrations of early deprivation there is a weak development of inward aggression, a low compulsion to channelize aggressive energies with reference to symbols of authority, and hence a weak superego. On the other hand, there develops in the Indian child a strong tendency for inward-directed motivations, an urge for "self-development," and thus a strong ego ideal. An important consequence of this is that moral energy does not come from the pressure of guilt feelings arising from a failure to live up to the superego, and depends crucially on a self-cultivated ego ideal. Self- development and fulfillment of the ideals set for

the ego rather than social obligation and the unconscious image of authority become the main drive for moral action.

This creates wide gaps in individual capacities. For the average Indian the constraints of authority are not intensely felt and as morality has reference to self-directed and introspective perfection, the compulsion to "perform" is not very great. On the other hand, the culture develops high and universalist ideals with which the creative and power-motivated individuals strongly identify: the theme that ego itself is the Absolute drives them to ever higher levels of perfection.[26] This gulf between the drives of ordinary men and those of "great men" results in abstract concepts of duty and morality and a personality ideal that is high and remote, realizable only by exceptional men whose authority derives from their capacity to embody virtues that are lacking in ordinary men.[27] Hence the emphasis on spontaneity and uncertainty. Hence too the exaggerated role of the guru, the ascetic, and the warrior, and indirectly of a hierarchy of roles, and of charisma.

2. There are characteristics of the Indian family structure which confirm the above tendencies, both during infanthood and when the child enters the stage of verbal interactions. Four points need to be noted here. First, there is a diffuse structure of authority and a dispersal of family roles. This is not so much because of the joint or extended family (which is more a cultural ideal and thus an intimate part of one's consciousness than a regular social reality) as due to the intimate structure of kinship ties, both paternal and maternal, and the crowded and exposed structure of households. It is also due to the belief that the father should not be much concerned with the bringing up of the child who is more a transient member of a group than an individual belonging to a discreet pair of adults; the father too is only one among a hierarchy of authority figures. The intimate interactions between father and son, resulting in a sense of conflict and rivalry, that are usually associated with the aggressive image of authority in other cultures are not as pronounced in the Indian family whose main idiom is in terms of mutual obligations rather than any clear-cut structure of authority.

Second, both because of its marked indulgence by different kins and the diffuse structure of authority in which it lives, the Indian child has considerable scope to maneuver for satisfying its demands, alternative models provided by uncles and aunts, grandparents and elder brothers and sisters, besides the parents, and on the whole a wide spectrum of images and ideals from which to choose. These factors further weaken the superego and strengthen the abstract idealism of the ego.

Third, although there is considerable indulgence and a ready response whenever the child cries for help, there is also a great deal of neglect in all other matters. Usually it is left alone, in the cot or on the hip, receiving attention only when it cries or creates a fuss. "Adult interaction with babies is generally aimed at producing a cessation of response rather than a stimulation of it."[28] Thus a baby is "never alone, never the center of attention."[29] Again, the fact of a large number of adults around and the notion of birth as a basis of status in family and kinship systems lead to a process of socialization that is impersonal. "The child has a sense of security in that there are many adults in the family with whom he can, or rather must, identify. But, by the same token, he cannot identify himself enough with any particular person."[30] This attitude is carried over when the child grows and enters the stage of conscious learning. The prevailing belief is that the young child learns more by observation and imitation than by formal instruction. While this adds to the individual's autonomy in deciding which among the conflicting role performances he should adopt, the minimal emphasis on conscious instruction and discipline keeps the salience of authority symbols low and less compelling.

Fourth, there are in India no sharp age or generational distinctions. Children, as soon as they can move about and speak, merge imperceptibly into adult life. They are not excluded from adult activities; there is no notion of specialized roles by age brackets, no cultural constraint to exclude the children from adult discussion, no deliberate putting them to bed early. In short, there is no clear- cut image of "bringing up" children in a particular way until their formal education begins. As an Indian official put it to a visiting psychologist from the West "you bring up your children, we live with ours."[31] On the whole a child is treated as part of the timeless and circular process of history while at the same time allowing considerable flexibility and manipulability in value choices and affective behavior. The internalization of restraints arising from linear and time-constrained symbols in other cultures is less compelling in India. The reinforcements needed for a strong superego are lacking in this respect too.

3. All the different characteristics of socialization mentioned so far — extreme indulgence of the infant leading to self-love and a strong ego ideal, the self-directed orientation of moral ideals, a weak internalization of external authority, and a diffuse structure of authority in the family—point to another important characteristic of Indian personality, namely its acceptance of diversity and differences. As the superego is weak there is no great urge to fall in line with the same values and standards; as the principal moral emotion is self-aspiration, the compulsion for centripetal behavior is not intense. Thus the cultural norm that each individual must work at his own destiny is reinforced by orientations developed in early socialization. Hence the easy acceptance of a gap between aspirations and fulfillment as, after all, "not everyone is equal." The structuring of lifestyle on the basis of plural identities, and the tolerance of ambiguities, disparities and uncertainties which were mentioned earlier, here find confirmation.

4. On the other hand, it was mentioned that there is a tendency in Indian culture for seeking order and predictability in the face of these diversities and uncertainties by recourse to rigid institutional hierarchies and strict conformity to formal rules and rituals of the social system. Again one finds elements in socialization that support this tendency. Extreme indulgence of the child whose every cry for pleasure and relief is agreeably solicited by the mother results in patterns of dependence and dominance that persist into adulthood. The role of women kin in early socialization as well as the great dependence on servants and menials in middle-class families greatly accentuate these patterns. Self-reliance is not insisted upon and a relationship of dependence on the mother and others in the family is encouraged, in return for which obedience to the elders and a formalized system of duties and obligations are easily forthcoming. When the individual grows up the pattern persists in the form of superior-subordinate relationships, conformity with formal rules and rituals, and a keen sensitivity to hierarchies of age and status. Observers have been struck by the retinue of subordinates and servants that Indian officers and politicians are used to, as much as by the regard

shown to "seniors" in every walk of life. This leads to an almost magical belief in the power of superior authority,[32] a sense of comfort whenever such authority is available, the tendency to pass on responsibility to higher echelons, and a sense of insecurity in dealing with equals. (In the Indian family, sibling rivalry is almost unknown, as brothers and sisters and cousins get almost automatically arranged hierarchically. Hence the weak socialization in dealing with others of equal status.)

5. From this follows the point that whenever either a primordial or a hierarchical condition is not met, Indians tend to be distrustful and suspicious. The support for such orientations to collective action comes not from any consistent pattern of socialization, as from the paradoxes of Indian personality formation. For instance there is extreme indulgence of the young child but the cultural ideal of adult life is that of self-realization and self-control. As the individual grows up, this ideal is stressed and there develops and unexpected strictness and harshness on behalf of the elders. This leads to an inner sense of instability and insecurity.[33] Or again, whereas there is a long and intense period of maternal indulgence there also comes a sudden withdrawal after this period: the mother withdraws her breast, attends more to father, gets involved in other duties, possibly turns to a younger brother or sister. Now such withdrawal is part of life everywhere; what is peculiar here is that it comes too late which makes it particularly painful and bewildering. The world to which the child had become accustomed, and ruled like a lord, suddenly ends. Nothing seems dependable any more. The lack of trust, insecurity, and the craving to recreate symbols and artifacts on whom one can fully depend can all be traced to this feeling of being let down at an early stage in life.

Such an experience of over-indulgence followed by sudden deprivation produces opposite strains in the personality. The early period of permissiveness and indulgence seems to lay a firm basis for the marked optimism — often unrealistic — of the Indian mind. (The experience of foreigners who find Indians very generous and pleasant to deal with but at the same time very self-righteous and moralizing toward others owes itself to this optimistic strain in the Indian personality.) It is later deprivation — much later as compared to children in other cultures — that creates insecurity and may lead to bouts of depression arising from a pervasive concern with the self and its effectiveness. The development of a perfectionist ego ideal adds to this concern, especially among the more creative individuals. Hence the great appeal of almost masochistic introspection and suppression of desires. The chief source of worldly comfort comes from primary group settings where it is possible to trust and share. Hence the main group affects are toward the biological family and similar in-groups. It follows that societal demands and interpersonal interactions, especially with those outside the biological family and primordial groups, need to be structured hierarchically, thus repeating the elements of primordial identity. Where the latter is lacking, feelings of insecurity and suspicion are likely to come to the fore. Indeed the great challenge of the egalitarian ideal in contemporary India is its negation of the principle of hierarchy which is so firmly rooted in Indian culture and personality.

There are many other societal outcomes of early and adolescent socialization; there have also been very suggestive hypotheses on India's peculiar approach to sexuality.[34] We do not have space to go into all of it here. We have indicated the personality orientations that are relevant to political action. We would also like to point out here that we do not subscribe to any deterministic view of childhood socialization. Indeed, as will become clear in the remaining pages, we are convinced that whatever the personality structure of a given culture, a great deal of learning takes place, both adult learning by the individual and social learning by individuals in groups. Even the enduring themes of political culture come more from the traditions and ideals and life-styles that the larger community has articulated through successive adaptations to new experiences than from the early influences on personality development, all the more so in a culture that has laid so much emphasis on institutional integration and formal rules of the system as a way of ordering diversity. And yet, granting all this, one must also admit that when the dimensions of personality formation and the traditions and structures of the wider culture reinforce each other as part of the ongoing socialization of individuals and groups, the resulting life style develops deep roots and a viability that cannot easily be either destroyed or wished away. The main question that remains is this: Given the continuous style of "endurance through adaptation" of the Indian culture and its proverbial capacity to absorb ever new elements in its structure, how has it been coping with the phenomenal challenges that contemporary modernization has let loose? To this question we shall now turn.

MODERNIZATION OF TRADITION

We have discussed how the traditions of an apolitical and highly diversified society bequeathed a flexibility to India in handling the challenges of modernization by adapting to a new kind of political center instead of an outright rejection of the old order. The focus of the discussion was how cultural continuities facilitate contemporary change and thus enable an apolitical society to be politicized. We now turn to the converse of this focus: how have the modern polity and it architects coped with the concrete traditions of an apolitical society? An ancient society like India that has shown such remarkable resilience through the vicissitudes of history must have developed strong traditions of handling successive challenges. The fact that traditional Indian society succeeded in integrating its almost fantastic variety into a common cultural milieu implies that, despite its strong emphasis on the tolerance of ambiguity and diversity, it must have developed norms of unifying this diversity, norms that must be deeply ingrained in Indian consciousness. How, then, did the new elite interpret or reinterpret these norms for establishing the legitimacy of a political society? In order to highlight our analysis, we shall focus on those norms that appear to be obstacles in the path to modernity.

REINTERPRETATION OF TRADITION

We may begin by considering the pervasive conservatism of Indian culture through a combination of two opposite norms: a situation-specific and pluralistic code of ethics on the one hand, and a transcendental and monistic world-view, in which all contradictions of time and space dissolve, on the other. As values were supposed to vary with appointed stations in life and with the "roles" of age, sex, occupation, and caste, there developed a high tolerance of ambiguity and contradictions and a capability to subtly neutralize dissent and radicalism by avowedly accommodating them in an ongoing consensus. The result was not an attitude of "choice among alternatives" according to a universal code of morality but rather an *avoidance* of choice situations, by evading pressing problems of morality, and by keeping the intensity of commitments low, especially in times of fluidity and change, thus maintaining the system's viability by underemphasizing hard biases and dogmatic positions. Even the concept of tolerance that resulted was often one of putting up with those who disagree rather than a positive value. The moral climate that resulted was not one of dualism as in societies governed by the Cartesian logic but of monistic pluralism in which infinite variety is admitted but no individual position is overstressed.[35] Such a world-view inevitably understressed the importance of interpersonal dealings and organizational skills, especially in non-primordial and contractual relationships. The notion that every dissenting voice was but a reflection of the same basic unity (which need not be positively spelled out) produced a low commitment to one's own value system and pronouncedly emphasized reconciliation and consensus. In politics this was a particularly costly heritage as it could tolerate both democratic permissiveness and authoritarian ruthlessness reminiscent of the *Gita* and the *Arthashastra*.

Elements of this world-view still persist despite the inherent radicalism of the social and political transformation of the last two centuries. How did the new elite handle such a debilitating heritage? First, it addressed itself to religious reform and the search for a new universalism as an attempt to do away with the extreme relativism of antecedent society. Right from the days of evangelical and reformist movements of men like Ram Mohun Roy to Gandhi's own search to provide a transcendental identity to an ethic of public responsibility and political commitment, a whole line of reformers and innovators sought to universalize antecedent traditions and graft a new world-view onto them, often drawing from older traditions that stressed the moral dimension of individual conscience. Concurrent use was made of the ethical pliability of Indian tradition to absorb and legitimize the ideals and institutions of Western culture.

Again, the situation specificity of earlier morality made it possible to dissociate the political sphere and enable it to develop its own value system and thus legitimize both the *role* of oppositional movements (at first against the British Raj) and the *authority* of the new political center (after independence). Along with all this, use was also made of the very lack of "fit" between disparate cultural norms and the values of the secular order in articulating the emerging national political culture. For only so was it possible to forge links between various primordial cultures and provide to secular authority the role of the new integrator of this ancient land. In the process the value system and ideological idiom of the new elite could be diffused in the form of the dominant political style around which new symbols and identities could develop. At the same time the traditions of transcendentalism and monism — according to which there was an ultimate unity underlying all differences — could be used as symbols of Indian greatness and spiritual supremacy as against the "materialism" of the West. This provided a good psychological balance to the intellectual humiliation of accepting "alien" forms and practices.[36]

Still later the monistic concept of reconciliation of seeming opposites allowed the new politics its bargaining and mediating roles in society, and thus its penetration at different levels of social reality. The familiar decision-making processes of village India with their emphasis on arbitration in disputes, combined with the eclectic universalism of the larger culture, permitted the development of new intermediate structures and traditions of political management that in part reflected traditional orientations but at the same time sanctified a new system of integrating society's diversities. Alongside the "great tradition" of Indian culture and the " little traditions" of village India there now began to develop *intermediate traditions* of a multi-group, multi-regional political culture.[37] Thus both the larger theme of an overriding consensus and the more operational theme of mediating between seeming opposites still continue and are slowly contributing to the peculiar bargaining culture of modern India. The peculiarity is manifested, for instance, in the operation of the party system. Here consensus is oriented less to policies and programs (which, being addressed to more obvious problems of under-development are hardly controversial) and more to group dynamics. The new ideas of representation, majority opinion and formal competition are being absorbed as part of the overall culture of bargaining and consensus. Indeed it is by utilizing and interpreting the classic concern with "striking a balance" between opposites that contemporary democratic politics has been legitimized in the world-view of India's cultural traditions, apart, of course, from the legitimacy that derives from its contemporary meaning and effectiveness.[38]

Almost as powerful as the criterion of monistic pluralism are the traditional Indian concepts of time and history, or rather of timelessness and *ahistory*. Emphasizing cultural continuity instead of manipulation of the future to fulfill the ambitions of the present (the "making" of history), the Indian world-view stressed a concept of cyclical history which transcends the distinctions between past, present, and future, emphasized passivity in the face of the inexorable laws of nature, and thought of this life as a transient affair in an eternal cycle of life and death. The result was an ascetic ideal that established self- control precisely by refusing to contest the laws of destiny. Clearly, such "fatalism" was considered pernicious by the great leaders of modern India who undoubtedly wanted to make history, and indeed abridge the process of history and establish their country in its rightful place in the world. Yet this leadership combined the urge to reject the negativistic doctrine with a desire to manipulate it in an attempt to develop a distinctive strategy of mobilization and integration. Thus while the earlier elite culture of Westernized intellectuals rejected the passive subjectivism and renunciative ideology of Indian traditionality, it was only when such outright rejection was replaced by a reinterpretation of the renunciative doctrine under Gandhi that a new dimension was added to Indian nationalism. While drawing his appeal from the antecedent subjectivism of Indian tradition, Gandhi made the saintly style a criterion of interference in the process of history.[39] His idea of active asceticism — "truth force" as he termed it — and his posture of non-violent militancy, epitomized in his famous campaigns of non-cooperation with the Raj, took the place of passive withdrawal from the hard realities of alien rule. At the same time, by emphasizing ideas of personal sacrifice and "service to the people" and by making his own exemplary life and struggles for self-potency a springboard for national education, he imparted both personal charisma and a moral dimension to the struggle.[40]

At the same time the new leadership used the antecedent tolerance of diverse belief systems, "a correlate of the tendency to undervalue history,"[41] as a means of integrating different religious and linguistic communities within the framework of the new secularism. Similarly participation in the modern sector could be pursued without anxiety, concern with personal suffering and social disparities contained by a subtle reference to traditional symbols, consumption demands held in check, and a style of mobilization worked out which was based less on motivations for personal advancement than on the calls of charisma and a new concept of destiny. Indeed the people's proverbial unconcern with the process of history itself became, in the hands of this post-Westernized elite, a facility in the making of history, in the process earning time and building political capital in the form of loyalties and symbols that bridged Indian traditionality and Indian modernity. As the new resources of time and affect were applied to the concrete tasks of nation-building, political penetration, and economic development, a step-by-step rejection of the older world-view became possible, more "materialistic" interpretations of tradition — by reference to the great empires, the commercial traditions of medieval India, and the writing of new caste and linguistic histories — emerged, and became meaningful for people who were by now engaged in new status aspirations. The "making of history" could be seen gradually for what it was.[42]

A similar process of fundamental change in the present through a reinterpretation of antecedent criteria can be seen with reference to the two great concepts of dharma and karma. The former (literally meaning "duty" but imbued with overtones of an impersonal and transcendental law) has always been the principal legitimizer of social hierarchy and political power by emphasizing man's obligations to the rules and restraints of social aggregates and the roles inherent in them. The latter (meaning "deed" but again related to an impersonal law according to which personal salvation was hitched to the goodness or badness of deeds), on the other hand, emphasized the individuality and eternity of each soul whose salvation was the responsibility of each individual. Although traditionally related to the notions of circularity of history, karma could also become the basis of achievement-oriented individual pursuits as against the duty to carry out ascribed roles. There was thus in the traditional transcendentalism a built-in ambivalence towards the constraints of ascriptive status. When the penetration of modern values began to emphasize personal initiative and individual rights, and as the wooden rigidity of the caste system began to loosen up, older identities and obligations tended to be under-valued and the new ideals of individuation and worldly achievement began to be sanctified by reference to the new aggregates provided by politics. The older notions were intimately connected with structures which were now being eroded whereas the new structures introduced quite different notions of rights and duties.

Thus while to the traditional elites politics became a means of grading everything in a hierarchy and establishing the superiority of the upper strata, to the more numerous social groups the same politics became a means of rising up the social ladder, including the traditional ladders of caste and local power. The very hierarchical embeddedness of the concept of dharma was now turned around once the social and political reality began to show a basic change. The use made by Gandhi and others of the concept of dharma to legitimize their struggle against alien rule as well as against social injustice legitimized the new aspiration of the downtrodden and underprivileged classes; it became their dharma to disrupt the very system that had held them bound for centuries.[43] The innate ambivalence and mutually contradictory norms of traditional culture thus enabled the new groups to establish their new claims and sanctify them by reference to neglected texts and ethnological sources. They resurrected genealogical histories and local myths that suited their status aspirations, and provided their new status demands with an aura of authority.[44] Consequently, while the new politics has been resurrecting traditional identities — a point that many modernists deplore — it is bringing about a fundamental change in the nature of those identities, providing them with a new value content,[45] and thus turning them into important levers of political integration. All of this only illustrates the twin reflexes of the process of historical change: the pliability of traditional identities on the one hand and the permeability of new values and structures into the older identities on the other.

An important aspect of this mutually supportive process of change has been the nature of leadership in India. Both in the course of the national movement and since independence there took place a significant shift in leadership from the Westernized *modernists* to the traditionalist *modernizers*, a theme we have discussed in Chapter 4. Gandhi with his unorthodox approach to political mobilization provided depth and meaning to the nationalist cause and transformed the movement from its Brahminic aloofness to a truly catalytic force. Both the personality and moral image of Gandhi and the tall and distinguished men who surrounded him and the symbolism that they imparted to the movement radiated a certain charisma that stood above the parochialism of traditional elites as well as the narrowness of Westernized intellectuals. The result was that a handful of "tall men" could abridge the process of history, impose quite a different system of values, and change the destiny of the subcontinent in the course of a generation. The readiness with which substantially novel interpretations of traditional themes were accepted owed not a little to this remarkable concentration of charismatic power in the half-modern, half-traditional leadership of the Congress movement.

Since independence a similar shift in leadership roles has taken place. The electoral and democratic process has shifted the levers of power from the hands of the first-generation leadership to those in charge of state and district organizations, caste federations, and rural panchayats and cooperatives. The important point here is not that this new leadership does not speak the *idiom* of the more Westernized elites at the national level—for in fact they are well socialized in the Nehruvian concepts of democracy and socialism which have acquired respectability at all levels—but rather that their *style* of communication and organization is not as remote and alien as that of the higher ups. Their interpretation of religious and caste symbols is more acceptable, and their crosscutting between the secular and the sacred establish them as the natural interpreters of the national political culture.[46]

NEW CENTER FORMATION

Underlying such shifts in leadership roles is the larger process of institutional and structural transformation which constitutes the kernel of historical change in modern India. Alongside reinterpretation of traditions with a view to modernizing them, has continued the accretion of *new traditions*, largely through the impact of this transformation in structures. As we have already seen, the nucleus of unity and order in the midst of India's baffling diversity and its lack of historical identity has been its hierarchical structure and the values and obligations that have upheld the integrity of that structure. To the extent that the structure is undergoing a basic transformation, the cultural moorings of traditionality may themselves be shaken.

There is no need to list the details of this transformation, which has been described in Chapters 2 through 6. The most outstanding change has been the establishment of a new political and governmental center and its penetration into the periphery. In bringing this about, the role of British rule has been important; even more far-reaching has been the role of the nationalist movement and its remarkable concentration of charisma. But the great historical jolt to the traditional structure came after independence when the new government took measures that upset the structures and privileges that had epitomized the old order.

The changes that now took place were visible, affected status systems by attacking, and in good part abolishing, feudal privilege, disturbed superior-subordinate relationships, broke the isolation of village communities, and established new media and centers of influence and power.[47] In the process it broke the perennial sense of fait accompli in respect to distribution of life opportunities, displaced ascriptive roles as a model of integration by secular-political roles, and exposed the hundreds of thousands of local communities to the central symbols of government, elections, parties, and bureaucracy.

The roles of adult franchise and periodic elections have been pivotal, not only in displacing the principle of hierarchy by the principle of numbers, but also in establishing a unified focus of attention and affect for the vast masses of people, even before the other learning processes of education and urbanization begin to play their role. In the words of a noted scholar of the new nations

> The granting of universal suffrage without property or literacy qualifications is perhaps the greatest single factor leading to the

> formation of a political society. The mere existence of the suffrage might in the course of a short time disintegrate the nascent political society, if it is not accompanied by other changes as well. Nonetheless, the drawing of the whole adult population periodically into contact with the symbols of the center of national political life must in the course of time have immeasurable consequences for stirring people up, giving them a sense of their own potential significance and for attaching their sentiments to symbols which comprehend the entire nation.[48]

Something positive can be gained if this larger identity is forged before the modernist differentiations and cleavages that are inherent in the processes of education, urbanization, and rapid economic development begin to play their role.[49] At any rate this seems to be the experience of India.

In his pioneering work on the dynamics of culture and personality of the twice born castes in India, Morris Carstairs was equally struck by the impact of the larger changes in politics and economic organization on the entire status hierarchy and historical experience of the village of Deoli. These wider changes were, according to Carstairs, "being assimilated in a process of referring them constantly to what has gone before, whether in public meetings or in the daily gossip of the bazaar. They represent instances of new learning imposed upon adults and children of all castes alike."[50]

Four important characteristics of this wider process of translation should be noted. First, alongside the use of traditional symbols for legitimizing the changes involved in modernization, there is an increasing tendency to utilize the new symbols of a secular political order for legitimizing a reordering of traditional relationships. Second, the consciousness of the new order arises not only from the adaptive process of socialization but also, and perhaps more crucially, out of a growing sense of contrast between the past and the present and thus as genuinely new learning that is conscious deliberative, and "rational.". Third, as this sense of contrast grows, there is an increasing readiness to see that there was something wrong in the past, that some kind of stagnation had set in, and that there is need for conscious and directed change. Fourth, there is an awareness of the novelty of all this. The changes to which Indian society was exposed in earlier periods were essentially ideological changes, with occasional disturbances in the mutual standing of status groups. But structurally the society had been remarkably stable and had displayed a chronic tendency to integrate everything in the prevailing structure and its hierarchy. It is realized now that it is this very kernel of stability that is under attack and that, however gradualist and incremental these changes are, they are in reality almost reordering the structure of society. Not everyone is comfortable at this realization — and some are uncomfortable because things are not changing fast enough — but it is spreading and is providing an important stimulus in the learning and socialization processes of contemporary India.

In the diffusion of this general realization, a pivotal role has been played by government and its associative agencies. The broadening of India's political community is a direct consequence of the enlargement of the role and status of government as a factor in social development. This is true not only in terms of the penetration of the governmental system and its resources, but also in terms of *government-mindedness* among the people at large. The point may be highlighted by presenting a tiny fragment of the data from a cross-national study. Posing a hypothetical situation (which in the case of India is a very real one) of financial need in times of serious crisis, the respondents were asked questions designed to tap "expectations" on the one hand and "preferences" on the other. To what extent are relatives likely to help? To what extent is government likely to help? And, if both sources were willing to provide similar help, who would they *prefer*[51] One would expect Indians, both because of their parochial orientations and their presumed dependence on "extended family," to expect greater help from relatives than from government, and if given a choice, to prefer family to government. In fact however, the contrary is true, as shown is Tables 7.1 and 7.2.

There are many problems of interpretation. Indians seem to expect help from government more than from relatives and if given a choice between the two prefer government even more. Part of this must be simply the propensity to avoid the frictions and humiliation that result from help received from relatives: the impersonal channel of government is much better to deal with. Similarly the little experience Indians had have in terms of *taccavi*

TABLE 7.1
A. Help likely from relatives (not living in the household);
B. Help likely from government

	Percentages		
	Yes	No	DK, NA, & other
United States			
A. Relatives	65.4	32.0	2.6
B. Government	69.4	20.3	10.3
Japan			
A. Relatives	69.7	24.1	6.2
B. Government	45.4	40.0	14.6
India			
A. Relatives	31.8	66.6	1.6
B. Government	50.5	42.4	7.1
Nigeria			
A. Relatives	54.2	41.2	4.6
B. Government	43.9	36.1	20.0

loans (advance money for agricultural improvements), loans from cooperative societies, and so on, may have inspired a more relaxed attitude towards public debts as opposed to family debts. It may also be argued that precisely because Indians have had little experience with government, they are less aware of the onus of contracting government debts. All the same the mutually reinforcing responses to both expectation and preference questions tend to support the general point that government is a legitimate symbol of reference and affect in India. And this is even more so than in the highly developed countries like Japan and the United States. Many other responses in the study support this contention but there is no space to go into them here. We must await a fuller analysis of the study for that.

TABLE 7.2
Help Preferred as between Relatives and Government (Percentages)

	Relatives	Government	Both	Neither	DK, NA, & other
United States	42.6	53.1	—	—	4.3
Japan	47.8	35.0	3.3	4.8	9.1
India	24.2	69.0	2.5	1.4	2.9
Nigeria	33.3	53.0	7.5	0.7	5.5

This general process of cognitive change may be called the process of *governmentalization.* There is increasing evidence in India of both attitudes and structures getting more and more governmentalized. Not only does government inspire political structures and economic programs, define goals and roles, and provide modal identities; it also stimulates the generation of various new inputs in the life style and productive processes of the individual and the family. Through this process of governmentalization and its concomitant structures of diffusion and cognition, the larger transformations described here become meaningful.

Not all of this is new, of course. The partriarchal image of authority and the propensity to look to the government for the good things of life are deeply ingrained in the Indian mind. Indeed it may be that such a radical "transformation" can be brought about in such a short time precisely because the new elite can use deeply ingrained images. On the other hand, the crux of political development is not just a positive attitude towards government but an ability to think of government as an object of manipulation and thus as something that is accountable for its deeds. There is evidence that increasing participation in politics is spreading such expectations. And this constitutes the major contemporary change in Indian society.

Such a change also throws light on a theme to which we have come back again and again in this book, the theme of "perception of change". Indians have shown a propensity to modernize themselves incrementally and without recourse to violent upheaval. The notion that results of forced change are less lasting and that the process of persuasion produces slow but enduring and constructive results have a long pedigree in India.[52] But the outsider's perception of the cumulative product of this incremental process has been dim and has led to a widespread feeling that not much is happening in India.[53] To this the Westernized intellectuals in the country, and even a section of the political elite, have themselves contributed. Cultural predispositions contribute to such a self-image. In some nations even though the general condition is one of stagnation an illusion of change prevails. In India the cultural mood has normally been in favor of an illusion of permanence. Unless there develops a significant input of systematic social and political analysis, the elite is likely to lose track of the true dynamics of the political process and appear increasingly ad hoc and uncertain in its moorings. India's social scientists carry a special responsibility in the respect.

SOME PERSISTING TRAITS

While it has been possible for the elites of modern India to utilize the ambivalences of Indian traditionality for legitimizing new ideals and institutions, many antecedent traditions and orientations have managed to survive in the modern period, and in some cases find a new lease on life. We have already noticed those that are proving functional to modern secularism and democratization. But others are impeding the pace and character of historical change.

The most persistent trait of Indian traditionality is its tendency towards hierarchical segmentation for ordering all differentiations, including dissent and diversity. During the national movement and the early phases of post-Independence political mobilization this trait was consciously resisted, and with considerable success. As the new political system crystallized and found its chief sustenance in the form of bureaucratic rules and procedures, however, the segmental characteristic found a new breeding ground in terms of excessive formalism and ritualization of roles and distances. Indians have always been impressed by fixed and codified rules which are supposed to transcend the mutations of personal aspirations and interpersonal relationships. The result is "rule-bound incompetence" in social and economic relationships, and in governmental functioning.[54] Hierarchy has also been a means of exercising authority in which legitimacy derives not merely from the roles and functions inherent in the hierarchy but also by endowing the hierarchy with extrapolitical meaning and charisma.

Traditionally the hierarchy which Indians have been used to is an ascriptive hierarchy. The capriciousness of impersonal laws and the insecurity and ambivalence resulting from diffuse systems of authority have been handled by recourse to fixed hierarchies differentiated by rigid distances and status-specific codes of conduct. This is also the case in modern India, with obvious adaptations. As the new universals embodied in modern secular-political institutions are in a fluid stage, the tendency towards an ascriptive ordering of the environment continues. Even modern education and new occupational opportunities tend to be integrated through segmentation and in-grouping in local hierarchies: they "have only managed to deepen the moorings of hierarchy as a group value."[55] Similarly the hierarchical style has been used for managing dissent: protests have often been directed at finding a place in the ongoing hierarchy of authority and status. Thus each catalytic change ends up by further articulating the antecedent structure of ascriptive relationships. On the other hand, Indians have been wanting when it comes to operating larger secular hierarchies in the economic and political spheres, except where these can be so differentiated as to lend themselves to smaller clusters of almost a primordial kind, as in the case of political parties and local bureaucracies. The ideal of "decentralization" thus very often gets translated into so many subcultures sharing the name structural characteristics but operating as distinctive entities with more or less ascriptive tendencies.

From this lack of experience in operating large-scale organizations and because of long socialization in familial and primordial settings, the Indian ineptitude for disciplined collective action becomes meaningful. Essentially it is a distaste for "giganticism". The result is a low intensity of collective orientations except under the spell of charismatic power, a point we have already discussed.

All this gives rise to further psychological handicaps. We have mentioned the tendency to feel uncomfortable among peers, whenever a clear superior-subordinate relationship is lacking. There is also a tendency not to confront a potentially divisive situation and to prefer to shelve an issue rather than resolve it and face the consequences. This again is an out-growth of the style of structural integration by which everything is absorbed into an ongoing structure of consensus. The result is a pathological consensuality even in spite of persisting conflicts and cleavages.[56] It produces, not infrequently, a state of deep bitterness and cynicism among the losing elements and leads to a non-expressive kind of resentment.

The main result of our discussion of the emerging mix of

traditionality and modernity in India's political culture is that while Indians seem to be eminently suited to operating the diversified and differentiated structures that modernization inevitably involves, and while they are also richly endowed for tolerating dissent and criticism, they are not as well equipped for developing collective commitments and the organizational discipline needed for large-scale enterprises which are also important correlates of modernization.

CONCLUSION: A COMPARATIVE OVERVIEW

In the end, it would be useful to provide some perspective to our analysis of the political culture of change as discussed in this chapter.

There is a difference between a culture in which the central system of institution and symbols has been continuous and dominant, and a culture in which identities have been more diffuse, where the center is remote and intermittent, the subcenters are autonomous, and there has been a general dissociation between the political and the cultural.

In the former type of culture, when changes of modernization set in, the challenge is to the whole authority system through which the individual and the group of which he is a part find their identity. In the latter type of culture the modernizing changes in the center fail to shake the system as a whole. By tradition the former is more secular where man is first a political being and where his principal allegiance is toward *authority*; in the latter by tradition the allegiances are segmented and a man's salvation lies in his *individual* self-realization and in the status of his *group* in the larger society. Authority in the latter is modaly diffuse and particularistic; a wide gap exists between the polity which is transient and unstable and the culture which is enduring and stable; and the "whole" is conceived as neither the sum of the individual parts, nor as something overriding the parts, but as a function of a series of ties, of a *network*.

In the latter type of culture there is also a different approach to the "patterning of aggression" than in the more secular cultures. As the management of aggression in the secular cultures is through sublimation under authority (the super ego), this facilitates the central role of politics in modern times. In the non-secular cultures like India, too, politics has assumed a central role, but for quite different reasons. Here it was the antecedent dissociation of politics from the rest of culture that gave to the "new politics" its autonomy and power; in this sense there has been a more basic discontinuity in cultures like India than in the historically secular cultures even if the latter experienced revolutions arising out of a struggle between the different "estates." On the other hand, although in India the political elite has assumed a catalytic role, it is still not the most important element in the ordering of community life-styles. It has achieved its importance not through the legitimacy bequeathed by history, nor by simply imposing its authority, but by dispersing its goods and mediating in other spheres through its resources and persuasive capabilities, thus taking on the roles that were hitherto performed by non-political elites.

Paradoxically, thus, "penetration" of the political center and its symbols downward through newly improvised channels of participation becomes both necessary and easy to achieve in the historically non-secular cultures, more so than in cultures that had identified with a particular form of secular authority. Penetration, in this case, becomes more a mechanism of indulgence and patronage than of simple bureaucratization and extraction. This leads to the further consequence that in such a culture government could rule and survive principally by becoming sensitive to the changes taking place in various segments of society; in the more secularly inclined cultures government could afford to be insensitive and impose the will of the ruling elite.[57] The point is that government in a hitherto apolitical society has to be both sensitive to the changes taking place in other segments and assume an active role in bringing them about. If it fails in either, it may soon lose its legitimacy.

Against such a perspective, the themes of political culture and political socialization achieve significance. In themselves the themes have only a heuristic value.

Notes

1. See, however, W. Norman Brown, "The Content of Cultural Continuity in India," *Journal of Asian Studies*, XX, August, 1961.

2. J.C. Hesteerman, "Tradition in Modern India," *Bijdragen Tot de Taat, Land-En Volkenkunde,* Deel 119, 3e, 1963. Hesteerman says that the reason for drawing such sharp contrasts between tradition and modernity is influenced by Westerners' own outlook, that is by the avidity for change that is proper to Western civilization.

3. China is probably the best case of such reaction. See Lucian W. Pye, *Spirit of Chinese Politics: A Psychocultural Study of the Authority Crisis in Political Development* (Cambridge, Mass. 1968).

4. The approach of British colonialism in India, and of the leaders of the nationalist movement, contributed to such a political articulation. The British ruled directly and negotiated directly with the intellectual leaders of the movement, so that when power was transferred to Indian hands, the princely vestiges of feudal India were soon reduced to a non-entity by the new Indian rulers. In many of their colonies in Africa, on the other hand, the British admitted the claims of tribal chiefs as part of the power equation. The results have been disastrous for political unity. There is little doubt that if power had been transferred to a council of princes in India, old animosities would have revived and the nation would not have survived as one. In fact the British very nearly did this under the Government of India Act of 1935. In rejecting the proposal, the Congress leadership saved the integrity of the future nation.

5. Lucian W. Pye, "The Political Cultures of India and China: Crises of Identity and Authority," in Rushikesh Maru and Rajni Kothari, eds, *India and China: Contrasts in Development* (New Delhi, 1970).

6. In Nehru's expressive words, the principal difficulty that Gandhi confronted in developing his unique strategy of nation-building was how to "overcome the hardness of heart of cultivated people." See André Malraux, *Anti-Memoirs* (New York, 1968).

7. S.N. Eisenstadt, " Tradition and Modes of Response to Modernity," in *India and China, op.cit.*

8. Amaury de Riencourt, *The Soul of India* (London, 1961).

9. Here the difference from the Hegelian concept of the Absolute as a generalized idea comes out. See T.R.V. Murti "The World and the Individual in Indian Religious Thought," in Charles A. Moore, ed., *The Indian Mind* (Honolulu, 1967).

10. On this see Surama Dasgupta, "The Individual in Indian Ethics," in *The Indian Mind, ibid.* On Gandhi's thinking on similar lines, see the Appendix to Philip Spratt, *Hindu Culture and Personality* (Bombay, 1966).

11. Nehru was the great exponent of such a synthesis. See his *Discovery of India* (New York, 1946). A later expression of this idiom was found in the ideological overtones of his non-alignment policy and the doctrine of "co-existence" in foreign affairs which was based on a reconciliation of seemingly contradictory policies in the period of the cold war. The same idea has been expressed in the country's economic philosophy and in many other spheres.

12. Ashis Nandy "The Culture of Indian Politics: A Stock Taking," manuscript (Delhi: Centre for the Study of Developing Societies, 1968).
13. There is no equivalent translation in Indian languages for the term "leader" as it is commonly used in secular English. All the terms used to denote authority, except the paramilitary use of *neta*, are either primordial or sacred.
14. On the factional character of Indian village life, see Bernard J. Siegel and Alan Beals, "Pervasive Factionalism," *American Anthropologist*, 62, No. 3, June, 1960. See also Alan Beals, *Gopalpur: A South Indian Village* (New York, 1962).
15. In this connection see Myron Weiner, "Traditional Role Performance and the Development of Modern Political Parties: The Indian Case," *Journal of Politics*, 26, No. 4, 1964.
16. Charles A. Myers, *Labour Problems in the Industrialization of India* (Cambridge, Mass., 1958). For thoughtful comments by prominent one-time trade unionists on arbitration as a means of negotiating industrial relations and restraining militancy, see V.V. Giri, *Labour Problems in Indian Industry* (Bombay, 1958), and Asoka Mehta, "The Mediating Role of the Trade Union in Underdeveloped Countries," *Economic Development and Cultural Change*, October, 1957. On the general issue of disputes and traditional legal norms, see the useful review by Bernard S. Cohn, "Anthropological Notes on Disputes and Law in India," *American Anthropologist*, 67, No. 6, December, 1965 (Special Publications).
17. We say "partly" because the orientation toward authority has only facilitated the more general rise in importance of the higher level elite in local affairs. A wider process of penetration has taken place from above as we discussed in previous chapters. The catalytic role that governmental and party leaders have assumed in this process has found legitimacy in the orientations discussed here.
18. See, however, Myron Weiner, *Politics of Scarcity: Public Pressure and Political Response in India* (Chicago, 1962) and the Foreword to it by Gabriel A. Almond. Weiner's attempt to apply the theory of organized interest groups to the Indian situation leads Almond to conclude that there is a weak bargaining culture in India. The point we make here is somewhat different. It is not so much that there is a weak bargaining culture — for a bargaining style in the settlement of disputes has been a long-standing tradition in India — but that it is not highly institution-alized, given the orientations towards authority and arbitration.
19. Riencourt, *op. cit.* Pye, *The Spirit of Chinese Politics*, *op. cit.*
20. Kautilya, sometimes described as India's Machiavelli, in his famous *Arthashastra* ("Treatise on Polity"), expressed an almost totalitarian role for the state and laid down detailed injunctions for the king and his ministers. Besides the authoritative *Dharmashastras*, the *Arthashastra* has been an influential source of *obiter dicta* in India. It is important, however, to stress the historical context of the work when the invasions of Alexander the Great

had given rise to great concern for order and unity. In this respect it is comparable to Hobbes' *Leviathan.* But in general "the idea of a body politic, of a state as an organism transcending its component parts ... does not seem to have taken any great hold on ancient Indian thought." A.L. Basham, *The Wonder That Was India* (London, 1954). See also T.N. Ramaswamy, *Essentials of Indian Statecraft: Kautilya's* Arthashastra *for Contemporary Readers* (Bombay, 1962).

21. To be sure, the philosopher Kant did talk at length of moral duties to oneself, but on the whole Western philosophy has followed the conception of morality as essentially social, as summed up so neatly by John Stuart Mill. For a recent examination of the two conceptions, see Paul D. Eisenberg, "Duties to Oneself and the Concept of Morality," *Inquiry*, II, No. 2, Summer, 1968.

22. For a good account of this doctrine, see S.K. Maitra, *Ethics of the Hindus* (Calcutta, 1925). For a discussion of the relevance of the karma doctrine to political culture, see Nandy, *op. cit.*

23. For an insightful treatment of this general theme, see the classic novel of E.M. Forster, *A Passage to India* (New York, 1924). See also the pioneering work of Morris Carstairs, *The Twice-Born* (London, 1957), where he dwells at length on the theme of interpersonal distrust.

24. Both his aggressive reaction to the rise of the Patel group in the Congress after Tandon became the party's president and his use of the "Kamaraj Plan" even while his health was failing are evidence of this basic mistrust, although in neither event was Nehru's own position really threatened.

25. See especially P.S. Naidu, *Mysteries of the Mind* (Allahabad, 1944); Gardner Murphy. *In the Minds of Men* (New York, 1953), Ch. 4; G. Morris Carstairs, *op. cit;* Dhirendra Narain, *Hindu Character: A Few Glimpses* (Bombay, 1957), Chapter VII; Leigh Minturn and John T. Hitchcock, "The Rajputs of Khalapur, India," in Beatrice B. Whiting, ed., *Six Cultures: Studies of Child Rearing* (New York, 1963); Philip Spratt, *Hindu Culture and Personality: A Psycho-Analytic Study* (Bombay, 1966).

26. Spratt, *ibid.*, characterizes this as "protective extroversion," a tendency by which the ego identifies itself with, and expands toward, the whole of the universe.

27. Carstairs, *op.cit.*, p. 55.

28. Minturn and Hitchcock, *op.cit.*, p. 317.

29. *Ibid.*, p. 318.

30. Narain, *op.cit.*, p. 179.

31. Murphy, *op. cit.*, p. 51. The official was Prem Kripal, until recently education secretary in the central government.

32. Hence the tendency in India both to feel comfortable under "charismatic" power and to credit it with Olympian and superhuman traits. The Indian ideal of leadership is not one who does better what others can do, but one who represents the negation of others' weaknesses, such as a self-composed yogi or a militant "fighter." Thus while Gandhi's image abroad was that of

a pacifist, in India it was that of a fighter who had "single-handedly" challenged the mighty British empire, reminiscent of the great epic figures.

33. Carstairs, *op. cit.*
34. *Ibid.*; Spratt, *op. cit.*; Narain. *op. cit.*
35. Riencourt, *op. cit.*; Nandy, *op. cit.*; Beatrice Lamb, *India: A World in Transition* (New York, 1963).
36. Lucian Pye, in *The Spirit of Chinese Politics, op. cit.*, says that the Chinese identity with a secular and materialistic rather than a spiritual tradition did not permit this escape from humiliation when at last China had to accept the superiority of the West in political and economic matters. As the "essential" values and identities of Indians were not greatly affected, there was no great feeling of being "dominated by barbarians."
37. Notice the relationship of such traditions to the "intermediate structures" described in Chapters 4, 5.
38. In the foregoing paragraphs and those that follow, I have benefited greatly from the paper of Ashis Nandy quoted above. I am grateful to him for making available his manuscript to me before this book was sent to press.
39. He meaningfully symbolized this by a display of his almost obsessive preoccupation with time. Gandhi is said to have measured everything in terms of time. He kept a watch dangling from his waist as a constant reminder. According to Professor N.K. Bose, Gandhi conceived of a disciplined allocation of time as intimately connected with realization of truth.
40. Gandhi published his autobiography as a series of weekly articles in *Navjivan*, his own mouthpiece for the struggle. For an interesting analysis, see Erik H. Erikson, "Gandhi's Autobiography: The Leader as a Child," *The American Scholar*, 35, No. 4, Autumn, 1966. See also Susanne Hoeber Rudolph, " The New Courage: An Essay on Gandhi's Psychology," *World Politics*, XVI, No. 1, October, 1963.
41. Nandy, *op. cit.*
42. It is in this process of grafting a new world-view that an "elite culture" emerged in India. In many ways this was a distinctive culture, and still is. It will be recalled that in our discussion of the Indian approach to morality, we emphasized the "self-regarding " orientation of moral energy in India. During the course of the national movement, however, a distinct emphasis on "other-regarding" values emerged. Gandhi's emphasis on the social dimension of spirituality ("service to the people") became an enduring element of the professional politician's ethos and is still very active.
43. After independence, Nehru repeatedly stressed what Gandhi had emphasized before, "Now India must struggle against herself."
44. The process has been helped by the existence in many parts of the country of specialized castes of genealogists. See A.M. Shah and R.G. Shroff, " The Vahivanca Barots of Gujarat: A Caste of Genealogists and Mythographers," in Milton Singer, ed., *Traditional India: Structure and Change* (Philadelphia, 1959).
45. Another transformation through interpretation of an old concept that is

relevant here is the concept of "justice." Traditionally justice belonged to the cosmic scheme of things, to the "natural" order of social and spiritual hierarchy. Now, using the same concept, the reformers of the nineteenth and twentieth centuries gave a new meaning to it. Justice now referred to notions of equality and compassion for one's fellow beings. Of course, in grafting these new values, the social reformers drew whatever support they could from other traditional notions, such as these of charity (*daya*) and "trusteeship."

46. The distinction between "idiom" and "style" is important inasmuch as the former is easier to diffuse at lower levels while the latter is more likely to prove functional and thus persist as a crucial component of political coalition-making. For an earlier analysis of different idioms, see W.H. Morris-Jones, "India's Political Idioms," in C.H. Philips, ed., *Politics and Society in India* (London, 1963).

47. Note that panchayati raj has become the vehicle of entirely new processes of mobilization while still using the symbolism and cultural overtones of the age-old panchayat.

48. Edward Shils, "Political Development in the New States," *Comparative Studies in Society and History*, II, No. 3, April, 1960, p. 287.

49. This view goes against the current notions of rates and sequences among Western scholars committed to the "social prerequisities" model of political development. According to these theorists, an optimal pattern of development is one in which things like adult franchise should come later, after national integration and the legitimacy of central authority have been established. For two recent statements of this approach, see Dankwart A. Rustow, *A World of Nations* (Washington, D.C., 1967) and Eric A. Nordlinger, "Political Development: Time Sequences and Rates of Change," *World Politics*, XX, No. 3, April, 1968.

50. Carstairs, *op. cit.*

51. The study was part of the "Cross-National Program in Political and Social Change" sponsored by the Centre for the Study of Developing Societies, Delhi, the University of Tokyo, Stanford University, and the University of Ibadan, Nigeria. In India the study was conducted in four states, West Bengal, UP, Gujarat, and Andhra Pradesh, based on a stratified random sample of the adult population. The exact wording of the questions was as follows:
    1. We are interested in this survey in finding out what individuals or families do when faced with serious financial crises. Suppose something were to happen to your family so that those in this household could not earn enough to support themselves. Where would you be most likely to go for help?
    (a) Are there any relatives not living in the household who you feel would be likely to help in a situation of this kind?
    (b) Do you think the government or a government agency would be likely to provide such support?
    2. In such a situation where there is not enough income and those living here needed help, suppose both the government and other relatives would

give you the same amount of material support. Where would you prefer to get the help from: other relatives or from the government?

52. Nehru played a seminal role in articulating this approach in the modern setting. Through attracted by dramatic achievements abroad and prone to be somewhat simplistic in the adoption of foreign models, he was disposed to show an almost obstinate faith in the rightness of the democratic path. He often brushed aside criticism of his bureaucratic contemporaries when it came to involving the people in the democratic process, as for instance in the programs of community development and panchayati raj. To the argument that the tempo of development might slow down, he replied that in the long run it was bound to bring more speed.
53. On this general problem see Albert O. Hirschman. "Underdevelopment, Obstacles to the Perception of Change, and Leadership," *Daedalus*, 97, No. 3, Summer, 1968.
54. Nandy, *op. cit.*
55. *Ibid.*
56. There is still an influential school of thought in India which emphasizes consensus as a paramount value. Exponents of this school oppose direct elections as being conflict-inducing and instead propose "unanimous elections" by mutual consultation between different groups or some scheme of "indirect elections" from lower to higher tiers, not unlike the models of basic democracy developed in Pakistan and Nepal. See Jayaprakash Narayan, *Plea for a Reconstruction of the Indian Polity* (Delhi, 1959). For a discussion of such attitudes, see Susanne Hoeber Rudolph, "Conflict and Consensus in Indian Politics," *World Politics*, April, 1961.
57. On all this the contrasts presented by China are revealing. See Lucian Pye, *Spirit of Chinese Politics, op. cit.*

8

Political Institutionalization and National Integration

In reading through the preceding chapters, the discerning reader would have noticed our running concern with the characteristic achievements of the Indian political system as it stands at present, as well as its peculiar lags in fulfillment. At the same time, he has every right to feel that such an evaluative concern has not been systematically brought out and documented. He is likely to say: I have read so far an analysis of the structures and processes of political change in recent and contemporary India, and the social and cultural variables that affect them. I have found such an analysis interesting. But I would like to know how the Indian political system is measuring up to the tasks and problems that it faces. How well has it succeeded? What have been its principal shortfalls? What does the future hold in store?

APPROACH TO PERFORMANCE ANALYSIS

Such questions are very much in order. Developmental analysis of the political process, even when it attempts to be "dynamic" inasmuch as it deals with changes through time, would still remain inadequate if it were not to lead to some measure of the performance of the system under investigation. Yet the fact remains that until very recently comparative political analysis has contributed precious little to our understanding of how different political systems have fared in dealing with the critical issue areas that they have encountered as they have moved from one threshold of articulation to another. Although modern political theorists have, for a long time now, talked of an "input-output model" they have largely remained preoccupied with the "input" side of the model and have only cursorily dealt with the "output" dimensions. Actually the outputs of the political system — elite decisions and policy penetration — become the principal inputs in the early articulation of a nation state.[1] Political elites in their capacity as actors and decision-makers appear to possess far more autonomy and creativity, indeed almost a causal power, than most developmental theorists care to recognize.

In recent years some useful theoretical constructs have been suggested for handling the performance dimension of political development.[2] Generally, however, analysts of political systems have either ignored issues of performance and problem-solving or, in the few instances where they have addressed themselves systematically to these questions, these have been almost exclusively in terms of aggregate measures of economic development, social mobilization, media exposure, and so forth, thus turning some of the *characteristics* of economically developed societies into *criteria* of political development. Reflecting the dominant ideology of modern social science research according to which political phenomena have to be explained by reference to economic and social "reality" and have no autonomy of their own, and generalizing from a specific historical experience of the West in which political development has often (though not always) taken place in response to pressures and demand from society, a majority of these theorists have by and large neglected the reverse process, namely the impact of political decisions on the structures and processes of society.[3] There has been until very recently no systematic attempt to relate and compare performance in social and economic spheres with measures of political development proper, such as the consolidation of a political center and its penetration into the periphery, its success or failure in institutionalizing political changes, and its ability to resolve issues of diversity and political demand. There has been much discussion of these issues and of the issues of economic performance, but the two tend to be isolated. While the consequence of the more general neglect of performance issues is that "behavioral analysis" of politics has often been little more than a Kremlinological treatment of cliques and factions, the consequence of not systematically relating indicators of economic and social mobilization with more clearly political indicators has been a conceptualization of political development as a purely dependent phenomenon that needs to be explained by reference to exogenous factors.[4] As we shall see in this and the next three chapters, however, it is in terms of comparing performance in different spheres that the real issues and dilemmas of a political system begin to crystallize, and give rise to some policy perspectives.

We have no intention here of suggesting ways in which to fill this gap in theoretical concerns: a country study is not a place for dealing at any length with broader issues of theory. Our own analytic framework of center crystallization and political penetration in the context of peculiar mixes of traditionality and modernity has been advanced for the limited objective of interpreting the Indian experience in political development; we feel no particular pressure to generalize from this experience. But our framework does raise important issues of performance and problem-solving, to which we intend to address ourselves in this and the next two chapters. In doing so we shall utilize whatever theoretical leads exist in the literature, identify the more important problem areas, consider what policies have been evolved in dealing with them, and with what success. In developing our analysis, we shall distinguish between problems that are central to political institutionalization and integration, those that stem from economic development and demographic movements, and those that are a consequence of operating in an international environment. We shall deal with the first set of problems in this chapter, the second set in the next chapter, and the last set in Chapter 10. In each of these, while principally looking at past and present trends, we shall also at some points try to project into the near future. This will be more as an aid in understanding, as a means of imparting a certain realism to the overall analysis, than with any claim to predict the hereafter with any degree of certainty. In the last chapter of the book we shall try to bring together the import of all this analysis from the perspective of policy-making.

DIMENSIONS OF INSTITUTIONALIZATION

In considering the specifically political issues of political development, the most basic issue which has enveloped all other issues seems to be that of integration: the crystallization and consolidation of a political center, its outward expansion, its institutionalization, and its assimilation of diverse identities and structures into a national political community; in short, the development of an "integrative capability." This issue continues to overpower all other in the values and actions of nation-builders; in the words of Nehru, the unity of India was his chief profession in life. In a society still in the process of "nation-becoming" it is inevitable that this should be so; what is of interest is the particular approach that was adopted. Two main characteristics of the Indian approach have been the growth and consolidation of unitary processes through the penetration of authoritative structures of government and the dominant party; and a process of accommodation of diverse interests and pluralities which are acknowledged as legitimate constituents of the slowly crystallizing center. Political unity in India has been a function of a balanced interplay between these two elements.— dominance and accommodation — and it has gradually emerged as political sense that the one provides strength to the other.

Such an approach to integration places a high emphasis on politicization and the legitimacy of the "political" in both the preservation and the transformation of the social order. Not an easy strategy by any means, it has worked in part because the apathy and passivity of a great majority of the people makes for a low intensity of demands, but more importantly because of an energetic penetration of structures of dominance represented by the bureaucracy, a towering leadership, and the Congress party. However, as the basic approach was designed to diminish the apathy, initiate a comprehensive process of change, crystallize new interests and coalitions, and challenge the status quo, it was unavoidable that such an approach to integration should run into difficulties and dilemmas from time to time.

The essential dilemma of dominant structures acting as dynamic agents of change is that their dominance must in time give place to more polarized and differentiated structures of power and legitimacy. The crucial tests of performance here are: How orderly and purposive is this process of diffusion? Are the demands of pluralism structured and assimilated into the dominant center? Does such a restructuring of authority provide the system with a broader base of legitimacy? In India such a challenge of adaptiveness to new crystallizations has been brought up in a series of issue areas.

NATURE OF COALITION-MAKING

One of the earliest institutional problems encountered by the new polity in India was the nature of the party system, a problem that has confronted every other new nation and has nowhere been satisfactorily solved. In India the problem was peculiar: the leadership had almost unanimously adopted a democratic Constitution of the parliamentary type which assumed the availability of a competitive infrastructure in the form of alternating parties and a structure of support groups that would provide competing resources to the opposing parties. Although the Constitution was silent on this point, the availability of such a structure of articulation and aggregation was implicit in its core political formula. In reality, such a party system did not exist and what took its place was quite different: a system dominated by one party which had, however, to admit in its internal structure the characteristics of party alternation and competing elite groups. The challenge of structural adaptation was basic; the Congress party had to replace its traditional emphasis (during the movement) on discipline and hierarchy by permitting in its scheme a new style of integration that was based on internal competition and elite turnover. To be sure, traditionally the Congress movement had been fairly wide-based and eclectic in its group structure. But the differentiations that it had encompassed were still within the narrow bounds of a strikingly homogeneous, "one class," English-educated elite. This elite had not yet experienced the dynamic pressures of mass politics based on adult franchise, or the divisive effects of having to distribute scarce resources of office and patronage among a swelling clientele.

The unavailability of a nation-wide and united opposition

party or parties forced the leadership of the Congress Party to admit to its organization an active and virulent factionalism without any significant reference to ideological or programmatic issues. Because the Congress Party managed to be in power continuously and there was no united or effective threat to its authority, the country's political process gained incomparable advantages of continuity and unity. As to the larger political system, however, the threat posed by continual internal factionalism was inherently more dangerous than the prospects of another party or parties replacing the Congress in power. It was precisely this factionalism, this struggle for "loaves and fishes," that has brought down the democratic edifice in many a new state.

We have, in earlier chapters, seen how the Indian polity has responded to these threats. From the beginning unity was emphasized through accommodation and consensus. It was realized that the Congress would remain dominant for a long time to come and thus the task was to ensure due accommodation to all the politically relevant groups in the interests of unity and stability. In the most definitive work on the making of the Indian Constitution to date, Granville Austin notes that India's two original contributions, to the process of constitution-making are "decision-making by consensus" and "the principle of accommodation."[5] Keenly aware of the damage that rule by simple majority can do to a nascent democracy in a highly plural society, and having recently experienced the traumatic consequences of political disunity, the leadership of the Congress sought consensus on basic issues essentially through a process of accommodation. But seemingly "accommodative" doctrines of representation such as proportional representation, indirect elections, special representation to religious minorities, and a Swiss type of cabinet were rejected in the interest of unity and with a view to enabling the polity to be autonomous of the basic cleavages of Indian society.[6] The chief value that the leadership sought to achieve through this simultaneous stress on accommodation and political autonomy was legitimacy. The leadership was highly aware that they were erecting a nation within the formal superstructure of a state that they had inherited, and they bent both tradition and resources to assure legitimacy to the democratic process through which they had chosen to evolve such a nation.

The same approach of combining the autonomy of the political process with accommodation of the relevant substructures has informed the politics of the Congress Party, which was placed in the ambivalent position of being an overwhelmingly dominant party that must still seek consensus on every major issue in order to avoid massive disaffection and secession. We have already seen how such an approach crystallized. Tolerance of factional disputes in state and local Congress units was matched by the insistence that all important changes in leadership be subject to approval of the High Command. The machinery of conciliation has been matched by procedures of arbitration from above. Although the law does not provide for any system of primaries, the Congress Party has adopted a highly institutionalized internal system of candidate selection, extending the opportunities for political participation and improvising competition through "internal democracy" even where the competitive situation outside was fairly one-sided.

We have already seen two other peculiarities of this approach at investing the Congress with characteristics of a full-fledged party system. One has been the peculiar communication system of Indian politics by which the position of each of the major opposition parties has been reflected in one or another of the factions within the Congress Party: the socialist faction, the Swatantra faction, the Jan Sangh faction, and so on. The other is the great emphasis that the Indian leadership has placed on "local democracy." The whole system of panchayati raj, and of the various participant and consultative devices around the structure of developmental administration in the districts and below, has been initiated and inspired by the national leadership from above. The system, apart from bringing handsome dividends in electoral and patronage terms, has also helped in further improvising competition at levels far beyond the crucial decision-making organs of government, thus building buffers between the center and its periphery and containing the forces of dissension and cleavage. Anticipation of potential cleavages and their containment, as with the abolition of feudal land rights or special protection given to depressed sections of the community, further contributed to the overall strategy of consolidating a framework of dominance through accommodation of dissent and diversity.

One final point about this approach at permitting competition despite the overall hegemony of the dominant party is found in the peculiarly personalized networks through which power positions have crystallized in Indian politics. Such personalized networks have contributed to the shifting rather than enduring nature of factional identities but they have at the same time galvanized local cleavages and politicized them, and have consequently prevented their "parochialism" from being destructive. One important outcome has been the diffusion of a surprisingly high information capability through these "networks of power" reaching up to the centres of the elite system.

On the whole, then, the dilemma of operating a democratic constitution for almost a generation without the availability of congruent structures of party competition has, in the Indian case, been resolved through some remarkable structural adaptations. Contributing to these adaptations are the autonomy of political elites, considerable improvisation at local levels and in regard to cleavage containment, the performance of representative roles by factional substructures within an otherwise dominant structure, and a high information capability despite desperately low levels of literacy and infrastructural resources.

THE ELECTORAL PROCESS AND SYSTEM ADAPTATION

The attempts to cope with what we earlier characterized as the "dilemma of dominant structures acting as dynamic agents of change" by incorporating plural identities and accommodative structures within the framework of dominance does not necessarily provide a lasting solution, especially when the democratic process is allowed a free and open play. Sooner or later the polarities of the system must emerge and pose a fresh challenge of adaptation for the prevailing structure of consensus. The issue now is how smoothly and willingly will the dominant structure adapt to the new articulation; how well will the new inheritors of power absorb the antecedent consensus on the fundamentals of the political system? If such a transition is accomplished without loss of nerve, the system would achieve a broader base of legitimacy by being able to further institutionalize the constitutional framework. If, on the other hand, the new response takes the form of either rigid confrontation or anomic fragmentation, the system would lose its legitimacy and enter a process of institutional disintegration.

Precisely this kind of challenge was posed in India by the increasing fragmentation of the Congress system of power in the wake of wars and successions, economic crisis, and a general election that brought to an end the long period of governmental stability. These events, crowded into a span of less than five years, caused a feeling of crisis in the political system and resulted in a pattern of response that, though still being worked out, provides clues to future possibilities.

The general reaction to the 1967 election was that it constituted a major change in the political system, as it ended the period of Congress dominance. Our analysis of electoral trends and post-election developments in the states casts doubt on such an assessment. However, for a fruitful discussion of the adaptive and integrative capabilities of the system, it would be useful to assume that the process started in 1967 will continue in subsequent elections, and to see what clues are available for the functioning of the system if the period of Congress dominance indeed comes to an end.

1. The Congress Party has not disintegrated in the face of effective challenge to its authority; the experience of other "movement regimes" that once they lose dominance they begin to disintegrate has not been repeated in India. In other words the fortunes of the Congress as a political party are not tied up in any hard and fast manner to its previously monolithic position as it has shown important adaptive capabilities both in terms of its staying and recuperative powers (as found in its impressive comeback to power in some state and local elections) and in terms of its ability to restructure its coalitional strategies (as found in its willingness to coalesce and bargain with other like-minded parties). The Congress also is still, and is likely to be for a long time, the most organized political party in the country, with a nationwide following and considerable depth in the localities. This has two consequences crucial to the system's functioning: it will continue to enjoy plurality at the center and thus a dominant voice in central coalition-making; and it will continue to control

widespread local power and patronage even where it is no longer in power at the state level.[7]

2. The other parties and party combinations that formed the government have, despite their militant "anti-Congress" stance during the elections, not shown any inclination of disrupting the fundamental institutional and programmatic consensus evolved under Congress rule. Indeed, as was discussed at some length in Chapter 5, there has been a remarkable continuity in both policies and political style despite the assumption of governmental power by almost all important parties of both left and right persuasions. It is now a familiar boast of many of these parties that they are implementing the Congress program better than Congress did when it was in power!

3. The factional structuring of competitive politics and group representation that emerged in the period of Congress dominance has continued to inform the politics of coalition-making since 1967. The defection of dissident groups from the Congress has made a majority of the new state coalitions possible. Even within relatively homogeneous parties like the DMK and the Jan Sangh and the ideologically inclined left parties, factional interactions similar to those found in the Congress have appeared. Lastly, just as left and right factions within the Congress reflected the ideologies and interests of important opposition parties, one now finds "Congress factions" within non-Congress parties and coalitions in power. So a crystallization of bargaining structures everywhere has facilitated both political communications across parties and a pressure towards the "center" of the ideological spectrum. The fact that each successive generation of politicians is being socialized into such a culture of politics has provided depth to the continuities noted above despite major shifts in the political structure.[8]

4. During this period trends also began to appear that pointed to important advances in political institutionalization. First, a significant change occurred in the coalitional style of the Congress leadership in regard to its various factions. Instead of the all-inclusive approach through which the leadership of the Congress had tried to retain all kinds of groups and interests within its boundaries, there now developed an emphasis on unity of purpose and a more cohesive team, with a willingness to allow

opposing groups to leave the party, and there was less anxiety about party defections.[9] Both the reduced margin of preponderance and the increasing differences over issues within the party contributed to this stress on a more homogeneous team. During the same period, the other major parties have also learned, through their experience of the fragility of improvised coalitions between disparate elements, that their strategy of "negative inclusion" against the Congress was proving costly and that they should return to the work of party-building in the constituencies. The experience of successive elections had shown that it was possible to carve out distinctive spheres of constituency strength; the task was to continue building this strength and confront the Congress on its own grounds.

5. Some trends in federal relations are likely to contribute to a strengthening of central initiatives and unitary tendencies. We have already noted in Chapter 5 how the Congress leadership at the center is finding it easier to deal with the more stable among the non-Congress ministries in the states than with the Congress ministries. There have been problems in containing the extremist impulses of some sections of the leftist united fronts of Kerala and West Bengal, but even here there is a shrewd combination of propagandist concessions to extremist opinion and pragmatic bargaining with the center. On the whole the fears of those who predicted a breakdown in federal relations as a result of other parties coming to power in the states have been belied. At the same time, wherever there has been instability in state coalitions the center has been able to intervene, in some cases by mediating in coalitional disputes, in other cases by utilizing the interventionist provisions of the Constitution. Other factors are at work here. Economically the center has assumed major new initiatives through nationalization of banks and greater control over credit and investment policies. The pressure to maintain the flow of basic necessities, the fact that the center has such a large say in the allocation of resources, and the growing realization on all sides that the Indian voter cannot any longer be taken for granted and will demand a concrete record of governmental achievement are all contributing to the acceptance of the role of central authority in the governmental process.

6. As against these trends in adaptiveness and further insti-

tutionalization of the democratic process, there are also some negative strains on the system and its performance capabilities. First is the obvious problem of governmental instability. Fortunately the extremes of "defectioneering" have ended following the realization that it damages the image and vote-getting power of the involved parties. Also the authority of the state governor, and of the center, to intervene have contributed to some sense of realism among contending parties. Yet the problem of the fragility of multi-party coalitions, arising in part from the fragmented character of party organization and the lack of stable party identities for the non-Congress parties, continues.[10] The question is: What if successive elections fail to turn up stable majorities? A fairly long period of governmental instability in a few states, interspersed by rule from the center, seems to be unavoidable, unless either the Congress shows a decisive comeback as it did in Haryana and UP, or a limited number of non-Congress parties can provide a stable alternative, as in Madras, Orissa, West Bengal, and Kerala.

Second, the inability of non-Congress parties and coalitions to maintain themselves in power owing to internal strains and the lack of stable electoral support is creating acute frustration in some of them. Until the Congress was the catch-all party, they seemed to have worked out a pattern of communication with different factions in the Congress and found satisfaction from debating and censuring opportunities that parliamentary politics provided. Once they have tasted governmental power, however, they are likely to want more and if this were not available, their frustrations are likely to seek more anomic and "radical" channels. The emergence of Indira Gandhi as a powerful national leader whose appeal cuts across parties, while welcomed by certain non-Congress parties, is likely in the end to accentuate these frustrations. What the 1967 elections did was to widen the base of political consensus by bringing in almost every important party to governmental power somewhere; unless this tendency gets institutionalized, the danger of disaffection on the part of a significant number of political groups is likely to grow. As the growing institutionalization of India's party system has been in terms of strong regional parties in opposition to the dominant national party (see Chapter 5), this danger can become really serious. We have argued that such an unaggregated party system facilitates political penetration and mobilization without turning these into loads on the central institutions of government. But by the same token, non-cooperation of the regional groups into the governmental system for long periods can lead to alienation and radicalization.

Third, coalitional instability and the continuous demands on central leadership for the maintenance of order and unity in the country are likely to lead to an overemphasis on issues of stability and political integration at the expense of other aspects of performance, especially in regard to economic development, although there seems to be no conclusive evidence in this regard. As we propose to consider these aspects of performance in the next chapter, we simply pose it here as a possible issue.[11]

7. All this leads to yet another issue: are the rules of the game fairly well accepted or are they still a matter of controversy and basic differences? It will be recalled that in the first phase of institutionalization the unavailability of alternating parties of "government" and "opposition" gave rise to a peculiar set of conventions and rules that were superimposed on the rules assumed by the Constitution. The developments leading to the 1967 election and its aftermath apparently brought the party system closer to the logic of the Constitution but, on the other hand, still retained important features of the dominant party system. While the ambivalences that arose from such patterns of continuity proved functional in socializing the new regional elites, they have also raised important issues on the detailed rules of the game, issues that have given rise to important controversies. At the same time the increasing differences and dissensions within the central leadership of the Congress Party have created an atmosphere of suspense about the stability of the center itself, and have consequently increased the temptation on all sides to pay scant respect to canons of propriety and decorum.

The chief issues relate to the manner in which the legislative strength of rival coalitions can be determined under fluid and fragmented conditions, the authority of a state governor in advising the center on whether or not the constitutional machinery has broken down in a state, the powers of presiding officers of legislative bodies, conventions of on the dissolution of the legislature, and most important, the powers of president of India in times of constitutional crisis. On all these issues the Constitution has something to say but the exact agreements must be worked out through conventions and precedents. While none of these controversies has threatened the core principles of parliamentary democracy and while no political party or group has utilized any crisis for undermining the Constitution, the detailed rules of the game cannot yet be said to be above controversy. Here is an area of indecision in the institutionalization of India's operating political system.

INSTITUTIONALIZATION OF POLITICAL CHANGE

An important index of political development is the ease with which change in incumbency at crucial levels of the system is routinized. In a majority of the new — and not a few of the old — states such changes have led to traumatic consequences, and the prospects of a wide variety of political systems seem to hang on this issue.[12] It is an old one in statecraft and only a handful of nations have been able to institutionalize changes in incumbency. In the case of India the issue was repeatedly expressed as critical to the future of its democratic Constitution. It was often argued that all the other developments, including changes in positions of incumbency at various other levels, were possible to absorb as the system was dominated by the Congress Party at the center and especially by such a towering, charismatic figure as Jawaharlal Nehru, and that the real test of the system would come when these critical conditions of stability were no long there. The issue was neatly posed in the question, "After Nehru, who?" sometimes rephrased as "After Nehru, what?" Increasing dissension in the Congress Party and its High Command, the lack of a clear choice of successor, the successive deaths of the "tall men" who came to power with Nehru, and the extraordinary domination of the political system by Nehru were responsible for such speculation and doubt. They created, throughout the late fifties and the early sixties, considerable interest in India's impending succession crisis.[13]

The country faced not one but two succession crises, and a third occasion for a closely contested choice of leader which earned the label of the "third succession," all within a span of three years (1964-67), years that were loaded with serious problems of internal and external survival. We do not intend to describe these events here but only to highlight a few points from the perspective of the capability of the Indian political system to effect crucial changes in an institutionalized manner. The points may have some relevance beyond India.

1. Nehru persistently and adamantly refused to name a successor. He often made the point that he had enough faith in democracy not to intervene in the selection process which should take its "natural course," that India's political system had achieved enough maturity to absorb his passing from the scene, and that he also had enough faith in the Congress party to select a person who would be equal to the tasks that this high office involved. Nehru showed not only a spirited conviction in the democratic process but also a remarkable appreciation of its dynamics: "If I nominated somebody," he said, "that is the surest way of his not becoming Prime Minister. People would be jealous of him, dislike him."[14] This is why he not only did not nominate a political heir; he also resisted any indirect institutional steps that might establish some kind of seniority, as in his refusal to appoint a deputy prime minister.[15] The contrast to Gandhi's unequivocal nomination of Nehru as his "natural heir" is striking. The different approaches of the two leaders also signify different stages in the country's institutionalization.

2. But Nehru was concerned about the succession issue. Supplementing his refusal to nominate a successor was his concern to avoid a sharp polarization that would lead to irreconcilable divisions in the party and in the central government. He sought to facilitate a slow consensus without forcing it. Keenly sensitive to the federal character of the country and the nature of coalition that the Congress represented, he wanted to avoid the decision's being made merely at the top. Through his active support of the "Kamaraj Plan"— a plan that ostensibly made important leaders of government resign and devote time to party work but in reality activated the federal structure of the Congress — Nehru himself concluded the chapter of Indian history that he had so overwhelmingly dominated and during which the party had been

reduced to an appendage. He revived the authority of the Congress president in times of crisis, recognized the role of chief ministers of the states in so important a decision as the choice of the next leader of a federal polity, and by a couple of shrewd moves — throwing his weight behind the election of Mr. Kamaraj as Congress president reappointing Mr. Shastri as minister without portfolio to assist the ailing Nehru in carrying out his duties as prime minister — laid the groundwork for an emerging consensus without going as far as to nominate his successor. (For he once again refused to nominate Shastri as deputy prime minister.)

The issue was still wide open when Nehru died but the emphasis had already shifted from engaging in a "struggle for succession" to evolving a "technique of consensus" that would come up with a solution acceptable to all. Such a technique was quickly evolved by the leaders of the party: it consisted of an attempt at not appearing to impose the decision of a caucus, to consult all the principal elements in the decision-making process, but at the same time to give to the decision the stamp of legitimacy derived from an authoritative "consensus." Thus no strong protest was raised when the Congress president, after a hectic round of consultations with the chief ministers, members of the Working Committee and office-bearers of the Congress Parliamentary Party, other leaders of the party, and about 200 Congress members of Parliament, declared Lal Bahadur Shastri to be the "consensus choice" of the party.[16] It was known that in effect the choice was of a united coalition of the most powerful elements in the party, welded together by the Congress president and by a pervading sense of somehow avoiding a polarization in the party. The rest was mere formality: the Congress Parliamentary Party met, with the Congress president in the chair, and unanimously elected Shastri as the leader, and the president of India invited Shastri to form the new government. The whole process of seeking consensus, though it involved such a large number of people, was completed in record time.

> At 9 AM on the 2nd of June 1964, 5 days and 19 hours after the death of Jawaharlal Nehru, the Congress Parliamentary Party met in extraordinary session in the Central Hall of Parliament and unanimously elected Lal Bahadur Shastri the party leader.

> Seven hours later, President Radhakrishnan invited Shastri to form a new government. With that act the succession to Nehru was complete. To those who participated in the drama of the six days that did not shake the world, no less than to those who observed it, this was a remarkably tranquil adjustment to the end of an era. People who had predicted dissension and turmoil, and there were many throughout the world, were proved prophets of gloom. Yet even those who had been optimistic were relieved, and even somewhat surprised, by the mature, sophisticated, and smooth internal transfer of power.[17]

Thus the first major "succession crisis," under conditions where one paramount consideration was how to maintain the unity of the party and the country, was handled through a subtle admixture of allowing the democratic process a free play and restraining the struggle for power from getting ugly and out of hand. While paying due regard to the opinions of the larger constituency, it was principally resolved by men who had a sense of the nature of the crisis, and the most appropriate resolution of it. Nehru himself contributed to it, though indirectly and with conscious circumspection.

3. None of these factors was present when Shastri died a mere nineteen months after he had become India's second prime minister. There was no great sense of gravity or impending disintegration: the country had already shown its capacity to fill a constitutional void. Shastri's death did not signify the end of an era as Nehru's did. On the other hand, the moment of choice came suddenly and without any forewarning or preparation of groundwork for a consensus. Shastri's death was sudden and dramatic, in far-off Tashkent, after a historic summit conference with President Ayub Khan following a bloody war between India and Pakistan. The question "After Shastri, who?" had never been asked and Shastri himself had played no role in paving the way for a succession. Furthermore there was no sense of a clear choice; indeed Mrs. Indira Gandhi, who emerged as the ultimate choice of the Parliamentary Party, was not even in the initial running. Many names were mentioned—Chavan, Morarji, Nanda, Mrs. Gandhi, Jagjivan Ram, perhaps Kamaraj himself—and there was no unity on any one name even among the core coalition of the Congress party (except perhaps a negative agreement to keep

Morarji out). New considerations were mentioned, such as who could best lead the party in the forthcoming general elections, but the issue was not decisive and the choice not clear.

This explains why a different set of rules emerged. An open conflict was not greatly feared, and ultimately the issue was settled through a secret ballot in the CPP. The decisive step that influenced the ballot was a meeting of the chief ministers who cast their weight in favor of Mrs. Gandhi who thus emerged as a consensus candidate though not a consensus choice. But even after the chief ministers' meeting, open and hectic campaigning followed and the election of the new party leaders turned out to be a closely fought contest, Mrs. Gandhi getting 355 against Morarji's 169. The politics of the succession was this time openly waged, carried out in dignity, and did not result in any deep scars as was feared during the first succession if an open conflict had taken place. The CPP, the rightful constituency for the election, had directly elected the leader; dissidence in the state delegations and defiance of the chief ministers were allowed free play. The outcome of the second succession was thus a more institutionalized procedure and a further show of confidence in the system's ability to fill a constitutional vacuum. At the same time both the federal character of the decision and the role of the party outside Parliament in crystallizing the nature of the choice were once again shown. What emerged finally was again a consensus but one that was more openly arrived at.

4. The selection of the prime minister after the 1967 general election, though not strictly a succession, was important in further testing the nation's ability to cope with problems of political choice at the apex of the system. The routine of electing a leader after every election was largely ritualistic and unimportant until Nehru was at the helm. Although there was an incumbent prime minister in 1967, her confirmation as leader of the party was far from certain; even when she was elected leader in January, 1966, it was clear that the issue of leadership would be freshly considered by the CPP after the election. Once again the political conditions under which the choice was to be made were different from those that obtained in the first two successions. The Congress Party had experienced a drastic diminution in its position in the country and its majority in the Parliament (44 in a house of

521) was just enough to keep it in the saddle; any dissident move would lead to its fall from power. The Congress had lost a majority in seven states, including Mr. Kamaraj's Madras (and Kamaraj had himself been defeated). This meant that the "Chief Ministers' Club" which had played such a key role in the 1966 succession was no longer available to assert its authority. Also, most of the powerful members of the party's "core coalition" had personally lost the election, and hence their authority to influence central politics: Congress President Kamaraj, the "king-maker," had been greatly humbled and was in no mood to seek a consensus and impose it as a solution.

Thus both the 1964-style technique of consensus which depended on the availability of an authoritative coalition in the party and the choice by ballot which would inevitably mean defeat of the minority group — which the 1966 ballot had shown to be fairly large — seemed inappropriate. Two points became clear as the leadership began to review the situation: the campaign for the leader's election had to be waged directly among members of the CPP, and as far as possible a contest should be avoided and all parties accommodated. The large incidence of dissidence during and after the elections haunted the decision-makers and united them in their effort to close all ranks.

Intense bargaining followed, in which the chief negotiators were the principal contenders themselves (Mrs. Gandhi and Morarji Desai) and their key supporters, a strategic group of mediators committed to avoid a showdown (Kamaraj himself and a couple of state bosses), and a new and powerful crystallization that emerged for the first time, a large group of young and committed "Nehruite" members of Parliament determined not to allow Mrs. Gandhi to lose ground in the name of party unity. There was free and open flow of information and negotiation, each party conceding less than the other asked; both finally agreed to a compromise. The final solution confirmed Mrs. Gandhi as party leader, brought in Morarji in the number two position with the formal title of "Deputy Prime Minister," and allowed Chavan to retain the powerful and coveted Home portfolio. (Morarji wanted Home but had to concede on that point; Mrs. Gandhi's supporters, especially Chavan, were not willing to give to Morarji the deputy prime ministership but had finally to concede the position to him.) The dignity of the bargain was maintained by Morarji agreeing not to fetter Mrs. Gandhi in the composition of her cabinet or in any other formal stipulation of the functions of the DPM.

The result was a composite cabinet, the return to an eclectic coalition that Nehru had all along presided over. The party remained united under a collective leadership that agreed to speak with one voice in the Parliament and the country. Morarji, always a party disciplinarian and an advocate of unfettered governmental authority, declared his resolve to back the prime minister. Mrs. Gandhi, by breaching her differences with Morarji and bringing him into the government, now had a balanced team which reduced her dependence on her own supporters (the so-called "kitchen cabinet") as well as her dependence on party bosses outside. A consolidated center coalition had emerged, a considerable asset in an otherwise fluid and unstable political situation in the country.[18]

One feature of the 1967 "succession" deserves to be noted because it throws light on the growing openness of the political process in India: the bargaining process was carried out openly and unashamedly; and there was a constant and open flow of information and communication. While mediators continuously played their role and eminently succeeded in driving home the moral that party interests should transcend personal ambitions and prejudices, the chief contenders themselves remained very active, laid their cards open, personally met a number of times, and did not allow misunderstandings to accumulate out of inadequate communication. Nor did they allow others to impose solutions or to deadlock conflict. This openness of the information process was a distinct advance over the earlier successions and contributed to the bargaining and accommodative capability of the Congress Party.[19]

This started a transition from the time when the political system depended for its image and its identity on a charismatic individual to a period of collective leadership and teamwork. This was another step in institutionalization.[20]

On the other hand, the transitional nature of political institutionalization was revealed during the same period. In the months prior to and since the fourth general election, party elites were continuously preoccupied with problems of forging and maintaining coalitions, bargaining for strategic rewards, and restraining personal ambitions. The manner in which the whole process of candidate selection in the Congress Party prior to the 1967 elections had been subjected to calculations of the coming struggle for leadership and the prime ministership showed deep divisions in the party all the way down to the electoral constituencies.[21] Still sharper divisions began to appear during 1969 in what seemed like another struggle for ascendancy within the "collective leadership" and an attempt to once again open the issue of who would lead the party. As this happened in an atmosphere of mutual suspicion, the very process of open communications that had been established in 1967 was reversed, and there took place a mutual closure and drifting away of opposite groups at the very center of the political system.

THE PRESIDENTIAL ELECTION, 1969

The governmental-organizational conflict that is inherent in the Indian party system was, until 1967, managed at lower levels, the national Congress leadership (the High Command) always maintaining a cohesive character and mediating in disputes at lower levels. Starting with the succession struggles, however, the process penetrated right at the apex of the system and by 1969 reached a climax at the Bangalore session of the Congress Party, where sharp divisions between Prime Minister Indira Gandhi and the party organizers led by the Congress President Mr. Nijalingappa, came out in the open. The divisions reflected a complex syndrome of personality conflicts, pressures from rival sets of constituencies, and programmatic differences. They led to a struggle for leadership which did three things. First, it brought out into the open an issue that had been suppressed throughout the operation of the Kamaraj Plan, namely the status and position of the prime minister and her government in the Congress Party's equation of power. Second, this intra-party split led to mobilization of support from outside the party, Mrs. Gandhi mobilizing the left parties, the DMK and other regional groups, and the organizational leaders finding support from the Swatantra and the Jan

Sangh. Third, the polarization that ensued also took on a regional character, with northern India, West Bengal, Kerala, and Madras going with Mrs. Gandhi, and western India, Rajasthan, and Mysore supporting the Congress organization. Together all this shook the complacency of the Congress consensus, nearly obliterated the boundaries of left and right that had so far preserved the identity of the Congress center, and plunged the country towards a new phase of competitive alignments.

The struggle reached a crisis point when the prime minister was voted out by the Congress Parliamentary Board on the nomination of the party's candidate for the coming election of the President of India in August 1969. Interpreting this as part of a design to weaken her authority and ultimately dislodge her from power, the enraged prime minister hit back by a series of moves: the virtual dismissal of Mr. Morarji Desai, the deputy prime minister, whom she had herself accommodated in 1967 to avoid a split; a hurried ordinance nationalizing the major banks as the beginning of a "radical" economic program; and the demand that Congress members of Parliament and state legislatures should be allowed a "free vote" in the presidential election which amounted to permitting them to vote for the opposition's candidate, Mr. V.V. Giri. The Congress president declined such a request and there took place an all-out bid to mobilize support for rival candidates. The electoral campaign that followed cut across all parties, took on an unprecedented momentum, and resulted in the defeat of the official Congress candidate, Mr. Sanjiva Reddy. This was the first time that an official Congress candidate was defeated in the presidential contest. It was a direct consequence of the struggle between the Congress organizational leadership intent upon establishing the discipline of the party and the prime minister's group in the government and the Parliament determined to authenticate the power and position of the prime minister's office. At the time of writing the prime minister and her supporters have emerged victorious and it seems likely that she will be able to re-establish the supremacy of the governmental leadership vis-a-vis party managers, as well as to re-establish a left of center consensus under Congress dominance.

On the other hand, the presidential election of 1969 showed the wide-open character of the Indian party system and the ambiguities arising out of such openness. Whereas mutual suspicions and recriminations at the highest level led to an almost complete blockade of communications, the campaign itself involved all the major parties and factional groups within the Congress. It was seen that alongside the usual situation of Congress dominance in which factions within the Congress Party utilize the existence of other parties to press their positions inside the party, the other parties like the Communists on the one hand and the Swatantra and the Jan Sangh on the other also tried to utilize rival factions in the Congress for pressing new alignments in the party system. The rival groups mobilized all their resources and the battle was openly waged, without fear of the system's breaking down under the strain of an almost even polarization of the party system, a polarization that took on both political-ideological and regional-communal overtones. While there was speculation during and for some time after the election regarding the stability of the Congress government at the center in the face of such an open split, there were no great premonitions of the breakdown of democracy. And even the much publicized "split" was avoided when the Congress Working Committee, meeting soon after the Presidential election under conditions of great tension, realized the seriousness of the situation and adopted a "unity resolution" moved by Y.B. Chavan who played a major role in saving the party from disintegration.

In some ways this latest crisis in leadership proved to be more important than the various succession crises. On the one hand, by straining the Congress system to the point of near breakdown, it tested the recuperative mechanisms of the system. On the other hand, it started a new chain sequence of alignments and confrontations at various levels, a period of raging debate and issue clarifications, and perhaps a new style in political competition. With this the democratic process in India is likely to come face to face with the dilemmas of operating a sophisticated political system under conditions of mounting pressures for resources and positions. These pages go to press as this process is still in midstream.

At the same time there is much disunity in the ranks of the other parties. A series of mid-term elections and continuous preoccupation with coalition-making have put their resources to severe test. Not only have the various non-Congress parties proved non-coalitionable; sharp cleavages based on interest, ideology, and personality have affected each of them too. Quite a few of them have a "succession crisis." The death of Ram Manohar Lohia has left the SSP, perhaps the most dynamic among the non-Congress parties, deeply divided. Ever since their ideological splintering in the early sixties, the Communists have lost their former unity and self-discipline. The PSP has been leaderless ever since Jayaprakash Narayan took to sarvodaya and Asoka Mehta was sold on the "compulsions of a backward economy" thesis. The Swatantra gives the impression of not believing in the need for a national leadership while the various dissident Congress groups seem to have too many leaders and hardly any followers. Only the Jan Sangh gives the impression of some cohesion and drive despite the inevitable factionalism in its ranks much on the lines of the Congress. But the Jan Sangh is still mainly a northern party, just as the DMK is a southern party. All of this underlines the fluid nature of political institutionalization in the post-Nehru, post-Congress preponderance phase of Indian politics. What gave the system its cohesion and unity through such fluidity so far was the leadership of the Congress Party which has shown its resilience and staying power despite the party's diminution of electoral standing and the passing away of its "tall men." Doubts are now being expressed whether the Congress will continue to perform this function.

ROLE OF BUREAUCRACY

Equally important to the resilience and continuity of the Indian system is its less noticed but pervasive structure of bureaucracy. Since we have discussed the role of the public bureaucracy in Chapter 4, we shall not go into it again here. But its importance to system performance can hardly be exaggerated. For at a time of political transition, like the present, not only does the structure of public administration provide the chief source of governmental continuity, but the key issues of performance also turn increasingly on what is achieved in specific areas of governmental output. The political leadership has to work closely with the bureaucracy and the technocracy, as is found in the increasing role of senior civil servants in India in higher level decision-making. Observers have been struck by the importance given to senior civil servants by Mr. Shastri and Mrs. Gandhi even in crucial political decisions. This was noticed during the conflict with Pakistan and at Tashkent,[22] and continues to be noted in New Delhi. The role of men like L.K. Jha, L.P. Singh, and P.N. Haksar in the making of crucial decisions, the growing importance of the cabinet secretariat and the prime minister's secretariat in political intelligence, and the participation of these secretaries in high-level committees signify the increasingly composite nature of governmental decision-making. It is a far cry from the days when even cabinet ministers were afraid to open their mouths before Mr. Nehru.

So far we have been concerned with the institutionalization of a political center, and the concomitant structures of coalition-making, political succession, and ideological consensus. However, it is widely recognized that another set of issues is generated in this very process of institutionalization, that as development proceeds it gives rise to new patterns of participation and bargaining, and that as these are diffused outwards from the political center they engender a new consciousness of diversities and distinctive identities which then become the rallying points of new demands and cleavages. These demands have a potential for both centrifugal and centripetal tendencies, their precise outcome depending on the peculiar interaction between processes of articulation and aggregation on the one hand and socialization and communications on the other. The issues that now confront the leadership are not cast in some simple framework of policy dichotomies or sequential choices but take the form of more realistic challenges that must be met if the system is to survive: how to assure unity *through* growth, how to consolidate the political center through the dispersal of both benefits and values, how to respond to parochial demands by involving them in the ongoing structures of coalition-making. While the challenges now become more pragmatic and less ideological, they put the capabilities of the elite to the more crucial test of political development: the continuous allocation of political resources and support structures to the resolution of pressing issues as the nation moves from one threshold of "unity in diversity" to another.

THE DEMANDS OF DIVERSITY

Because the principal contextual variables of Indian civilization are its great size, antiquity, and multi-ethnic character, the "politicization of diversities" has been crystallized along a variety of dimensions. Chief among these are caste, religion, language, and region. We have devoted a full chapter to caste and its transformation under the politicizing impacts of an adult democracy. We need not repeat the conclusions of that analysis. As regards religious diversity, we have seen in Chapter 2 how the very birth of the new nation witnessed a deep schism in Indian society leading to the division of the country, and led to an outbreak of violence and bloodshed that has few parallels in modern history. We have discussed the communal problem there at some length. Here it is only necessary to note the significance of this experience for contemporary nation-building.

With all its terrible cost—some of which still continue to be paid—the partition of the subcontinent bequeathed two distinct advantages in the learning and socialization of the new nation. The first of these was to place a very high value on unity and order, on the need at all costs to preserve central authority, and on the political necessity to hold the country and its diverse elements together. This was evident not only in the considerations of the Constituent Assembly and its various decisions which gave to the federal Constitution both its unitary and its accommodative characteristics; the value on unity has informed the national political idiom ever since. The second advantage was even more far-reaching. The partition and the violence that attended it, and the considerable problems of reerecting the nation's political edifice, made the Indian elite highly sensitive to the elements of statecraft, and what is takes to preserve political autonomy and dominance.

The problem is very significant to the nation-building enterprise. A number of new nations of Asia and Africa inherited a unified national territory essentially as a ready-made package from their colonial predecessors. Since they had no need to construct the "state" or build the "nation" from its elements, this unity turned out to be not only precarious but highly deceptive. In the first few years of independence the leaders of these nations thought in terms of their dominance over national politics; in reality what they enjoyed was what may be called the *illusion of dominance.* While it lasted these leaders seemed to be peculiarly insensitive to the issues of authority and consensus, so that when the issues came dramatically to the fore, they were taken wholly by surprise. Ghana under Nkrumah and Indonesia under Sukarno manifested extreme versions of this illusion; the "Nasser appeal" over large parts of the Middle East symbolizes the pervasive instability of national identities born out of the accidents of history. On the other hand, the civil wars of the Congo and Nigeria may well prepare those nations with a deeper feeling of what unity and national identity involves. At any rate in the Indian case such an experience did produce a realistic feeling for the elements of nationhood and the politics of dominance.

In post-independence India caste and religion as population characteristics are fairly widely dispersed and the process of politics has tended to attenuate such widely dispersed identities by rendering them as subconstituents of larger political and coalitional identifications. It is in respect to more clustered identities that political demands emanating from ethnic divisions create greater threats to national unity. That takes us to the remaining two of the dimension mentioned above—language and regionalism.

LINGUISTIC DIVERSITY AND NATIONAL UNITY

The linguistic configuration of India is in many respects unique. Analogies from other countries—Canada, Belgium, Switzerland, USSR—have little relevance in understanding its problems. Nor are conceptual categories or empirical insights drawn from the European experience of the nineteenth century of great relevance. The assertion of a decisive relationship between language and politics which formed an important part of the European nationalist creed[23] applies quite differently in a situation where the language problem is, to say the least, multi-dimensional. It needs to be understood that India has always been a multi-lingual civilization with a complicated system of communications both laterally and vertically, special elite languages, and a constant interplay between local, regional, and all-india languages. Patterns of language development in different historical group cohesion, secular accommodation, and emulation of dominant cultural standards that has characterized India's general approach to unity and assimilation. The hesitant, groping character of contemporary language policy reflects the same approach and underlines both the inherent difficult of enacting an easy solution and the imperative of moving slowly[24] towards some negotional agreements.

One needs also to grasp that the doctrine that a single language is essential for national identity is hardly relevant to the Indian case, that even the self-assured radicals have been reluctant to provide a neat formula as they are prone to do in other fields, and that the language fanatics (in the Congress, the Jan Sangh and the SSP on the one side and the DMK on the other) have been steadily moving towards accepting a center position. While the language problem is no doubt putting to test India's overall design of national unity, it is also forcing all parties to accept a pluralist solution, and has lately, after encountering a series of crises, led to important break throughs in policy crystallization. Let us look at some of the facts.

The Linguistic Survey of India, published in 1927, spoke of 179 languages and 544 dialects (and in all 1,652 "mother tongues"), while the latest Census of India (see Table 8.1) recorded speakers of 1,018 different languages. The seeming variety, however, conceals a number of *central tendencies*. First, all these languages and dialects fall under four language families (Indo-Aryan, Dravidian, Tibeto-Chinese, and Austro-Asiatic), and all but 2 per cent under the first two families (73.3 per cent Indo-Aryan and 24.5 per cent Dravidian), which, in turn, by constant borrowing from each other, are part of a single linguistic area.[25] Second, throughout history there has been concentric convergence within regional language belts, as between the local village dialect, the subregional dialect which may or may not have been standardized, and the regional standard language with a distinctive literature and political usage.[26] The Constitution of India recognized this when it listed fourteen "languages of India" in the Eighth Schedule; according to the 1961 Census, 87 per cent of the population gave these fourteen languages as their "mother tongue." These regional standards have become greatly consolidated with fixed characteristics and a thriving literature during the last hundred years under the impact of education, urbanization, and political development. Underlying the persisting diversity of India's language situation has been this striking process of regionalized unification which has largely gone unnoticed except among a few linguists and anthropologists.

TABLE 8.1
Language of India (1961)

	Languages	Speakers	Percentage of Indian population
Indo-Aryan	574	321,721,000	73.3
Inner Sub-Branch		212,482,000	
*Hindi		133,435,000	
*Urdu		23,323,000	
*Gujarat		20,304,000	
Rajasthani		14,933,000	
*Punjabi		10,951,000	
Pahari		4,562,000	
Other		4,974,000	
Outer Sub-Branch		109,239,000	
*Bengali		33,889,000	
*Marathi		33,281,000	
Bihari		16,807,000	
*Oriya		15,719,000	
*Assamese		6,803,000	
Other		3,199,000	
Dravidian	153	107,411,000	24.5
*Telugu		37,668,000	
*Tamil		30,563,000	
*Kannada		17,416,000	
*Malayalam		17,016,000	
Other		4,749,000	
Austro-Asiatic	65	6,192,000	1.5
Tibeto-Chinese	226	3,184,000	0.7

*Indicates the languages that are listed in the Eighth Schedule of the Constitution of India

Source: Census of India 1961, I, Part II C (ii), *Language Tables*. The figures have been rounded to thousands.

Third, beyond these circles of convergence there has continuously been in India (except in the very ancient past) one or more languages that could be used throughout the land, and especially for cultural and political purposes. First it was Sanskrit, then Persian, then Urdu, and since the nineteenth century English and Hindustani (which is a mixture of Hindi and Urdu). The heart of the present controversy on the language problem derives from this very issue: what should be independent India's official ("national") language, English — the ambivalent legacy of the British Raj — or Hindi as proclaimed in the Constitution? For the moment we may simply note that operating in and through the bewildering variety of India's languages have been these central tendencies, and that these have been further consolidated through the process associated with India's political modernization.

The early impact of this modernization, however, created a sharp dichotomy between the elite and the masses of India. Groomed in the English language as a necessary passport to officialdom, the professions, and the national movement, the former were drawn away from their cultural moorings and ignored the development of their own languages and local cultures. The hiatus thus created was deep and still persists. The later thrust of modernization, under Gandhi and the mass mobilization phase of the movement, revived the original relationship between the language of the elite (English), the presumed language of the "nation" (Hindi), and the regional standard languages. Local elites began to develop regional literary and political forms, communicated the ideology and techniques of the movement through regional media, undertook a number of "educational" tasks, and as implored by the Mahatma, " built bridges" with the villages. It was during the movement that these identities were strengthened, and the demands for "linguistic autonomy" and the replacement of English by Hindi and the regional languages spread. While these demands were accepted in principle, the kind of issues inherent in implementing them were not squarely face. They were not readily faced even after independence when the misplaced antipathy of Nehru and the modernist elite towards "parochial tendencies" served only to postpone the problems. Only when the regional elites gained self-confidence and insisted on bringing the issues out in the open was sufficient pressure created for definitive policies. Indeed, it was largely under the influence of crisis-like events that apparently intractable issues were openly confronted and a measure of response generated.

We have previously discussed the first of these crises, that associated with the demand for territorial redistribution of state boundaries on the basis of language. Although the Congress movement was openly committed to, and its own organization based on, the linguistic principle, it took a "fast unto death" and serious disturbances to force the issue. This led to a mammoth political and administrative reorganization of this vast country. It was in many ways a historic transformation. There is little doubt that the reorganization, once accomplished, led to considerable political consolidation, ease of communication between the government and the people, and greater integration of the political community. The hiatus that had divided the English-educated elite and the vast masses and their immediate leaders has at long last been broken and the channels of mobilization have been able to penetrate into the countryside with speed and effect, in the process generating a major information and communications breakthrough. A commitment to planned programs and a basic consensus on institutional and procedural norms have also been facilitated by this approximation of the nation's territorial design with the "natural" boundaries of its people.

But the role of regional linguistic autonomy in the crystallization of administrative and political relationships and the ordering of regional identities toward a "federal consensus" constituted only one part of the language problem. An equally important part was the question of the all-India medium, or media, of communication. For reasons already discussed, and given the symbolic legacies of the national movement, English could not be accepted to continue as the nation's lingua franca. The only other candidate was Hindi but the independence movement had not been able to spread the use of Hindi in non-Hindi areas on an adequate scale and neither the government of India nor the various Hindi Prachar Samitis (agencies for the spread of Hindi) had done their homework in the 15-year moratorium on the issue provided by the Constitution. The Constitution had stipulated that, while Hindi be designated as the "official"—the term "national" was avoided—language of the Union, English might continue to be used until 1965, after which the Parliament was to review the position.

When the end of the moratorium drew near, regional identities had been sufficiently articulated, the poverty of Hindi in comparison with more richly endowed languages like Bengali, Tamil, Telugu, and Marathi had become glaring, the "Hindi fanatics" has pushed their case in an exclusivist and purist style thus alienating other language groups, and the fact that Hindi was no more than one among several regional languages — even if more numerous—had been emphasized in the consciousness of the non-Hindi language elites. On the other hand, the Official Languagerests. Commission and the Committee of Members of Parliament on the same issue recommended, along with a few notes of dissent, that Hindi should progressively replace English as the official language, possibly with effective changeover in 1965. There was some flexibility in these reports as to the date of media change in various fields but the reports nonetheless aroused great anxiety in the non-Hindi areas where agitations were mounted to register protests against the recommended course of action.

The pressure that ensued led to an immediate response from Nehru who gave a "pledge" to the non-Hindi areas that English would remain for an indefinite period (as long as the non-Hindi-speaking people wanted) as "an associate official language." His emphasis that Hindi could not be imposed both restrained the agitation against Hindi and led to a shift in emphasis in official statements, as in the resolution of the Congress Party at its annual session at Gauhati in 1958, in the Presidential Order of 1960, in resolutions of the National Integration Conference of 1961, and in the Official Languages Act of 1963, to which all were added Nehru's personal "assurances."

True to the consensus through ambiguity style of Indian politics, however, the assurances were not clearly translated into the Act; Nehru—whose personal guarantees proved more effective than anything else in allaying southern fears—passed away in 1964, routine administrative circulars on the "switchover" to Hindi continued to irritate the southerners and fray their tempers, and the day of reckoning arrived on January 26, 1965 without adequate preparation of a groundwork for national consensus. The result was a precipitous crisis that took a dramatic form: the unprecedented act of self-immolation by two DMK leaders in Madras city, violent outbreaks in large parts of Madras state, the formation of a highly organized Student's Agitation Council, and, above all, a dramatic resignation of two Madras ministers, one of whom was a highly esteemed Congress leader, from the central government. Such a cumulative and massive pressure finally led to a policy change which, while still obscure on a few points, committed the country to a specific language formula.

The outcome—long in the making but clearly announced only after the crisis and after protracted negotiations between various groups in the government and Congress Party—was the "three language formula." Every state was to have freedom to transact its own business in the state language, which was also to be the medium of instruction in the state universities; English was to continue as the language of interstate communications (if these were written in Hindi they would have to be accompanied by an official English translation); non-Hindi states were to continue to correspond with the center in English; English was to continue as the official language at the center, including the Parliament; official examinations were to be conducted in English, Hindi, and all the regional languages; and there was to be a phased program for the development of Hindi. Although no section was fully satisfied with this compromise formula, the announcements—made by the president in his Address to Parliament and by the Congress Working Committee—became the basis for a slow process of consensus.

The main difference that remained was whether the assurance should be translated into an amendment to the Constitution or into a simple resolution of the Parliament. The war with Pakistan shelved this particular issue but a parliamentary resolution incorporating the various assurances was eventually passed, and, although some drama was created when the Madras Assembly adopted a unilateral resolution rejecting any role for Hindi, it was realized that this was done mainly to forestall fresh disturbances. The DMK leadership soon made amends by agreeing to confer with other parties and defining steps to implement the "three language formula." What is even more reassuring is that the Jan Sangh, which had traditionally adopted a doctrinaire pro-Hindi position, has accepted the formula, largely as a concession to the south and the east where it is keen to consolidate a political base in its attempt to emerge as a "national party." In the case of the DMK, too, accession to power has helped modify its posture of hostility and has instead turned it into a proponent of the "middle way." Power, it seems, has been the great modifier of positions.

On the whole, both the crisis of the fifties leading to states' reorganization and the crisis of the early sixties leading to the three language formula helped crystallize the main issue by an open confrontation between opposing groups, and ultimately led to a way out of what, at one time, appeared like a situation in which any decision would jeopardize the country's unity. The nation survived both crises and, from all evidence, perhaps with a greater capability to handle fresh outbreaks of linguistic subnationalism. In the meanwhile studies have indicated that, despite the known animosities, Hindi has been spreading rather fast as a second language in non-Hindi areas, through education, trade, and the mass media (according to the 1961 census, Hindi and Urdu as second languages were slightly ahead of English as a second language); English as a second language has also been spreading fast (it is compulsory in secondary schools, is a medium of instruction in an increasing number of "central" institutions of learning, and dominates the national press and the publishing trade); and both are being used with varying degrees of familiarity by all aspiring groups.[27] The situation is not very different than it always was in India: a special language for the elite (English), a lay language spoken fairly widely in the land but with many regional variations (Hindi), and regional standard languages dominating and bringing together the more numerous sub- regional and local dialects. The main difference now is that the regional standards are becoming important all-state vehicles and the gap between these standards and the local dialects is fast narrowing. Building upon this process of local integration are the emerging national languages—English and Hindi—both of which are likely to survive in India, most probably for all time to come.

REGIONALISM AND THE DANGERS OF SECESSION

The point made a little while ago about power being the great modifier of positions can be made also in regard to the accommodation of other regional strains in post-independence India. One of these is the threat of "secession" from the Union or from one of its constituent states. It has been speculated by some pessimists that the country faces the "dangerous" alternatives of either Balkanization or authorization rule as the movement for regional autonomy gains ground.[28] There have indeed been such movements in the past as well as in the present. Based partly on historical mythology and partly on caste, ethnic, and regional hostility, there developed a powerful intellectual movement for autonomy in the Dravidian south, mainly in the old Madras state. Broadly in continuation of a movement for the rights of non-Brahmins against the monopolistic hold of Brahmins on administrative and political positions, started by the Dravidian Association and the South Indian Liberal Federation (the Justice Party) in 1917, the militant Tamils set up, in 1914, the Dravida Kazhagam (DK) which called upon the Dravidian peoples of south India "to guard against a transfer of power from the British to the Aryans." It asked for a separate south Indian state, Dravidasthan, and for complete separation from the Indian Union.[29]

By 1954, however, when political power shifted from the Brahmins to a distinctly indigenous "Tamilized" and non-Brahmin leadership under the new chief minister, Kamaraj Nadar, the DK threw in its support to the Congress ministry. This led to the formation of a splinter group, the Dravida Munnetra Kazhagam (DMK) which pledged itself to carry on the movement for Dravidasthan. But both the increasing Tamilian character of the Congress and the growth of the DMK as a strong political party— first by its capture of power in the Madras city corporation and other urban governments in 1959 and then by its emergence as the largest opposition party in Madras after the 1962 elections— chastened the militant posture of the DMK. By a series of moves it shed its extra parliamentary character and decided to win power through the ballot box.[30] This, no doubt, led to another splinter group led by E.V.K. Sampath who sought to carry on the torch of Tamil separation. Upon this followed a characteristic process of factionalism and coalition-making from which the most skillful of the Dravidian leaders, C.N. Annadurai, emerged victorious. Under Annadurai the party grew in strength, spread its appeal into the rural areas, invested more in issues of economic and caste equality and linguistic autonomy than in the futile search for a separate political identity, and ultimately succeeded in capturing political power in the state in the 1967 elections. Since then, apart from continuing a slightly different emphasis on the language issue, Madras (renamed Tamil Nadu) is proving to be one of the most loyalist and orderly of the Indian states.

Since 1967 the DMK in power has been subject to the same kind of internal factional pressures as has the Congress Party which has now become the principal opposition party in the state. Thus the usual processes of party pluralism are found to be operating in Tamil Nadu. This secular transformation of primordial sentiment [31] has led to a process of regional articulation that is, as elsewhere in the country, contributing to the polyarchal nature of the functioning political process. Here it is important to recognize that both the assertion of a regional identity and its assimilation into a larger national identity have been essentially political-coalitional processes.

On the other hand, it is important that separatist identities in India have been more potent in regions inhabited by distinctly non-Aryan ethnic groups which have experienced varying degrees of assimilation into the all-India cultural mainstream. Thus the more serious problems confronting India's territorial integrity come from the unassimilated tribal periphery in the northeast region of the country.[32] Here too the processes of political competition and governmental penetration are opening up the possibility of greater assimilation through politicization. But such integrative tendencies are still at an early stage, modernization also tends to create awareness of separate identities, and the situation calls for considerable ingenuity in the development of new patterns of federal association. The secessionist demands in the Naga region are being managed by the establishment of an independent Naga state known as Nagaland and the adoption of a flexible attitude in New Delhi towards the " Naga rebels" which has resulted in dissensions and divisions among the rebels. In Assam the aspirations of the tribal party, the All Party Hill Leaders Conference (APHLC), have been accommodated by the establishment of a new kind of political arrangement, a "subfederation" within the state of Assam with considerable internal autonomy and access to resources. Another constitutional innovation was tried earlier with respect to giving a special status to Jammu and Kashmir.

Some other areas still remain unaccommodated, as for example the small militant tribe of Mizos in the northeast, the Chhota Nagpur area in Bihar, the tribal enclaves in MP; and the movements of autonomy in the tribal regions of south Gujarat and Orissa. As political participation grows and education and economic development produce new differentiations, such demands are likely to grow. Some of these issues are accentuated by the fact that many of these tribal enclaves are on the border with China and Pakistan, and there have been attempts at "training" some of the discontented elements in guerrilla activities. The challenge from across the borders is likely to continue for a long time to come and the country will have to face up to the continuing task of evolving new policies for dealing with increasing political mobilization of the border regions. The Home Ministry has been handling these issues imaginatively but there does not seem to be any easy way out of this composite challenge of domestic political mobilization and international interventionism.[33]

India's territorial situation presents a continuing problem of integration, a greater incidence of subregional mobilization within individual states (rather than secessionist movements against the center), the development of specially tailored policies to deal with specific situations, and the natural strains emanating from increasing participation of the periphery in the central symbols and institutions of politics.

ISSUE OF MINORITIES

Two other issues have called for a policy response. One is the continuation of linguistic and religious minorities within the states. On an average about 18 per cent of a state population has as its mother tongue a language other than the official state language (the figure varying from 5 per cent in Kerala to 35 per cent in Mysore, with the exception of Assam where the non-Assamese speaking people constitute as much as 44 per cent of the state population). The problem has not caused much trouble except in areas where the "outsiders" occupy strategic administrative or industrial positions and are perceived as "exploiters" as in the case of Gujaratis and south Indians in Maharashtra, Bengalis in Assam and Orissa, and Marwaris in West Bengal. Militant movements of the "sons of the soil" against these outsiders have emerged in the urban areas of those states, notably the Shiv Sena in Maharashtra and the Lachit Sena in Assam. Organizations like the Maharashtra section the Rashtriya Swayamsevak Sang (RSS), a militant wing of the Jan Sangh though functioning autonomously from the party, have also mobilized some of this parochial sentiment. The sentiment against the Marwaris in West Bengal and, in part, Tamil Nadu, is also getting vociferous. As some of these movements, such as the Shiv Sena, are led by highly obscurantist elements and employ the symbolism of extremist chauvinism and a paramilitary appeal, they pose a source of great danger. Unless the government demonstrably evolves a policy of firm suppression of such excesses, pockets of fascist tendency are likely to develop in the country, fanning middle-class frustrations, distorting the instruments of "democracy," and turning the natural competition between "majority" and "minority" into irreconcilable opposites.

A related issue, though one that expresses itself sporadically and largely due to some local and personalized conflicts, is Hindu-Muslim communalism. During 1967 in a number of small towns in Uttar Pradesh a series of violent events took place, some of them quite ugly and manifesting deep religious hostility. Even more shocking was the condition in Ahmedabad and some other cities of Gujarat in September 1969 when, following a chain reaction of chance incidents, rumors, and deliberate provocation, communal frenzy spread like wild fire, led to arson and vandalism on a large scale, and resulted in the death of several hundred people. Here is another issue for which only long-term secular development will provide the ultimate answer but which does call for short-term policies of vigilance and accommodation, not only on the part of the government, but also on the part of political parties and organized groups in educational and cultural fields. (Thus in Aligarh the University has become the scene of communal incidents.) The prospect of electoral reprisal in inhibiting the various parties from getting too closely associated with such events, but local temptations for making political capital out of such unfortunate events often defeat such directives from above. Incidents like these are often sporadic and unaggregative but they continue to pose as threats to the overall image of the country as a secular, democratic polity.

SIZE AND DEMOCRACY

The other issue area to which no great thought has yet been given in official circles concerns the general incidence of size and optimality in the territorial design of the country. It is one thing to agree to the principle of linguistic autonomy in the organization of states. It is quite another thing to implement this principle in the form of a "one language, one state" formula. But this is precisely what the States Reorganization Commission recommended, except in the case of the Hindi speaking region where there are four states. The result of not attending to other criteria of regional organization, such as size, level of development, administrative optimality, social homogeneity, and political feasibility, has been that the country has such unmanageable and grotesque units as Uttar Pradesh with its 75 million population, a sprawling Madhya Pradesh with four historically distinctive and heterogeneous regions, and states like Andhra Pradesh which encompasses the extremely backward Telengana region and the very prosperous delta regions giving rise to the inevitable charge of "discrimination" and deliberate deprivation of the former. All this leads to fissionary tendencies, as found also in Mysore and Maharashtra. Many of these states could perhaps be split into administratively more efficient and politically more homogeneous units. The center too would find it easier to deal with smaller and more numerous but politically more homogenous states. Similarly the question of special treatment of the large metropolitan areas, through the establishment of autonomous governmental and developmental institutions in these areas, and providing them with planning resources that are independent of state allocations, has not received any systematic attention so far. And yet the "urban problem" is continuously growing. Some students of the Indian situation, including the present author, have therefore argued for a fresh review of the country's territorial organization from the perspective of size, social cohesion, effective administration, efficient center-state relationships, and the possibility of having single-party governments.[34] The issue will have to be faced sooner or later, and the sooner the better. For the alternative is to face recurring crises and to respond only after the event. The fore of inertia and the usual fear of not doing anything that involves some unknown factor may, on the other hand, indefinitely postpone the issue.

CONCLUSION: DEMOCRACY AND NATIONAL INTEGRATION

There are many other kinds of political demand. There is, for instance, the whole problem of "regional disparities" in regard to economic development, the allocation of financial resources, location of industry, and other indicators.[35] But enough has been said and analyzed here to indicate the range of problems that a mutli-ethnic federal polity trying to consolidate a nation state through the open processes of democracy has to face. Seen in conjunction with the other issues of political institutionalization discussed earlier in this chapter, they provide us with an outlook on the opposite pulls of centrifugal and centripetal forces generated in the process of crystallizing a political center.

Politics in India have served to provide a "model" for the integration of the various diversities and cleavages into a common framework, led to an interplay between parochial demands and systemic outputs, and through such an interplay challenged the established system of institutions and symbols towards new thresholds of performance. Such a model has inevitably brought to the surface the inherent issues in the interrelationship of the various constituents of the polity: there seems to be no easy approach to the development of a manifest and categorical "national identity." As already pointed out, the Indian identity will continue to evolve in the form of a complex network of relationships rather than a unit relationship. In the crystallization of this network the political center is playing a crucial role. The "cost" of such a model of integration is the likelihood of an increasingly issue-oriented polity as it passes from its low-mobilization quiescent phase to one of political activation, institutional dispersal, and decentralization. With this the "loads on the system are likely to grow and the very capabilities that have been generated so remarkably in such a short time will be put to severe test.

It has been our underlying contention in this chapter and in the book that a country as vast and pluralistic as India can be effectively united only through a participant and accommodative model of politics. (It is impossible to rule India from New Delhi.) A concomitant of such a model is the autonomous and creative role of politics, and its penetration all the way down to the social infrastructure. The integrative capabilities that we have noticed in our analysis, insofar as they have developed at all, owe a great deal to such autonomy and creativity (though no doubt they have been greatly helped or hindered by the persistence of cultural themes noticed in Chapter 7). At any rate it is in terms of the performance of such a "political model" of development, instead of any reductionist view of politics as found in both the "social origins" and the "prerequisites" models, that we have approached the subject of integrative outputs in this chapter.

Notes

1. Those who have invested a great deal in the traditional version of the input-output model may frown upon a reversal of terms. It is possible, however, to consider the input-output process in a circular manner. Rajni Kothari, "Implications of Nation-Building for the Typology of Political Systems," paper presented at the *Seventh World Congress of the International Political Science Association*, Brussels, 1967.
2. Gabriel A. Almond, "Political Systems and Political Change," *The American Behavioral Scientist*, VI, No. 10, June, 1963; and Almond, "A Developmental Approach to Political Systems," *World Politics*, XVII, No. 2, January, 1965.
3. Such theorists dominate every field. Examples are Neil Smelser, William Kornhauser, S.M. Lipset, Karl Deutsch, Daniel Lerner, and Barrington Moore. For a recent crtitique of the literature, see Joseph LaPalombara, "Macro-theories and Micro-applications in Comparative Politics: A Widening Chasm," *Comparative Politics*, 1, No. 1, October, 1968. On the importance of politics and power from the perspective of social theory, see Reinhard Bendix, *Nation-Building and Citizenship* (New York, 1964).
4. Economics themselves have done better in this respect, although those who think in terms of linkages between economic and political variables are still in a minority. See Albert O. Hirschman, *Strategy of Economic Development* (New Haven, 1964); Charles E. Lindblom, *Intelligence of Democracy*) (New York, 1965). For a recent attempt by a political scientist to compare political systems by reference to their respective performance in different spheres, see Samuel P. Huntington, *Political Order in Changing Societies* (New Haven, 1968). So far as we are aware, this is the only systematic attempt of this kind by a political scientist.
5. G. Austin, *The Indian Constitution: Cornerstone of a Nation* (London, 1966), Ch. 13.

6. *Ibid.*
7. Myron Weiner, *Party Building in a New Nation: The Indian National Congress* (Chicago, 1967).
8. A characteristic instance of this continuity in style and idiom was noticed when, following factional disputes in the ruling DMK in Madras, there was a demand for a "Kamaraj Plan" for the party under which a section of the governmental leadership should resign and return to party work.
9. For perceiving such an eventuality even before the 1967 elections, see a suggestive article of W.H. Morris-Jones, "The Indian Congress Party: A Dilemma of Dominance," in *Modern Asian Studies,* No. 2, 1967.
10. See the table on party identities in Chapter 5. It should be pointed out here that the non-Congress multi-party coalitions in India differ in important respects from their counterparts in Western Europe. While the latter (including France of the Fourth Republic) are based upon relatively stable structures of support in the constituencies, which, however, fail, to "aggregate" at the national level, thanks in part to the nature of the franchise, the former are essentially based on a constantly shifting support structure in the constituencies and a legislative paten work resulting from it. As their constituency base is not stabilized, non-Congress parties in India, with the possible exception of the Communists and the Jan Sangh, do not yet feel "accountable." Electoral reprisal is something to which only Congressmen seem to be sensitive so far.
11. It is precisely on this issue of restructuring the political coalition by rallying the country around issues of growth and performance that Indira Gandhi's offensive against Congress Party managers in 1969 gains significance. Although essentially a political move, culminating in an unprecedented presidential election, it drew its momentum by reference to issues of economic growth and social justice. With this the politics of the Congress Party is once again pitched to the consolidation of a left of center ideological consensus, as under Nehru.
12. Countries that are engaged in a variety of political experiments and have in other respects shown the viability of these experiments still must pass this crucial test before their systems can be said to have been properly institutionalized. Prominent among these are the Soviet Union, Yugoslavia, France, China, Cuba, Pakistan, and Egypt.
    Among the democracies Malaysia, Tanzania, and Kenya, and in part Ceylon, must still pass this test. Israel seems to have passed the latest both when Ben-Gurion was succeeded by Levi Eshkol and when Eshkol died and was succeeded by Golda Meir. And Mexico has passed it eminently well by resorting to a peculiar formula of incumbency change.
13. The issue was posed in a series of speculative writings by foreigners. It was summarized in a popular kind of essay by Wells Hangen, *After Nehru, Who?* (New York, 1963). In India the issue led to a public opinion survey carried out after Nehru's serious illness in 1963. See "After Nehru, Who?" *Monthly Public Opinion Surveys*, No. 101, 1963. (Indian Institute of Public Opinion.)

14. Televised interview with Arnold Michaelis. See Michael Brecher, *Nehru's Mantle: The Politics of Succession in India* (New York, 1966).

15. Sardar Vallabhbhai Patel was deputy prime minister from 1947 to 1950 and constituted, with Nehru, a ruling duumvirate. The position was not filled on his death. In 1960 the issue was put to a vote in the Congress Parliamentary Party (CPP), but in the sharp divisions that were revealed, Nehru declined to fill the post. The pressures were revived during his long illness prior to his death but, certain that such an appointment would virtually amount to the nomination of a successor, Nehru declined to give in. On details of cabinet seniority and the struggle for the coming succession, *ibid.*, pp. 94-103.

16. Shastri's chief contender was Morarji Desai whose differences with Nehru were well known; he was opposed by a majority of the chief ministers, and had developed an image of being a "rightist." Both Kamaraj and Shastri, on the other hand, were known to be centrists and likely to continue the core of the Nehru program. In addition, Kamaraj, who was to earn the label of being a "king-maker" in the two successions, enjoyed the reputation of being a judicious and disinterested arbitrator. For a detailed chronicle of the various events, see *ibid.*, Chs. 2, 3. See also R.J. Venkateswaran, *Cabinet Government in India* (London, 1967), Ch. X.

17. Brecher, *ibid.*, p. 6. For the details of the consensus technique and its application by Kamaraj, see pp. 59-66.

18. The consolidation was revealed in yet another crucial election in 1967, that of the president of the Indian Union. The non-Congress parties which together represented a majority of the electoral college (which consists of members of all state legislatures and the Parliament, on a weighted scheme) put up a senior judge of the Supreme Court as an agreed candidate against Dr. Zakir Hussain, a Muslim candidate of the Congress Party. The Congress, and especially Mrs. Gandhi, deliberately took the risk of sponsoring a Muslim candidate, declared that the country's commitment to secularism was at stake and, despite its factional divisions in the states, put up a united show and won the election. The election of the president proved a shot in the arm for the Congress Party and its leader. The non-Congress parties, on the other hand, showed marked dissidence among their ranks.

19. The Indian press was able to report almost every move each day in the bargaining process: who met whom, at whose house, in whose presence, and at what stage in the negotiations. The general observation that Indians tend to shy away from open confrontation and bargaining apparently does not apply to this important case study in decision-making. The highlights are chronicled in concise detail in Michael Brecher, "Succession in India, 1967: The Routinization of Political Change," *Asian Survey*, VII, No. 7, July, 1967.

20. On the other hand, such a pattern of leadership, and inexperience in it, creates major strains in governmental and political functioning, and suspicion as regards the other person's or group's loyalties. It was precisely this that led, only two years after Mrs. Gandhi's election as leader in 1967,

to a series of political and economic steps on her behalf to forestall an alleged attempt to "topple" her. These steps included the virtual dismissal of the Deputy Prime Minister, Mr. Morarji Desai, an ordinance by the President of India nationalizing the major banks, and a general thrust to rid the government and the party of "groupism." We have discussed the general issue of trust and distrust in India's political culture in Chapter 7.

21. On the politics of candidate selection prior to the 1967 general election see Rajni Kothari, "Congress System on Trial," *Asian Survey*, VII, No. 2, February, 1967. See also Stanley A. Kochanek, *The Congress Party of India: The Dynamics of One Party Democracy* (Princeton, 1968).

22. Brecher, *Nehru's Mantle, op. cit.*, pp. 115-20, 167-68.

23. For a useful survey, see Elie Kedourie, *Nationalism* (London, 1960).

24. P.B. Gajendragadkar, former chief justice and a prominent intellectual of India, stated the matter picturesquely in the subtitle of a recent address on the language problem: "A Plea to Consider the Problem Rationally, Decide Wisely and Hasten Slowly" (Convocation Address to the MS University of Baroda, *Medium of University Education*, October 14, 1967, published by the Bombay University Press).

25. The term "linguistic area" was applied to India by Murray B. Emaneau, the linguist. In his words, "the end result of the borrowings is that the languages of the two families, Indo-Aryan and Dravidian, seem in many respects more akin to one another than Indo-Aryan does to the other Indo- European languages." See his "India as a Linguistic Area," in *Language*, 32, 1956. Commenting upon this mutual borrowing, Bernard Cohn, the anthropologist, says: "The history of the relationships among the language families in India illustrates by analogy a general process in Indian civilization—that what appears on the surface as great and real diversity can be seen to have underlying connections, if not unity." Bernard S. Cohn, *India: The Social Anthropology of a Civilization* (New York, 1969).

26. Thus in the case of Hindi, the educated speakers of a variety of local and regional dialects (including those like Bihari and Rajasthani with regional followings) have accepted a standard "true" Hindi known as *Khari Boli* as against local dialects of Hindi known as *dehati* ("of the village"). Similar convergences to literary standard languages such as Bengali, Tamil, and Marathi are found in different regions. As for the association of such regional standards with persistent political centres, see John J. Gumperz, "Speech Variation and the Study of Indian Civilization," *American Anthropologist*, 63, October, 1961.

27. On these various trends, see the excellent study of Baldev Raj Nayar, *Language Planning in India* (New York, 1969).

28. Selig S. Harrison, *India: The Most Dangerous Decades* (Princeton, 1960)

29. For a brief survey of the genesis of the Dravidian movement, see Robert L. Hardgrave, Jr., *The Dravidian Movement* (Bombay, 1965).

30. Opinion in other parts of the country no doubt contributed to such a dilution of the DMK's aims. Following the excesses of separatist sentiment, and on

the recommendation of the Committee on National Integration and Regionalism of the National Integration Council, the Indian Parliament unanimously amended the Indian Constitution "to prevent the fissiparous, seccessionist tendency in the country engendered by regional and linguistic loyalties and to preserve the unity, sovereignty and territorial integrity" of the Indian Union. The Amendment, among other things, led to a revision of the DMK's own constitution with a view to enabling the party to function within the framework of the Constitution.

31. Hardgrave, *op. cit.* See also Hardgrave, "The DMK and the Politics of Tamil Nationalism," *Pacific Affairs*, XXXVII, No. 4, Winter, 1964-65.

32. For a recent survey, see Arthur J. Dommen, "Separatist Tendencies in Eastern India," *Asian Survey*, VII, No. 10 October, 1967.

33. Separatist demands against individual states rather than the nation's political center are also to be found in non-tribal regions. Most important among these is the demand of the Telangana region in Andhra Pradesh for autonomy. Disappointed at the non-fulfilment of "promises" by the state leadership of a fair share in development benefits and political opportunities, and following the failure of the chief minister to hold factional elements in the Congress Party together, some of the Telangana leaders led, during 1969, an organized movement for autonomy. The agitation and violence that followed brought activity in Hyderabad, the state capital, and other urban areas to a standstill. To this the central leadership responded by mediating in the dispute and offering a series of concessions, but these have failed so far to satisfy the leaders of the agitation, and it is likely that some major concession, such as a change in the leadership of the state government, may be needed for arriving at a satisfactory solution. Similar, though far less vociferous movements have from time to time occurred in other states like Maharashtra and Mysore.

34. Rajni Kothari, "National Unity in Danger: Case for Smaller Units," *The Times of India*, February 10, 1968; M.N. Srinivas, "Towards Smaller States," *The Times of India*, August 14, 1969. See also an earlier article by M.N. Srinivas, "Future of Fission," *The Times of India*, November 16, 1967.

35. On this issue, see the detailed analysis of K.N. Raj, "Regional and Caste Factors in India's Development," in J.C. Daruvala, ed., *Tensions in Economic Development in South-East Asia* (Bombay, 1961). See also P.K. Chaudhuri, "Balanced Regional Growth," *The Economic Weekly*, XII, October 8, 1960. A conference on regional and social disparities was organized under the auspices of the Indian Statistical Institute and the International Social Science Council in New Delhi in 1967. Papers of the Conference are available from Professor Ramkrishna Mukherjee of the Indian Statistical Institute of Calcutta.

9

Political Economy of Development

IN OUR CONCERN with the crystallization of a political center and its penetration and institutionalization, we have emphasized the autonomous role of the political process and the issues of "performance" that it raises. Political institutionalization, however, involves a series of policy issues regarding social and economic goals, the performance of which affects the viability and legitimacy of the constitutional order. The penetration of the system and the processes of participation and coalition-making that it has generated themselves crystallize these issues and convert them into demands on the political center. This is especially so in a model of development that is wide open and is committed to the welfare and development of its citizenry, as is the case in India. Furthermore the very concern with national unity and legitimacy of the political system leads to a growing preoccupation with problems of growth and acceleration.

The relationship between economic growth and political development is not by any means simple; certainly there is no one-to-one relationship. It seems clear, however, that any political system that fails to systematically deal with problems of poverty and deprivation as pressing *political* problems cannot be said to have achieved viability and stability. Just as the more sensitive among the economists are getting increasingly concerned with the contribution of the political process to economic performance, with what they call the "politics of economic development," the political scientists have to be concerned with the economic content of political performance or the "economics of political development." Actually, as the issues involved in this area are more interactional and cut across strictly economic or strictly political variables, and as a number of other kinds of variable — demographic, environmental, socialization — enter into the picture, we need to turn to an older and more dynamic tradition of thinking about these issues. We may call it the "political economy of development."

THE BROAD STRATEGY OF TRANSFORMATION

The present is a somewhat difficult point from which to evaluate the performance of India's strategy of social and economic change. Two successive years of serious drought (1965-67) and the industrial recession that followed, the war with Pakistan and the abrupt interruption of the expected pattern of economic aid in its wake, the eventful election year and the period of political uncertainty that followed, and above all a comprehensive, still continuing review and restructuring of the whole development strategy and its administrative framework—these events have turned the decade's closing years into a particularly fluid time in the nation's developmental history. They have thrown the institutional structure of development out of gear and have momentarily halted—and in some aspects set back—the country's pace of development. To be sure, the years 1967-69 brought some reversal of these setbacks and the process of development seems to be just beginning to resume its course from where it left off in 1964-65. But on many aspects of developmental performance there is still great uncertainty. However, as we are not concerned here with either the very short run or the very long run, as natural calamities seem to visit India every so often and should thus be treated as recurrent themes, and as recent changes in political structure and economic strategy suggest important clue to the shape of the unfolding future, we may still be able to pursue our task of evaluating India's developmental performance, even if tentatively. Indeed, the recent setbacks and the present review of the overall strategy serve to highlight some of the continuing issues of performance.

The most general observation often made on the relationship between the political system and economic mobilization is that of a conflict between the objectives of growth and justice, of production and accumulation on the one hand and distribution and equity on the other. These and other objectives should, however, be seen less as conflicting ends—though of course they often work at cross-purposes—than as simultaneous goals. The main point here, made early in this book, is that the new states do not have the option of "phasing" their processes of growth into a developmental sequence; they must necessarily pursue diverse goals simultaneously. Thus from almost the beginning India's developmental strategy has grown around the pursuit of four more or less well-defined goals: independence of the economy from its reliance on strategic imports and foreign aid (the goal of "self-sustained growth"), resource mobilization and capital accumulation leading to increasing rates of saving and investment (the goal of a high "rate of growth"), reduction of sectoral and social disparities (the goal of "equality"), and the simple concern with providing minimum conditions of subsistence and survival (the goal of equity and "justice"). And apart from the pursuit of these specific goals there was also a wider political concern with promoting integration, avoiding sharp cleavages, and assimilating diverse interests into the new political center.

A number of measures were taken in the pursuit of these goals, measures which underline the imperative of pursuing all of them simultaneously. In a sense the imperative arose out of the mandate that the leadership carried from the nationalist movement, a mandate that was repeated in a series of resolutions of the Congress Party after independence. Thus among the early steps taken by the new regime were land reforms designed to undermine the feudal order in the rural areas and replace it by more equitable land rights, the setting up of a planning machinery to start a coordinated effort at resource mobilization and planned development, and the initiation of a community development movement and allocation of new resources to the cooperative movement for promoting self-help in the villages and the construction of basic facilities for village development. By the time the necessary administrative framework and a basic infrastructure were created (by the mid-fifties), the planned effort moved towards creating a design for "self-sustained growth" through emphasis on investment in heavy industries, and by diverting foreign exchange to the import of strategic plant and equipment. Though the long gestation period that such a design involved and the piling up of unutilized capacity that followed from a speedy building up of plant perhaps slowed down the immediate rate of growth and even led to some hardship in the availability of consumer goods, the approach was defended from the point of view of reducing the country's dependence on imports and foreign aid for the supply of industrial goods, a dependence that was likely to compromise the country's independence and integrity. Hence the emphasis on "import substitution" and on giving priority to those components of the industrial economy that would enablé the country to meet its internal needs. To use a cliche, the design was to produce "machines that would make machines."

As it turned out, the strategy lacked in realism: in trying to reduce the country's dependence on imports for industrial goods, it in fact made this dependence more humiliating as the country had to import in large quantities the most basic necessity of all, namely food. We shall consider shortly the failures of this policy. Here we may simply more that the broad approach of the planners was to try to meet the diverse goals the country had set before itself by placing the highest value on achieving economic independence and "self-sustained growth," and by concentrating on the development of a capital goods sector within the country in as short a time span as possible.

THE GOAL OF SELF-SUSTAINED GROWTH

For more than a decade, Indian planning was characterized by considerable insulation from the pressures for distribution and welfare. It succeeded in concentrating on the accumulation of capital and its investment in heavy industries and, except for meeting immediate needs of equity in the form of a modest program of village and agricultural uplift and short-run relief from drought and floods, was able to neglect the distributive goals of socialism. Although the full payoff of the strategy is yet to come (from more intensive utilization of capacity and reaping the full benefits of import substitution), the rate of growth has been by no means negligible. If we leave out the two years of acute shortages, between 1951 (the beginning of the modest First Plan) and 1965 (the fourth year of the Third Plan) the national income in aggregate terms and at constant (1960-61) prices increased by 69 per cent, or a compound rate of growth of 3.8 per cent per year. The rate has slightly increased from plan to plan: 3.4 per cent during the First Plan period, 4 per cent during the Second Plan, and 4.2 per cent in the first four years of the Third Plan. The Third Plan as a whole, not just in its worst last year of 1965-66, was ridden with difficulties—two bad harvests, two wars, and a serious shortage of foreign exchange. Now an average 4 per cent rate of growth is not high performance, but if it is remembered that the country started from an almost stagnant economy (the economy during the first half of the century has been estimated, from being at a standstill, to having progressed at a .5 to 1 per cent gross rate of growth), the performance can be seen in its proper perspective, though such comparisons can be no source of complacency for a country as poor as India. If we discount for the phenomenal rise in population during this period (21.5 per cent during the decade 1951 to 1961), the per capita growth has been about 2 per cent per year.

Aggregate statistics are often not very useful in assessing performance. Breaking the figures up sectorally and in certain other specifics, the record becomes more clear. During this period, foodgrain products rose by 50 per cent, an average of a 3.5 per cent rate of growth per year, a marked improvement considering the fact that throughout the first half of the century agricultural production had remained static and had in fact declined in per capita terms,[1] but hardly satisfactory given India's desperately low standard of living and its population "explosion" during this period. The performance was much better in the industrial sector, which shows the impact of the plan effort. The index of industrial production during these 14 years went from 74 in 1951 to 187 in 1965 (taking 1956 as the base), an increase of more than 152 per cent in 14 years. (The index, however, does not reflect more spectacular growth rates in strategic sectors because of the larger weight given to traditional industries.) During the same period coal production went up by 100 per cent, steel by 400 per cent, electric power by 600 per cent, and a prospering machine tool industry was established from almost nothing. Important strides were made in the production of other necessities of a growing industrial economy, including certain strategic producer goods, commercial vehicles and petroleum. By the end of this period India was the third largest world producer of railroads, third in woven cotton fabrics, seventh in coal, ninth in pig iron, ninth in hydraulic cement, tenth in coke, and twelfth in electric power. It had the eighth largest gross national product in the world. In terms of potentials that were laid bare through surveys but were only now beginning to be explored, the country has the largest deposits of iron ore in the world, it is third in manganese and seventh in coal, and it has a hydraulic potential of 41 million kilowatts (at 60 per cent load).

These potentials are beginning to be exploited. The Indian government has initiated the development of a key public sector which has pioneered some of the more crucial areas of industrial development which, because they have a high gestation period, are not readily undertaken by the private sector.[2] Investment in the public sector has gone up from rupees 55 crores in the First Plan to Rs. 520 crores in the Third; the corresponding figures for the private sector are from 233 crores to 1,050 crores. As a proportion of the national income net domestic savings were stepped up from 5.3 per cent in 1951-52 to an estimated 10.5 per cent in 1965-66 and net investment from 5.3 per cent to an estimated 14 per cent.[3] Even more remarkably, such a pace of development, modest though it is, was maintained through a high degree of monetary stability: wholesale prices rose by about 40 per cent over the whole 14-year period. This includes the period of Chinese hostility and the marked stepping up of defense expenditure that followed as well as a moderate dose of deficit financing by the Indian government. Resource mobilization through taxation rose from approximately 7 per cent of national income to about 14 per cent. All of this enabled the country to achieve a progressive if modest increase in national income throughout this period except in one year of bad harvest.

Again, all these magnitudes are less impressive than they seem for, after all, India is the seventh largest and the second most populous country in the world. But compared to where it started from, the performance can be said to be moderately successful insofar as the pursuit of industrialization is concerned. By and large its goals of capital accumulation and an increasing rate of investment and output in the industrial sector, and gradual independence from imports of strategic industrial goods were, though somewhat short of plan targets, fairly well realized. And despite the simultaneous striving after other goals, the pursuit of capital accumulation and self sustained growth was fairly well insulated from them.

MISSED OPPORTUNITIES

But the full potential of this period of relative freedom from other pressures was not exploited owing to a reluctance to take calculated risks. Thus, while land reforms removed some of the worst vestiges of feudalism, the full implementation of their redistributive and mobilizational components was not carried out for fear of the divisive effects of such action. Resources of new irrigation facilities were diverted more to conspicuous drought relief operations than to selected high yield areas. The rate of fertilizer production was held up owing to largely academic arguments between the proponents of private and public sectors. A soft policy of food imports to cushion scarcity conditions was adopted rather than an aggressive policy of turning these conditions into crisis-impelling pressures for a major drive in agricultural productivity.

In the industrial sphere the policy of import substitution in a variety of fields, while induced by a genuine concern for achieving economic self-sufficiency, was in actual implementation allowed to become a protectionist wall that shielded incompetent enterprise and led to a mushroom growth of inefficient plants. Evidence suggests that the attempts to create "too broad a range of industrial capability too rapidly" lowered individual plant efficiency by spreading critical resources too thinly and creating "external diseconomies in the form of escalated costs throughout the economy."[4] There was a general lack of readiness to shift resources and improvise new techniques in the face of adverse conditions of demand and supply. There was also a timid approach to the allocation of resources, the usual temptation being to satisfy a large number of pressures and to give in to institutionalized vested interests in existing patterns of investment and capital formation. And there was a general suspicion of the market mechanism, a fear that it might release unpredictable pressures on prices and wages. There was especially too great a preoccupation with keeping inflationary conditions under check rather than utilizing price levels as stimuli for increasing productivity: thus low prices of marketable farm output and consequent high real costs of inputs to the farmer provided a design for stagnation. This fear of inflation was carried so far that when the drought years brought a threat of price rises, the government cut back its own investment program, thus further depressing the economy.

Lack of a clear policy of matching production with effective demand, sectionally and by each industry, led to a curious situation where, while the economy suffered from shortfalls in critical inputs and raw materials, production of machine tools and other industrial items started piling up with no takers. That this should have happened with the output of public sector industries, including the most prized units like Hindustan Machine Tools, indicated a clear failure in policy. In sum, while important strides were recorded during the three plans, the available opportunities were not fully exploited and there was a lack of intensity of effort and concentration of energy and resources in selected areas of priority. The "postponement of gratification" capability is best attained when the pressures arising from social mobilization are not too pressing as was indeed the case during the first decade of Indian planning. Although to some extent this was achieved, the performance in this respect was by no means optimal. There was also much waste and distraction, many prestige projects, and an enthusiasm for conspicuous development.

More striking for our analysis, however, is the extreme contrast in performance between the agricultural and the industrial sectors, and within the latter between consumer goods on the one hand and capital and intermediate goods on the other. Indian developmental effort during the second and third plans provides a manifest case in "unbalanced growth." Owing to the general model employed, to particular policies such as an overcautious pricing, and to lack of implementation of certain other policies such as land reforms and irrigation, development during the 14 years under review resulted in a situation of marked disequilibrium in sectoral rates of growth. Because more than half the national income of India comes from the agricultural sector which accounts for three-fourths of the population and for much of the country's effective demand, and which also provides important raw materials for industry, the consequences of such a disequilibrium were bound to affect the entire economy.

The issue was brought up dramatically when the country was faced by a cumulation of events: two successive years of drought, a fall in export earnings and foreign aid (following the war with Pakistan), consequently a shortage of crucial raw materials and spare parts, a peculiar combination of industrial recession and rising prices, and conditions of acute scarcity and political uncertainty all around. The disequilibrium between agriculture and industry, under such conditions, virtually halted the economy, and created a situation of grave crisis. These conditions set in motion a decisional process that ultimately led to a comprehensive review of economic strategy, an overhaul of program priorities and administrative routines, and a rethinking in ideological attitudes and coalitional style.

DISEQUILIBRIUM AND DEVELOPMENT

Situations of "unbalanced growth," however, need not result in permanent loss.[5] The crises to which they lead often prove to be catalysts of not only a change in strategy but also of considerable increments in energy and imagination, a better grasp of a complex reality, and a reconstruction of the elements of the developmental process. Developmental crises are like moments of truth in the life of a society. Provided the culture is capable of a basic optimism and has had experience and skill in adapting to new challenges, developmental crises are likely to bring it to new thresholds of cognition and problem-solving potentiality. They reveal new latent capabilities, change the salience of issues and information on issues, lead from simplistic notions and theories to an appreciation of the complex interactions that reality is made of, galvanize hardened and centralized structures and routines, bring forward groups at intermediate and lower levels in functional roles, neutralize antecedent antagonisms, in short lead to "new motivations, new allies and new insights."[6] More than anything, such crises instil in the leadership and the governmental structures a new sense of autonomy from the usual pressures as well as from their own inhibitions and preconceptions. Precisely by administering a shock and stirring developmental elites out of their complacency, they lead to a new self-assurance and a new drive. Things that were thought to be unthinkable now become both possible and acceptable to the different constituents of the operating coalition. Especially in a culture long given to apathy, inertia, and to taking a line of least resistance and risk, developmental crises turn out to be the principal agents of action.

The 1965-67 food crises in India resulted in this kind of a total shift in the country's developmental outlook. We have already discussed in an earlier chapter the change in plan strategy and the forces that combined in favor of such a change. Heralded by the government's "new agricultural policy," there took place a series of other steps in the revision of economic strategy: a new irrigation policy with emphasis on minor irrigation, a concentration of inputs—improved seeds and fertilizers — on high-yielding areas as the principal way out of stagnation, a comprehensive soil survey, a reassessment of plan priorities and a reallocation of scarce resources including foreign exchange, liberalization of controls and an "incentives" policy in regard to industrial development, a change in emphasis from import substitution to export promotion, a more positive approach to price policy, and a shift in emphasis from a proliferation of projects to utilization of existing capacity.

More important than these changes in strategy are the shifts in basic attitudes that they reflect: from exhortation and administrative fiat to an accent on profitability, from a policy of restraints and deprivation of the peasant to his indulgence, from an attitude that the peasant has to be "motivated" to a conviction that the real need is to divert capital resources to strategic inputs, from a thin spread of these inputs to their intensive application to areas of high yield, from too much concern with stability of prices and "cushioning" devices to an awareness that prices and the market mechanism can act as stimuli of growth. More generally there has been a shift from considering agricultural production as a function of planning and extension to treating it as a genuinely economic problem, and from too great a reliance on the tnchnocracy and the bureaucracy to a resumption of initiative by their political masters. The latter, a great many of whom now come from the rural sector, have shown a greater appreciation of the role of new entrepreneurial groups (the "kulaks" of the Indian countryside) and have been willing to impose their own outlook on the ivory tower bureaucrats in the Planning Commission.

The administrative bureaucracy itself showed new reserves of capacity and commitment, as for instance in the manner in which the food and agriculture ministries at the center and in the state handled the situation in the drought-stricken regions. In other areas too there has been a noticeable shift from vague generalities of policy-formulation to a hard-headed attention to the minutiae of execution and implementation. And the net result of the new policy and its detailed execution, albeit helped in part by good monsoons, has been a dramatic improvement in food production and in a general optimism in the ruling quarters. For the first time the government has felt confident about the future and has announced that it will be able to discontinue food imports and become self-reliant by 1970. Even if this estimate is overoptimistic by a few years, there is now greater hope of a steady pace of improvements in the near future and an eventually self-sustaining process of growth. The prospect of the latter is now more secure because the crucial sector of agriculture is likely to turn from being a bottleneck to a stimulus. Alongside the new policies, the earlier policies of industrial development, while they may have produced serious developmental lags in the very short run, are now likely to reap their advantage.

POLITICAL ISSUES

In order to understand the political implications of such a change in strategy under the impact of a situation of crisis, several points emerge after close examination. First, the policy change was initiated some time before the onset of the two droughts: a great deal of thought had already gone into discovering the real dimensions of the problem, with the consequence that when the droughts precipitated a serious crisis, the administration was not entirely unprepared. But it was the onslaught of the droughts that really enabled the central leadership to deal with the political hurdles in their way, mainly the hurdles posed by a combination of autonomy-conscious surplus states and demand articulating deficit states that direct all their demands toward the center. Second, there was available a leader of outstanding administrative and political skills in the person of Food Minister C. Subramaniam who used every opportunity and "crisis"—including external war and external pressures as from the United States government—to forge common agreements and decisional outcomes. Third, one needs to distinguish between a short-run "food crisis" and a long-run "agricultural production crisis," both of which involved center-state bargaining and joint implementation of decisions. The important point that emerged, when we separated out the content of the decisions in this manner, was that it was easier to make an impact on the long-run production issues (which were more a function of central initiative and creativity) than on the short-run food crisis which involved issues of distribution and interstate cooperation. This goes to show that whenever serious vested interest are involved, even the threat of a crisis may not produce quick results, and there is need to continuously work on several fronts and at various levels. Finally, the real solutions that emerged were not so much a result of the center's imposing its decisions on the states but of working *through* the states and impelling their own decision-making units such as the National Food Council (made up of the state chief ministers and the central ministers of food, planning, and finance, under the chairmanship of the prime minister) to take the critical decisions. The decision-making was thus highly involved and characteristically federal. While this minimized the loads on the center, it also meant that the decisional process was not easy to predict.

Many issues remain to be resolved; the lessons of the crisis have not been fully learned and there persist both ideological resistances and vested interests in less than optimal outcomes of policy. For instance, the studied reluctance of most chief ministers to abandon the "zonal system" (according to which food grains are not allowed to move out of state boundaries except through negotiated procurement by the center) impedes the implementation of an efficient price and distribution policy by the center. It was often said during the 1965-66 (though not the 1966-67) drought that the conditions of scarcity were in part created by the distortion of the distribution process for which the zonal system was responsible. Also, the policy of maintaining high procurement prices is strongly resisted by political and ideological groups who want to bring cheap food to the city-dwellers. The same ambivalence characterizes the execution of the government's inputs policy: the decision to assign top priority to fertilizer production and imports continues to be slow in implementation, thanks to the continuing controversy between exponents of public and private sectors, while the implementation of the intensive irrigation policy is meeting the traditional resistance of ideologues and drought-relief engineers.

There is also perhaps not enough grasp of the varied technical details of implementation and the need to develop differential capabilities in an effort to "plan against failures."[7] Again, the shift of attention to agriculture and the considerable political support for this strategy, which seems to insure against any serious backsliding from it, risks giving inadequate attention to the industrial sector which may, in turn, also affect the supply of critical inputs to agriculture.[8] Even the much publicized and dramatically adopted policy of nationalization of the major banks in mid-1969 seems to be addressed more to making credit available to the farmers and small retailers than harnessing investment surpluses to a new industrial policy. Thus there still remain facets of policy that are far from satisfactory. The process of learning that began under the impetus of the situation of crisis is still under way and while there is hope that the shortcomings will be progressively overcome, there is no guarantee that this will in fact happen, certainly not in all areas of policy and implementation. But the broad economic strategy seems to have taken a turn for the better and is likely to show results in the years to come, with or without further crises. Given the experience of the past and the constant danger in India of slipping into a complacent mood, the recurrence of such crises cannot be ruled out and may indeed prove functional in restoring the lost sense of urgency that such a mood engenders. (Here we are not discussing the role of external factors, such as balance of payments crises and foreign aid shortfalls, in accentuating or alleviating such crises, as we propose to deal with them separately in the next chapter.)

ISSUES OF DISTRIBUTION AND EQUITY

Having considered the critical issues of policy and decision-making in regard to economic development, we may now turn to the heart of the traditional concern of political analysis: who gets what? Two kinds of issues are involved here, those arising from the elite's own pursuit of distribution and equity as desirable goals (simultaneously with other goals), and those arising from the elite's own pursuit of distribution and equity as desirable goals (simultaneously with other goals), and those arising from the pressures from below in the wake of cleavages and inequalities that have resulted from the distribution of the gains of development. A host of subissues and many autonomous trends that contribute to these general issues are involved here, but we can only briefly deal with these, our chief concern being the effects of distribution and welfare on the decisional processes of politics.

The striking point about the Indian concern with issues of distribution is its concentration on a single focus of attention: the urban-rural dimension. Most other issues—unemployment, population pressure, price policy, taxation policy, even education policy—seem to be treated under this larger rubric of "sectoral" relationships. Even the within-sector disparities and cleavages seem to have so far been glossed over in national discussions, although we intend to deal with them here as they point to some crucial issue areas in the years to come. The ideology that dominated the nationalist movement, and has since been expressed in the directive principles of the Constitution, the resolutions of the Congress Party, and the plans themselves, is heavily weighted in favor of rural development and the "awakening of the villages." And this is despite the plans' concern with rapid industrialization and acceleration in rates of growth based on heavy industries.

The planning model started with the usual formula of industrialization: a shift of resources and the labor force from the agricultural sector into industry and urban areas. Given the pressure of population on land, the low marginal productivity of labor in agriculture, and the fact that every increment of surplus devoted to industry yields far more return than injecting the same in agriculture, this seemed like a reasonable presumption. Yet the net impact of planning did not lead to such changes. An examination of the census returns on the distribution of workers shows that the share of the primary sector was 72 per cent both in 1951 and 1961. (If we take male workers only, the proportion fell slightly from 69 per cent to 68 per cent.) The structure of the capital stock also shows the same results: in 1950-51, 40 per cent of India's reproducible tangible wealth was in the agricultural sector and it remained the same in 1960-61, whereas the estimated share of agriculture in the national income fell a little from 49 per cent to 46 per cent. Even the latter shift seems to be more an indication of the lag in agricultural production than of basic redistribution in sectoral positions. Thus, as far as the general structure of employment, income, and capital stock goes, the idea of an effective shift away from agriculture has not worked. (These percentage figures, of course, conceal a considerable absolute increase in factory production and the industrial work force.)

SECTORAL REDISTRIBUTION

Perhaps more important are the figures on governmental extractions and inputs through fiscal measures and developmental outlays, as these would revel a policy thrust in this regard. Even during the heyday of the strategy of rapid industrialization, when the planning process was practically immune to distributive pressures, the net benefit accrued to the rural sector. Thus whereas money taxes collected from the rural sector during the decade 1951-1961 rose by 80 per cent, annual outlays covered by taxes spent in that sector rose by 180 per cent. The net inflow of tax-financed expenditures into the rural sector increased by about 150 per cent after adjusting for price increases and the cost of living index. This flow of outlays came from an excess of receipts over expenditures in the urban sector which remained constant at a little short of Rs. 200 crores in both years. Even in terms of plan outlays, an estimated 45 per cent of the outlays under the first two plans and 40 per cent under the third plan were in the rural sector.[9] Thus although investiment in agriculture was on the whole a neglected item in government planning (except during the First Plan), the outlays in the rural (as distinct from the strictly agricultural) sector were still substantial.

On the other hand, as should be expected from widely differing rates of productivity in the two sectors, the gains from a rising national income were, both per capita and per worker, higher in urban areas than in rural areas. But this is so only at factor cost; they represent the situation before the intervention of the government's fiscal measures. The after-tax situation still favors the rural sector in comparison with the urban sector. The government's reluctance to impose direct taxes on the agricultural sector has, of course, contributed greatly to this imbalance in the distribution of development gains. The main direct tax on agriculture is the land revenue which, not having been adjusted since the last war, has considerably declined in real terms. This was one calculation that recently persuaded many state governments, irrespective of party labels, to abandon the tax altogether. But even the incidence of indirect taxes is higher in urban than in rural areas, adding to the imbalance in resource mobilization.

The recent shifts in economic strategy are likely to consolidate this imbalance. Agriculture is now in the process of becoming a modern occupation, with modern inputs, increasing yields, a growing scope for managerial talents, and a fertile field for profitable investment. For a field whose ptential is only now beginning to be exploited and where the prospects are not of a few percentage points' increase in yields but a quite substantial increase, it is likely to draw both private and public resources on an increasing scale. Agriculture may not any longer seem like a "dismal" enterprise. The increase in power of the institutions of panchayati raj, cooperative societies, and nationalized banks disposing of crucial loans and investment opportunities is further likely to consolidate this shift. Prominent local leaders of the Congress Party, once eminent princes and *zamindars* returning from their urban hideouts,[10] important members of the dominant castes and other economically entrenched groups, even civil servants and retired military officers all seem to realize the great potential of the agricultural sector for both economic and political benefits. The newest power group in Indian politics is that of the kulaks, the class of independent owner-cultivators drawn from a variety of social groups, who are making of agriculture a thriving business propositiion and one that provides them with a base for effective political bargaining at higher levels.[11] Their pressure for sustaining, and carrying further, the recent changes in economic policy is likely to increase.

Thus both the general ideology of India's developmental elite and the effective distribution of political power seem to be underwriting a redistribution of the gains of development from urban to rural areas. There are good functional reasons for such a shift, in part because for centuries the real potential of the populous Indian countryside was not exploited, and in part because this agriculture-based strategy of economic development may well provide a distinctive model that may enable India to surmount its massive problems of poverty and deprivation.[12]

DEMOGRAPHIC SHIFTS

Partly reflecting this general flow of net benefits is another interesting aspect of Indian development: its slowing down of the rate of urbanization. During the decade of progressive development that we have been discussing, the proportion of total population living in urban areas remained almost constant: whereas in 1951, 17.29 per cent of the population was urban, in 1961 it was 17.97 per cent. Although there was a net addition to the urban population of 16.5 million (21.2 million after adjusting for definitional changes made by the Census), in terms of relative proportions the share of the urban sector gained by only 0.68 per cent (1.76 per cent after adjusting for definitional change). In terms of the *rate* of urbanization (percentage variation in the proportion that is urban), it was barely 3.9 per cent for the whole decade as compared to 24.8 per cent for the previous decade.[13] The rate of urbanization is thus falling; in fact it was lower than in all previous decades since 1921, as shown in Table 9.1

It was a rate much below that expected by the authorities and clearly goes against the usual notion that modernization is neces-

TABLE 9.1
Rate of Urbanization in India: 1901 to 1961

Decade	Percentage of total population in urban areas	Variations in percentage urban	Percentage variation in percentage urban (rate of urbanization)
1901	10.84	—	—
1911	10.29	-0.55	-5.07
1921	11.17	+0.88	+8.55
1931	11.99	+0.82	+7.34
1941	13.85	+1.86	+15.52
1951	17.29	+3.44	+24.84
1961	17.97 (29.05)[a]	+0.68(+1.76)[a]	+ 3.93(10.18)[a]

[a] Adjusted for definitional changes, assuming the same definition of "town" in 1961 as in 1951.

Source: Ashis Bose, "Six Decades of Urbanization in India: 1901-1961," *The Indian Economic and Social History Review*, II, No. 1, January 1965.

sarily accompanied by a fast rate of urbanization.[14] No one can say that India was not being modernized in this decade; its performance in technological and economic development was fairly steady from 1951 to 1965, during which time it also experienced a high degree of educational expansion and political modernization. The fact is that the Indian development strategy, while relying no doubt on *absolute* increases in the urban working force, is not necessarily tied to an increasing *rate* of influx from the villages.[15] Although we have no reliable figures for any changes in urban-rural proportions in the years since 1961, it seems likely that the increasing modernization of the rural sector, the growing profitability of agriculture as an occupation, and the increasing decentralization of political functions are all contributing towards the maintenance of the slow tempo of urbanization noticed during the decade 1951-61.

The increase in urban population is composed of two factors: natural increase within urban areas and migration from rural to urban areas. The latter provide us with a measure of net urban flows. Here again one notices a slowing down of the "push" effect from rural to urban areas. The situation is brough out very well if we look at Tables 9.2 and 9.3 on migration from rural areas during this decade. Table 9.2 shows that very few agriculturists are leaving the villages. (The data presented here are only in respect to larger cities but the same occupational breakdown is found in other towns and cities.) Table 9.3 shows that contrary to the usual belief about the relationships between pressure on land and migration to the cities, the greatest incidence of migration occurred in states with low population density. (The exceptions are Madras, West Bengal, and Rajasthan.)[16]

Two other facts are hidden in these tables. One is that there is in India a great deal of what Ashish Bose has called "turnover migration": people go to towns and cities and then come back. Whereas the net migration between 1951 and 1961 was about 6 million, a year-by-year calculation pushes up the migration figure to 24 million: there is a "push" and "pull" effect on both sides, urban as well as rural. The second fact is that the most significant migration in India is not rural to urban but from small towns to large cities: from "quasi-urban" to urban areas. The process of urbanization takes place by making urban areas more urban rather than any hypothetical shift in rural-urban ratios.

Finally, let us note another significant summary fact: while the rural population as a whole increased by 20 per cent between 1951 and 1961, agricultural cultivators rose by 43 per cent. In the aggregate, the proportion of those engaged in agriculture as an occupation increased from 74.40 per cent in 1951 to 76.44 per cent in 1961.[17] The net result is the relative stabilization of the rural-urban relationship in India. It presents a peculiar demographic setting for the country's development—and this at a time when power and influence are steadily shifting from urban to rural areas.[18]

Such a stabilization of sectoral distribution should not, however, lead to any conclusion of tranquility or lack of cleavages in the country. Both the diminution in the dominant position of the industrial and professinal groups in the urban areas and the fact that large natural increases in the urban population do not permit a sizeable migration from the rural areas can lead to a rising state of frustrations. Among other things it would increase the pressure on land and accentuate the cleavages within the rural sector. Meanwhile the ranks of the unemployed in the urban areas—and especially of the educated unemployed—may keep swelling. This may well lead to a new coalition of disaffected interests in both

TABLE 9.2
Migration to Major Cities by Occupational Groups (Percentage)

	Cities	Cultivators	Agr. lab., farmers, fishers	Prof., adm., clerical, sales	Miners, trans. & com., and craftsmen	Services, sports, & recreation	Workers not classifiable	Non-workers
1.	Bombay	0.10	0.65	17.85	27.01	8.10	0.03	46.26
2.	Calcutta	0.01	0.34	22.80	21.22	9.34	0.17	46.12
3.	Delhi	0.17	0.46	19.26	16.58	5.01	0.08	58.44
4.	Madras	0.01	0.75	19.05	16.08	6.12	0.11	57.86
5.	Ahmedabad	0.04	0.63	11.80	26.80	4.36	0.01	56.36
6.	Hyderabad	0.29	1.08	18.11	15.87	6.67	0.03	57.95
7.	Bangalore	0.91	1.13	16.73	19.94	5.20	0.22	55.87
8.	Kanpur	0.22	0.63	13.27	27.63	2.96	0.79	54.50

Source: *Census of India 1961*, *I*, Part II C (iii), Migration Tables.

rural and urban areas, a coalition on "class" lines which may mount an effective protest against the present "caste" and "interest" configurations. Let us look at some of the trends in this regard.

WITHIN-SECTOR DISPARITIES

Within the agricultural sector are wide differnces in the distribution of the gains of development.[19] To be sure, the land reforms

TABLE 9.3
Rural Density and Migration to Urban Areas

State	Rural density (1961) (workers/1,000 acres)	Percentage of rural population migrating to urban areas
A.P.	467	6.20 (1,842,328)
Assam	635	2.01 (220,460)
Bihar	737	2.94 (1,248,661)
Gujarat	242	8.47 (1,297,163)
Jammu & Kashmir	706	2.33 (69,242)
Kerala	440	3.20 (59,633)
M.P.	330	4.26 (1,181,852)
Madras	602	8.04 (1,986,276)
Maharashtra	291	12.34 (3,504,816)
Mysore	286	6.66 (1,220,682)
Orissa	405	2.06 (338,221)
Punjab	242	5.70 (924,783)
Rajasthan	226	3.44 (580,863)
U.P.	506	3.24 (2,081,785)
W. Bengal	460	8.01 (2,113,179)
All India	386	5.46 (19,679,797)

Notes: "Rural density" is the ratio of agricultural workers (laboers and cultivators) to net area sown. The units of measurement for the land is an acre. Migration figures are only of those migrating from rural to urban areas. The percentage is the ratio of these migrants to total rural population.

These data were computed at the Data Unit, Centre for the Study of Developing Societies, Delhi.

Sources: Government of India, *Indian Agricultural Statistics*, I (1960-61).
Census of India 1961, Union Primary Census Abstract — India, Part II A.
Census of India 1961, 1, Part II C (iii), *Migration Tables.*

program has brought about a marked alteration in the structure of rural power. Not only has the traditional feudal class been shorn of its oppressive monopoly of power; the abolition of intermediaries and tenancy reforms have also brought a substantial part of the total land surface under control of owner-cultivators engaged in managing their own land. According to the 1961 Census, 77 per cent of the cultivating households were located in ownership holdings, about 8 per cent in pure tenancy, and about 15 per cent in mixed tenancy. However, failure to implement the land reforms rigorously and the fact that the support of the large peasants was electorally essential for the ruling Congress Party have led to continuing disparities in both the command of resources and the distribution of economic gains from development programs. A Reserve Bank of India study on the distribution of total assets held by cultivating households shows that when the households are classified according to an ascending order of the reported value of assets, 25 per cent of the households in the highest assets brackets own as much as 75 per cent of total assets while the remaining 75 per cent of the houseolds own 25 per cent.[20] This big assets group generally corresponds to the group of rich peasants and managerial farmers which has benefited the most from development plans. A number of earlier studies[21] had shown that both because of their greater creditworthiness and because of their status in the structure of rural influence, as also no doubt because of their greater enterprise and know-how, this group drew the maximum out of the cooperative, the community development, and the agricultural extension movements. More recently with the added impetus to per acre yields and the considerable flow of modern inputs, the same group has benefited the most. Many recent government policies like the concentration of irrigation waters on high yield areas, agricultural price support, and procurement are likely to further boost up this new class of rural entrepreneurs.

There is another point of interest here. So long as such a group enjoyed the traditional privileges of a "closed" society, the sense of deprivation among the others was likely to be low. However, when such a class no longer owes its position to traditional status, indeed includes a significant stratum of the nouveaux riches, and derives much of its prosperity from government-initiated programs, its advantage need not go unchallenged.[22] Much would depend on the extent to which these gains from development percolate outwards, how far the short run compulsion to be selective in distributing scarce inputs can in turn transform such peaks of prosperity into "leading areas" from which adjoining farms and households, as well as those without land of their own, could also derive some benefit. Lacking such diffusion of the gains of economic growth, the perpetuation of inequalities will not only retard further growth but also create conditions of social and political turmoil. A special report of the Union Home Ministry in 1969 warned that, thanks to the "tenuous" tenancy system under which owners of land in high yielding regions were replacing sharecroppers with casual labor, the problem of rural unemployment was becoming serious and was likely to give rise to an increasing incidence of agrarian unrest. The very success of the "green revolution," in the absence of basic structural reforms, is thus likely to accentuate inequalities[23] is well taken, but if carried too far and for too long these inequalities are likely to become dysfunctional for both growth and the political conditions sustaining growth.

If we divide the rural class structure among large and medium-sized cultivators, small cultivators, and the landless (including landless laborers), the first group seems to have benefited the most for reasons already mentioned, and the second group has also benefited, thanks to land reforms, the new inputs, and the general improvements in agriculture. The 43 per cent rise in the number of cultivators as shown in the 1961 Census suggests that the number of small landholders increased as a result of land reform, especially the ceilings on landholdings (despite widespread evasion). The redistributive effects of the land reforms seem to have gone further. The two Agricultural Labour Enquiries conducted by the government, covering the period 1950-51 to 1956-57, found that while the general lot of the agricultural laborer had not improved, the number of these laborers had declined.[24] It seems likely that the better off among these laborers (those with some land) were able to acquire more land and leave the ranks of agricultural labor. The 1961 Census estimated an absolute increase in the numbers of agricultural laborers, but there was a relative decline. While the rural population as a whole increased by about

20 per cent and the numbers engaged in cultivation by 43 per cent, the number of laborers declined from 20 per cent to 17 per cent. In more prosperous districts in states like Punjab, Gujarat, and Andhra Pradesh it is even found that laborers are in short supply, especially during peak season. There is another indirect gain: since per acre yields have increased, land owners are found to gradually evict sharecropeers and employ casual labor instead. Thus as a class—as caste groups, as families—even the lowest class in the rural social structure seems to have gained a little.

However, in wages and other benefits the absolute increase in the number of laborers and a general situation of surplus population has managed to keep the condition of the laborers very depressed; the Agricultural Labour Enquiries found a decline of about 10 per cent in their incomes. While such a conclusion has since been found to be unreliable because of definitional and estimation problems, there is little doubt about the highly precarious economic condition of this class.[25] Even more important, though, is the fact that a few members of this class have improved their condition and hence the level of aspiration has been rising. Meanwhile, the general environment of the countryside has acquired a "demonstration effect," and socially proximate groups, such as the small landholders, have been rising in both status and material well-being. On the whole things are on the upswing. It is a well known maxim of revolutionary theory that it is not from a continuing state of misery but from a demonstrated possibility of change that the temper of discontent arises.[26] In the next ten to fifteen years the Indian countryside is probably going to witness a growing demand for more change. The very success of the kulaks is likely to expose them to a struggle with both the sharecroppers and the landless, although the interests of the latter two may often pull in opposite directions. And in all likelihood the old issues and policies that have been collecting dust in government bureaus— redistributive land reforms and taxation of agricultural incomes among others—may be revived under pressure from below.

An examination of trends in respect to both increase in production and distribution of the gains from development, and the developing linkage between the two, would support such a prognosis. In the beginning both the bringing of new land under cultivation and the stimulation of proprietary interests in land through land reforms increase output. As further increases in production depend on new techniques and inputs, and in good part on access to the political and bureaucratic structures, the elite groups draw the maximum advantage, and there develops a high correlation between economic development and an increase in disparities. In course of time, this affects adversely both production and distribution goals. The leveling off of the former motivates higher-level elites to start a process of political mobilization of the uninvolved strata of the population instead of simply relying on bureaucratic structures. (Hence panchayati raj.) The nonfulfillment of the latter results in increasing polarization of interest alignments locally, a good deal of disaffection and anti-government feeling, and significant electroal reprisal. The two together produce mounting political pressure for policies of drastic change.

On the other hand, the likelihood of general movements of rural protest against the political system as a whole seems to be slight. As a rule, when there is relatively low production leading to a maintenance of high prices for the produce, the agricultural sector experiences a stimulus and benefits not only the prosperous peasants but also other agricultural strata through more jobs and a general climate of expansion. Projecting into the near future, it seems that domestic production is likely to trail behind the needs of the economy for the next several years (especially since consumption standards are likely to rise in both urban and rural areas), thus leading to a maintenance of high procurement and market price. Meanwhile population increases and a cutting back on foreign imports are likely to continue this favorable relationship between output and prices. There will, no doubt, be pressures from the spokesmen of the urban sector for bringing down the price of food but the strategic political weight of the agricultural sector is likely to resist these demands. Thus there seems to be a greater threat from class conflict within the rural sector as discussed above than from any general movement of protest against the "system" as a whole.

The situation is likely to develop somewhat differently in the urban sector. Here the structure of group interests is far more differentiated and the gains of development have diffused unevenly. Although some broad inquiries have been carried out on the general issue, there is no clearcut picture of the distribution of per capita gains and losses. Without going extensively into these we may present here the rough picture: profits in the corporate sector have gone up; real wages of factory employees have gone up; the real earnings of upper level employees of the private sector, both in terms of the great expansion in employment and in terms of incomes, have gone up; the real incomes of other salaried classes in private employ have remained steady but employment opportunities have multiplied; the earnings of those employed in wholesale and retail trade (including the large numbers of self-employed) have gone up. On the other hand, real incomes of both the higher salaried classes and the great bulk of the lower middle classes in government employ have declined, the former more sharply than the latter, largely because of the decision of the government not to raise their salaries. The earnings of factory and manual workers in government employ have remained constant because of the recommendation of the Pay Commission to maintain their real wages in the face of a rising price level, while the total numbers of these wage-earners have increased significantly. Perhaps the worst affected group is school and college teachers, including university teacher, although once again the number of people employed in this profession has gone up manifoldly, thanks to the unprecedented expansion of the educational system, thus perhaps raising the total income of the families in this class.

This continuous increase of employment opportunities for the members of the lower middle class families constitutes a net gain from the development process. But, at the same time, there has been a closing of the income gap between this class and the laboring class and a widening of the gap with the upper middle class, especially with those in private employ and in trade and commerce. Thus the lower middle class groups seem to have gained absolutely but lost *relatively* both to higher income groups of whom they are jealous and to the organized wage sector, ahead of which they would like to stay. As a "class" they cosntitute the greatest source of disaffection in the urban setting. Simultaneously, the dramatic decline in the hitherto privileged position of the higher level bureaucrats, intellectuals, and professionals seems to have created a general intellectual environment of protest and anomie. The usual threat of a class war waged by an industrial proletariat is less potent in India where the real threat comes from a disaffected lower middle class, the typical *lumpenproletariat*, and its coalition with an intellectual class that has been disinherited from its earlier status and power.

THE PROBLEM OF UNEMPLOYMENT

The potential of such a coalition has been greatly increased by the vast numbers of unemployed in Indian society, including a sizeable section of educated unemployed who are concentrated in the urban areas. The rate of growth of the economy, while it has kept ahead of the rate of population expansion, has not been sufficient to absorb all the additions to the labor force. According to official estimates, between 1951 and 1961 the labor force increased by 21 million. Against this employment rose by only 17 million. At the end of the Second Plan, the number of unemployed is estimated to have been about 7 million. During the Third Plan the labor force increased by 17.5 million while employment went up by only 14.5 million. Thus, at the end of the Third Plan (1965-66) the backlog of unemployed is estimated to be on the order of 10 million, about a fourth of which was found in the urban areas.[27] (Many feel that these are very conservative estimates and that 15 million may be nearer the truth.) Projecting into the future, at the end of the Fourth Plan (1970-71), despite the government's intention to step up employment-inducing factors, the ranks of the unemployed are likely to rise to anywhere from the officially estimated 14 million to almost 20 million. In part such increases in unemployment are due to a phenomenal rise in population and thus in the work force, in part due to a strategy of growth that is more concerned with raising the accumulation and self-generative capabilities of the economy, and in part due to the underutilization of existing capacity because of paucity of raw materials and strategic imports.

There are three alternatives for raising employment: lowering of capital-labor ratio, pressing more labor into the present technological structure, and full utilization of unused capacities. The first is difficult to achieve economic and technological targets, while the second would diminish labor productivity. During the

TABLE 9.4
Percentage Distribution of Unemployment Population 1961, by Educational Levels (15 years and above)

States	Illiterate	Literate	Primary/ junior	Matric & above
A.P.	9.27	13.21	33.28	44.24
Assam	51.01	22.51	18.60	7.88
Bihar	26.42	25.42	22.62	25.54
Gujarat	25.75	16.74	47.26	10.25
Jammu & Kashmir	27.00	21.71	21.18	30.11
Kerala	7.54	27.34	20.67	44.45
M.P.	27.62	32.94	24.62	14.82
Madras	11.59	24.10	31.37	32.94
Maharashtra	23.30	19.36	40.57	16.77
Mysore	16.57	29.07	19.66	34.70
Orissa	22.43	36.11	26.97	14.49
Punjab	16.96	8.29	30.61	44.14
Rajasthan	35.66	39.37	7.06	17.91
U.P.	29.48	22.76	22.18	25.58
W.Bengal	29.13	27.91	26.68	16.28
Delhi	20.81	19.91	18.83	40.45
India	22.25	24.03	28.25	25.47

Sources: Census of India 1961, I, Part II B (iii), "General Economic Tables."

decade 1951-61 increases in labor productivity contributed about 65 per cent of the growth of output as against 35 per cent by additional employment. Hence the main course left open to the planners is to take concerted steps in raising rates of utilization which in turn depends on the availability of strategic imports and thus on increased export earnings. The government intends to concentrate on these steps in the coming years. Although the magnitude of unemployment and consequent inequality is quite large, the country's planners have decided to accord high priority to rapid growth in production and productivity, and wait till such growth is able to provide increasing opportunities for employment.[28] In the intermediate period they have undertaken to alleviate the acuteness of hardship and suffering by creating some opportunities at low levels of income and technology, such as the large rural works program envisioned in the Fourth Plan. More recently, following Indira Gandhi's initiative on the economic front which has shifted the emphasis from a technocractic view of the planning process to a political approach to issues of poverty and inequality, a major push is likely to be given to the rural works program, in the process alleviating the unemployment and underemployment of both technical personnel in the urban areas and of sharecroppers and landless laborers who are out of jobs. But the plan is still at the stage of discussion and formulation. Meanwhile the spectacle continues of a growing class of dispossessed amidst all the planning to relieve misery and deprivation.

The capacity of India's uneducated masses to put up with hardship, of caste and extended family structures to absorb tensions, of migrant labor to remain satisfied with intermittent jobs and subsistence incomes, and of the larger culture and polity to retain the commitment of even the dispossessed are all proverbial. The real threat comes from another source: the educated unemployed in the urban areas. The incongruence between the rapid expansion in the educational system and the rate of economic growth has made for a continuous increase in the ranks of this potentially volatile segment of the Indian population. Table 9.4 shows that in many states the number of unemployed who are educated (not just literate) exceeds that of the illiterate and the barely educated. This is especially true of the more urbanized and industrialized states like Punjab, Andhra, Madras, and Mysore and the politically more active centers like the Delhi area and Kerala. In Gujarat and Maharashtra, the other two industrialized states, the situation is better in respect to the highly educated but there are large numbers of unemployed in the intermediate category. The number of educated unemployed registered with employment exchanges throughout the country rose from over 200,000 in 1955 to approximately 600,000 in 1961. It is officially estimated that only about half of the total unemployed actually register themselves, which means that more than a million people who were educated were unemployed in 1961 and the numbers have since been rising. A recent breakdown shows that of those registered at employment exchanges more than 150,000 were professional and technical people, over 650,000 had graduated from high school, and over 73,000 were university graduates and above. (See Table 9.5.)

TABLE 9.5
Applicants on the Live Register of the Employment Exchanges, by Occupational Groups

	Number on Dec. 13'66	Percentage of total
Professional, technical, & related workers	153,058	5.8
Administrative, executive, & managerial workers	4,364	0.2
Clerical, sales, & related workers	94,316	3.6
Agriculture, dairy, & related workers	9,702	0.4
Miners, quarry men, and related workers	2,481	0.1
Workers in transport & communication occupations	62,156	2.4
Craftsmen and production process workers	195,323	7.4
Service workers (e.g., cooks, chowkidars, sweepers, etc.)	99,536	3.8
Laborers with work experience not elsewhere classifed	103,371	3.9
Persons without professional or vocational experience		
(a) Below matric. (incl. illiterate)	1,173,749	44.8
(b) Matric. & above but below graduates	650,802	24.8
(c) Graduates and above	73,599	2.8
Total	2,622,460	100.0

Source: India 1967, A Reference Annual

In India the magnitude of absolute figures is more important than percentage estimates. All the unemployed, with the most liberal estimates, would not be more than 4 per cent of the total population, much less of the actual working force. And this would not compare badly with other industrial and industrializing countries. But this is hardly relevant. Even a half per cent of India's population comes to more than two and a half million people. While the slow rate of urbanization and the fact that only a fourth of the unemployed persons live in urban areas prevent the situation from becoming volatile, they also conceal the real magnitude of the problem. Unemployment in the cities and, conditions of overcrowding contribute in part to the continuing preponderance of the rural sector, while in urban areas they furnish material for demonstrations of protest like the bandh and the gherao discussed in Chapter 5. Generally speaking, the protest is still unorganized and sporadic; the trade union movement is a conservative force, the student strikes lack any coherent ideology and pose no great challenge to the system, and the law and order machinery of the government has been able to handle movements of protest without any great play of violence. While the political structure has shown a capacity for tension absorption, the preponderance of the agricultural sector, a family structure that binds rural and urban areas together, and the fact that employment opportunities are rising even if slowly have all held the tide of discontent within bounds. It should also be noted that while agriculture has assumed a pivotal role in India's economic development, the Indian elite—both metropolitan and provincial—does not subscribe to typical agricultural values any more; in fact the whole appoach is one of political and institutional diffusion of modern, urban values throughout the country. All this will help. Looking at the future, however, unless the performance of the economy markedly improves, industrial capacities are utilized to the fullest extent, and a proper climate of expansion is created, the demographic situation appears to pose a source of continuous frustration and anomie.

Some recent steps, whose origins lie in a struggle for leadership within the Congress Party (already discussed in Chapter 5), may well be utilized by the planners as auguring a new "climate of expansion." The nationalization of the major banks and the decision to tighten up governmental control of the economy to combat its monopolistic tendencies and spread the gains of development to less privileged strata of the population may provide a benchmark from which new innovations in economic policy can be worked out. These can be specifically addressed to the problems of unemployment and capacity utilization. On the other hand, unless accompanied by tactical moves that will continue to stimulate voluntary effort, these very steps may have a dampening effect on the entrepreneurial class. There is also need to contain the distributive pressures that are bound to emerge as a consequence of recent policies. A developing economy in a populous country gives rise to a conflict between the pressures of equity and the usual criteria of efficiency and growth; the challenge is to develop policies that reconcile the two. Much would depend on the government's ability to mobilize the aspiring strata in the various sectors towards a new elan of productive orientations.

The big unknown in the situation is the position of the youth. We do not have adequate studies on this issue. A fast multiplying population has lowered the average age of the nation: in 1961, 57.7 per cent of the population was 24 years old and under, 41 per cent under 14 years. old. Considering the facts that these are also the recipients of an expanding educational system (enrollments in secondary and higher education are being doubled every seven and six years, respectively), that a majority of those migrating to towns come from the age bracket 15-34 (Table 9.6), and that unemployment rates are highest among the young (Table 9.7), the

TABLE 9.6
Migrants to Major Cities, by Age Group (Percentages)

Cities	0-14 yrs.	15-34 yrs.	35-59 yrs.	60 yrs. & above	Age not stated
1. Bombay	15.02	51.41	29.46	4.09	0.02
2. Calcutta	14.25	48.58	32.81	4.35	0.01
3. Delhi	19.40	48.55	26.40	5.63	0.02
4. Madras	15.62	48.35	30.14	5.88	0.01
5. Ahmedabad	18.64	46.23	30.72	4.40	0.01
6. Hyderabad	21.02	48.30	25.80	4.88	0.00
7. Bangalore	18.21	48.24	27.67	5.87	0.01
8. Kanpur	15.50	49.60	29.96	4.93	0.01

Source: Census of India 1961, I Part II C (iii), *Migration Tables*.

problem of generational discontent may be presumed to have high political relevance. In the chapter on political culture we have seen that generational differences are much less marked in India than in the West, socialization patterns tend to underemphasize age differentials, and there is a high degree of deference to the authority of the old. All this may serve to contain the tensions that would normally arise from the changing age struc-

TABLE 9.7
Percentage Distribution of Unemployed Population 1961, by Age Groups

States	15-34 yrs.	35-59 yrs.	60 yrs. & above	Age not stated
A.P.	88.20	10.82	0.97	0.01
Assam	75.64	19.54	4.78	0.04
Bihar	86.41	12.00	1.54	0.05
Gujarat	77.41	19.65	2.92	0.02
Jammu & Kashmir	83.67	15.01	1.25	0.07
Kerala	89.66	9.64	0.68	0.02
M.P.	80.61	17.02	2.35	0.02
Madras	86.62	12.13	1.24	0.01
Maharashtra	81.09	16.43	2.46	0.02
Mysore	87.65	11.56	0.71	0.08
Orissa	82.45	15.72	1.74	0.09
Punjab	90.17	7.70	2.10	0.03
Rajasthan	71.82	24.00	4.01	0.17
U.P.	82.79	14.94	2.23	0.04
W. Bengal	76.08	21.29	2.62	0.01
Delhi	85.50	13.03	1.47	0.00
India	82.30	15.65	2.03	0.02

Sources: Census of India 1961, I, Part II B (iii), "General Economic Tables." pp. 540-571 and 601-621.

ture of the population. The fact that student protests in India, given the general condition of competing for scarce opportunities, aim more at finding a place in the establishment than at challenging its legitimacy is further likely to keep the challenge of youth within manageable limits.[29] The increasing attractiveness of agriculture as a vocation may also act against the desertion of the youth for job-hunting in towns and cities. There is also some evidence that suggests that those who were born after independence show a more realistic approach to life than those who were exposed to the nationalist movement and its often utopian promises.[30]

All this may help. But it is also well known that education and the exposure to mass media and other artifacts of modernization are everywhere acting as powerful forces against the cohesion of traditional structures, and that the "realism" of the youth can also mean that it is not prepared to be fed on daydreams and looks for concrete results in jobs and rising incomes. The evidence in India so far is not decisively in favor of either greater basic acceptance of the system or greater disaffection from it. But even if there has not as yet been a clear patterning of attitudes, there is reason to believe that mounting frustration in life opportunities would turn this crucial segment of the population against the status quo. Thus once again the expansion of employment opportunities seems to be a crucial variable for the future, at least until population growth is brought under control.

Aware of the long-term tasks involved in dealing with these trends, the Indian government has launched an ambitious program of population control and family planning. Aiming at a reduction in the rate of growth of population from 40 per thousand to 25 per thousand, it has greatly stepped up the plan outlay on family planning (from Rs. 270 million in the Third Plan to Rs. 3,000 million in the Fourth Plan). Operationally the goal is to create facilities for the adoption of family planning in (1) group acceptance of a small-sized family, (2) personal knowledge of the techniques, (3) ready availability of supplies and services, and (4) training facilities for a large number of experts. A major outlay on research of both methods and attitude changes has also been undertaken. With all this the program is still in its infancy, has begun to show results so far only in urban areas and in districts where intensive drives have been undertaken,[31] and much yet remains to be done. Evaluation studies have brought up serious gaps in supply and distribution systems, the requisite educational drives, information feedback, and above all in the administration of the program and its ability to attract personnel of high quality. One other handicap is the lack of enthusiastic support from local political leaders. All this will have to be rectified. However, a bold step has been taken and though the results can only affect the long term while the real issues of performance must be faced now and in the near future, the importance of the program is self-evident.

EDUCATIONAL CHANGE AND LIFE OPPORTUNITIES

It should be clear by now that a crucial variable in political development which affects certain basic relationships is education. Not only has the importance of education as a critical input in social and economic development increased many-fold in modern times; it also seems to have become a dynamic transformer of motivation, life-styles, and aspirations. A major agent of socialization, it also tends to uproot men from their traditional moorings. And to the extent that it prepares human beings for opportunities that are not easily forthcoming, it creates a climate of frustration and leads to a general demand for change.

The old view that education is preparation for life and for a gentlemanly status, though still of some relevance, seems to work as a handicap in adapting to the challenge of modernization in which education itself plays an increasingly catalytic role. There is also, especially in a democracy, the further dilemma of evolving a policy of manpower development and allocation even while "open" channels of enrollment and admissions are conceded. Also, in a much less than full employment economy education tends to be looked upon as *the* medium of job opportunities while the discrepancy between educational output and employment openings creates great frustration and disaffection. All these dilemmas are manifesting themselves in India, sometimes with very disturbing consequences.

Once again, the issues in India are somewhat different than in other new states (although it appears that the Indian case only highlights what all other newcomers to modernization will have to face sooner or later). The key problem in India is not too slow but too fast a rate of educational development. It is true that the literacy level (24 per cent in 1961) is rather low, but this is largely a function of population expansion, and as already pointed out, what matters in India are absolute and not percentage figures. Between 1951 and 1961, enrollments nearly doubled for boys and trebled for girls.[32] Present indications show that enrollments in secondary and higher education are being doubled in a period of seven and six years respectively. If these trends continue, which they seem likely to do, by 1980 enrollments in secondary education are likely to be about 80 per cent of the total population of the relevant age-group while enrollments to higher (university) education are likely to be as high as 10 per cent of the population.

Again, the tendency to continue at school from one stage to another is growing very fast. It is estimated that within the next

10 to 15 years most of those who have completed middle school will continue in secondary school and about 60 per cent of those who complete secondary school will enroll in college. Of course, the main tendency here is for everyone who complete a stage of education but does not get a job to continue into the next stage. (Hence the great expansion of education among girls.) And this may change if economic expansion is fast enough to absorb more and more people at lower levels of training. But what may work against this is the attitude of employers who demand high academic qualifications even where these are not necessary for the job. All these pressures are likely to produce in India a system of universal (elementary, secondary, and higher) education in about 30 years.

Such a rapid expansion of the educational system, thanks largely to an "open door policy," has created a host of problems. Adequate attention to quality improvement and vocationalization has not been possible, the chief preoccupation being an expansion of opportunities.[33] A marked imbalance has developed between general degree holders in aall branches of knowledge, including the sciences and engineering, and the availability of specialized manpower. One offshoot of this is that a high proportion of educational resources are spent on the education of girls which, from the short-term point of view, is highly uneconomic because far fewer girls than boys put their knowledge to use by taking up gainful employment.[34]

The general picture is one in which, while there may be a few manpower shortages, there is an overproduction of educated personnel in most branches of knowledge. The Education Commission has recommended a double attack on the problem: fulfillment of manpower needs of the economy and a restriction on the proportions of those completing middle school from entering secondary and higher education. Even at the present proportions, the stock of educated manpower would be well in excess of needs. From mid-seventies onward, this will become especially serious; by 1986 there would be 4 million "too many" matriculates and 1.5 million "too many" graduates. In higher education alone, total enrollments are likely to be between 7 and 8 million by 1986, more than twice the estimated manpower requirement.

The growth in educated unemployment in India has been a

function not only of expanded opportunities in education, but also of the fact that the expansion has been very lopsided. Table 9.8 shows that while enrollments in lower secondary education as a whole went up from 6.5 per cent of the relevant age group in 1950-51 to 19.1 per cent in 1965-66 (a three-fold increase), the proportion of these students enrolling in vocational schools declined from 3 per cent in 1950-51 to 2.2 per cent in 1965-66. At the higher secondary stage vocational enrollment declined from about 44 per cent in 1950-51 to 40 per cent in 1965-66. Even if the optimistic projections of the Education Commission in regard to vocational—20 per cent at lower secondary stage and 50 per cent at higher secondary stage by 1986—are realized, total vocational enrollment would work out to about 100 per cent of all enroll-

TABLE 9.8
Enrollment in Secondary Education in India: General and Vocational

	Enrollment as percentage of population in relevant age group			Enrollment in vocational education as percentage of total enrollment		
Stage/years	Boys	Girls	Total	Boys	Girls	Total
Classes VIII-X						
1950-51	10.9	1.8	6.5	2.2	8.8	3.1
1955-56	14.9	3.3	9.3	2.0	7.9	3.0
1960-61	20.4	5.4	13.1	2.2	4.7	2.7
1965-66	28.7	9.1	19.1	1.9	3.3	2.2
1970-71	34.2	12.2	23.4	3.4	5.0	3.8
1975-76	40.8	16.9	29.1	6.0	7.6	6.4
1980-81	49.1	22.6	36.3	11.0	12.4	11.4
1985-86	60.4	30.6	46.0	20.0	20.0	20.0
Classes XI-XII						
1950-51	3.3	0.5	1.9	42.7	53.6	44.2
1955-56	5.2	0.9	3.1	41.6	49.4	42.7
1960-61	8.0	1.6	4.9	41.7	44.9	42.2
1965-66	11.5	2.3	7.0	40.7	38.5	40.3
1970-71	14.6	3.5	9.2	42.5	40.2	42.1
1975-76	17.0	4.8	11.0	46.3	44.5	45.9
1980-81	21.7	7.4	14.8	48.1	47.2	47.9
1985-86	28.8	11.4	20.4	50.0	50.0	50.0

Source: *Report of the Education Commission* (based on Ministry of Education, Form A, for 1950-51 to 1960-61).

ments, a figure far short of the requirements of an industrial economy. (The proportion of vocational to general education in schools in West Germany is 70 to 30 per cent, in Japan, 60 to 40.) As regards professional education at higher (university) levels, the Indian proportion was about 23 per cent of total enrollments in 1965-66, again far short of what is desirable.

However, in absolute numbers India has shown a marked improvement in higher professional enrollment, from 54,000 in 1950-51 to 249,000 in 1965-66, a four-and-a-half-fold expansion in 15 years. The dilemma is again clear: while the rapid growth and diversification of the economy calls for an expansion in professional and technical manpower, the restricted expansion of employment opportunities turns such a necessary development into a liability. The latest crisis occurred when even among trained engineers there was reported unemployment of almost 40,000 people, a fact that created a sense of insecurity among students in science and engineering colleges and led to widespread strikes and demonstrations. This happened in 1967 and was in part due to the economic recession following two years of serious drought. But in part it was due to faulty planning and served to highlight the consequences of rapid educational development in an under-employed economy. The figure has since gone up to about 60,000 as of September, 1969 and is expected by manpower experts in the country to go up as many as 100,000 unemployed engineers, despite the reduced intake in universities and polytechnics. The government has stimulated the development of high-level technical institutes, agricultural universities, research laboratories and institutions, and government-sponsored "special projects." The diverse needs of the economy are thus likely to be met at reasonably high levels of proficiency. The establishment of advanced centers in various disciplines, with additional resources and facilities, and the Education Commission's stress on developing a few "peaks of excellence" in the midst of rapid expansion will also promote the same ends. The issue that would remain unattended is the opposite: how to provide employment to the turnout?

The outcome is clear and poses a serious dilemma. The country and its entire developmental ideology have stressed high value on education as a means of self-development and achievement. Any going back on this is inconceivable. Yet education, if not accompanied by commensurate opportunities for fulfillment, can prove to be the greatest source of disaffection and anomie for the political system. This is one of the more serious developments that has taken place anywhere at any time. It is likely to provide a source of considerable strain for the political system, and is certain to contribute further to urban unrest.[35]

The situation may not be as desperate as it sounds. The government has been taking steps for changing the internal distribution of the system: more seats for the rural poor, greater enrollment in vocational and technical schools as against general education, greater regional and rural-urban diversification, and a better correspondence between educational output and manpower needs. There is evidence that educated sons of farmers are returning to the villages and to agriculture as an occupation; in this the impressive performance of a number of new agricultural universities are playing an important role. Emphasis on utilization of existing industrial capacity as a matter of top priority is likely to open up new employment opportunities for the educated. Expansion of social services and welfare agencies (including the expansion of the school system itself in the rural areas) is likely to take on a growing number of lower middleclass graduates in the humanities and the basic sciences. The plan for a massive rural works program is likely to offer opportunities to engineering graduates. Furthermore the ability of the country to absorb a high incidence of "underemployment," the tendency for a large number of people to engage in seasonal and intermittent employment, commuting between rural and urban and within rural areas, and the fact that income and employment are in large part still considered in family rather than individual terms, are all factors that help contain the strains caused by lack of adequate opportunities. Finally, despite the immediate and short-run problems discussed here, the cultural and political consequences of an increasingly well-educated population—including women—should not be underestimated.[36]

These are some of the hopeful signs in the situation. On the other hand, the archaic nature of the university system, its courses and curricula, administrative structures, and teaching personnel, are all creating serious issues which inhibit the educational process from playing its due role in the socialization and integration of the younger generation in the mainstream of national life. At the level of economic policy too the government has not yet evolved a clear approach to relating education to the larger framework of development; the process of adapting the plan strategy from the point of view of increasing employment is not receiving due attention; there is lack of any imaginative drive at turning this vast reserve of unutilized talent into a developmental resource; and there seems to be a sad lack of understanding of the political consequences of the problem of educated unemployment.

CONCLUSION: CRISES AND DEVELOPMENT

In fact on many of the issues discussed in this chapter—utilization of industrial capacities, allocation of agricultural inputs, attacking the problem of unemployment, arresting the rate of population growth, and involving the educated unemployed and the youth of the country as a force for change and reconstruction— it needs to be said that while the Indian government is vaguely aware of the problems and is taking some steps to resolve them, the requisite energy and drive that are needed are lacking. Much detailed work is possible in the utilization of idle capacities and the implementation of already adopted schemes; the education system offers unlimited scope for improvement; and the vast masses of unemployed and underemployed in the country can be turned into a powerful force for rapid development by initiating specially tailored programs. The administrative structure needs to be stirred from the present inertia and salvaged from the vestiges of obsolete rules and archaic structures. More capable personnel need to be brought in at every level of the developmental hierarchy. There seems to be a frightening lack of imagination in all this.

From the experience of the past, it may be that a few more "crises" will be needed for eliciting creative responses to the pressing issues of under-development, somewhat comparable to what happened in agriculture. It is likely that in a few years the convergence of various conditions of disequilibrium discussed above may provide another jolt to the system and take it to a more efficient threshold of developmental performance. The issues facing the Indian system are so large and complex that such a periodic jolt out of the complacency of normal development becomes almost a necessity. There is, of course, always the danger of "cumulative disequilibrium," as could conceivably arise from a combination of an intransigent zonal system, mounting prices affecting both the real earnings of the laboring and middle classes and the cost of exports, a serious balance of payments crisis, a further drop in capacity utilization resulting from the unavailability of crucial imports, and all this leading to more unemployment and mounting urban unrest. And if this happens, the achievements of the system may well go under. Thus the analysis of crises as correctives has its obvious limitations. Yet the alternative of tranquility through stagnation is perhaps even more corroding to national well-being and is anyway no longer available in this dynamic age.

India has shown a surprising capacity to survive various kinds and degrees of crises so far, and generally to profit from each of them, though not necessarily always institutionalizing the resulting insights and correctives. Which brings us once more to the problem of elite perceptions to which we have referred from time to time in this book. What has emerged from an attempt to relate the various sectorial and environmental trends described in this chapter is that in "attending to the affairs of one's society" one is faced by a benevolent combination: the impossibility of total premeditation on the one hand and an increasing possibility of information and feedback on a large number of "variables" on the other. While the former makes creative response to unexpected situations and disequilibria possible, the latter enables an elite to respond constructively to such situations and to move to a new threshold of performance. But such beneficence is available only to a responsive and sensitive elite. To others the combination may prove doubly confounding.

Notes

1. See K. Mukerji, *Levels of Economic Activity and Public Expenditure in India* (New York, 1965). The agricultural production index at the time of independence stood 6 per cent higher than it had in 1900 and 12 per cent below the peak year of 1936-37. During the same period there was a shift from food to cash crops and a net drop in per capita availability of food.

2. Public sector undertakings, which do not follow the usual formula of nationalizing the private sector, have instead tried to fill critical gaps. Among the more important of these undertakings are Bharat Electronics, Hindustan Machine Tools, Hindustan Cables, the three locomotive and coach factories at Chittaranjan (West Bengal), Varanasi (UP), and Perambur (Madras), and a chain of fertilizer factories. In the critical sector of iron and steel the government has launched four major "integrated" complexes at Rourkela, Bhilai, Durgapur, and Bokaro, through technical and financial collaboration with foreign countries.

3. The estimates are based on the *Fourth Five Year Plan—A Draft Outline* (New Delhi, 1966). For the benefit of the reader, 1 crore = 10 million; 1 lakh = 100 thousand. At current exchange rate, 1 rupee = 0.13 United States dollars, Rs. 1 lakh = $13,333 and Rs. 1 crore = $1,333,333. More simply, Rs.3 crores = $4 million.

4. On these issues, highlighted by the experience of trying to produce locally a hitherto imported manufacture, see Jack Baranson, *Manufacturing Problems in India: The Cummins Diesel Experience* (Syracuse, 1967).

5. See, in this connection, Albert O. Hirschman, *Strategy of Economic Development* (New Haven, 1964), and *Journeys Toward Progress* (New York, 1963), where he goes so far as to make unbalanced growth "functional" to the development process.

6. Ibid., Journeys.

7. For an excellent article on this theme of not allowing success to blind against future failures, see Rushikesh Maru, "Planning for Failure in Agriculture," *Economic and Political Weekly*, Annual Number, January, 1968.

8. This fear has been expressed by Max F. Millikan in a recent article, "India in Transition: Economic Development— Performance and Prospects," *Foreign Affairs*, 46, No. 3, April, 1968.

9. This includes outlays both on agriculture and on social services, communications and rehabilitation, as well as on non-inventory, miscellaneous items.

   The various figures given above are taken from different official publications such as the *Census of India 1961*, "Final Population Totals" (New Delhi, 1962), relevant appendices in the *Third Five Year Plan* (New Delhi, 1961), and *Basic Statistics Relating to Indian Economy, 1950-51* to *1965-66* (New Delhi, 1966) and from George Rosen, *Democracy and Economic Change in India* (Berkeley, 1967). Rosen's analysis is mainly in terms of sectorial distributions and is thus directly relevant to this section.

10. On this see Thomas R. Metcalf, "Landlords without Land: The U.P. Zamindars Today," *Pacific Affairs*, XL, No. 182, 1967.

11. For a characterization of this class and the kinds of men attracted to it, see a series of four articles by Daniel Thorner, "New Class Rises in Rural India," *The Statesman* (New Delhi and Calcutta), Nos. 1-4, 1967.

12. For an ex post rationale of this model see two papers by Charles E. Lindblom, "Political Democracy and Disciplined Development: The Case of

India" (Manuscript, 1968) and "India's Economic Prospects," *Ventures* (magazine of the Yale Graduate School), VII, No.1, Spring, 1968.

13. Ashish Bose, "Six Decades of Urbanization in India: 1901-1961," *The Indian Economic and Social History Review*, II, No. 1, January, 1965. It should be said here that the decade 1941-51 was exceptional in that it was accompanied by a major war, the mass exodus of refugees after the country's partition, and the general climate of expectancy after independence.

14. This view is so prominent that when faced by India's different experience of a slowing down of the rate of urbanization in a decade marked by development out of a stagnant economy. Kingsley Davis, the noted expert on population, explains it by "*relative* slowness of economic development" (italics mine). See Kingsley Davis, "Urbanization in India: Past and Future," in Roy Turner, ed., *India's Urban Future* (Berkeley, 1962). For a different approach, questioning the orthodox view and considering the Indian case as in some ways unique, see Ashish Bose, "Urbanization in the Face of Rapid Population Growth and Surplus Labour—the Case of India," *Indian Population Bulletin*, No. 3, 1964.

15. The rate of urbanization was much faster in the larger towns and cities (Classes I, II, and III in the Census, which include towns of 20,000 and above) than in medium-sized and smaller towns. The former increased by 42.2 per cent as against 52.6 per cent in the previous decade) while the latter in fact *decreased* 7.2 per cent (as against an increase of 22.4 per cent in the previous decade). This relatively slow growth of small towns is noteworthy and further highlights both the importance of large industrial towns in the process of modernization and the retentive capacity of the village in India as against the simple "push" of moving to the nearest town as indicated in the theory.

16. The largest migration is from rural to rural areas. Between 1951 and 1961, 27.51 per cent migrated from rural to rural areas, 13.71 per cent from urban to urban, 6.10 per cent from urban to rural, and only 5.46 per cent from rural to urban areas. It should be mentioned, however, that a good proportion of the "rural to rural" migration is traditional—the movement of married women. *See Census of India 1961*, I, Part II C (iii), Migration Tables (New Delhi, 1967). See also *Internal Migration in India* (NSS Report No. 53, 1953).

17. Several studies have been made of the changing occupational structure of India, including the reports published by the Census of India and the Planning Commission. For a useful summary, See J. Krishnamurty, "Secular Changes in the Occupational Structure of the Indian Union: 1901-61" in *The Indian Economic and Social History Review*, II, No.1, January, 1965.

18. The term "rural areas" in India encompasses a wide variety of sizes from villages of less than 100 to those that have a population of more than 10,000. Furthermore from the political point of view the district structure of the rural sector provides both a hierarchy of concentric circles of population and a sufficiently large base for both economic and political power, as well as for a great variety of services and facilities. Similarly the terms "town"

and "city" may conceal many a rural characteristic. Cutting across both are the power centers of India: the district and state capitals.

19. In the discussion that follows I have drawn from the perceptive work of P.C. Joshi and from reports of the Reserve Bank of India and the Program Evaluation Organization of the Planning Commission. See especially P.C. Joshi, "Farms and Food: The Problem," *Seminar*, No. 81, May, 1966.

20. The study is known as the All India Debt and Investment Survey, to which a follow-up survey was also conducted. For details, see the *Reserve Bank of India Bulletin*, June, 1965 and October, 1966. There are regional variations from state to state. "Gini's concentration ratio" (which expresses the degree of inequality in asset distribution) was 0.65 for all-India, was lowest in Jammu and Kashmir (0.48) and highest in Andhra Pradesh (0.73) with other states falling between.

    For a perceptive analysis of the relationship between land reform and economic development, see Raj Krishna, "Some Aspects of Land Reform and Economic Development in India" in Walter Froelich, ed., *Land Tenure, Industrialization and Social Stability: Experience and Prospects in Asia* (Milwaukee, 1961).

21. Some of these are Reserve bank of India, *Rural Credit Follow-Up Survey*, 1958-1959 (Bombay, 1961); S.C. Dube, *India's Changing Villages* (Ithaca, 1958): D. and A. Thormer, *Land and Labour in India* (Bombay, 1962), See also the excellent study of K.N. Raj, "Some Features of the Economic Growth of the Last Decade in India," *The Economic Weekly*, XIII, Annual Number, 1961.

22. The lucrativeness of agriculture seems to have drawn, in the last few years, a wide variety of social groups, including businessmen and money- lenders, retired civil servants, and members of the armed forces. Some of these come from castes fairly low in the traditional hierarchy and raise many jealous eyes.

23. Albert O. Hirschman, *Strategy of Economic Development, op.cit.*

24. See especially *Report on the Second Agricultural Labour Enquiry*, 1956-57 (Simla, 1960). For calculations of the relative gains and losses of different agricultural groups, see George Rosen, *op.cit.*, pp. 165-176.

25. On this see the contributions of K.N. Raj and V.K.R.V. Rao to V.K.R.V. Rao, ed., *Agricultural Labour in India* (Bombay, 1962) and D. and A. Thorner, *Land and Labour in India, op.cit.*

26. Alexis de Tocqueville, in his classic study of the French Revolution, commented that it was not during the long centuries of deprivation and misery but under conditions of economic improvement that the *ancien régime* appeared to be truly oppressive. The experience has since been repeated over and over again.

27. This is in addition to "underemployment" which is estimated to be somewhere between 15 and 20 million. Not all underemployment, however, is involuntary.

28. Another source of inequality comes from disparities in income and wealth. The issue had attracted great public attention in India during the early

sixties and the government of India had appointed a committee to inquire into the whole question of the distribution of wealth and the concentration of economic power. The committee's findings have thrown little light on the issue, largely owing to the unavailability of requisite data. For this reason, and because income inequalities seem to us to be less politically salient at the present stage, we have not dealt with the issue here. See, however, *Report of the Committee on Distribution of Income and Levels of Living* (popularly known as the Mahalanobis Committee Report), (Delhi, 1964); for a study of concentration of wealth in the industrial sector, see R.K. Hazari., *The Structure of the Corporate Private Sector* (Bombay, New York, 1966).

29. Joseph Lelyveld, "India's Student Demand—A Safe Job in the Establishment," *The New York Times Magazine*, May 12, 1968. Mr. Lelyveld says, "Indian students don't want to upset the old order; they want to come to rest in it."

30. See Joseph W. Elder's study of changing conceptions of national loyalty across generations in India, in which he distinguishes between the "nationalists" of the older generation and the "patriots" of the post-independence generation. Joseph W. Elder, "National Loyalties in a Newly Independent Nation," in David Apter, ed., *Ideology and Discontent* (New York, 1964).

31. In the state of Maharashtra these drives have produced striking results. The Maharashtra government has been so impressed by its efforts so far that it thinks that a proper climate has been created for undertaking bolder steps. Among these are a disincentives scheme under which parents with more than three children will be penalized in many indirect ways, such as by being disqualified from free or subsidized social services. With a view to stop short of a direct infringement of individual rights, the idea is to resort to various means of "pressure."

32. The statistics that follow are all taken from the report of the Education Commission, 1964-66: *Education and National Development* (Delhi, 1966).

33. The expansion, however, has been inequitable to the poorer and rural sections of the community, sections which offer the most serious and highly motivated students. Students from the rural areas which account for more than 80 per cent of the population get only 41.4 per cent of the seats in vocational and technical institutions; families of an income less than Rs.150 per month, which again represent about 80 per cent of the population, get only 50.5 per cent of total seats.

34. At the primary level the number of girls enrolled per 100 boys has increased from 12 in 1901 to 39 in 1950, to 55 in 1965. At the secondary level the corresponding figures are 4,15, and 26. In higher education the growth is more phenomenal. Total enrollment of girls grew from a mere 264 in 1901, to 40,000 in 1950, to 240,000 in 1965. As against this expansion, employment of educated female population has shown a very slow rate of growth, including in the scientific and technical fields. Thus a census of scientific and technical personnel in 1961 pointed out that unemployment in female scientists and technicians is much greater (31 per cent) than in males (8.7

per cent). The imbalance is likely to be even more pronounced in humanities and social sciences where the tendency is to treat a degree as a necessary qualification for marriage rather than for a career.

35. We have already seen in Tables 9.4, 9.6, and 9.7 that there is a high correlation between education, the younger age bracket, unemployment, and migration to the urban areas.
36. For a rigorous demonstration of education as a powerful variable in citizen orientations, see Alex Inkeles, "Participant Citizenship in Six Developing Countries," *American Political Science Review*, forthcoming. The countries reported include India.

10

Coping with the International Environment

ANY DISCUSSION of the performance of a political system must sooner or later come to grips with the fact that it forms part of a larger world setting with which it interacts almost continuously. Thus, no important analysis of the European experience in state- and nation-building in the seventeenth, eighteenth, and nineteenth centuries would be possible without a consideration of the viability of the concerned state within the "states system" of which it was a part: wars, invasions, secessions, and treaties played a major role in the establishment and consolidation of nation-states in Europe. In thinking about the state-and nation-building experience of the newly independent countries of Asia and Africa, apart from recognizing the fact of their newly won independence, this wider setting of the international system is often left out, as if the processes of "development" were autonomous and self-generating.

There are many reasons for such a manner of thinking. With the diffusion of the democratic ideal all over the world, the analytic concerns of the social sciences have shifted from thinking of states as juridical wholes confronting other similar states to a political-sociological study of internal structures and processes. Second, there is perhaps a greater threat to the integrity of these states and their development toward nationhood from internal upheavals than from external confrontations. Third, the long period of hegemony of a "bi-polar" world institutionalized through a "cold war" and a "nuclear stalemate" which coincided with the first decade of independence turned the external variable into more or less a constant, into a condition of equilibrium. Finally, many issues of external relationship have become variables in the process of internal development—economic and military aid, "self-sustained growth," balance of payments issues—and could be handled as such.

In our analysis of political development in India too, while we have been broadly concerned with the external impacts of colonization and Westernization, our analysis has been mainly directed to internal developments.

It is necessary now to fill this gap. To omit consideration of the wider world setting within which the new state and the new nation have strived to achieve an identity would be to omit a great deal, both because the post-war situation of a world dominated by superpowers raised serious issues of the preservation of national autonomy, and because the country's achievements and failures in accommodating external pressures and mobilizing external resources have been an important variable in domestic development. More recently the bi-polar equilibrium of the world has been breaking down, there is increasing fluidity in certain regions, and countries like India are called upon to take on new roles and produce new policies.

We do not intend to undertake a detailed examination of India's foreign policy and international relations, or even to document our discussion at any length, but only to briefly draw attention to some of the main themes in the development of India's contemporary encounter with the external world. The encounter has taken place at various levels. At the most general level, through colonization and related processes of cultural conveyance, the country has been exposed to—and is in turn modestly contributing to—a worldwide diffusion of ideas, techniques, and institutions. A related but slightly more specific level is that of world power relationships which seem to be increasingly affecting the development of India's identity and status as a nation. Involved in this are the characteristic problems of the defense of the country and its boundaries from the threats posed both by its immediate neighbors and by the armed encirclement of the world by the "great powers". Finally, the development of international economic relationships and the role of foreign economic aid are vitally affecting the country's overall strategy of growth. All these encounters also play a role in the articulation of domestic issues: the place of the military in political development, the consequences of external conflicts for national solidarity, the relationship between defense and economic development, the role of foreign aid and international loans in the development of not only the "material balances" of the country's developmental model but also the whole policy process of political preference and choices. More basic issues of self-image, identity, and morale have also arisen. Through all these issues runs a basic developmental theme: reconciliation between political independence and aspiration to acquire a position of influence and leadership on the one hand and a state of economic dependence arising from a weak industrial base at home on the other. Viewed in this way, an international capability has to concern itself not only with the traditional problems of defense and diplomacy but also with the more general problems of "underdevelopment," problems that tend to compromise the integrity and standing of the nation in the world.

GROWTH OF A POLICY

Independence came to India at a time in world affairs when it was natural for India to adopt the approach that it did under the stewardship of Jawaharlal Nehru. The world was divided into two blocs; the chief new thrust of the period was the emergence of new nations in Asia and Africa; massive tasks of political consolidation and planned change required concentration of attention at home and minimum involvement abroad. India's own ideological background favored world peace, freedom and self-determination for the colonies, preservation of links with the Western democracies, and at the same time an advocacy of non-involvement in foreign military and ideological entanglements. Although during World War I the Indian National Congress had declared its loyalty to the Western allies and supported the use of the Indian Army in the war, a distinct change took place in its stand on foreign affairs in the twenties and the thirties. Henceforth the emphasis of the Congress was to support all movements for independence and national self-determination. Nationalism became India's dominant creed. There also developed among the younger generation of Indians an ideological fascination towards Marxism and communism that had been spreading over large parts of the world, some Indians taking an active part in the extension of the Communist International to the Asian countries.[1] Finally, there was the element designed by Nehru himself, namely a bid for leadership among the newly independent nations of Asia and Africa.

In many ways, the Indian posture in the external world, in the decades before and the years after independence, was in the nature of a response to the impact of the Renaissance and the Enlightenment that came to it during the nineteenth century. It seemed as if the long suppressed Indian universalism was at last finding an expression. In Nehru's memorable words quoted at the beginning of this book, the coming of independence was like a moment "which comes but rarely in history, when we step out from the old to the new, when an age ends, and when the soul of a nation, long suppressed, finds utterance." The result was an idealistic view of the world and its problems, characterized by a refreshing if naive optimism countering, as it were, the hardened cynicism and opportunism that appeared to prevail all around.

NATIONAL AUTONOMY

Underlying such idealism, however, was a thoughful conception of national interest and a profound awareness of world currents; the idealism was by no means empty. Nehru realized before any of his contemporaries in the "third world" that World War II had drastically altered the nature of the world order; that precisely when the ex-colonial states were acquiring national autonomy, this autonomy was liable to be threatened. Not only did the new nations themselves lack the means to preserve their autonomy but the new power balance in the world threatened to reduce all smaller powers to mere appendages in a global tug-of-war. Also, the United Nations charter by the terms of which the new world order was created in the San Francisco meetings in 1945, while no doubt an improvement on the prewar situation, was not satisfactory from the point of view of countries like India. It created a world of super-powers and subordinate power—or at best groups of power—not a world in which each nation was equally autonomous. Finally, India felt that the big powers (especially the now all-powerful United States) threatened to engulf the whole region from the Mediterranean to the Bay of Bengal and the South China Sea in which India has such a vital stake as a power.

Nehru strove to alter all of this. It was an ambitious undertaking but that did not deter him. He knew that he could not do this on the traditional lines of power politics by building a mighty army; the new world conditions, military technology, and India's limited resources and urgent domestic tasks, as well as Nehru's own inclinations, did not permit this. Instead he strove through a new vision and a new doctrine, backed by incessant pressure on the outside world, and utilizing the new atmosphere of idea in the thinking sections of all nations. The result was a foreign policy designed to fulfill three aims: to assure a degree of autonomy to nations who lacked the means to resist great powers (hence the accent on anti-imperialism and anti-colonialism), to restrain the power politics that were a logical consequence of the United Nations settlement (hence his persistent and stubborn opposition to power blocs), and to keep free from big power domination the area from North Africa to Indonesia (hence the Asian Conference as Nehru's first diplomatic act and the series of Afro-Asian meetings). Such an approach soon led to a clash with the Americans whose aims directly conflicted with his; so Nehru solicited a Russian counterforce in the region when he saw that the Americans could not be fully restrained, and he also generally played East against West to maintain India's own autonomy.

Nehru's success in defeating the "Dullesian design" is outstanding and will receive recognition in due course (when the scholarship on international relations becomes less parochial and ethnocentric). His later failures on particular aspects of his policy have to be balanced against this larger accomplishment. What informed his various policies was a passionate striving for transforming political independence into genuine national autonomy, a necessary counterpart of nation-building at home. Other aims like maintenance of peace at home and in the region surrounding it, and the securing of economic aid from Western and Eastern powers, were a by-product of this principal thrust of his foreign policy.

The approach was informed by other remarkable insights and ideas. Nehru was the first to make a historic theme out of the changing power relationships of the interwar period: "the days of colonialism were over," he said. Nehru was also the first non-Communist leader to draw the world's attention to the positive achievements of the Soviet Union and to the theme, which he pronounced after his first visit to Russia in 1927, that with technological advance there would be internal pressures within Russia for liberalization, a more pragmatic approach to the other world powers, and an eventual rapprochement with the United States. India was the first non-Communist country to have invited Soviet leaders to personally visit the outside world, a visit that started with India, and was later followed by invitations from the Western countries to these leaders. There is reason to believe that Khrushchev's various visits to the non-Communist countries contributed to the "thaw". Even more perceptive was Nehru's view, expressed long before others realized its importance, that a conflict of interests between Russia and China was bound to take place, that nationalism was a more powerful force than communism, and that there were "different shades" to communism. Based on these insights, Nehru developed the doctrine of "peaceful co-existence" between seemingly opposite ideological systems, vehemently pleaded for nuclear arms controls in the absence of a total ban, developed the concept of "non-alignment" in power blocs, and called for "aid without strings" in the economic relationships between the developed and the underdeveloped countries.[2]

NON-ALIGNMENT

Nehru himself preferred to think of non-alignment not as an ideological doctrine but as a policy based upon "elightened self-interest." India needed the friendship of both Eastern and Western powers, it intensely disliked any evidence of interference from outside, and it realized that keeping the big powers out of the region was a vital pre-condition of political autonomy and national reconstruction. Following this line of approach was his interest in mobilizing the support and assistance of the richer nations of the world for India's economic growth, in avoiding conflict with China and Russia, the two great powers on its northern frontiers, in cultivating the friendship of the emerging countries, and in speaking authoritatively in their behalf in the councils of the world.

In pursuit of such an approach shortly after India's independence, Nehru convened the first Asian Conference in New Delhi in 1949 for the support of the cause of Indonesia against the Dutch. His next important steps in this direction were: India's participation in the Bandung Conference held in 1955; the signing of the Panch Sheel ("five principles of peaceful coexistence") treaty with China in 1954; the strong support given to Egypt at the time of the Suez Crisis in 1956 and to the Algerian cause against France; its role in arranging a cease-fire and working out the involved problem of exchange of prisoners in the Korean War and in convening the Geneva Conference on Indo-China and Laos; its participation in the U.N. forces in the Congo and efforts to maintain political stability in that strife-striken country; its constant pleading for China's right of admission to the United Nations; and its "constructive" role, along with Yugoslavia and Egypt in keeping open lines of communication with the great powers at the Belgrade Conference of non-aligned nations in 1961.[3]

For a newly independent country still struggling to create a nation, this involved a remarkably wide-ranging role in world politics. Because India's policy sought to combine non-alignment with active support to "anti-imperialist" movements and displayed greater sensitivity to opinion within the socialist and the non-aligned countries than in the West, it carried within itself a measure of ambivalence and created not a little misunderstanding in certain quarters.[4] Later on, with growing threats from across its borders on the one hand and the increasing burden of foreign economic debt on the other, the policy was tested severely. Despite such growing strains, the country resisted too close an identification with any one bloc, and by the time a need arose for a reappraisal, the world system had already entered a period of confusion and drift.

The policy of non-alignment, while also an outgrowth of India's ideological background and position in the third world, seems to have served her immediate interests rather well. A period of peace and lack of any external involvement permitted the consolidation of the country, incorporation of the formerly independent native states, and the strengthening of the country's ties with outlying areas, including the "buffer state" of Nepal and the principalities of Sikkim and Bhutan. It could hold to the Valley of Kashmir and wrest Goa from the Portuguese in December, 1961, despite criticism in the West, continue its ties with the Commonwealth, and at the same time command the respect of the new states by being their principal spokesman in the world, reap the advantage of the doctrine of "coexistence" by mobilizing economic support from both sides of the ideological spectrum, and above all keep its defence expenditure low and thus direct its resources to planned economic development. The idealism underlying the policy gave the country and its intellectuals a degree of self-assurance; its operational returns, under the peculiar conditions of the cold war, enabled it to turn its energies to urgent tasks at home. The overall effect was considerable freedom of maneuver in the mobilization and direction of the nation's energies.

CHALLENGES TO NATIONAL INTEGRITY

Such a momentum in the country's development could have conceivably continued but for four at first unrelated sources of disturbance: the politics of the cold war, an ill-defined tradition from the British days, the entangled Kashmir issue, and economic planning at home.[5] The first source of disturbance to India's containment of external pressures was the policy of the United States, under John Foster Dulles, of encircling the world with a network of military bases and security pacts with a view to filling the "power vacuum" in the world, and as part of a strategy of "massive retaliation" against Communist threat. The strategy permeated South Asia and the Indian subcontinent itself with the United States-Pakistan alliance, Pakistan's membership in SEATO and CENTO, and the establishment of military bases on the subcontinent.

COLD WAR PENETRATION

The decision, implemented in the face of vehement protests from India, caused great bitterness in India and forced it to deal with the threat through a series of steps: arms build-up (India's defense expenditure in 1958 went up by more than 50 per cent above its usual Rs. 200 crores annually and steadily increased thereafter); its moving closer to the Soviet Union in an effort to increase its bargaining power, diversify its sources of economic support, and elicit big power support for its position on the Kashmir issue; and, more important than both of these, its effort to arrive at an understanding with China which involved recognition of Tibet as part of China and termination of India's special rights in Tibet in return for an agreement by China on the principles of non-aggression and mutual co-existence. During this same period, India, unhappy with its dependence on foreign supplies for conventional weapons, stepped up indigenous manufacture of ammunitions. All this involved a change in attitudes. As a result of the United States policies which created a state of uncertainty in the region and provided teeth to Pakistan's belligerent posture, and genuinely fearful of the extension of the cold war into the subcontinent, India sought to avoid simultaneous trouble with its other two large neighbors in this halting and defensive manner. Together these various moves enabled India to contain the threat posed by the United States-Pakistan pact, in spite of apprehension that Pakistan might violate its undertaking under the pact that United States arms were only to be used against "communist aggression" and under no circumstances against India.

A BORDER WAR

India's second, and until now most serious and humiliating, source of disturbance to its policy of external containment came from a protracted border problem with China. The Indian government inherited the British view of the country's "natural frontier's" whereas the Chinese held that the boundaries were never clearly demarcated and wanted a reconsideration of the problem on fresh grounds rather than on the basis of "imperial" arrangements.[6] More generally India had followed a policy of weaning China away from any cold war entanglements despite its historical and ideological association with the Soviet Union, and to bring it closer to the Afro-Asian cause. Inspired both by the idealism characteristic of the resurgence of Indian universalism and by pragmatic considerations of containing the cold war, India had pinned great hopes on Sino-Indian collaboration in the post-revolutionary world. What obstructed realization of this aspiration was an extraordinary lack of candor and frankness on both sides, a preoccupation with generalities and neglect of operational details and strategic conditions, and cumulative misunderstandings on both sides arising from the Chinese habit of circuitous dealings and the Indian predisposition to wish away unpleasant reality.

The issue crystallized after the Tibetan revolt in 1959 when China felt pressed to find an alternative route to the difficult terrain that marked its direct route to Tibet. China's devious, underhanded ways of asserting its claims and the difficulty of selling any compromise border settlement to the Indian parliamentary and public opinion which had become sympathetic to the plight of the Tibetans, especially after the gruesome manner in which the Chinese had suppressed the revolt, accentuated the misunderstandings; while the Chinese felt they were confirmed in their view that the Indians were playing the "British game" in Tibet, the Indians became convinced that China had aggressive designs on India. Looking back, a compromise would not have been impossible to work out fairly early in the bargaining process, either at the time of the Tibetan treaty in 1954 or when in 1957-58 it became clear that the Chinese were not prepared to accept India's claims and were instead looking for a settlement that would give them access to Aksai Chin in the Ladakh region of Kashmir in return for recognizing India's claims on the Himalayan ridge (along the McMahon Line) in the northeast. Instead the Chinese began to move in so many devious ways — showing Indian-claimed areas on Chinese maps, building a secret road in Aksai Chin, and through inspired border skirmishes — while India tried to respond by stepping up its defense reinforcements in the border regions, slowly and cautiously, and moving its forces forward in Ladakh during 1961-62. It was only in April,

1960 that Chou En-lai suggested to Nehru, when they met in New Delhi, the compromise border settlement. By this time it was too late and border incidents and mutual misunderstandings resulted in the Chinese being "provoked" (through India's advance into Ladakh and Nehru's over-reacting statements of throw-the-Chinese-out) into a massive act of aggression on Indian territory. It is not improbable that the very symbolism and pedantry of friendship and "brotherly" relationships impeded the working out of a realistic settlement.

This sudden attack, which took the Indian largely unawares, produced a humiliating defeat for India and turned China and India into hostile neighbors for a long time to come. The fact that the Chinese "unilaterally" withdraw from the territory beyond the disputed borders in Ladakh, had earlier proposed clear lines of a border settlement, and also later withdrew from the NEFA (North East Frontier Agency) region, show that Chinese intensions were limited. But once the die was caset, once the aggression was perpetrated, the road to any honorable settlement became very difficult, at least in the foreseeable future.

The results of the fighting, for India, were negative. The country and its leadership—most of all Nehru himself—suffered a deep blow as the event shook them out of their complacent idealism; as Nehru graphically put it, "India will never be the same again." Confronting two hostile neighbors at the same time, the country not only lost the freedom of maneuver that it had hitherto enjoyed but had also to undertake a defense build-up which pushed up its expenditure from a little over Rs. 300 crores in the 1962-63 budget to between Rs. 800 and 900 crores in the following years. (It has since gone up to approximately 1,000 crores annually, roughly 5 per cent of GNP). Though the precise effect of defense expenditures on general economic development is difficult to assess and although defense outlays do provide some stimulus to industrial production, not to speak of the psychological energy that they release, there is also no doubt that such a heavy commitment of resources of guarding the country's 2,000 mile frontiers tends to distract from other developmental tasks, creates inflationary pressures, and affects production priorities. Moreover, the crisis with China created a long period of uncertainty regarding India's ability to guard its own frontiers, exposed the country to continuous border skirmishes, and made Indians suspicious of anything that smacked of Chinese or Pakistani intentions, including an unhealthy suspicion of political groups at home such as the left Communists and the various Muslim parties.

But the Chinese attack also had some positive effects. An amazing outburst of patriotic feeling all over the country included a spontaneous surrender on a large scale of young sons and property in the national cause. The conflict led to a heightened national identity and an increased solidarity behind the government. It also served the nation well in another respect. It was forced to shed its illusions and simplistic ways of looking at problems of international relations, and prepared for a long, hard effort at building up its defenses. Responding to the crisis, a state of emergency was created, a "defense *and* development" strategy worked out, internal resources mobilized through a series of schemes, plan activities accelerated in strategic industries and target dates advanced, and an Industrial Truce Resolution worked out between employers and workers.

Externally too, considerable opinion was aroused in favor of India among the democracies and the non-aligned countries (with the exception of Indonesia). The most vocal support came from Egypt, which said that the Chinese attack was a "blow to the concept of non-alignment," Yugoslavia, and Malaya (which started a "Save Democracy Fund"). The Colombo powers (Ceylon, Ghana, Burma, Indonesia, and Cambodia besides Egypt) sought hard to work out compromise proposals which were acceptable to both India and China; the proposals have been accepted "in toto" by India but only "in principle" by China. Arms and equipment were rushed by western powers, especially the United States, United Kingdom, and Canada, and long-run agreements involving military aid and import of military hardware were signed with these powers as well as with the Soviet Union. Slowly an approach was developed which received a flow of both Western and Soviet arms. Not wanting to rely on the West alone, and watchful of not creating any Sino-Russian entente on India, the country moved towards a new version of non-alignment, namely an acceptance of military assistance from both the West and the East, similar to the existing acceptance of economic aid from both, At the same time India considerably expanded indigenous output of modern arms, including ordnance supplies, fighter aircraft, electronic equipment, and radar, and a Department of Defense Production was set up. All this helped when the country faced its next external crisis in 1965.

WORSENING OF INDIA-PAKISTAN RELATIONS

India's apprehensions that the United States security pact with Pakistan, followed by a supply of the most modern military equipment and establishment of American bases in Pakistan, would some day turn against India, as well as its fear of a Sino-Pakistan collusion against India following their border agreement of March, 1963, all came true with the outbreak of hostilities between Pakistan and India in 1965. The first conflict, which occurred in April, was a limited border engagement. It took place when Pakistan tried to assert its claims on the Kutch-Sind border by attacking Indian posts, deploying 16 of its battalions, and using, on their own admission,[7] American and British arms and equipment (including American tanks). It was stopped through a cease-fire on June 30 mediated by the British prime minister, restoration of the status quo, and an agreement between the two countries to refer the dispute to a three-member international arbitration tribunal whose award was to be binding on both countries.[8]

The relations between the two countries took a serious and dramatic turn when Pakistani armed infiltrators moved into Kashmir across the cease-fire lines[9] on August 5, 1965, followed by an open military confrontation between the armies of the two countries, at first in the Chhamb sector across the international boundary and then, in an attempt to relieve pressure on the north and forestall further aggression, by Indian forces moving into west Pakistan. The Indian forces also occupied the Haji Pir pass and a number of other posts in Pakistan-held Kashmir. In the 50-day war that ensued, India successfully repelled the Pakistani attack despite the latter's open and extensive use of American, British, and West German arms and equipment. The Indian land and air forces put up an impressive display of strength and resilience, India's indigenously manufactured arms and equipment (especially the bomber aircraft) amazingly reaching up to the much superior American equipment, and the Indian military command showing skill and finesse, as in their opening of the western flank in Lahore which caught the Pakistanis unprepared.

The Indian leadership also showed great patience and courage, as when they refused to yield to a Chinese threat and "ultimatum" of September 16 that it would open a simultaneous attack in three days unless India were to "dismantle all its military works" on the Sikkim-Chinese border. In order to back up the ultimatum with some claims, the Chinese demanded a return of "kidnapped border inhabitants," and a return of "seized livestock." Prime Minister Shastri offered joint inspection of the border but at the same time declared India's "grim determination" to fight the two countries simultaneously if attacked. Actually the Chinese ultimatum proved to be a bluff and by calling it the Indians achieved a tactical and psychological gain. (In a lighter vein the common man in New Delhi joined the government's more serious reply by leading a massive herd of sheep and other livestock to the Chinese Embassy and embarrassing the embassy officials, who evidently were not able to accept the live animals despite their government's demand.)

In the end, following continuous efforts by U.N. Secretary-General U Thant and the Security Council and especially the Soviet Union's active intervention and initiative for a personal meeting between President Ayub Khan and Prime Minister Shastri in Tashkent, a cease-fire was agreed to between the two countries with effect from September 23, 1965. The two leaders eventually met in Tashkent January 3-10 and signed the famous "Tashkent Declaration" which provided for a restoration of the status quo of August 5 and pledged the two countries to the principles on non-interference, restoration of economic and diplomatic relations, and a reaffirmation of their obligations under the U.N. Charter "not to have recourse to force and to settle their disputes through peaceful means." Russia played a leading part in these negotiations and, although Prime Minister Shastri died the day after the Declaration were carried out despite protests within India against surrendering positions within (Pakistan-held) Kashmir, especially the strategic Haji Pir pass. Similarly, despite parliamentary opposition to the Kutch Award which deviated somewhat from India's position, the Indian government has agreed to honor its commitment to implement the Award.

Border incidents still continue sporadically between the two countries but the state of hostilities has become more manageable. Negotiations on restoration of telecommunications and trade channels have taken place, military and technical personnel have also met, and recently Prime Minister Indira Gandhi made a symbolic overture by a message of congratulations to President Ayub Khan on Pakistan's completion of the Mangla Dam built on Kashmiri territory held by Pakistan. The prime minister was severely censured in the Indian Parliament for tacitly agreeing to Pakistan's continued occupation of Kashmiri territory but the government has, for some time now, favored a de facto partition of Kashmir along the ceasefire line.

CHANGING CONTEXT OF INTERNATIONAL ENVIRONMENT

The Pakistan conflict in some ways proved a shot in the arm for India, especially because the Indians were able to repel the technically superior Western arms in Pakistan's possession. But the war involved serious costs. Any aggravation of the conflict with Pakistan should be in itself a cause for concern insofar as it increases the state of strain in the subcontinent and involves it in the wider confrontations of international politics, accentuates problems of Hindu and Muslim identities, and transforms problems of domestic discontent into continuous and difficult issues of international accommodation. This conflict proved more serious since it involved not only the contesting parties but big powers also whose concern at maintaining the status quo in the subcontinent led to some drastic moves, as in the American cessation of all economic aid during and for some time after the conflict. In Tashkent the USSR began slowly to crystallize a neutralist position in its efforts to freeze the existing balance of power in the subcontinent and to contain the expansion of Chinese influence. While still broadly supporting India on Kashmir and other issues, the Soviet Union has been trying to make up with Pakistan too by providing it with military supplies and adopting an approach of equal friendship toward the two countries.

Thus even more than the Chinese conflict of 1962, the "war" with Pakistan resulted in a shrinkage of India's diplomatic freedom and led to a climate of disillusionment with the big powers. Together the two conflicts have slowly and imperceptibly produced a general mood of detachment and negativism in the country, a mood of wanting to withdraw from world issues, indeed even from taking a position on Afro-Asian issues which has for so long been India's chief strategic and ideological forte. It is in respect of these psychological consequences, accentuated by the immediate aftermath of an economic recession and political problems with the big powers, that India's self-image and identity appeared to have suffered the most.

It is not simply that the "victory" against Pakistan proved so very costly for India's position in the world environment. The world environment itself has undergone a striking change. The neat logic provided by the cold war is no longer available, the big powers have adjusted more carefully and often cynically to the new era, including their own version of "non-alignment" in the conflicts of the third world. With all this, India's traditional role and position have lost their raison d'être. When no great power wants India to "align," indeed when everyone professes non-alignment, following Nehru's great doctrine for peace, Indian non-alignment loses in meaning both as a strategy and as an ideology. And yet India has so far not been able to produce an alternative strategy.

What is important here is not any weakening of India vis-a-vis the external world—if anything India's military as well as industrial potential has improved—but rather the loss of confidence in its own vision and idealism, and the assumption of an overly defensive posture to world issues. At a time when the need is to reconstruct the country's foreign policy and the basic philosophy underlying it by a more positive approach to the institution of a world order, it is a pity that India of all countries should so withdraw into a shell. The basic Indian approach to the world and to the region in which it has a lasting stake have been held out despite her local entanglements with her neighbors. Indeed the approach has had a powerful impact both in the preservation of its own autonomy (and the acceptance by other new nations of its basic position) and in by and large keeping free the region in which it has such a vital role to play. The present mood is thus quite artificial and temporary. The reasons for it are two-fold: the psychological strain of extended military engagement has been something to which Indians have not traditionally been accustomed (India escaped the ravages of both world wars); and India's own economic base is still too weak to sustain the freshness and optimism that were Nehru's principal attributes. To occupy a position of great power potentiality without great power status, while on the other hand being unable to enjoy the comforts of a small power, creates ambivalence and self-doubt and prevents the development of an effective posture vis-à-vis the external world. But it must before long give place to a more positive approach.

When we turn to more concrete developments, the country faces a new balance of advantages and disadvantages. Militarily it has gained steady ground—India has the fourth largest military establishment in the world—and has perhaps already acquired a position where it can successfully contain joint attack from China and Pakistan. Its nuclear capability has also steadily increased and it has already the potential to emerge as a nuclear power if it so desires. Diplomatically, too, since 1965 the situation has become somewhat favorable. China has been increasingly isolated from the rest of Asia and the world—witness its alienation of at one time staunch allies like Burma and Indonesia and of almost the whole of the African continent. Pakistan, too, has been losing in self-esteem and the esteem of other powers, especially since its increasing dependence on China diplomatically. There is increasing concern within Pakistan that its desire to obtain maneuverability vis-à-vis India has involved heavy costs to its national autonomy, without leading to any gains over India. Not a small part of its current political crisis is the failure of the country under former President Ayub Khan to evolve a positive national identity.

STATUS QUO POWER

Meanwhile India has steadily moved in the direction of being a status quo power, projecting a political image that much of the

Afro-Asian world sees as a clear alternative to the Chinese image, and urging a constructive attitude that would keep the third world in active communication with the West as well as the Soviet Union, both of whom continue to compete for a position of influence in Asia, West Asia, and Africa. With all its difficulties, India continues to symbolize the voice of reason and sobriety in international affairs.[10] Its recent economic revival and its success in handling severe domestic strains without compromising its democratic commitments are likely to add to this image. And its recent display of some firmness, as shown in its refusal to sign the Soviet-U.S.-sponsored nuclear nonproliferation treaty, has shown that it cannot be taken for granted and represents — together with countries like Japan — a body of international opinion that needs to be shown due respect and consideration.

There are also new problems. A major difficulty arises from the fact that Indian foreign policy must favor a status quo position but operate in a region where the dominant cry is for change and revolution. China is the revolutionary power par excellence, inspires in every other nation of Asia fear and awe, and provides the vanguard for "national liberation movements" everywhere, including among the minority tribal groups on India's borders. Pakistan, though domestically a conservative political system, has staked its entire identity on a disturbance in the status quo of the subcontinent, in Kashmir to begin with and possibly beyond. It has been argued that even if the border conflict with China had not led to an armed aggression, Indian and Chinese interests are so much at variance that the rivalry between the two powers was bound to come out in the open sooner or later.[11] It has similarly been argued that even if the Kashmir issue was settled, Pakistan and India would still continue to pull in opposite directions. Tied as they are by a deep-seated "negative identity", Pakistan being founded on such an identity, such rivalry is deeply ingrained.[12]

Second, pressed by this continuous dilemma of an "anti-imperial" power having to pursue a status quo position, India has been forced to translate operationally its policy of non-alignment by gradually allowing a remarkable increase of the Soviet presence in South Asia. This is not a comfortable position for a country like India, firmly committed to a democracy, seriously embarrassed by Russia's policies in Eastern Europe (à la Czechoslovakia) and its arms aid to Pakistan, and still heavily dependent on Western economic aid. Third, the issue of economic development poses another dilemma for India's freedom of maneuver: how to reconcile political independence with dependence on foreign countries in vital economic matters, including supplies of basic necessities and raw materials.

All these factors, together with the country's inability so far to negotiate a settlement with either China or Pakistan, have greatly limited the country's initiative, produced a highly defensive and circumspective style, and prevented it from articulating a new foreign policy. This has been manifested in both the assertion of a policy position — as when India was forced to support the Arab cause against Israel in the 1967 war—and in its non-assertion—as in India's ambivalent opposition to the United States war in Vietnam and to the Russian occupation of Czech territory. Indeed much of what remains of India "non-alignment" is this policy of extreme caution and drift, not any positive posture, either in its definition of national interest or in day-to-day diplomacy. The learning process on which the country has entered through its grim encounters in the two wars and through a strain in its relationship with the great powers will have to go still further before the old self-confidence is restored, a new policy is worked out, and hopefully a more effective version of the old vision reemerges. Much will depend on the performance in other sectors and the growth of domestic capabilities. Meanwhile the urgent task is to acquire economic independence. As this poses a series of interconnected and difficult issues which go beyond the analysis of Chapter 9, it would be worthwhile to consider them now.

ACHIEVING ECONOMIC INDEPENDENCE

One of the main requirements of speedy industrialization is to mobilize resources in the form of capital goods and machinery, and until these are not produced indigenously, to import them from abroad. There is need therefore to develop a policy, or a combination of various policies, of external resource mobilization. Among these are a cutting down on import of "non-essential" consumer and manufactured goods in favor of machinery and scarce raw materials (reallocation of imports), producing domestically what was hitherto imported (import substitution), increasing earnings from trade abroad (export promotion), and filling the gap in foreign exchange caused by an excess of imports over exports by recourse to external loans, grants, and other forms of assistance (foreign aid) as well as by attracting foreign capital for investment in the country (foreign capital investment). The Indian government has followed all these approaches to the mobilization of external resources for the achievement of economic independence, and has had to evolve a policy toward each of them.

CORRECTING THE TRADE DEFICIT

Dependence on foreign aid and capital arises essentially from a continuing deficit in the balance of external trade, a deficit that increases with the strategy of rapid industrialization, especially in its early stages. In India a trade deficit existed even before planned industrialization began and the sterling balances that had been accumulated during the war were being gradually depleted. When the country became independent there were acute shortages of foodgrains and raw materials like jute and raw cotton, caused mainly by World War II and the partition of the country as some of the best granaries of the subcontinent went to Pakistan. Exports on the other hand remained static with the exception of 1951-52 during the Korean War. The First Five Year Plan sought to correct this disequilibrium by concentrating on agricultural production and thereby reducing the drain on foreign exchange reserves. The plan was a great success in this regard. Once the economy was consolidated at this level, however, the plan strategy took a leap towards the development of heavy industries. Starting with the Second Five Year Plan, this strategy immediately led to a sharp increase in the import of developmental inputs like machinery, transport equipment, chemicals, metals, and metal manufactures. Although some improvement in exports was noticed in the latter part of this plan, imports rose even more, pushing up the trade deficit during the plan period from Rs. 165 to Rs. 400 crores.

The Third Five Year Plan registered an even bolder effort at rapid industrialization, pushing up the import content of India's economic structure with the aim of raising its technological level. At the same time bad weather conditions in three out of give years of the plan, including a severe drought, and the country's involvement in two wars resulted in failures to meet production targets, led to underutilization of capacity due to maintenance shortages, and kept exports down while pushing up imports of both essential and non-essential goods. To these were added imports of strategic defense items. During the same period population was increasing rapidly and led to a strong upward swing in demand for all goods.

One of the more difficult problems of economic development derives from the nature of the colonial economy, which is characterized by a subordinate relationship of exchange in which the colony produces primary and semi-manufactured goods and exchanges them for manufactured and machine goods. Although a country as vast as India, endowed with rich resources and entrepreneurial skills, could not be turned into a plantation economy as was the case with many African and some other Asian countries, the bulk of India's exports consisted of what are now known as "traditional items." These were tea, spices, tobacco, coffee, mineral ores, cotton textiles, and choir and jute manufactures. Such a concentration on primary products and consumer goods is disadvantageous because it makes for dependence on imports for industrial products — which may be defended on the grounds of "comparative costs" though this argument has ceased to be persuasive — and also because the terms of trade between primary and industrial goods have for several decades now been steadily moving against the former. Also the low income and price elasticities of traditional items have led to a decline in demand for them, thus further sharpening the trade gap.

In view of all this, one of the main policy thrusts of India's economic planning was to improve this imbalance. Exports of new items such as engineering goods and machine tools, petroleum products, a few steel items, iron ore and concentrates, chemicals and chemical compounds have all been increasing in recent years. On the import side, the policy of import substitution and increasing fulfillment of local demand from indigenous manufacturing has contributed to some improvement. Imports of machine tools, metal manufactures, mineral fuels and transport equipment have all declined as have the imports of raw materials like cotton and jute, paper and paper board, and dyeing and tanning materials.[13] The significant fact here is that in spite of a sharp increase in demand caused by population rise and general economic expansion, the proportion of this demand met by indigenous production has increased. The trend is likely to continue. It is estimated that by the end of the Fourth Plan indigenous production will take care of 75 per cent of the demand for machine tools, the entire demand for special steels, and the entire demand for aluminium, with possibly a surplus for export.[14]

NEW MARKETS

There is generally great difficulty for an underdeveloped country to enter the world market with new industrial products in the face of competition from more developed nations and other obstacles like customs and tariff barriers. As internal demand is constantly growing and the domestic market is protected due to the policies of import restriction and import substitution, the disincentives to export expansion are formidable. The position is made worse since even the traditional items of export, because of their low demand elasticities and growing competition from countries still specializing in primary goods, suffer a decline. All these factors have led to India's drive for a more diversified world market with special effort devoted to Eastern Europe, Southeast Asia, and the continents of Africa and Latin America, while still continuing to trade in the traditional markets of United Kingdom and Western Europe. A series of bilateral trade agreements have come into effect in recent years, most prominently with USSR, Yugoslavia, Hungary, Poland, Czechoslovakia and East Germany, Argentina and Chile, the UAR and Iraq, Japan, Burma, Ceylon, and Malaysia. Government to government collaboration has also been developed, as for example with Yugoslavia and Czechoslovakia (with whom a "joint commission" of experts has been set up.

Collaboration between foreign private firms and Indian industrialists has been increasing, and lately Indian industrial houses and the government have also been establishing joint industrial enterprises, as in Kenya, Tanzania, Iran, Malaysia, Philippines, Ceylon, and in Ireland. To the countries of Africa and other underdeveloped countries, there has been an increasing flow of Indian professional and technical know-how, including the supply of senior civil servants (as in Nigeria and East Africa) and military personnel (as in Ethiopia). On the other hand, despite a perennial controversy between the right and the left of the Congress Party, there has been an increasing flow of foreign private capital, mostly in industries that have hitherto depended heavily on imports, and generally in collaboration with indigenous entrepreneurs.[15] All this is part of the effort to diversify the country's international trade and economic relationships. Their full contribution will take time to show results, as their magnitude is still small, but they provide us with a trend for the future.

In the meanwhile India's dependence on imports continues, thanks largely to its attempt at rapid industrialization on the one hand and lagging agricultural output on the other. Thus while the share of machinery in total imports went up from about 14 per cent in 1950-51 to about 30 per cent in 1965-66, it is the country's "food problem," only now beginning to respond to planned efforts, that has been the greatest drag on the import bill, which must also take care of a large proportion of the increasing demand for fertilizers and other agricultural inputs. New industrial plants, and replacements and spare parts for old plants, have also maintained a high pressure on the balance of payments. Many of India's policies until recently, such as protection of the indigenous market, the absence of sufficient differential incentives to local manufacturers for preferring exports to selling locally, and the absence of a well thought-out price policy have all contributed further to this deficit in the balance of payments. What holds some promise now is that on each of these counts there is evidence of both a cumulative outcome of past efforts and the evolution of policies that are sensitive to the various issues. The former include a reduction in the import content of whole machinery produced locally, diversification of the export market, increases in productivity arising out of greater utilization of capacity, and increased local production of agricultural inputs and industrial raw materials. Among the new policies that have been adopted but will take some time to make an impact are cost reduction in new lines of export through rationalization of these industries, various steps in the direction of quality control, and introduction of new processes discovered through industrial research (such as those which allow for a substitution in metallic base and raw material components).

Apart from mobilizing the economy for narrowing the trade gap, there is need for a concerted export drive abroad. Indians have been rather slack and unaggressive in "selling" themselves abroad, both politically on controversial issues and in the pursuit of economic interests. Also, following a defensive policy arising out of the "self-sufficiency" model, the planners had pinned more hopes on import substitution, while the continuous flow of economic aid had provided a false cushion to their policies. It was the serious balance of payments crisis during the Third Plan that led to a shift in policy here, both in respect to moving the emphasis from import substitution to export promotion, and to giving to the departments dealing with foreign trade and to bodies like the Board of Trade their due status in the decision-making structure of the government. Export Promotion Councils, one for each commodity, have been set up and have been entrusted with responsibilities for market research, commodity research, and quality promotion. The work of earlier bodies like the State Trading Corporation, known to the sluggish and bureaucratized, the been under review. There is also evidence of the diminishing role of ideological considerations in this regard: steps in the direction of lessened controls and liberalization have been adopted, a policy on extending export credits and guarantees to firms engaging in foreign trade has come into being, and various media of commercial publicity and competition in the world market are being at long last developed.[16]

CURRENCY DEVALUATION

Apart from attending to these minutiae of economic efficiency which is of highest importance, there have also been certain large policy changes. One such step that was taken specifically to reduce the balance of payment deficit was the decision to devalue the Indian currency as of June, 1966. The presumption was that devaluation would increase export earnings and reduce the demand for imports. The results of the step (which aroused bitter controversy in the country and led to the allegation that the government had sold out to foreign pressure) were for long not reflected in trade statistics. In part this was because traditional items which constitute almost 70 per cent of total exports have a very low price elasticity, in part because of the high import content of the new industries to whom devaluation came as a mixed blessing, in part because of the government's view of devaluation as some kind of panacea so that various other schemes of export promotion were simultaneously abolished, and perhaps more than all this, because the aid-givers and the World Bank failed to meet their *quid ·pro quo* which was to back the decision by significant increases in economic aid at easy terms. Lack of firm bargaining and political pressures within the aid-giving countries were responsible for this lack of timely assistance with which critical maintenance imports could have been bought and existing capacity raised before price rises and other pressures had wiped off a good part of the incentive supplied by devaluation.

While the government expects and claims that the effects of devaluation are beginning to show as exports with low import content pick up and the local supply of raw materials increases, economic experts are sharply divided as regards the causes of recent increases in exports which are responsible for a narrowing of the trade deficit. Clearly, devaluation was a step hastily taken without proper bargaining, probably under duress, and without proper regard to supplementary measures to make it work. So regarded, it stands in sharp contrast to the "new agricultural policy" initiated in depth and executed in detail by C. Subramanian and his departmental aides. Such a contrast illustrates the kind of social engineering involved in carrying out what look like purely economic decisions.

EXTERNAL RESOURCE MOBILIZATION

We have explained at some length the various facets of India's external balances, as it helps us to bring out the kind of comprehensive restructuring needed in moving from a colonial economy to a modern planned economy aiming to bring about rapid growth. The transition is probably as difficult to bring about as is the transition from a colonial polity to a truly independent nation-state, with the added difficulty that whereas the availability of political resources is a function of culture, charisma, and institution-building capabilities which can all, with some luck, be found within the country, economic resources are inherently more scarce and almost as a rule unavailable in sufficient measure within the country at the start of the modernization process. Because of this particular issue of filling the gap in much needed resources a new branch of international relations known as "economic aid" has opened up in the post-war world, with direct and obvious repercussions on the economic and political life of underdeveloped nations, and with implications for the world order as a whole.

The controversial issues involved in a country's dependence on foreign aid are now well known. At the most general level the issue is posed in terms of a dilemma: political independence versus economic dependence. Attempts have been made to substitute the current typology of "developed" and "underdeveloped" (or "developing") nations by a more direct typology of "independent" and "dependent," or alternatively, "donor" and "recipient" nations.[17] The question that is raised in this way is straightforward: given the fact of the vast disparities in national living standards, and living in an age dominated by the "end of colonialism," how best to reconcile economic dependence with national freedom? The political advantages that flow from economic aid are obvious. It can reduce the immediate problem of scarcity, widen the range of choices open to the elite, provide the necessary cushion to the ruling coalition by releasing part of its resources for pressing political needs, allow the regime to undertake relatively comprehensive social and economic change, enable optimum preference schedules in the planning process, and as all this constitutes an investment in the future, raise the nation's postponement of gratification capability. The disadvantages may not be as obvious but are equally pertinent. The availability of economic aid may distort economic aims and priorities by going after projects for which aid is available, accentuate conditions of scarcity by inducing unwillingness to undertake hard internal tasks, reinforce existing disparities and favor particular economic and political groups against others, lead to inflexibility in future choices by trying up resources to particular programs, and above all, introduce an element of uncertainty and constant anticipation in the entire policy process, not infrequently leading to a humiliating experience and an explosive political situation. On balance economic aid may still be an advantage—as is evident from the fact that no new state has done without it—but it is not an unmixed blessing.

FOREIGN AID

India has by now experienced much of what is listed above, has sometimes resented such a state of dependence, but there has been little doubt about its conscious preference: it is in favor of seeking external resources, including economic aid, until the economy "takes off" into self-sustained growth. The issue has been immune from a great deal of controversy except among extremist intellectuals; in fact all political groups are agreed on the need to mobilize such aid, although there are important differences on specific issues such as whether aid should be bilateral or multilateral, how much of it should come from "capitalist" of "socialist" camps, and how far to accept intervention in its dispersal and administration.[18] Actually, in India foreign aid came almost as a logical extension of its plan strategies and its foreign policy, while on the part of the aid-givers it constituted a response that was a mixture of international trade and monetary policy, cold war strategy, and either plainly humanistic or subtly ideological philanthropy.

We have already seen how planned economic change involved massive investments and large-scale imports of machinery, equipment, and supplies which exerted a heavy pressure on the country's foreign exchange resources. While this was at first met from the sterling reserves built up during World War II and the Korean War, these were soon depleted as the Indian model of growth necessitated an increasing volume of imports of capital goods. This produced, about the middle of the Second Five Year Plan, the first of the country's foreign exchange crises which, while it led to some talk of reappraisal in terms of distinguishing the "core" of the plan from the rest of it, did not produce any change in basic strategy.[19] On the contrary the pressure on foreign exchange only served to reinforce the planners' view that the capital base of the economy should be rapidly expanded, and in order to ward off both the gap in foreign exchange resources and the inflationary pressures during the transition, foreign credits and loans should be contracted, to be repaid at a later date when the economy produced an export surplus.[20] Since then India has contracted an increasing volume of foreign aid. It has gone up from Rs. 382 crores during the period of the First Plan to Rs. 2,531 crores in the Second and Rs. 2,936 crores in the Third Plan, with an estimated need of over Rs. 4,000 crores during the Fourth Plan (after adjusting for the new exchange rate).

A few more facts may be noted before evaluating the role of foreign aid in India's economic and political development. The bulk of the aid has gone to the building of India's strategic public sector. In fact, the implications of the growth of the public sector for India's economic and political system would have been quite different if external assistance of this order had not been available: external assistance accounted for 12.6, 37.0, and 39.0 per cent respectively of public sector investment in the first three plans. See Table 10.1.

TABLE 10.1
Public Sector Dependence on External Assistance

Plan period	Total investment (Rs. crores)	External assistance utilized (Rs. crores)	External assistance utilized as percentage of total investment
First Plan	1,560	196	12.6
Second Plan	3,650	1,352	37.0
Third Plan	6,300	2,479	39.0

Source: Government of India, *Economic Survey*, 1965-66

BI-POLAR AID

Second, however, in part reflecting India's policy of non-alignment and the advantages it drew from the politics of the cold war, and in part genuinely fearful of the Dullesian threat to the subcontinent, the sources of external assistance have been increasingly diversified. As can be seen from Table 10.2, while the United States accounts for over 50 per cent of the aid, the balance comes from other national and international sources, including substantial aid from the Soviet Union. (In fact the aggregate figures do not reflect the reality, because while aid from the Western countries has been spread over a number of planned programs including infrastructural and welfare programs, Soviet aid has concentrated in the more "strategic" sectors such as steel and power.) The flexibility provided by this policy came out when the Soviet Union stepped in to finance the Bokaro steel plant when the United States backed out of it.[21]

BURDEN OF DEBT

Third, while such aid has proved handy in relieving immediate pressures and in enabling the pursuit of plan objectives, it has created a mounting burden of debt for the future. Although the

TABLE 10.2
External Assistance, by Source

Source	Authorization up to the end of Third Plan		Utilization up to the end of Third Plan	
	Actuals (Rs. Crores)	Percentage of total	Actuals (Rs. Crores)	Percentage of total
USA	3,027.12	51.55	2,588.18	57.32
USSR	489.27	8.33	287.04	6.36
IBRD	462.81	7.88	379.98	8.42
Federal Republic of Germany	449.96	7.66	347.33	7.69
UK	366.43	6.24	293.53	6.50
IDA	278.55	4.74	200.63	4.44
Canada	222.43	3.79	161.61	3.58
Japan	174.01	2.96	113.35	2.51
Others	402.06	6.85	143.46	3.18
Total	5,872.64	100.00	4,515.11	100.00

Source: Government of India, *Economic Survey*, 1966-67

term "economic aid" is used for all kinds of resource flows from foreign sources, it is for the most part misleading as an increasing proportion of it is in the form of loans and credits and not outright grants as the term suggests. (See Table 10.3.) Consequently, repayment obligations as a proportion of export earnings and foreign aid have been steadily rising: from 7.8 per cent in 1960-61 to 18.4 per cent in 1965-66 to an estimated 28 per cent in the Fourth Plan. (As a proportion of foreign aid alone more than 36 per cent of the aid sought for the Fourth Plan will be utilized for debt-servicing payments.) India has all along been emphatic about its obligation to repay all its debts, urging only that loans may be made on "soft terms," namely a longer period of maturity and a low interest rate. The hope is that, given a sufficiently long period, the country will be in a position to meet its obligations without undue strain on its economy.

A number of political issues have arisen in the course of India's developing experience with foreign aid. For a long time the bulk of the aid was "tied" to specific projects. While this increased and diversified the basic industrial capacity, resources for the utiliza-

TABLE 10.3
External Assistance Utilized, by Mode of Repayment
(Rs. Crores at pre-devaluation rate of exchange)

Mode of Repayment	Up to the end of First Plan	During Second Plan	During Third Plan	Between April 1, '66 and Sept. 30, '68	Total
A. Loans repayable in foreign currencey	124.13 (61.55)	607.93 (42.51)	1,752.09 (61.07)	662.23 (62.25)	3,146.38 (56.54)
B. Loans repayable in rupees	2.29 (1.14)	116.82 (8.17)	156.39 (5.45)	8.16 (0.77)	283.66 (5.10)
C. Other assistance[a]	5.07 (2.15)	544.81 (38.09)	853.22 (29.74)	321.80 (30.25)	1,724.90 (31.00)
D. Grants	70.18 (34.80)	160.64 (11.23)	107.15 (3.74)	71.55 (6.73)	409.52 (7.36)
Total	201.67 (100.00)	1,430.20 (100.00)	2,868.85 (100.00)	1,063.74 (100.00)	5,564.46 (100.00)

[a] Includes PL 480, PL 665, and Third Country Currency Assistance

Note: Figures in parentheses represent percentage to total assistance under each plan-period.

Source: Government of India, *Economic Survey*, 1967-68.

tion of this capacity in the form of maintenance and raw material imports were not easily available. This resulted in the greatest bottleneck of all: low capacity utilization owing to an inability to finance maintenance imports. As this most hit the performance of new growth-inducing industries and especially of the new export industries, it further accentuated the pressure on balance of payments, led to still more dependence on aid, distorted the structure of planning, and consequently kept the economy tied to the aid-giving countries in an almost "colonial" relationship. Lately this has been realized on both sides and there is now a shift from aid tied to specific projects to program aid, or what in the Indian parlance is known as "non-project aid."

In reality, however, this shift in aid strategy has created its own problems. While project aid involved a discussion with the aid-givers of a particular and normally tiny segment of the economy, the new kind of aid has led to a comprehensive review of the whole policy process, not excluding aspects of social and political structure.[22] Both the Russians and the Americans have intervened on an increasing number of issues: the Russian attitude to the participation of Indian engineers in the Bokaro steel plant and the role of American and World Bank "experts" in the devaluation of the Indian currency have come to the Indians as signs of warning of the political coasts of increasing foreign aid. Even more serious was the American embargo on the release of aid already committed during and after the Indo-Pakistan conflict in 1965-66, in the process upsetting a number of planned schedules, leading to unemployment of both men and plant capacity, contributing to the economic recession, and generally producing considerable hardship. The recent Russian attempt to force the sale of aircraft not suited to Indian needs has brought home the realization that the policy of mobilizing resources from the opposite poles of the world spectrum may also produce simultaneous pressures from both sides which may be hard to contain.

FUTURE AID

There is reason to believe that the heyday of increasing economic aid is now over. The end of the bi-polar world, a re-distribution of economic power among the developed nations, consequent balance of payments difficulties experiences by the leading aid-givers, other commitments broad, and growing pressures within these countries for concentrating on internal problems are all contributing to levelling off and possibly a decline in the quantum of aid commitments. There is also a general mood of not bothering about the problems of others, a feeling that aid creates more problems than it solves, that it produces ingratitude and unpopularity rather than appreciation. Here the main fact — though this may be an over-simplification — is that willingness to give economic aid as a deliberate national policy was part of the general context of the cold war which involved a keen competition between the two blocs, each of which was convinced of the strategic importance of the "uncommitted" nations of the world. India was the foremost among these nations: its policy of non-alignment proved a great facility in this regard. Now with the end of the cold war and with it the end of India's own foreign policy posture, the approach to economic aid is bound to be more ad hoc and less systematic. Within India too is growing a persuasive body of opinion which thinks of aid as an unnecessarily constraining factor that detracts from the "real tasks."

The emerging trends now seem to be closer regional co-operation as shown in the realization in both Japan and India that they must develop an "Asia" policy (although here again the trends seem to be more competitive than cooperative), attempts to attract foreign private capital for industrial investment (a role that is being pressed by international agencies like the World Bank), and a greater concentration at mobilizing internal resources. There is also a growing awareness that economic aid on a large scale produces subtle but far-reaching intellectual dependence, an awareness that has been heightened by the activities of intelligence agencies of the big powers, and has led to increasing suspicion of anything that smacks of "pleasure." Disillusionment with both the Americans and the Russians at the political level has further contributed to this mood.

Meanwhile, a considerable investment in basic capacity has been created in India, resources have been released for politically pressing tasks, both militarily and economically the country is now better equipped, and a diversified social and economic infrastructure has come into being. In the next few years aid will still be needed but it will be increasingly a product of businesslike bargaining, a stringent application of efficiency criteria, and perhaps more as part of the normal flow of economic give and take than due to any involved political logic.

A PERIOD OF TRANSITION

India must now function in an international environment characterized by increasing plurality, growing conflicts of interest in different regions, a lot of policy drift everywhere, and a big power commitment to the status quo in the China-India-Pakistan region. The country's nuclear capacity is on the increase, it has been able to resist the big-power sponsored non-proliferation treaty unless enough guarantees against "nuclear blackmail" (especially by China) are provided, and the coming issue is likely to be whether India should produce its own nuclear bomb (which it can do, technically), the economic and political costs involved in this, and how this would fit the country's emerging but still very inarticulate foreign policy.[23] India must henceforth increasingly think in regional rather than global terms, develop a *quid pro quo* with countries like Japan, Indonesia, and Australia, develop a fresh approach to China, and treat the problem of producing the "bomb" as part of this new regional articulation. The paramount need in all this is to develop a well thought-out policy of both containing the pressures from the two superpowers and utilizing their respective regional strategies for promoting India's own objectives. Failure to do this will turn the "presence" of these great powers in the region—a presence that cannot be wishe away — into a permanent constraint.

A WORLD ROLE

Politically and ideologically the whole world has entered a phase of stalemate and fluidity. It provides yet another transition, yet another "breathing space" to India during which there is likely to be a greater preoccupation with internal problems of integration and growth. It will take time before the country will be able to resume its natural role in international politics. This may occur only after it has acquired greater internal strength and a stronger self-identity and confidence. The role is so natural that, short of long-tern stagnation or disintegration, it can not be foresaken. The Nehruvian prognosis is independent of the particular doctrines that were developed for a given period; while the doctrines may cease to be relevant under changed world conditions, the basic prognosis is as true today as it was when Nehru first articulated it. India is a large nation, occupies a strategic position in the world both geographically and ideologically, and is endowed with big power potentialities and corresponding responsibilities.

The assumption of such a natural role will, no doubt, involve not merely industrial prowess and political stability at home, but also symbolic evidences of "greatness" such as nuclear power and a satellite program, a determined regional articulation as an anchor for the country's foreign policy, and perhaps more than all this, a self-sure and clear-headed leadership which is able to shift the various elements in the situation and emerge with an articulated approach. Until then, India's standing and image in the world are likely to remain vague and ambivalent—shaped more by its internal accomplishments than external maneuverability. But the tasks are as real in the latter as in the former.

Notes

1. A number of Indian revolutionaries and Marxists were involved in the international communist movement, some of them operating from abroad. The most distinguished among these was M.N. Roy, ex-revolutionary and latter-day radical humanist, who worked closely with Lenin and was responsible in Moscow for directing the communist movement in Asia. See Gene D. Overstreet and Marshall Windmiller, *Communism in India* (Berkeley, 1959).
2. For a discussion of some of these contributions of Nehru, see Michael Brecher, *Nehru: A Political Biography* (New York, 1959).
3. The Belgrade Conference was sharply split between the protagonists of an exclusivist approach to non-alignment favored by Indonesia, Cuba, Guinea, Mali, and others who wanted to make the meetings a rallying point for militant "anti-colonialism" and the proponents of a more open definition of non-alignment who aspired to give to the meetings a truly international and

global character. Nehru was the leader of the latter group and his presence ultimately brought around Egypt and Yugoslavia to the same approach.

4. At the same time it needs to be said that the socialist countries have all along expressed unambiguous support of non-alignment; the same cannot be said of the Western nations whose comments on non-alignment have ranged from being patronizing to openly hostile.

5. See also analysis of William J. Barnds, "India in Transition: Friends and Neighbors," *Foreign Affairs*, 46, 3, April, 1968.

6. It is significant that Chiang Kai-shek and his government also share the approach of the People's Republic to the border issue.

7. This was admitted personally by President Ayub Khan on May 4, 1965. For a detailed diary of events, see *India 1966* (Delhi, 1966).

8. The award has since been made and accepted by India, despite much opposition from the right-wing political parties. Pakistan has also accepted the award.

9. Following an early confrontation between Pakistani forces and Indian troops in 1947 on the issue of Kashmir's accession to India. India had referred the issue to the United Nations, under whose auspices a cease-fire had been negotiated which took effect on January 1, 1949. The cease-fire has since been the basis of the division of Kashmir between the two countries. For a full and authoritative treatment of the Kashmir issue, see Sisir Gupta, *Kashmir: A Study in India-Pakistan Relations* (Bombay, 1966).

10. This is acknowledged in other quarters. It became more clear with India's role in Korea and Indo-China and came out forcefully on the Congo questions where India, along with other non-alignment nations, had to assume both a peace-keeping and a political role. As United States Secretary of State Dean Rusk acknowledged, India had often been "called upon to serve the United Nations in ways which we ourselves could not." For a fuller treatment of this aspect, see Cecil V. Crabb, Jr., *The Elephants and the Grass* (New York, 1965).

11. Leo Rose, "India, China and the Afro-Asian Bloc" in *Contemporary China*, 1967.

12. On this, and generally on India-Pakistan relations, see the perceptive treatment of Sisir Gupta, *India's Relations with Pakistan 1947-57* (New Delhi, 1958). Gupta is one of India's foremost thinkers on International affairs and on the relationship between external relations and political development.

13. A few statistics will show the trends: whereas 91.6 per cent of machine tools were imported in 1950-51, the proportion fell to 44.5 per cent in 1964-65 (with a few items being exported). The corresponding decline in import of sugar machinery was from 100 per cent to a mere 1.4 per cent, textile machinery from 100 to 56.5 per cent, commercial vehicles from 35.7 per cent to 0.5 per cent , petroleum products (other than kerosene) from 91.5 to 1.6 per cent, and aluminium from 74.8 to 29.7 per cent.

14. In the case of industrial metals on which the country has been heavily

dependent on imports and for which demand is constantly growing, the proportions supplied indigenously are also expected to rise: zinc from a bare 5.8 to 53.8 per cent at the end of the Fourth Plan, black carbon from 52.0 to 89.3 per cent, and copper from 12.5 to 21.4 per cnet. There is also evidence of increasing exports of metallic and engineering goods which have resulted in a narrowing of the trade deficit with practically every major region of the world — Asia and Africa, Western Europe, Russia and Eastern Europe, and the American region. Among other things, India is now supplying transmission line towers and conductors to the United States. *The Statesman Weekly*, January 18, February 1, 1968.

15. The issue of attracting foreign capital continues to bedevil India's development effort. Suspicion on both sides, a lack of frank bargaining, a wrong image abroad regarding India's "prospects", and tiresome administrative procedures have all contributed to the continued ambivalence on the issue. Lack of a policy one way or another also leads to great uncertainty and a sense of drift. On the other hand, insistence on at least a parity between indigenous and foreign enterprises is well taken: the spectacle of entire economies being controlled by foreign investors has been avoided in India.

16. All this will take time to show results. Without prejudging the results, however, it is necessary to reemphasize India's lethargy and lack of imagination in promoting exports. The evidence to the contrary is still very slack. At a time when the affluent nations of the world are providing an easy market for flooding "non-Western" products, there is no reason why India, with its vast heritage of diverse skill and products, should be lagging behind its competitors. There is no reason why the new craze for Nehru jackets should be exploited more by South Korea, Japan, and Venezuela than by India!

17. Albert O. Hirschman, "Underdevelopment, Obstacles to the Perception of Change, and Leadership," *Daedalus*, 1968, pp. 925-937, where he uses the terms "independent" and "dependent." Hirschman has apparently acquired the terms from the Latin American literature which he candidly acknowledges. For the use of "donor" and "recipient" in the context of foreign aid, see Albert O. Hirschman and Richard M. Bird, "Foreign Aid — A Critique and a proposal," *Essays in International Finance*, No. 69 (Princeton, 1968).

18. In fact, the "salience" of foreign aid as an issue is very low. A study based on a content analysis of party resolutions between 1948 and 1964 showed that foreign aid figures in only 2 per cent of the Congress Party's resolutions on foreign policy, not at all in Jan Sangh and Swatantra, and in 12 per cent of the foreign policy statements of the Communist Party of India, largely on the issues mentioned above. See Warren F. Ilchman, "A Political Economy of Foreign Aid; The Case of India," *Asian Survey*, VII, No. 10, October , 1967. For a fuller report of the study which shows a general absence of controversy on foreign policy issues, see Warren F. Ilchman, "Political Development and Foreign Policy: The Case of India," *Journal of Commonwealth Political Studies*, IV, No. 3, November, 1966.

19. Two documents produced by the Planning Commission during this crisis are relevant: *Appraisal and Prospects of the Second Five Year Plan* (May, 1958) and *Reappraisal of the Second Five Year Plan: A Resumé* (September, 1958).

20. For a defense of the basic strategy despite foreign exchange difficulties, see K.N. Raj and A.K. Sen, "Alternative patterns of growth Under Conditions of Stagnant Export Earnings," *Oxford Economic Papers*, XII, No. 1, February, 1961.

21. Even in respect of Western aid, there has been a shift from bilateral aid to some kind of a package deal involving all the leading Western nations as well as other international agencies. This has led to the "Aid India Club" which meets regularly and reviews possibilities and prospects of future aid in the light of past performance and the short-run problems of the Indian economy. This has led to some institutionalization of economic aid and has reduced simple bilateral transactions which often involve high "political" costs.

22. For a theoretical discussion of different institutional alternatives for routing foreign aid, see Hirschman and Bird, *op.cit.*

23. The Indian government has so far resisted the growing pressure for the bomb from intellectual soucres within the country, through it says it wants to keep "the option open." For a technological appraisal of India and Japan, the two countries threatened by China's possession of nuclear power, both resisting the non-proliferation treaty, see William R. Van Cleave and Harold W. Rood, "A Technological Comparison of Two Potential Nuclear Powers: India and Japan," *Asian Survey*, VII, No. 7, July, 1967.

11

Future Perspectives

WE MAY NOW TRY to piece together the analysis and conclusions of the various chapters into some kind of perspective. The perspective we have in mind is that of the future. For, without doubt, the key question is: What are the prospects for the future? We intend to approach this question by treating the principal focus of out study, the relationship between political institutionalization and the system's performance, as a basis for future prognosis. In attempting to present such a prognosis, however, we are faced with a dilemma: the achievements and lapses of the past may provide important clues to the future but the structural propensities and leadership styles through which problems were tackled in the past may cease to be relevant; they may even become inhibitory and hence a "negative resource." There is in the history of nations an unfolding dialectic. The problems encountered in the next phase are likely to be different; a non--aggregative and non-cumulative political style must come face to face with increasing aggregation of structures and cumulation of issues; and the more politically institutionalized the system becomes, the greater is the range of problems that the central institutions and symbols of that system will need to cope with.

In other words, the question, "Is the system's capacity to cope increasing or declining?" must be related to the question, "Are the problems going to be the same or different?" The discriminating reader must have already noticed a developing tension in the Indian system between the tendencies towards political institutionalization and integration outlined in Chapter 8 and the increasingly range of unresolved problems described in Chapters 9 and 10. The "capacity to cope" is a direct consequence of political institutionalization and its penetration at various levels; the "problems to cope," on the other hand, come from other spheres. To what extent is it possible to resolve this dilemma? What leadership capabilities are called forth? And what are the policy implications?

In order to tackle the issues posed above, it would be useful first to recapitulate the Indian model of development thus far, to follow this by reiterating the problems of the future in more specific terms, and finally, to identity the tasks that are involved and the policy priorities that are entailed in tackling those problems. We shall deal with these three aspects.

THE INDIAN "MODEL"

As we perceive it, it was the crystallization of a dominant political center in the midst of plural identities and segmental distances that had characterized Indian civilization for centuries that the foundation of modern India took place. In the crystallization of such a center the colonial, political, and educational impacts played a key role but it was not until an elite emerged that thought of itself as the spokesman of all India, sought to assert its legitimacy by systematically pursuing that role, and institutionalized this role in the form of a premier political institution with a nation-wide organization and a membership that encompassed segmental differentiations of all kinds, that the dominant political center was established. The consolidation of this center after independence, its close identification with an enacted structure of institutions and the ideology inherent in this structure, and its imaginative penetration at various levels and into different segments have been the core processes through which the Indian political system has achieved its identity.

Since then, acting in and through various other processes and policy thrusts, has been one overriding dimension of Indian politics: the incorporation of various pluralities and segmentations into the dominant political center. The approach has been not of denying the autonomy of these differentiations but their incorporation, not imposing the dominant center as a different and alien system but as an *establishment* in which diverse groups and individuals should try to find a place. This has been the meaning of an "open" political system in India: not just a system providing means of competition and conflict but also a coalitional arena in which both ruling and oppositional groups can enter their diverse claims.

ROLE OF PLURALITIES

We have gone at some length in this book into the role of party politics and adult franchise in this general process of penetration and incorporation. Far more than "social mobilization"—education, urbanization, mass media, and the rest—it is through the political involvement of existing differentiations into a common framework of institutions that the historic consolidation of the Indian polity has come about. What has enabled the political process to integrate pre-existing pluralities—it should be stressed that the pluralities were pre-existing and not just a consequence of "democracy"—is the authority of a dominant elite which has then sought to legitimize its role through seeking a consensus at various levels, respecting rival claims on the basis of electoral and competitive criteria, and structuring the diversity of Indian society into a network of linkages. In the institutionalization of this network both the unitary processes provided by the Constitution, the federal structure of government, and the party system and the decentralizing processes inherent in the same structures have played complementary roles. (The very concept of "dominance" involved diversity and dissent; it needs to be distinguished from the concept of centralization or of hegemony.) Mediating in such an interplay are the true modernizers and integrators of Indian society, namely the coopted elites at intermediate levels. They operate from all parties and coalescing and dissident groups, and are in fact responsible for the peculiarly open party system in India in which both governmental and oppositional groups dissolve into a "ruling class." We have described the features of this system at some length in Chapters 5 and 8.

The "resources" for such an interplay have been provided by

other mechanism of penetration and incorporation. A number of policy initiatives, both legislative and administrative, have accompanied the development of a political infrastructure. Specific legislation aimed at removing and containing major cleavages and gross disparities, a wide-ranging strategy of planning and development in the rural areas, dispersal of financial resources, and the establishment of new kinds of federal and local self-government structures have all contributed to the catalytic role of politics. The initiative for all this has generally come from above, with a few exceptions *before* demands began to mount from below, but the fruits of such initiative have gone to those at lower levels in the national hierarchy. The role of government and what we have called "governmentalization" of society have been central in such an articulation.

Responding to such penetration of the political center there has taken place a remarkable restructuring of social and economic forms and a growing politicization of the "traditional" subcenters of Indian society. New elites have seized the organization of these subcenters and have on the basis of a newconsolidation—caste federations, cooperative societies, and panchayati raj—pushed themselves upward to state and national levels. Utilizing the opportunities of cooptation offered by the metropolitan elite, they have occupied crucial positions at higher levels and have generally succeeded in outnumbering and outwitting the modernists. (We have conceptualized this change as a displacement of the "modernists" by the "modernizers.") It is in this sense rather than in terms of any sectoral transfer of power or in the sense of any populist movement of "power to the people," that the usual observation of a shift of power from urban to rural areas has to be understood. Indeed, the diversification that is taking place is in the context of values and institutions that are essentially urban and "modern." It is all part of the penetration and incorporation model of political integration.

NON-AGGREGATION

Three other factors have contributed to such integration—a simultaneous rather than sequential model of development, an antecedent consensus and its institutionalization before the new state came into being, and a political culture that is non-aggregative and has a low salience of "demand." We have discussed all of this in previous chapters. In simultaneously pursuing the goals of political participation, social mobilization, and economic development, and at the same time trying to project a world image, the Indian elite spread its energies too broadly on too many tasks but this also enabled it to articulate an incremental and cumulative style of nation-building which, because it focused on coalition-making, enabled it to contain the pressures that inevitably emerged with increasing politicization. That this was possible to bring about owed not a little to the fact that the Congress movement had thrashed out most of the basic issues, evolved a consensus, and institutionalized this consensus through the authority of a dominant party. But it was also due to the very segmentation and plurality of India's political culture which are decried by some as "parochial" and "divisive." That the revolution of rising expectations has hit no more than a tiny and dispossessed class of urban intellectuals in India is due to this non-aggregative style of Indian politics. The model of a dominant center penetrating downwards through differential assimilation, mediated by intermediate elites, and maintaining the autonomy of various subcenters, has been greatly helped by these characteristics of India's contemporary pontical culture and its historical antecedents.

APPROACH TO DEMOCRACY

It follows that the Indian approach to "democracy" is not one in which an "elite" derives its legitimacy from an amorphous and unstructured "mass." In many ways India does not present the picture of a mass society. At the same time Indians are not convinced that an authoritarian regime directly ruling the masses and unencumbered by a variety of "constituencies" is a good recipe for an underdeveloped society. There are a few intellectuals who still think this way, prefer the orderly and efficient image of "strong rule," get exasperated with the uncertainties and ambiguities of democratic politics, and argue for at least an interregnum of authoritarian rule. Experience of contemporary dictatorial regimes, however, fails to confirm such a view. Indeed such regimes are found to be at least as inefficient as the democracies, and certainly less amenable to self-modification. At least in a democracy there is the fear of electoral reprisal, and the doctrine of "responsibility" compels the elite to be accountable to a variety of constituencies. It is also well known that while an authoritarian regime usually rides on the crest of intellectual discontent, once in power it drops its intellectual disguises and tends to invest heavily in control and manipulation. It tends to be a clique of "vested interests." In time it promotes neither freedom nor efficiency. The examples of Ghana, Indonesia, and Pakistan have influenced political opinion in India considerably; even monarchical regimes like Nepal and Thailand are attempting to introduce democratic elements in response to restive elements within their countries; and China—the "model" for so long—pays high costs for institutionalizing revolutionary communism. The Indian model, if not better than any of these, is at least providing a viable alternative to them.

Two kinds of revolution are going on in the third world. In one there is a single monolithic force, a personality or an ideology, seeking to collapse everything that stands in its way. In the other there are different and supplementary elements, operating at various levels, and assimilating various centers of creative output. India is undergoing the second kind of revolution. For want of a better name it may be called an "incremental revolution," contradictory though it may sound. It seeks to maintain the present structure by assimilating the forces of change, in the process leading to new thresholds of developmental initiative. Innovativeness in such a model of revolution is a function of maintaining the system, institutionalizing and adapting it to new conditions, and in the process enlarging the horizons of its potentiality. It does not rule out teleological direction, or even discontinuities, but the latter are continuously conditioned by evolutionary criteria and operational values, rather than an all-embracing messianic zeal.[1] In effect it is at least as open to creative transformations, and probably more, than the monolithic revolution, and it is certainly more durable.

STRAINS ON THE MODEL

The real tests of such a model incremental democratic modernization came in the period 1962 to 1967 when in a short span of time the system encountered a series of crises. It faced two successions to the highest political office in the country, producing not only a change in leadership but also in leadership roles and in the range of pressures upon those roles. Almost simultaneously, the political system had to contend with two major challenges to long-established policies, in agriculture and economic development on the one hand, and language policy on the other. In both areas the system had failed in its performance and the failure was widely perceived and made all the more intense by two droughts in succession, a strange combination of severe economic recession and rising prices of items of bare necessity, and a consequent spurt of mass demonstrations and protests, including an attempted attack on the Parliament.[2] During the same period of increasing domestic difficulties the system had to contend with serious entanglements abroad: the nation's boundaries were penetrated, and it went to war twice. Upon heels of the second of these entanglements, that with Pakistan, the country and the economy faced a major disturbance in the flow of aid and imports, and was virtually forced by foreigners to accept a drastic devaluation of its currency. By 1967 when the effects of the droughts and external crises began to have serious consequences, the country went to polls, which brought to an end the long period of Congress dominance, an era of political instability, and challenge to the national leadership.

For any system to cope with such a cumulation of stresses is a formidable task. For a nascent political order, operating in the context of massive poverty and underdevelopment, the task would seem impossible to cope with. Yet cope it did. The wars were contained. The agricultural and economic development policies were shifted and reconstructed. The language crisis was sorted out through a working compromise. The successions took place peacefully. The overall performance of the system, in its encounter with this unprecedented influx of issues and the atmosphere of challenge and unrest that accompanied it, was creditable. The basic structure of the system came out of it all fairly intact.

PROBLEM-SOLVING CHARACTERISTICS

We have dealt with each of these crises in some detail in the chapters on performance. There is no need to go into them again. But it would be useful to try and account for the factors in leadership style and political structure that contributed to such an overall outcome. For by doing so we may not only perceive the sources of strength and endurance in the past but also assess their import and relevance for the future. (What is said below also applies, in a broad sense, to the system's propensities in general.)[3]

NON-CUMULATION

There is in India a tendency to deal with issues in a segmental and non-cumulative fashion. This is so even in respect to seemingly simultaneous issues. Cleavages cut across each other; they are not additive. Thus the states split in different ways on the agricultural and language crises. While the center was pressured by both these crises, the two wars and the successful handling of the two successions gave it strength and a sense of unity. Specifically, the language crisis threatened unity but the war with Pakistan, superimposed on the language crisis, reduced its impact. Although the key actors played their roles in each of the crises, they shifted positions from issue to issue. While linkages did occur between resolution of a crisis and the next crisis, there were none *across* crises and issue areas, leading to a low salience of cross-issue pressures.

SHIFTING ALIGNMENTS

Closely related to such a non-cumulative approach is a tendency towards shifting rather than continuous alignments. Issues are defined and redefined thus narrowing areas of disagreement and increasing the incentives toward consensus. The locus of leadership tends to shift from one crisis to another: different leaders played key roles in the language, agricultural, and succession crisis. A mediatory style operated in each but the mediators were each time different. Functions and powers were shifted; new bargaining structures and formulae for resolution of crisis were instantly created; and when they were found unworkable, they were scrapped just as quickly, as in the language crisis. The "rules of the game" were incrementally adjusted each time. Thus in each succession crisis the new leader was chosen with a different decisional structure. In all this, the very newness and weakness of a structural tradition turned into advantages and there appeared a high propensity to separate the substantive and the procedural issues with a view to moving gradually toward a resolution.

OPEN-ENDEDNESS

There is, third, a considerable open-endedness and tentativeness in the bargaining process. The dominant feature of crisis resolution is bargaining between actors, each of whom—including those who resort to violence—has a partial claim to legitimacy. There are no fixed and final "resources" and "constituencies" for the bargainers. Demands are expressed loudly but are soon muted and subdued. The objective indices of demand do emerge; riots and demonstrations are not infrequent. But they are hardly ever converted into a generalized pressure on the political system. They are in effect different forms of issue articulation, seldom forms of "anti-system" confrontation. Moreover, the area of conflict and bargaining is around a specific issue; there is very little tendency towards log-rolling coalitions. In fact the precise coalitions are hard to identify and are generally transient and unstable. The result is a continuous redefinition of the overall crisis situation. It may be said that there are at any time a number of crises but these do not precipitate a *crisis*.

LOW INTENSITY

Underlying all this is a low intensity of allegiance and affect. Firm and unwavering allegiances are not expected or demanded. Political actors at each level move in and out of temporary alliances with comparative ease. Retribution and reprisal are not frequently used as sanctions. Ideology imposes fewer constraints than most social scientists have come to expect. While the Congress Party's decline in 1967 owned not a little to defections from within, the non-Congress coalitions brought together parties of all shades and policy commitments. The matter is helped greatly by the lack of involvement of the vast periphery living in the hinterland; there is in India a significant rural cushion to any situation of strain. It is also helped by the wide distances between levels and non-aggregation between them; here, too, there is a cushion provided by what we have called "intermediate aggregation" in the polity. Both of these factors contribute to a general autonomy of the political center from social and substructural pressures. On the other hand, the *imploration* toward unity and integration is a running theme: the wars, the successions, and the challenge to the new survival of the Congress involved the theme and, on balance, proved integrative. It is hard to mount a generalized challenge to the political system under such conditions.

Each of these mechanism serves to limit the appearance of a final "crisis," of what the game theorists call a "zero-some game." There seems to be a powerful built-in resistance to a zero-some game. Demands can be muted by implicit pressures for consensus. Crises become catalysts of significant change with damaging the basic constitution of the system and the fundamental consensus underlying it. The general result is survival and incremental adaptation to changing conditions.

COSTS OF THE MODEL

We have said enough to indicate the basic institutional and leadership capabilities that have emerged in India's confrontation with problems of nation-building so far. Such a record of performance and of wide-ranging strategy of response to serious situations of crisis should provide grounds for optimism with which to face the future. Yet when all of this is taken together, it fails to answer the key developmental questions that are likely to emerge in the next few decades. Indeed, it is possible to see that the model described above involves some serious costs. In a sense the costs are the obverse of the advantages just discussed. The autonomy of the policy process from social pressure resulted for a long time in a doctrinaire approach to modernization, a highly bureaucratized implementation process, and a cumulation of developmental lags and disequilibria. Too great an emphasis on integrating and assimilating various diversities into the "establishment—an eminent goal given the divisive antecedents of Indian society—has resulted in a fragmented process of feedback and serious blocks in information channels. Lack of an aggregative framework of political parties and interest organizations has meant that the coalitional structures remain fragmented and dispersed. The low salience of "demand" has also produced a low confrontation of polarities and issues, and a halting and ad hoc approach to performance and administrative drive.

Only through the bold vision and energy of charisma, or through the precipitation of crises, have large-scale reversals in structure and policies been possible. Among other things, this puts an accent on demonstrated strength, on violence and uproar, before an issue is forced to a decision. Routinization of feedback and responses which is an important criterion of political institutionalization has been weak and uncoordinated in India; for any system that relies so much on charisma and crises as aggregative devices must remain weak and uninstitutionalized. Our analyses of the linguistic, agricultural, and external crises, each of which brought about significant alterations in the basic framework of policy, highlight this particular characteristic of Indian politics.

Now, with the coalitional arena of Indian politics expanding and the varied constituencies of the dominant elite getting activized on the basis of new groups and parties, the polity enters a new state of political articulation. As this happens, social and economic cleavages, contained at lower levels for so long, will tend to gravitate upward toward the policy process. At the same time the urbanized middle classes that dominated the political scene for so long are being displaced and feel alienated. The result is a "coalition of protest" which will not any longer be contained through the traditional style of coalition-making. The accent must now shift to issue manipulation and governmental performance, greater specificity in this performance, and an ability to perceive the sources of strain, anticipate their transformation into public issues and group demands, and *act* before the latter precipitate a crisis.

We spoke above of the Indian model as one of "incremental revolution." This is an eminently worthwhile model, one that offers a viable alternative to both violent change and authoritarian reaction. But its success cannot for all time depend on the presumption of consensual behavior on the part of a majority of actors and the persistence of a fragmented political structure resulting in a low salience of aggregative demand. Instead, its success will henceforth depend on continuous (rather than discontinuous) performance, on the availability of a highly sensitive and "reconstructive" leadership,[4] and on the willingness more energetically to force the pace of change without disrupting the achievements of the past. The propensity towards continuity and adaptation, on which the Indian genius of politics rests, does not rules out such a pursuit of goal intensity. But it may nonetheless call forth a degree of new stirring and new image-building which may appear to disturb the values of continuity and stability.

EMERGING ISSUE AREAS

The above points become more clear as we begin to see that the problems that the system will have to face in the future are going to be of quite a different order than in the past. The capabilities developed in the past will not doubt serve as important resources, and above all as a source of abiding optimism which is so necessary for purposive action, but by themselves they will not be sufficient.

Many of the emerging issue areas have been spelled out in previous chapters. Thus, as we saw in our party system analysis, a 40 plus per cent support for the Congress Party is proving increasingly inadequate as a statistical base for stable government; so is a 6 to 8 per cent base of each of the other major parties. And yet it is difficult to see how, in the absence of a real effort to penetrate the periphery of the population with positive policies, such an arithmetic of electoral alignments can be effectively altered. As these pages go to press,[5] the process of polarization within and beyond the Congress Party discussed in Chapter 5 has gone further. Two Congress parties have come into being at the national level itself, one dominated by Prime Minister Indira Gandhi's group keen on subordinating party organizational structures to the pursuit of governmental power and presumably a new policy drive, and the other by the traditional custodians of the Congress who insist on the primacy of the organization and loyalty to it above everything else. As the conflict widens and influences the behavior of other parties at the center and in the states, the resulting party structure is likely to consist of rival coalitions, representing marked differences in ideological and programmatic emphases. While such a rearticulation of the structure of politics may hold the long term promise of clarifying issues and stirring the country out of a long spell of complacency and stagnation, in the short run it raises acute problems in the maintenance of necessary support for the ruling coalition. Issues of stability and order thus arise at the very center of the system.

Again, with increasing modernization of agriculture and the short run disparities that it engenders, the so-called "rural cushion" for governmental stability will soon begin to give way to class cleavages in the rural areas and a growing politicization of these cleavages. The very success of the green revolution has resulted in an accentuation of disparities and a consciousness of the injustice of these disparities. It is true that India presents a unique demographic context of modernization in which for a long time to come the rural sector will continue to predominate, influence patterns of migration, and leave the urbanized middle classes in a minority status. But such a demographic picture gives rise to its own problems, chief among which is what we have characterized as a coalition of protest between the alienated and impoverished segments of both urban and rural sectors. We have discussed this in some detail in Chapter 9.

Or again, the ongoing educational revolution is already beginning to produce a growing hiatus between a rapidly expanding educational output and lagging opportunities of employment and economic mobility. Education is known to destroy traditional values of want limitation and deference for authority; in the absence of meaningful participation in developmental outputs, it is also known to be strongly correlated with separatist identities and anomic behavior. Both economic modernization and the expansion of modern education will thus raise the salience of issues and accentuate both subregional and ideological polarities. The changing pattern of political coalition-making will be fed by such polarities.

Above all, as political loyalties begin to be channeled along such cumulative (rather than dispersed and decentralized) modes, there is likely to be greater aggressiveness in nationalist postures, a different outlook on foreign affairs, and a search for a different structure of identity and national realization. While such a posture may not yet lead to an assault on the system (especially if it is still "performing" moderately well and is able to maintain satisfactory standards of political morality as it has done so far), the central institutions of the system are likely to experience a higher incidence of both internal and external loads. It may also be added that in such an intellectual context the ability of crises to prove as catalysts for positive reconstruction, which has been a characteristic of the Indian model so far, may prove difficult as the occurrence of crises will tend to produce a sense of defeat and humiliation, and a feeling of despondency. And as this happens, "anti-system" behavior may get more pronounced.

REVERSE DIALECTIC

We can perceive in all this the elements of a dialectic of history which is the reverse of the Marxian dialectic. It occurs not because the basic relations of production have outstripped the archaic superstructure of political institutions, but on the contrary because a highly sophisticated institutional superstructure rests on a weak and immobile foundation. The situation is also the reverse of what Samuel Huntington has characterized to be the key issue in developing societies. Huntington has suggested that sudden increases in modernization, and its concomitants of mobilization and participation, without corresponding advances in the institutionalization and adaptiveness of governmental forms, produces "political decay."[6] The problem in India, however, is that a sophisticated and adaptive institutional framework may begin to give way if it is not matched by corresponding advances in social and economic modernization.[7] The country may continue to adapt and readapt the pieces of its political puzzle without enhancing aggregate welfare or sustaining a satisfactory rate of social and economic development. Without the latter developing before the pressures emanating from greater politicization begin to accumulate, the system's ability to survive may soon become a thing of the past. For as pressures on its meagre resources begin to pile up, its institutional superstructure may be exposed for disguising a whole series of latent incapacities.

As will be recalled from Chapters 3 and 4, an important measure of India's political success has been its ability, especially during the fifties, to press policies in a number of areas before demands began to pile up; in the process a large investment in symbolic and substantive allegiances was also brought about. Since then the nation has been drawing on these reserves of identity and loyalty. The task is once again to move forward, make fresh policy thrusts, and instead of simply drawing upon past investments, to undertake new penetrations, build new supports, and evolve new coalitions. The era of political consolidation must be followed by a period of fresh appraisals of the evolving situation and new policies designed to resolve the issues arising from the new situation. Without such a sequence in developmental performance—from institution-building to substantive outputs—the system may cease to sustain a climate of cooperation and basic acceptance that it has received so bountifully so far. Instead, it may enter a period of stagnation and ultimate reaction.

There is, of course, no need to exaggerate these problems. What is said above is relevant only if governmental performance is not adequately generated. The institutional foundations and experiential grounds for such performance — as well as the relevant technological and intellectual infrastructures — are all there. What is needed is speedily to fill the growing gaps between potentiality and actual performance, to anticipate problems and devise congruent policies, and to press the advantages of political autonomy and cultural tranquility before the latter begin to give in to mounting pressures from the constituent elements in the system.

POLICY PERSPECTIVES

We owe it to the reader to back up our general appraisal by a consideration of some policy dimensions. It would, of course, a presumptuous to think that intellectual (even "scientific") analysis can ever do better than the informed judgement and insight of the politician. It has often been found that the practising politician is in closer touch with reality and more sensitive to the actual distribution of need and pressures.[8] And yet how often has it happened that intuition and "practical" sense are based on selective information and obsolete facts, with the consequence that new developments catch the politician unawares. In a rapidly changing society, the judgements and concerns arising out of dispassionate analysis may well be in order. Without offering any further apologies, let us present some policy perspectives that emerge out of the analysis in this book for whatever they are worth.

AN EFFECTIVE POLITICAL CENTER

A stable and effective political center is crucial to the system's performance. It is quite clear that if the ruling faction of the Congress Party wants to maintain even its present position, it must both restructure its coalitional arena and cut deeper than its present electoral base. Our analysis in Chapter 8 has brought up two points in this regard: the need for a concerted organizational drive in the constituencies (in place of reliance on "vote-getters"); and the need for a new policy drive designed to win the allegiance of the peripheral and deprived sections of the people. But in the changed political picture since 1967 much more than these strategic considerations of partisan effectiveness is involved. In India an effective center entails effective federalism, a viable regional policy, and a rational approach to coalitional tasks across the nation. In Chapter 5 we emphasized the role of a "federal consensus" in the successful articulation of the Indian model. The need now is to turn the increasingly competitive interactions of federal politics into a lever of national decision-making; the growing confrontation between intraparty and interparty groups at national and state levels can itself be turned into a device for containing regional politics in the new framework of central coalitional politics. And as such a confrontation moves from a simple struggle for power to a confrontation on issues that cuts across regions, the processes of coalition-making and bargaining can be turned into channels of central influence and regional feedback, and as agencies of bringing hesitant and recalcitrant states into line. The alternative is that aggressive state postures will undermine central authority.

REGIONAL POLICY

There is already enough knowledge to identify the critical elements in regional politics — intrastate and interstate — to lead to a well thought-out "regional policy" as part and parcel of the national policy profile. This should be done if necessary through a special organ of the Home Ministry or the Cabinet Secretariat. Of equal importance is the need to evolve a conscious policy of institutionalizing the involvement and participation of all the major parties in the governmental process. There has been not only a considerable neglect of this dimension but also a tendency to give in to partisan pressures from the states, often leading to a lot of mistrust, an irrational apprehension that the constitutional machinery is being threatened by some conspiracy of leftist or rightist parties, and a general atmosphere of allegations and counter-allegations.[9] Even from the limited perspectives of "maintaining" the system it is absolutely vital that a party that has a significant electoral base is not deprived of political power by resort to formal constitutional devices; the story of Kerala in 1959 and West Bengal in 1967 should not be repeated. While it would be unrealistic to ask for a cessation of partisan considerations, the need for fairness in operating the rules of the game — including the need to appear to be fair — cannot be stressed too much. It may sound "idealistic" but it in fact makes good political sense. And it is only on such a basis that a strong and effective center can be institutionalized.

Inherent in the Indian political system are strong unitary tendencies; the real threat of a "weak center" arises not from state pressures but from an *isolated center* that is insensitive to the regional profile over which it presides. It has been relatively easy so far to "coopt" non-elite strata at lower levels into an ever expanding political structure; the real challenge is to integrate *counter-elites* at the various levels of the system without leading to any sharp reversal of its democratic character. These counter-elites are now on the increase; they are found all the way from rival Congress groups at national and state levels to the "Naxalite" communists and the right-wing communalists. The threat posed by these counter-elites seems to be inversely correlated with the center's ability to contain them in the operating framework of Indian federalism. Here lies the real test of India's model of incremental development.

All this, however, necessitates the existence of a cohesive political center which, on account of such cohesion is ensured of stable support from the regions. Since 1967 this cohesion has been under continuous strain. While a degree of "confrontation" between opposing groups in the Congress Party is to be welcomed, at least for the clarification in issue positions that it brings, a prolonged period of strife at the very apex of the system can only produce an atmosphere of drift and indecision all around. A better alternative may be the formation of a viable coalition consisting of proximate groups, a coalition that provides both governmental stability and the necessary strength for making and enforcing critical decisions. Democratic politics are everywhere the politics of coalition-making and entail the inevitable strains of such a system. The chief challenges are two-fold: the maintenance of a "team" in the face of the inevitable strains of collective leadership; and the maintenance of autonomy of this team from the inevitable pressures from other levels and subsystems of the polity. Failure to accomplish the former will lead to failure in the latter, and eventual breakdown of the system's consensus. Regional integration, in other words, presupposes a cohesive and authoritative political center.

SOCIAL INTEGRATION

What was said above of regional integration applies also to issues of social integration. One of the more difficult issues of Indian politics which will become more pronounced as the democratic framework expands, but which has so far been dealt with in an ad hoc and hesitant manner, is that of enabling the religious minorities, especially the Muslims, to resolve their "identity crisis" in terms of active and equal citizenship. The problem is especially difficult in urban areas; urban life tends to be more prone to produce a consciousness of polarities than rural life. We have seen in Chapter 6 that there is evidence of increasing self-confidence among the Muslims who have begun to organize themselves politically, but that there are also signs that this has often led to a chain reaction of communal tensions and violence. A number of political parties, the Jan Sangh on the one side and the Communists on the other side but also sections of the Congress Party, make capital out of such a situation. At a time when the whole problem of Muslim identity is still under strain and Pakistan continues to provide a counter-stimulus, the political dimensions of the problem are wide-ranging: all the way from disaffection of local groups to an attempt on the part of some political groups to disrupt national unity and weaken the center. The whole issue needs careful study, purposive bargaining and support-building, and backing this with an imaginative handling of the usual complaints of discrimination in jobs and the like.

DEMOGRAPHIC POLICY

While the strictly political dimension of national consensus-making spelled out above is of crucial importance for stability and effectiveness, in itself it will be extremely difficult to achieve without attending to more basic transformations taking place in the country and devising concrete policies to deal with them. There are many dimensions to such policy-making—demographic policy, social mobilization (rural, urban), the involvement of the youth, economic policy and its critical linkages, and external political and economic relations.

There is need to evolve a deliberated policy towards the larger demographic structure of the nation. India presents a potential for a wholly different structure of social change from that found in the early arrivals to industrialization; the task is to turn this potential into a unique model of growth and development and, on that basis, build powerful reserves for political stability and sustenance. It is possible to maintain a predominantly rural base for an indefinite period of time, pursue a policy of rapid modernization in and through such a base, develop urban and metropolitan centers as peaks over a structural continuum that cuts across town and country, and turn to advantage more modern technology for the consummation of such a unique structure. Contrary to some oversimplified constructs of modernization, a thriving and prosperous agricultural sector is not inconsistent with a modern industrial society; indeed it may provide a very viable economic and social base to the latter. Also, more basic demographic changes like population expansion and a changing age structure which in the eighteenth and nineteenth centuries in Europe led to such violent upheavals, uncivilized conditions of urban life, and economic exploitation may, with the aid of modern forms of government and planned change, turn into sources of vitality and substructural strength. The next couple of decades will bring about in India a major shift in basic demographic conditions. The choice is between evolving a policy of meaningfully containing these potentially revolutionary changes and allowing the changes to take control of the situation.

RURAL SOCIAL STRUCTURE

Apart from evolving a general design of demographic development, a series of differentiated policies are involved in carrying out the design. One is in regard to the rural social structure. While the "new agricultural policy" has led to major breakthroughs in the productivity and modernization of agriculture, there are some real questions as to whether the productive potential of agriculture is itself spreading outward from the "leading areas," and from the point of view of social justice whether the planned programs are benefiting all strata of the rural population, even if unequally. While there is no need to retract from that policy of concentrating inputs in areas of high potential, there is a need to initiate policies designed to contain an accentuation of rural class cleavages, to stimulate differentiated technological and incentives schemes as between the large and the small farmer, and to revive certain "redistribute" policies that would benefit the vast periphery of the landless, the wage-earners, and the underemployed. Inadequate attention to the social costs of development and the ability of entrenched interests to dictate governmental policy have elsewhere led to massive alienation and movements of protest. Without giving up its basic incremental approach to such issues, the government needs to evolve such a policy before it is too late. The alternative may be a series of Telanganas and Naxalbaris,[10] an influx of the frustrated rural elements into the urban areas, and a further accentuation of the conditions of mass violence.

URBAN DEVELOPMENT

An equally important area of policy is in regard to urban development. This has been the most neglected aspect of India's strategy of planning. Dominated by the overall ideology of "village development" and motivated by the numerical and electoral strength of the rural areas, the Congress Party has failed to respond to the constantly deteriorating conditions of urban life. While it is true that in proportional terms India's urban sector is very small, we have been that this is not true in absolute terms. What is more, politically the urban areas are still crucial to Indian democracy. Here the nerve centers of the polity are still to be found; from here, even rural-based organizations like caste federations and regional parties operate; and here even small numbers turn into powerful movements of military (including the militancy born out of separatist identity and chauvinist ideology like the Shiv Sena in Bombay). It is well known that one of the strongest reasons for anti-center sentiment in Calcutta has been the continuing neglect of the gruesome problems of that city. And conditions of economic deterioration and declining opportunities in small towns have in no small measure contributed to the growing incidence of communal violence in recent years.

The needs are two-fold. The more obvious one is to provide minimum conditions of living for the less fortunate among the urban dwellers: the lower middle classes, the students from poor families, the scheduled castes whose condition continues to be a matter of concern, and the migrant non-factory workers. The more fortunate classes must be made to pay for this. (This is the urban counterpart to the argument for social equality in the rural areas urged above.) The second need is to evolve an approach towards urban self-government. Here the need is to endow urban authorities, especially in the large cities, with autonomy from state governments and direct allocation of plan resources. Urban life, to be at all conducive to national well-being, requires the cultivation of truly urban values which can come only from pride and attachment to one's city, a capacity to influence one's environment, and the hope of a "good life." All this necessitates a special approach to the problem of urban government.

POLICY ON YOUTH

Then there is the whole area of policy in regard to the youth of India. One of the most depressing sights in India is its colleges and universities with their overcrowding, archaic conditions of work, uninspiring and substandard teachers, and obsolete standards of academic courses and syllabi. The need is to break up the massive report of the Education Commission into operational tasks, and to begin to make an impact in this regard. Directly related is the problem of the output of schools and colleges. (We have already dealt with this issue in Chapter 9.) There is here a vast reserve of energy and talent. Random inquiries suggest that on the whole the new recruits to the educational system are creatures of hope, enthusiasm, and optimism, especially those coming from poor families and lower castes. But lacking a positive approach towards mobilizing this talent — although there is a Ministry of "Education and Youth Services" there is little systematic attention given to youth services — such hope and enthusiasm are likely to turn into symptoms of despondency and anemic behavior, and feed into the general "politics of protest."

It would be wrong to think of these protests as just the handiwork of conspiratorial groups, for the fact is that underlying their rebelliousness is a basic commitment, a sense of aggressive nationalism that is potentially creative, and an energy that only needs to be channeled. The elements for a still more viable political order are all there. But their style may not any longer be one of waiting to be incorporated in the establishment. It is more likely to be one of challenge and confrontation. The need once again is to evolve an approach to these elements.

APPROACH TO ECONOMIC DEVELOPMENT

All of this leads logically to issues of economic and technological development. Our analysis in Chapter 9 has brought out the critical problem areas in economic policy and there is no need to repeat the cycles of crises, accomplishments, and new and potential crises spelled out there. What bears repetition is the central point involved in that analysis. This is that while increasingly the fate of the Indian political system will be decided in its farms and factories, it will be decided even more in terms of the political sensitivity of its economic decision-makers.

The crucial issues are: (I) how to reorient modern technology to sustain a demographic structure that is "continuous" between rural and urban areas; (2) how to make the plans and the economic technology underlying the plans increasingly oriented to generating greater employment; (3) how to fill the lag between the rate of educational development and the rate at which commensurate economic opportunities are growing; (4) what measures to take to prevent the social disparities that arise from economic development in both rural and urban areas; and (5) how to orient the strategy of resource mobilization so that it becomes a conscious lever for the realization of these political goals.

These questions must be tackled with imagination and without loss of time. Indian economists and economic administrators are among the best in the world, the research and information infrastructure that they have built is impressive, and important steps are being taken for adapting the technocratic structure to the new tasks of development. What is still lacking — and it is a big lack — is the capacity of the economic and political elite to inform the policy process with a well thought-out developmental perspective in place of an ad hoc approach to problems only after they arise. And while this is lacking there is also the temptation to hand over these problems to an ongoing administrative machine. When the innovativeness of comprehensive thought gives place to rush and routine, such a surrender to bureaucracy is inevitable. There is urgent need to evolve institutional mechanisms of screening every major proposal from the perspective of its implications for the system as a whole. A political unit in the present Perspective Planning Division of the Planning Commission or the prime minister's secretariat may be one way of dealing with this problem. Even the head of this division could be a specialist on the politics of economic development.

SPECIAL SEGMENTS

One way of approaching these various issues is to develop a "critical segments" policy under which a special plan is evolved for each of the critical social and demographic segments of the population — the educated youth and the educated unemployed, the urban lower middle class, the small peasantry and the landless, the scheduled and other low castes, the religious minorities, and the tribal population in the different regions. Economic development generates special stresses for these strata which are then translated into generalized symptoms of discontent and disaffection. For any plan strategy to be politically sensitive, there is need to develop and approach to each of these special segments.

CRITICAL LINKS

We may pause here to take brief note of the erosion of two of the most vital links in the country's development process — education and public administration. The educational system is perhaps the weakest constituent of India's institutional structure, at nearly all levels and in all regions. Archaic courses, uneducated teachers, chaotic administration, and unimaginative policies whose chief contribution is to resist all attempts at innovation have reduced this vital linkage in the nation's growth into a deadwood of history. Here, as in many other aspects of India's public policy, the corrective measures are largely known: the *Report* of the Education Commission contains a mine of recommendations. What is lacking is an instrument for carrying out these recommendations. The worst linkage here, of course, is the Education Ministry at the center, an epitome of inefficiency and bureaucratic malaise. The other big hotch-potch is the university system, presided over by a huge bureaucracy in the University Grants Commission. Even the "centers of advanced study"—which are supposed to implement the recommendation of creating "centers of excellence"—continue to be conducted as mere extensions of outmoded departments. Of the school system, of course, the less said the better. In all this, nothing short of a total reconstruction is called forth. But unless the structure of the Ministry, and the priorities in its program, are drastically overhauled, there is little hope of a revival. The issue is serious because on the quality of education depends the quality and efficiency of the country as a whole. And, what is more, the quality of a whole generation that is now in schools and colleges.

Of almost equal importance is the quality of public administration. The periodic innovativeness of public policy and the bold experimentation of higher level elites run into a serious obstacle: the creeping bureaucratization of implementation structures. A colonial-style administration is wholly unsuited to an imaginative implementation of developmental goals. The bureaucracy has to be an equal partner in, and equally committed to, the nation-building process. Basic issues of structure, ethos, training, political sensibility, and esprit de corps are involved here. A review of each of these elements would produce a pessimistic outlook. Thus it was instructive that the lurking suspicion even among the ardent supporters of bank nationalization was that the declared goals of the measure may not be fulfilled since it would be subject to "bureaucratization."

Once again, the remedial steps are known: the massive studies of the Administrative Reforms Commission and a number of other inquiries have laid bare the basic problems to be tackled. The task is to carry out the most urgent among the agreed measures, and to do this with as much authority as the government of India can wield. The Union Home Ministry, which has shown a commendable record of achievements in more sensitive areas of public policy, seems to have given much less attention to this rather important dimension of political and institutional development. In some ways it is more urgent than almost everything else.

APPROACH TO EXTERNAL AFFAIRS

In spelling out the different policy perspectives on the next phase of India's political development, we have stressed one running theme: the need for a new thrust of policy-making and support-building on the basis of a fresh appraisal of the developing political situation. Now it is clear that such a thrust entails some critical psychological energy. While some of this energy may come from the process of leadership and decision-making within the country, it is more usually generated by some aspect of what is loosely known as "national identity." In this context, the issues of external relations become directly relevant, for in the absence of the external environment furnishing symbolic confirmation of self-identity and self-respect, the requisite psychological stimulus for domestic reconstruction may not be forthcoming.

Here lie some of the more urgent challenges before the post 1967 leadership. We have seen that the great accomplishment of the Nehru era lay in manipulating the external situation to the purposes of national autonomy and regeneration despite a woefully inadequate technological and economic base, and despite a threatening atmosphere of "big power" politics. Since Nehru's time the country has lost its grip on the international environment, has become unduly "dependent" in its posture, and apologetic and defensive in its political style. The conditions arising from the hostility of China and Pakistan, and the changed relationship with both the United States and the USSR in the wake of an uneasy thaw in the world, coupled with the last few years of dependence on these powers for vital imports, have all compromised the country's freedom of maneuver. And yet there have been some significant improvements in internal conditions to warrant a different approach to foreign policy. Food shortage is no longer pressing enough to allow others to use it as a leverage, the country's defenses are more secure, and the realism that has followed the disenchantment with the great powers is for the first time enabling Indian statesmanship to develop a more self-reliant attitude of mind.

PRICE OF NATIONAL AUTONOMY

But the point is not to "learn the lessons" in a mood of caution and shrinking back, but to be consciously willing to pay the price of national autonomy, to generate a new self-confidence, and to move forward once more towards carving out an identifiable "area of influence." A country like India cannot afford to be isolationist; the whole context of world politics has entered a stage of fluidity, and what is needed is clear-headed initiative, articulated goals, and patient diplomacy. India may still be only a potential world power, but it already has a developed technological base and defense capability, and in its own region a unique chance of making an impact, given the wide-ranging power vacuum all around. Once more the need is to develop a fresh "approach" to this whole area of policy.

Undoubtedly the reverse of the above is also true: While the external environment can furnish critical resources for an internal psychological push, as long as internal politics is not extricated from its confusion and equivocation, a confident external image would be hard to bring about. What is said above under domestic political tasks is thus directly relevant to India's position in the world. But while the relationship is interactive, it is not circular, and given the willingness to reappraise and reconstruct, it can reap advantages on both sides.

AID POLICY

But it will involve other concrete decisions too. The country has far too long maintained a "dependent" posture in its economic relations with other nations. In many ways this is unwarranted; India is not really that dependent economically and technologically any more. A more meaningful approach would be to devote greater attention to indigenous technological development and a "take-off" on that basis, aided no doubt by foreign trade earnings and a sustained exploration of the kinds of economic markets that would buttress such an overall design. (In turn, this is bound to stimulate the economy internally.) This will not only put a premium on relevance and optimality — for too long the country has undertaken projects that were determined by external factors — it will also bring an end to the present sense of inferiority that is affecting the entire political profile. We do not suggest any abrupt "end to aid," but we argue for making the country's own appraisal and articulated needs the basis of aid negotiations, dropping the stance of being only an innocent recipient, and evolving an approach to aid as part of a larger international strategy.

There is also need to consider the long-term implications of various kinds of aid for the general design of Indian development. Thus the immediate advantages of aid should be balanced against tying up the future of the economy to servicing a mounting burden of debt. Also, the implications of certain projects for social and economic structure should each time be related to the country's preferred model of development. Only by attending to such perspectives can external resource mobilization be made to sustain the psychological drive spoken of above, and the self-respect needed for the same. The importance of such self-respect for economic growth has not yet been adequately appreciated in India; it is probably greater than a great deal of aid. Continuing to maintain our political perspective on developmental tasks, we would say that much in India depends on the morale of the elite. Prolonged economic dependence defeats the maintenance of such a morale. Hence if the conditions imposed by some kind of aid appear to be not functional to the country's own strategy or compromising its self-respect, it should be rejected. (The same argument applies to "pressures" for purchasing obsolete armaments or machinery.)

THE NEXT PHASE

Our consideration of the emerging issue areas and the policy perspectives that they occasion suggests that the "dialectic of development" spoken of earlier has nothing inevitable about it. It is in fact no more than a "conditional": if this and this is not done, then that might follow. Actually when the real issues are broken up in operational terms, the tasks that face the elite are not really that insurmountable. By the same token, while we have been deliberately critical in the latter part of this chapter, there is no need to read any exaggerated sense of doubt or pessimism in our appraisal. Indeed what is said here should be read in the context of the general analysis in this book. That analysis has underlined the great potency of the Indian model and has brought out how Indian society since 1947 is turning an entirely new leaf in its long history, and has already achieved a series of breakthroughs. But the analysis also suggests that national political development is now entering a new and critical phase, and there is need for a fresh appraisal and a corresponding policy thrust for taking Indian society forward from its present threshold of institutionalization and consensus.

There is no great need to change the basic contours of the Indian political profile. The strong points about contemporary Indian society are its very diversity and its peculiar approach to secularization and integration which preserves differential identities and builds incrementally from those identities. There is richness in this approach, and it is humane. The mechanistic-aggregative model of Western political thought should not be allowed to tantalize Indian modernizers. They must seek and express their own innovative style. What is said in these pages is more with a view to resolving impending and relatively specific problems that must be tackled for continuing and consolidating India's unique secular thrust. Preservation and innovation are thus only two sides of the same basic thrust. Without the innovative component, preservation may not be possible for long.

ROLE OF ELITE

In our analysis we have continuously emphasized the role and perceptions of elites in society; according to us it is the decisions of these actors that constitute the critical inputs. A study of the achievements and shortcomings of the Indian case brings this out quite clearly. Despite all its penetration and institutionalization, the future of India's political system depends crucially, as has its past, on the quality and creativity of its political, administrative, and intellectual elite.

It depends on the ability of the elite to occasionally take stock of the changing contours of reality, to respond to these changes by reconstructing the policy process and forcing the pace of change, and — what is crucial — to prepare the minds of the various constituents of the political coalition, and indeed to shift the relative position of these constituents, for bringing about the desired changes. In effecting such a reconstruction the elite can draw upon the vast reservoir of talents and resources that already exist: the highly committed but rebellious intelligentsia, the vast numbers of educated unemployed, the recently activized small peasantry and the landless, and the seething mass of students and youth. The defensive style of coalition-making within the limited range of inner party ranks, the corrosive dependence on foreign powers and foreign intellectuals for resources and developmental models, and the fear of random and unexpected reprisal at the hands of the electorate need to give way to a more self-conscious and assertive political style. If in the process the political framework becomes less eclectic and more structured, this may be a net gain.

We have seen that crises produce important transformations and bring about higher thresholds of system performance. But in a culture so used to continuities and "functional change" too frequent a dependence on crises may bring about disenchantment among leading social strata and lower the system's legitimacy. Rational anticipation and reality perceptions must also play a role, as indeed they did in the first several years of India's independence. Crises then become shorthand catalysts of an ongoing policy drive instead of throwing the whole political process into confusion and provoking adventurism.

THE LEADERSHIP ISSUE

One final question remains; some may consider it to be the key question. If the next decade in Indian development is going to necessitate a resolution of the range of issue areas mentioned in this chapter, and if the basic need in all of them is to provide a major organizational and policy thrust as suggested here, is the present Indian leadership capable of delivering the goods? More specifically can the ruling faction of the Congress Party provide the necessary personal and intellectual resources needed for these tasks? Can it mobilize the necessary support from the Parliament and the public as it undertakes a series of major policy initiatives? Or will it be further fragmented and lead to a period of chronic instability? Can Indira Gandhi provide the necessary combination of a "consensus leader" and a "reconstructive leader"? Or will her pressing the latter role lead to a decline in her capability as a consensus leader? Is there a need to bring about a change in the top leadership?

It is not the business of a political scientist to provide recipes on who ought to govern. At best, he can assess and evaluate. There are also likely to be wide disagreements on such matters and the judgments that are advanced tend to be polemical and biased. But it seems to us that the Congress Party has done remarkably well in seeing the country through a major political transition without disrupting its basic consensus, and that since 1967 Mrs. Gandhi has been the kind of consensus leader who has commanded the minimum acceptance necessary in such a transition, both within her own party and among other parties that have been in power in some of the states. In carrying the latter along and making them part of the same policy frame, there is little doubt that the role of Indira Gandhi has been of great value.

But there can still be questions as to whether a consensus leader is not, by the very nature of being a consensus leader, too much of a compromiser and a drifter; and a reconstructive leader, by the same logic, does not put a premium on change at the expense of the system's preservation. The issue may not be that simple, of course: the overwhelming need in a stage of flux and readaptation, and when the country is still faced with challenges to national unity, is for a leadership that can combine a youthful and purposive image with wide-ranging acceptance of its authority. While a case can be made for seeking a leader who can collapse the usual obstacles and inhibitions in his way, this need not necessarily imply one with charismatic appeal only. In normal and peaceful times democratic politics require more the efficiency of a collective leadership that is sensitive to the larger coalitional arena than the power of one who rides above it. The more relevant issue is whether such a collective is made available, kept cohesive and united in the face of challenge, and made an instrument of purposive decision-making. A new generation of leaders is already in office in India and perhaps the more relevant issue is "what is to be done" rather than "who will do it," although undoubtedly failure to respond to the former would resolve the issue in terms of the latter.

Here the Indian situation provides ground for concern. All that has been said so far in respect of reconstructive initiatives presupposes the ability of such a leadership to preserve the integrity of the political structure and to lend cohesion to its coalitional components for carrying out the new policies. The danger arises not so much from ideological polarities as from lack of communications and an atmosphere of mutual trust and camaraderie. This has given rise to oscillations between an urge to stay aloof from conflict for fear of being drawn into a partisan position and a tendency to make surprise moves to forestall any opposition and short-circuit the decision-making process. The former approach reduces the appeal of a leader and gradually undercuts his position vis-à-vis the larger constituency, while the latter produces a climate of suspense within the effective coalition and deprives politics of all predictability. Both together can undermine the authority of the ruling coalition and dislocate the very structure from which a "reconstruction" would have been possible. It is in respect of these deeper bases of collective orientations that the recent initiatives of Prime Minister Indira Gandhi become significant. These initiatives hold the promise of providing the country with a new climate of confidence and consolidation. To the extent that she can maintain the tempo of these initiatives, re-establish the left of center consensus of the Congress Party, retain the by now well-articulated "federal consensus," and at the same time make the new coalition at the center a cohesive and effective instrument for further action, she is likely to retrieve the ground lost since the death of her father. Her failure to effect such a combination of strategies, on the other hand, can lead to yet another spate of crises and uncertainties.

As we approach the end of the nineteen-sixties, political systems are almost everywhere in turmoil — including those in the "bastions" of democracy and the "vanguards" of socialism. Many hidden ambiguities of each system are coming out in the open as the complacency of the last two decades gives place to a more probing self-analysis. This is a new phase in world politics; it will not do to reduce it in terms of some simple struggle between ideologies, or even forms of government. It is, rather, a phase of acute self-evaluation everywhere, of testing the implications of each system by subjecting it to new demands, and in and through this, finding meaningful self-expression as nations. Everywhere the forces of reason and change are in conflict with forces of irrationality and reaction. In such a world context, the political challenge facing India acquires greater urgency and a wider significance. If the "model" it has adopted succeeds and overcomes the strains that it faces, it would be more than just a success at home; if it goes down, the chances are that the strategists of reason and reform may suffer a setback in a number of other places too.

DRIVE TOWARD UTOPIA

Democratic politics has proved to be the creative force behind India's historic transformation. The issue before such a model is how to keep the activism and élan — the urge toward the utopia — alive in the middle of the pragmatic trends that inevitably accompany democratic politics; how to continuously endow politics with a moral purpose. It is this challenge of keeping alive the flame of national reconstruction as a means of self-realization that haunted India's great political consolidator, Jawaharlal Nehru. The inspiring lines of Robert Frost Framed Nehru's desk when he died:

The woods are lovely, dark and deep.
But I have promises to keep
And miles to go before I sleep,
And miles to go before I sleep.[11]

The theme is as relevant today as it was in Nehru's time. There is a difference between a society that has seemingly achieved most of its pronounced goals and thus begins to doubt the very directions of its utopia (as in the West), and one that can still look forward to a long process of realizing its goals and ideals. The latter presents an exciting panorama, one that may prove frustrating at time for it is a race with time itself; but it is also one where the mainsprings are futuristic and where there is no scope for either complacency or self-doubt. To quote, once again, Nehru, with his genius for fathoming the dialectics of nation-building, "We are concerned with the shaping of the future of India. It is therefore with a sense of the burden of history upon me, upon us upon this House, that I face this problem.[12]

The post-Nehru generation still faces this "burden of history." Its creativity will be tested by the extent to which it translates the bold vision of its predecessors into issues of performance and coalition-making modes of anticipation and reconstruction, and by such application legitimizes the political order on which the country has staked its destiny. The accumulated experience of the past may prove of great help in this but it is not likely to provide adequate guides to the future.

Notes

1. Such a formulation of innovative behavior in the course of maintaining existing structures and ways of life is, of course, not new to evolutionary theory. It has been recently formulated as a law of behavior called "Romer's Rule" after the paleontologist A.S. Romer. The rule has been stated thus: "The initial survival value of a favorable innovation is conservative, in that it renders possible the maintenance of a traditional way of life in the face of changed circumstances." It should be noted that such a rule is not anti-teleological and permits purposeful innovation. See Charles F. Hackett and Robert Ascher, "The Human Revolution," *Current Anthropology*, 5, No. 3, June, 1964.
2. On November 7, 1966 a motley assortment of groups, in part agitated by the religious symbolism of cow slaughter, in part taking advantage of mounting disturbances and chaos, led an attack on the Parliament in New Delhi, when it was in session, and clearly attempted to disrupt constitutional government. The attempt fizzled out almost immediately and badly exposed the "lunatic fringe" of Indian politics. Home Minister Gulzari Lal Nanda had to resign for failure to anticipate and deal firmly with the political *sadhus* (ascetics turned politicians) who were responsible for the event. See my "The Congress System on Trial," *Asian Survey*, VII, No. 2, February, 1962.

3. The points made here are drawn from an analysis of this period in Indian history as developed in a paper by Rajni Kothari and Thomas Headrick, "Crises and Non-Crisis Development: India 1962-67" (Mimeo., Centre for the Study of Developing Societies, Delhi, and Institute of Political Studies, Stanford, 1969). The paper was prepared for the Political Development Seminar at Stanford University run by Gabriel A. Almond.

4. On these points I have benefited from discussions with Albert O. Hirschman and Charles E. Lindblom, two economists who have been seriously concerned with the role of political and institutional variables in economic development. On "reconstructive leadership," see Lindblom, *India's Prospects* (Mimeo., December, 1967). In writing this chapter I have also benefited from discussions with Gabriel A. Almond.

5. Recent events in the Congress Party leading to a split in the Working Committee, the "expulsion" of Prime Minister Indira Gandhi from the party by her opponents, and their establishment of a rival parliamentary party took place after this book was printed. It was only possible to marginally include the implications of these events in these last few pages of the book (just as it was only possible to briefly include at the galley stage the events from the Bangalore Session of the Congress to the Presidential Election of August 1969 in Chapter 8). On the other hand, the general analysis of this chapter in terms of a shift from an autonomous center and non-aggregation of issues to a more polarized and aggregated polity, and the implications of this shift for future tasks, appear to be further emphasized by these events. For an analysis of recent developments, see Rajni Kothari, "Political Consensus in India: Decline and Reconstruction," *Economic and Political Weekly*, IV, No. 41, October 11, 1969.

6. Samuel P. Huntington, *Political Order in Changing Societies* (New Haven and London, 1968). Huntington is careful to single out the Indian case for high praise. "... a country may be politically highly developed with modern political institutions while still very backward in terms of modernization. India, for instance, was typically held to be the epitome of the underdeveloped society.... Yet in terms of political institutionalization, India was far from backward. Indeed, it ranked high not only in comparison with other modernizing countries in Asia, Africa, and Latin America, but also in comparison with many much more modern European countries .... The stable, effective, and democratic government of India during its first twenty years of independence rested far more on this institutional inheritance than it did on the charisma of Nehru." It is nonetheless, interesting that Huntington should consistently use the past tense in describing Indian performance. It is as if he is afraid that since 1967 reverse tendencies have set in.

7. A study of differences within India shows that, insofar as the two are related, high modernization is supportive of high political institutionalization and stability, whereas low modernization, while not a cause of political instability, is compatible with it. An instance of the former is Madras, of the latter UP. See Paul R. Brass, "Political Participation, Institutionalization and Stability in India," *Government and Opposition*, 4, No. 1, Winter, 1969.

8. For a charming and provocative essay on the value of intuitive judgement of the politician against the claims of the rationalist, see Michael Oakeshott, *Political Education*, Inaugural Address to the London School of Economics (Cambridge, 1951).
9. A reaction to such a state of affairs is the declared resolve of parties like the Communist Marxists to make center-state relations an "issue" in their political platform. There is no reason why, even while such a slogan is stressed for the consumption of doctrinaire elements in these parties, a reasonable "understanding" cannot be evolved through personal discussions and patient bargaining. The initiative of Prime Minister Indira Gandhi after the 1967 elections, of assuring the non-Congress chief ministers of central cooperation, which has since cooled off, should be revived and followed up.
10. Soon after independence a Communist-led insurrection took place in the Telangana region of what is now Andhra Pradesh. The movement was ultimately suppressed. It should not be confused with the more recent demand for a separate state of Telangana. In 1967, following on the heels of the leftist United Front victory at the polls, the left-most fringe of the Communist movement in West Bengal led a revolt in the rural area of Naxalbari based on the extremely depressed condition of the landless and their exploitation by the *jotedars*, the large landowners with a feudal background. In this case the revolt was suppressed by the United Front itself, with the active assistance of the central police.
11. From "Stopping by Woods on a Snowy Evening," in *Complete Poems of Robert Frost*. Copyright 1923 by Holt, Rinehart and Winston, Inc. Copyright 1951 by Robert Frost, Reprinted by permission of Holt, Rinehard and Winston, Inc. and of Laurence Pollinger Limited.
12. Quoted in *The New India: Progress Through Democracy* (Delhi., 1957).

Index

administration, 9, 32, 38-9, 79, 87, 110, 118, 129, 450, 451;
power of local, 128-9
adult franchise, 9, 104, 126, 157, 170, 284;
new power centre, 126
Africa, 79, 103, 156, 390, 393, 398, 405, 407, 410, 411
agriculture, 5, 15, 21, 140-1, 356, 358, 359, 362, 363, 364-8, 374, 433, 439, 446
Akali Dal, 125, 167, 186, 189, 196, 197, 212
Ali, M. Mohammad, 66, 67
M, Shaukat, 66, 67,
All India Congress Committee *See* Congress Parties Conference, 58, 67, 103
— Party Hill Leaders Conference, 332
Ambedkar, B.R., 107
Andhra Pradesh, 113-4, 122, 175, 191, 197, 236, 335, 367, 372
Annadurai, C.N., 194, 331-2
Ansari, M.A., 67
Appleby, Paul, 118
Arya Samaj, 44
Asia, 79, 103, 156, 390, 393, 398, 405, 407, 410, 411
regional cooperation, 421, 422
Asian Conference, First, 394, 396
Asian associations in India, 6, 43, 213-5, 245-7
Atlee, Clement, 73-4
authority, 15, 109, 428-31
cultural roots of, 274-6
as arbitration, 265-6
Avadi Resolution, 115
Azad, M.Abul Kalam, 67, 74

backward classes, concessions to, 112
See also reservations, Scheduled Castes
Bandung Conference, 396
Banerjee, Surendranath, 43
bank nationalization, 141, 356, 359, 374
'bargaining culture', 92-3, 267, 279, 435
See also authority, consensus
Belgrade Conference, 396
Bengal, 3, 34, 45-9, 74, 121-4, 168, 184, 189, 190, 196-7
Bhakti (devotional movement), 30

Bharatiya Kranti Dal, 186, 196
Bihar, 122, 123, 124, 184, 188, 192, 196, 212, 236
Bose
  Ashish, 361, 362
  Subhash Chandra, 55, 58
  brahmins, 24, 29, 63, 84, 91, 96, 99, 233, 241, 331
  See also caste, elite
Brahmo Samaj, 43
British Cabinet Mission Plan, 72-3
British Raj,
  contributions of, 38-41
  impact on politics, 21
  bureaucracy 9-10, 12, 14, 87, 110-2, 122, 131-2, 213, 289-90, 307-8, 353-4, 449-50;
  and political development, 135-6
  See also administration
Calcutta, 43, 123, 447
Carstairs, Maurice, 285
caste, 23-5, 34, 96-7, 214, 229,
  aggregative aspect of, 243-5
  associations, 245, 247
  consciousness, 235-7
  federations, 245-7, 283, 430, 447
  fragmentation, 239-40, 242
  integration dimension of, 234-5
  new identity of, 243-7
  and politics, 123, 232-5
  secular organisation of, 232-4, 246
center, 291-2
  authority of, 38
  power of, 165-6
  -periphery institutionalization *See* center-state
center-state relationship, 116-20
  consensus system in, 192;
  importance of central leadership in, 119;
  pressures on, 123;
  role of party in, 120
change
  ideology of, 2;
  perception of, 288
  See also modernization
  traditions of, 256-61
  See also Hinduism
Chavan, Y., 193, 194, 318
chief ministers, importance of, 116, 118, 120
  See also center-state, Congress Party
China, 396, 398-402, 406-8, 422, 432, 452
Christians, 24, 106, 248
civil disobedience, 51, 52, 59
  See also protest
coalition, 58, 183-7, 191-2, 437, 456
colonialism
  and Indian society, 41-3
  institutional rigidity of, 2, 86-7
communal
  award, 60, 68-9;
  problem, 62;
  representation, 66;
  violence, 67, 74-5
communalism, 34-5
  politicization of, 65-7
community development, 115, 129, 11, 132, 140
Communism, Communist Parties, Communists, 167, 168, 175, 182, 184, 187, 189, 190, 195, 197, 202, 205, 207, 211, 212, 216, 393, 395, 445
competitive dominance, 197
Congress Party, 43, 45-9, 53, 66, 71-7, 80-1, 121-2, 165, 169, 171, 198,
  as agent of change, 99-100;
  competitive dominance, 156-8;
  future trends, 187-91
  as coalition maker, 182-3;
  consensus party, 159, 195;;
  defections, 180-1;
  dissidence in, 177-8, 181, 201;
  District Congress Committees, 128;
  electoral strength of, 188;
  elite turnover in, 178-80;
  factionalism, 266;
  as Government party, 76, 102, 158-9;
  hierarchy of, 110;

High Command (Congress Working Committee), 55, 56 119;
ideology of, 82, 115;
leadership, 69
See also leadership
organisation, 55-6, 83; 207;
as political center, 189;
split in, 114, 190, 439
consensus, 267, 431, 434, 457, 458;
change in, 195;
making, 109;
institutional, 115;
politics, 218-9;
structure of, 290-1
Constituent Assembly, 72, 73
Constitution of India, 103-17
background, 103;
debate on, 104;
making of, 105-6
See also adult franchise, parliamentary democracy
constitutionalism, 45, 50, 59
cooperative societies, 359, 430
cultural identity, 257-60
Congress Socialist Party, 59, 158
Cripps, Stafford, 71

Dange, S.A., 167
Dayananda, Saraswati, 44
decentralization of politics, 118, 124-7
democratic decentralization, *See* Panchayati Raj
Desai, Morarji, 311, 313-4
devaluation of currency, 413-4
development
crises, 352-4, 383-4;
See also economic development planning
models,
Indian, 8-19, 428-33;
Western, 3, 9
strategy, political implications of change in, 354-7
'dharma', 27, 281, 182
differentiations,
new, 96;
traditional, 96
dissent, goals of, 162, 164-5
See also Congress Party.
distribution, urban-rural dimension, 357-9
district, political importance of, 129-30
deregulation, 128
See also regulation, state control
DMK (Dravida Munnetra Kazhagham), 167, 184, 187, 190, 194, 196, 197, 204, 208, 212, 328, 330-1
Dulles, John Foster, 394, 397
'dyarchy', 47

economic
crucial issues, 449-50;
development, 433;
drain, theory of, 44-5, 48;
education, 39, 450;
development of, 378-83, 439;
imbalanced growth, 351-2;
planning, 112, 115, 410
policy, 141;
See also planning, Planning Commission, trade deficit
English, 39, 45, 98-9;
and Hindus, 63;
importance of, 377-8;
and Muslims, 64
educated unemployed, 370, 372, 383, 450
See also employment
elites, 84, 91, 92, 429-31, 444;
intermediate, 94;
role of, 92-3;
national, 48, 85, 89, 97;
ideology of, 97;
new, 98, 102
role of, 267-9;
role of, 6, 29
See also brahmins, caste, Hindu social order, leadership
elections, 170-7, 181-4, 284
system, 126
employment, 368, 439;
raising of, 370-2

See also industrialization,
migration, unemployment
ethics, code of, 26-9
exports, 409-10, 413, 414, 420
See also imports
extremists, 45

factionalism, 182
family planning, 377
federalism, 91, 118, 442-4, 458;
political patterns, 121-4
Five Year Plans, 115, 370, 372,
409-10
See also economic planning,
Planning Commission
foreign
aid, 408, 415-55, 453-4;
sources of, 418;
utilisation of, 419;
exchange, 416-7;
policy, 452-3;
growth of, 393-3,
peace-keeping missions abroad,
396
trade, 411-3;
agreements, 411;
deficit, 409-11

Ganatantra Parishad, 175, 196
Gandhi
Indira, 141, 190, 193, 194, 372,
404, 457, 458;
M.K. (Mahatma), 51-2, 57-8, 60,
61, 66-8, 74, 75, 80, 82, 97, 99,
157, 158, 268, 270;
institution-building, 55-6;
reinterpretation of tradition, 54-5
Gandhians, 57, 91
Gokhale, Gopala Krishna, 43, 44, 46
Government of India Act, (1919),
47, 49;
(1935), 60-1
government
and mass attitudes, 201;
and party, 162, 165;
as political focus, 192-3;
power, 162-3;
and social development, 10,
286-8
governmentalization, 288-9, 430
Gujerat, 122, 196, 236, 237, 367, 372

Harijans, 24, 30, 52, 56, 60, 106, 247,
248
See also reservation, untouchables
Haryana, 186, 191, 192
hierarchy, 276
See also authority
Hindu
-Muslim relationship, 62;
unequal development of, 63-5;
unity, 53, 67
See also communalism, Muslims,
secularism
revivalism, 35, 63, 65;
social order, 22-5, 28-9;
dissent in 29-31;
Muslim impact on, 33-5;
and modernist influences, 237-
reform, 44,
Home Rule League, 46
Huntington, Samuel, 440
Hyderabad, 110, 123, 175

ideology and politics, 267-9
imports, 350, 410, 416, 420
India
-China border conflict, 398, 402,
403;
cultural identity, 84, 257-60;
heirarchical segmentation,
289-91;
incremental democracy in, 431-3;
costs of, 436-8;
strains on, 433;
Independence, 72-5;
international role, 423;
See also foreign policy;
leadership, 49, 283
See also leadership;
non-alignment policy, 395-7, 405;
nuclear policy, 422;
-Pakistan conflict, 402-4;
See also Pakistan;
as status quo power, 406-8

Indian National Congress, *See* Congress Party
Industrial Policy Resolution of 1956, 115
industrialization, 115, 140, 357-8, 408-12
industry, 350-1;
  role of kinship structure in, 213-4
institutionalization, process of, 143-4
integration, politics of, 4
interest groups, 213-4
  See also caste
intermediate aggregation, 93, 429, 436
  See also issue orientation of politics, 217

Jan Sangh, 107, 167, 182, 186, 188-90, 192, 195, 204, 208, 212, 310, 445
Japan, 421
Jinnah, M.A., 59, 66-70
Justice Party, 59

Kamaraj, K., 175, 330
  Plan, 178
karma, 281, 292
Kashmir, 402-4, 407
Kerala, 121, 123, 168, 175, 178, 184, 186, 187-9, 192, 194, 212, 216, 306, 372
  central rule in, 196-7
Khan, Sir Syed Ahmed, 64
Khilafat movement, 58, 66-7, 68

labor laws, 112
language problem, 211, 433
leadership, 3-4, 111, 434, 456-9;
  ideology of, 144;
  roles, shift in, 283, 433
Legislative Councils, 47
Liberal Federation, 50
linguistic reorganization of states, 113-4
local
  elites, 118;
  power, levers of, 128;
  solidarity, 25-6
  See also caste, district, panchayati raj
Lohia, Ram Manohar, 160, 183, 204
lower castes, mobilization of, 240
  See also caste , reservations
Lucknow Pact (1916), 47, 66

Madhya Pradesh, 122, 124
Maharashtra, 122, 207, 372
Marathas, 31, 36
Madras, 113, 121, 122, 124, 175, 178, 184, 186, 190, 194, 196, 372
Mehta, Asoka, 160, 318
middle class
  creation of, 39, 40;
  educated, 50;
  lower, 369
minority groups, 24
migration, rural-urban, 362, 364, 375, 448
  See also employment, urbanisation
modernists, 134-5, 430
modernizers, 134, 135, 430
modernization, 40, 42, 65, 87
Mountbatten, Lord, 73, 74
Mukerjee, S.P., 107
Muslim, 24, 31-5, 59, 62, 106, 247, 248, 445
  and British Raj, 64;
  League, 47, 66, 68-73;
  nationalism, 70-1;
  political consciousness, 66;
    groups, 248-9;
  rule in India, 31-3;
    impact on Hinduism, 33-5;
  separate state for, 69,70
  See also Pakistan
Mysore, 121, 122, 123, 372

Narayan, Jayaprakash, 160, 317, 318
Naoroji, Dadabhai, 44, 48
nation-building,
  concept of, 16-7;
  processes of, 9-10
national
  autonomy, 393;
  consciousness, 48;

Development Council, 139;
identity, 7, 48, 95
See also cultural identity
nationalist movement, 46-53;
development of, 49-50, 81-3;
and Hindu civilization, 84-5;
ideology of, 97;
origins, urban middle class, 80
Nehru, Jawaharlal, 57-9, 61, 73, 74, 80, 92, 97, 99, 105, 107, 111, 112, 158, 159, 169, 170, 179, 181, 195, 217, 268, 270, 392-5, 400
Nijalingappa, 316
non-alignment, 407 *See* India, non-alignment policy of
non-cooperation movement, 60, 67
non-officials, 139
role in politics, 133

opposition parties, 177;
and elite turnover in Congress Party, 180-1;
government party factions, 163;
power, 168
role of, 159-60, 163
Orissa, 121, 122, 124, 175, 186, 189-91

Pakistan, 75, 397, 398, 401, 405-8, 432, 433, 445, 452;
demand for, 70-1
security pact with USA, 398, 402
Panch Sheel *See* peaceful coexistence
panchas, caste, 23-4
panchayat, 24
panchayati raj, 92, 115, 129, 134, 139, 359, 368;
features of, 132;
significance of, 130-3
Parliament, Members of, 202-7
parliamentary democracy, 104-6
party
ideology, 211-2;
organization, role of, 159;
penetration, 198, 200;
preferences, 198-200;
system, 19, 156-7;
evolution of, 161-2, 168;
and government, 165;
regionalization of, 193
parties,6,
social composition of, 202;
support structure, 207-11
Patel, Vallabhbhai, 74, 99, 111, 158, 169
patronage, 125
Pax Britannica, 41
'peaceful coexistence', 395, 396
See also non-alignment
planning, 114, 124-5, 157, 356-7;
Commission, 112, 119, 138, 139
policy making, 87
political
centre, 11, 283-9, 292, 443-4;
culture, 262-7;
development, 2-8
See also development models of
dissent, 162;
influences, 21-
integration,92, 115;
legitimacy, 166;
organization,238-47;
leadership, changes in, 240-1;
personalities, importance of, 167;
power, diversification of, 9;
protest, 164, 216-8;
socialization, 271-7;
stability, 2,3,6-7
population control, 377
Praja Socialist Party (PSP), 204-5
Prasad, Dr. Rajendra, 107
President of India, 107
public administration, 136-8
See also administration, bureaucracy
sector, 138-9,349,351,417
Punjab, 74, 121, 184, 186, 190, 191, 367

Quit India movement, 61, 71

Radhakrishnan, S., 106
radicalism, 45
Rajagopalachari, C., 167, 178, 180
Ranade, M.G., 43, 44

religious minorities, 106, 247, 248, 445, 450
reservation policy, 108-9, 247
See also Harijans, Scheduled Castes
'revolution, incremental', 432, 438
See also India, incremental democracy
rightist parties, 196-7, 212
Roy, Ram Mohun, 39, 40, 42-3
rural
development, 357, 358;
sector, 135, 359, 439;
disparities wi'hin, 364-7;
social structure, 446-7;
and politics, 125-7

Samyukta Socialist Party (SSP), 167, 182, 188, 192, 204-5, 208, 211
sanskritization, 236-7, 250;
See also caste
satyagraha (moral persuasion), 51, 59
scheduled castes, 24, 30, 108, 247-8, 448, 540;
special privileges for, 108, 247
secular identity, 260
secularism, 6, 60, 243, 250
self-government, 43, 45, 46
separate electorates, 60, 65
sustained growth, 347-50, 413
Shafi, Sir Mohammad, 67, 68
Shastri, Lal Bahadur, 181, 195, 403
Shiv Sena,
Sikhs, 30, 36, 106, 248
social
integration, 444-5;
norms, institutionalization of, 269-71
reform, 40-4
See also Hindu social order
socialism, 40, 89, 115, 283, 307, 396
socialists, 207
Socialist Party,
Soviet Union, 395, 396, 398, 401 403-5, 407-8, 418, 420, 452
special
electorates, 47;
representation, 65
States
administration, 118, 122;
diffusion of political power in, 124-7;
leaders, power of, 117, 125-6;
politics, 120-4, 127-30;
social structure, 122-3
See also center-state relationship, chief ministers
Swadeshi movement, 48
'Swaraj' (self-rule), 46
Swaraj Party, 58,59, 67
Swatantra Party, 167, 180, 182, 184, 189, 204-8, 212
electoral gains, 187

Tandon, Purshottamdas,
Tashkent Declaration, 403
Tibet, 398, 399
Tilak, B.G., 46, 49, 50, 80
trade unions, 24, 112
tradition, reinterpretation of, 277-83
tribals, 24, 56, 108, 450;
politics of, 123;
special privileges for, 108
See also scheduled castes
'two-nation' theory, 70
unemployment, 77, 145, 370, 372-7, 376;
Unionist Party, 59, 69
united front politics, 123
United Nations, 393-4, 403
United States of America (USA), 397, 401, 408, 418, 420, 452;
Asia policy, 397-8
universal franchise, 28
See also adult franchise
untouchables, 65
See also Harijans
Untouchability Offences Act, 112
urban
development, 447-8;
sector, 359, 368
See also distribution
urbanization, 65, 360-2
See also migration
USSR *See* Soviet Union

Uttar Pradesh, 67-8, 122, 123, 124, 184, 188, 190, 192, 204

varna *See* caste
voters, importance of, 118
See also adult franchise

Westernization, 35, 98, 250, 283, 288
See also education

youth, 56, 375-6, 450;
policy on, 448-9